LANGUAGE ENGINEERING FOR LESSER-STUDIED LANGUAGES

NATO Science for Peace and Security Series

This Series presents the results of scientific meetings supported under the NATO Programme: Science for Peace and Security (SPS).

The NATO SPS Programme supports meetings in the following Key Priority areas: (1) Defence Against Terrorism; (2) Countering other Threats to Security and (3) NATO, Partner and Mediterranean Dialogue Country Priorities. The types of meeting supported are generally "Advanced Study Institutes" and "Advanced Research Workshops". The NATO SPS Series collects together the results of these meetings. The meetings are co-organized by scientists from NATO countries and scientists from NATO's "Partner" or "Mediterranean Dialogue" countries. The observations and recommendations made at the meetings, as well as the contents of the volumes in the Series, reflect those of participants and contributors only; they should not necessarily be regarded as reflecting NATO views or policy.

Advanced Study Institutes (ASI) are high-level tutorial courses to convey the latest developments in a subject to an advanced-level audience.

Advanced Research Workshops (ARW) are expert meetings where an intense but informal exchange of views at the frontiers of a subject aims at identifying directions for future action.

Following a transformation of the programme in 2006 the Series has been re-named and re-organised. Recent volumes on topics not related to security, which result from meetings supported under the programme earlier, may be found in the NATO Science Series.

The Series is published by IOS Press, Amsterdam, and Springer Science and Business Media, Dordrecht, in conjunction with the NATO Public Diplomacy Division.

Sub-Series

A.	Chemistry and Biology	Springer Science and Business Media
B.	Physics and Biophysics	Springer Science and Business Media
C.	Environmental Security	Springer Science and Business Media
D.	Information and Communication Security	IOS Press
E.	Human and Societal Dynamics	IOS Press

http://www.nato.int/science
http://www.springer.com
http://www.iospress.nl

Sub-Series D: Information and Communication Security – Vol. 21 ISSN 1874-6268

Language Engineering for Lesser-Studied Languages

Edited by

Sergei Nirenburg

University of Maryland Baltimore County, USA

IOS Press

Amsterdam • Berlin • Oxford • Tokyo • Washington, DC

Published in cooperation with NATO Public Diplomacy Division

Proceedings of the NATO Advanced Study Institute on Recent Advances in Language Engineering for Low- and Middle-Density Languages
Batumi, Georgia
15–27 October 2007

ISBN 978-1-58603-954-7
Library of Congress Control Number: 2008941928

Publisher
IOS Press
Nieuwe Hemweg 6B
1013 BG Amsterdam
Netherlands
fax: +31 20 687 0019
e-mail: order@iospress.nl

Distributor in the UK and Ireland
Gazelle Books Services Ltd.
White Cross Mills
Hightown
Lancaster LA1 4XS
United Kingdom
fax: +44 1524 63232
e-mail: sales@gazellebooks.co.uk

Distributor in the USA and Canada
IOS Press, Inc.
4502 Rachael Manor Drive
Fairfax, VA 22032
USA
fax: +1 703 323 3668
e-mail: iosbooks@iospress.com

PRINTED IN THE NETHERLANDS

Language Engineering for Lesser-Studied Languages
S. Nirenburg (Ed.)
IOS Press, 2009

Preface

Technologies enabling the computer processing of specific languages facilitate economic and political progress of societies where these languages are spoken. Development of methods and systems for language processing is, therefore, a worthy goal for national governments as well as for business entities and scientific and educational institutions in every country in the world. Significant progress has been made over the past 20–25 years in developing systems and resources for language processing. Traditionally, the lion's share of activity concentrated on the "major" languages of the world, defined not so much in terms of the number of speakers as with respect to the amount of publications of various kinds appearing in the language. Thus, much of the work in the field has been devoted to English, with Spanish, French, German, Japanese, Chinese and, to some extent, Arabic also claiming strong presence. The term "high-density" has been used to describe the above languages.

The rest of the languages of the world have fewer computational resources and systems available. As work on systems and resources for the "lower-density" languages becomes more widespread, an important question is how to leverage the results and experience accumulated by the field of computational linguistics for the major languages in the development of resources and systems for lower-density languages. This issue has been at the core of the NATO Advanced Studies Institute on language technologies for middle- and low-density languages held in Batumi, Georgia in October 2007. This book is a collection of publication-oriented versions of the lectures presented there.

The book is divided into three parts. The first part is devoted to the development of tools and resources for the computational study of lesser-studied languages. Typically, this is done on the basis of describing the work on creating an existing resource. Readers should find in this part's papers practical hints for streamlining the development of similar resources for the languages on which they are about to undertake comparable resource-oriented work. In particular, Dan Tufis describes an approach to test tokenization, part of speech tagging and morphological stemming as well as alignment for parallel corpora. Rodolfo Delmonte describes the process of creating a treebank of syntactically analyzed sentences for Italian. Marjorie McShane's chapter is devoted to the important issue of recognizing, translating and establishing co-reference of proper names in different languages. Ivan Derzhanski analyzes the issues related to the creation of multilingual dictionaries.

The second part of the book is devoted to levels of computational processing of text and a core application, machine translation. Kemal Oflazer describes the needs of and approaches to computational treatment of morphological phenomena in language. David Tugwell's contribution discusses issues related to syntactic parsing, especially parsing for languages that feature flexible word order. This topic is especially important for lesser-studied languages because much of the work on syntactic parsing has traditionally been carried out in languages with restricted word order, notably, English, while a much greater variety exists in the languages of the world. Sergei Nirenburg's section describes the acquisition of knowledge prerequisites for the analysis of meaning. The approach discussed is truly interlingual – it relies on an ontological metalanguage for describing meaning that does not depend on any specific natural language. Issues of reusing existing ontological-semantic resources to speed up the acquisition of lexical semantics for lesser-studied languages are also discussed. Leo Wanner and François Lareau discuss the benefits of applying the meaning-text theory to creating text generation capabilities into multiple languages. Finally, Stella Makrantonatou and her co-authors Sokratis Sofianopoulos, Olga Giannoutsou and Marina Vassiliou describe an approach to building machine translation systems for lesser-studied languages.

The third and final part of the book contains three case studies on specific language groups and particular languages. Shuly Wintner surveys language resources for Semitic languages. Karine Megerdoomian analyzes specific challenges in processing Armenian and Persian and Oleg Kapanadze describes the results of projects devoted to applying two general computational semantic approaches – finite state techniques and ontological semantics – to Georgian.

The book is a useful source of knowledge about many core facets of modern computational-linguistic work. By the same token, it can serve as a reference source for people interested in learning about strategies that are best suited for developing computational-linguistic capabilities for lesser-studied languages – either "from scratch" or using components developed for other languages. The book should also be quite useful in teaching practical system- and resource-building topics in computational linguistics.

Contents

A. Tools and Resources

Language Engineering for Lesser-Studied Languages
S. Nirenburg (Ed.)
IOS Press, 2009

doi:10.3233/978-1-58603-954-7-3

Algorithms and Data Design Issues for Basic NLP Tools

Dan TUFIŞ
Research Institute for Artificial Intelligence of the Romanian Academy

Abstract. This chapter presents some of the basic language engineering pre-processing steps (tokenization, part-of-speech tagging, lemmatization, and sentence and word alignment). Tagging is among the most important processing steps and its accuracy significantly influences any further processing. Therefore, tagset design, validation and correction of training data and the various techniques for improving the tagging quality are discussed in detail. Since sentence and word alignment are prerequisite operations for exploiting parallel corpora for a multitude of purposes such as machine translation, bilingual lexicography, import annotation etc., these issues are also explored in detail.

Keywords. BLARK, training data, tokenization, tagging, lemmatization, aligning

Introduction

The global growth of internet use among various categories of users populated the cyberspace with multilingual data which the current technology is not quite prepared to deal with. Although it is relatively easy to select, for whatever processing purposes, only documents written in specific languages, this is by no means the modern approach to the multilingual nature of the ever more widespread e-content. On the contrary, there have been several international initiatives such as [1], [2], [3], [4] among many others, all over the world, towards an integrative vision, aiming at giving all language communities the opportunity to use their native language over electronic communication media. For the last two decades or so, multilingual research has been the prevalent preoccupation for all major actors in the multilingual and multicultural knowledge community. One of the fundamental principles of software engineering design, separating the data from the processes, has been broadly adhered to in language technology research and development, as a result of which numerous language processing techniques are, to a large extent, applicable to a large class of languages.

The success of data-driven and machine learning approaches to language modeling and processing as well as the availability of unprecedented volumes of data for more and more languages gave an impetus to multilingual research. It has been soon noticed that, for a number of useful applications for a new language, raw data was sufficient, but the quality of the results was significantly lower than for languages with longer NLP research history and better language resources. While it was clear from the very beginning that the quality and quantity of language specific resources were of crucial importance, with the launching of international multilingual projects, the issues of interchange and interoperability became research problems in themselves. Standards and recommendations for the development of language resources and associated processing tools have been published. These best practice recommendations (e.g. Text Encoding Initiative (http://www.tei-c.org/index.xml), or some more restricted specifications, such as XML Corpus Encoding Standard (http://www.xml-ces.org/), Lexical Markup Framework (http://www.lexicalmarkupframework.org/) etc.) are language independent, abstracting away from the specifics, but offering means to make explicit any language-specific idiosyncrasy of interest.

It is worth mentioning that the standardization movement is not new in the Language Technology community, but only in recent years the recommendations produced by various expert bodies took into account a truly global view, trying to accommodate most of (ideally, all) natural languages and as many varieties of language data as possible. Each new language covered can in principle introduce previously overlooked phenomena, requiring revisions, extensions or even reformulations of the standards.

While there is an undisputed agreement about the role of language resources and the necessity to develop them according to international best practices in order to be able to reuse a wealth of publicly available methodologies and linguistic software, there is much less agreement on what would be the basic set of language resources and associated tools that is "necessary to do any pre-competitive research and education at all." [5]. A minimal set of such tools, known as BLARK (Basic LAnguage Resource Kit), has been investigated for several languages including Dutch [6], Swedish [7], Arabic [8], Welsh (and other Celtic languages) [9].

Although the BLARK concept does not make any commitment with respect to the symbolic-statistical processing dichotomy, in this paper, when not specified otherwise, we will assume a corpus-based (data-driven) development approach towards rapid prototyping of essential processing requirements for a new language.

In this chapter we will discuss the use of the following components of BLARK for a new language:

- (for monolingual processing) tokenization, morpho-lexical tagging and lemmatization; we will dwell on designing tagsets and building and cleaning up the training data required by machine learning algorithms;
- (for multilingual processing) sentence alignment and word alignment of a parallel corpus.

1. Tokenization

The first task in processing written natural language texts is breaking the texts into processing units called tokens. The program that performs this task is called segmenter or tokenizer. Tokenization can be done at various granularity levels: a text can be split into paragraphs, sentences, words, syllables or morphemes and there are already various tools available for the job. A sentence tokenizer must be able to recognize sentence boundaries, words, dates, numbers and various fixed phrases, to split clitics or contractions etc. The complexity of this task varies among the different language families. For instance in Asian languages, where there is no explicit word delimiter (such as the white space in the Indo-European languages), automatically solving this problem has been and continues to be the focus of considerable research efforts. According to [10], for Chinese "sentence tokenization is still an unsolved problem". For most of the languages using the space as a word delimiter, the tokenization process was wrongly considered, for a long time, a very simple task. Even if in these languages a string of characters delimited by spaces and/or punctuation marks is most of the time a proper lexical item, this is not always true. The examples at hand come from the agglutinative languages or languages with a frequent and productive compounding morphology (consider the most-cited *Lebensversicherungsgesellschaftsangestellter,* the German compound which stands for "life insurance company employee"). The non-agglutinative languages with a limited compounding morphology frequently rely on analytical means (multiword expressions) to construct a lexical item. For translation purposes considering multiword expressions as single lexical units is a frequent processing option because of the differences that might appear in cross-lingual realization of common concepts. One language might use concatenation (with or without a hyphen at the joint point), agglutination, derivational constructions or a simple word. Another language might use a multiword expression (with compositional or non-compositional meaning). For instance the English *in spite of*, *machine gun*, *chestnut tree*, *take off* etc. or the Romanian *de la* (from), *gaura cheii* (keyhole), *sta în picioare* (to stand), *(a)-şi aminti* (to remember), etc. could be arguably considered as single meaningful lexical units even if one is not concerned with translation. Moreover, cliticized word forms such as the Italian *damelo* or the Romanian *dă-mi-le* (both meaning "give them to me"), need to be recognized and treated as multiple lexical tokens (in the examples, the lexical items have distinct syntactic functions: predicate (*da/dă*), indirect object (*me/mi*) and direct object (*lo/le*).

The simplest method for *multiword expression* (MWE) recognition during text segmentation is based on (monolingual) lists of most frequent compound expressions (collocations, compound nouns, phrasal verbs, idioms, etc) and some regular expression patterns for dealing with multiple instantiations of similar constructions (numbers, dates, abbreviations, etc). This linguistic knowledge (which could be compiled as a finite state transducer) is referred to as tokenizer's MWE resources. In this approach the tokenizer would check if the input text contains string sequences that match any of the stored patterns and, in such a case, the matching input sequences are replaced as prescribed by the tokenizer's resources. The main criticism of this simple text segmentation method is that the tokenizer's resources are never exhaustive. Against this drawback one can use special programs for automatic updating of the tokenizer's resources using collocation extractors. A statistical collocation extraction program is based on the insight that words that appear together more often than would be expected under an independence assumption and conform to some prescribed syntactic patterns are likely to be collocations. For checking the independence assumption, one can use various statistical tests such as mutual information, DICE, log-likelihood, chi-square or left-Fisher exact test (see, for instance, http://www.d.umn.edu/~tpederse/code.html). As these tests are considering only pairs of tokens, in order to identify collocations longer than two words, bigram analysis must be recursively applied until no new collocations are discovered. The final list of extracted collocations must be filtered out as it might include many spurious associations.

For our research we initially used Philippe di Cristo's multilingual segmenter MtSeg (http://www.lpl.univ-aix.fr/projects/multext/MtSeg/) built in the MULTEXT project. The segmenter comes with tokenization resources for many Western European languages, further enhanced, as a result of the MULTEXT-EAST project, with corresponding resources for Bulgarian, Czech, Estonian, Hungarian, Romanian and Slovene. MtSeg is a regular expression interpreter whose performance depends on the coverage of available tokenization resources. Its main advantage is that for tokens with the same cross-lingual interpretation (numbers dates, clitics, compounds, abbreviations etc) the same label will be assigned, irrespective of the language. We re-implemented MtSeg in an integrated tokenization-tagging and lemmatization web service called TTL [11], available at http://nlp.racai.ro, for processing Romanian and English texts.

For updating the multiword expressions resource file of the tokenizer, we developed a statistical collocation extractor [12] which is not constrained by token adjacency and thus can detect token combinations which are not contiguous. The criteria for considering a pair of tokens as a possible interesting combination are:

- stability of the distance between the two lexical tokens within texts (estimated by a low standard deviation of these distances)
- statistical significance of co-occurrence for the two tokens (estimated by a log-likelihood test).

The set of automatically extracted collocations are hand-validated and added to the multiword expressions resource file of the tokenizer.

2. Morpho-lexical Disambiguation

Morpho-lexical ambiguity resolution is a key task in natural language processing [13]. It can be regarded as a classification problem: an ambiguous lexical item is one that in different contexts can be classified differently and given a specified context the disambiguation/classification engine decides on the appropriate class.

Any classification process requires a set of distinguishing features of the objects to be classified, based on which a classifier could make informed decisions. If the values of these features are known, then the classification process is simply an assignment problem. However, when one or more values of the classification criteria are unknown, the classifier has to resort to other information sources or to make guesses. In a well-defined classification problem each relevant feature of an entity subject to classification (here, lexical tokens) has a limited range of values.

The decisions such as what is a lexical token, what are the relevant features and values in describing the tokens of a given language, and so on, depend on the circumstances of an instance of linguistic modeling (what the modeling is meant for, available resources, level of knowledge and many others). Modeling language is not a straightforward process and any choices made are a corollary of a particular view of the language. Under different circumstances, the same language will be more often than not modeled differently. Therefore, when speaking of a natural language from a theoretical-linguistics or computational point of view, one has to bear in mind this distinction between language and its modeling. Obviously this is the case here, but for the sake of brevity we will use the term *language* even when an accurate reference would be *(X's) model of the language*.

The features that are used for the classification task are encoded in tags. We should observe that not all lexical features are equally good predictors for the correct contextual morpho-lexical classification of the words. It is part of the corpus linguistics lore that in order to get high accuracy level in statistical part-of-speech disambiguation, one needs small tagsets and reasonably large training data.

Earlier, we mentioned several initiatives towards the standardization of morpho-lexical descriptions. They refer to a neutral, context independent and maximally informative description of the available lexical data. Such descriptions in the context of the Multext-East specifications are represented by what has been called *lexical tags*. *Lexical tagsets* are large, ranging from several hundreds to several thousands of tags. Depending on specific applications, one can define subsets of tagsets, retaining in these reduced tagsets only features and values of interest for intended applications. Yet, given that the statistical *part of speech (POS) tagging* is a distributional method, it is very important that the features and values preserved in a tagset be sensitive to the context and to the distributional analysis methods. Such reduced tagsets are usually called *corpus tagsets*.

The effect of tagset size on tagger performance has been discussed in [14] and several papers in [13] (the reference tagging monograph). If the underlying language model uses only a few linguistic features and each of them has a small number of attributes, than the cardinality of the necessary tagset will be small. In contrast, if a language model uses a large number of linguistic features and they are described in terms of a larger set of attributes, the necessary tagset will be necessarily larger than in the previous case. POS-tagging with a large tagset is harder because the granularity of the language model is finer-grain. Harder here means slower, usually less accurate and requiring more computational resources. However, as we will show, the main reason for errors in tagging is not the number of feature-values used in the tagset but the adequacy of selected features and of their respective values. We will argue that a carefully designed tagset can assure an acceptable accuracy even with a simple-minded tagging engine, while a badly designed tagset could hamper the performance of any tagging program.

It is generally believed that the state of the art in POS tagging still leaves room for significant improvements as far as correctness is concerned. In statistics-based tagging, besides the adequacy of the tagset, there is another crucial factor[1], the quantity and quality of *the training data* (evidence to be generalized into a language model). A training corpus of anywhere from 100,000 up to over a million words is typically considered adequate. Although some taggers are advertised as being able to learn a language model from raw texts and a word-form lexicon, they require post-validation of the output and a bootstrapping procedure that would take several iterations to bring the tagger's error rate to an acceptable level.

Most of the work in POS-tagging relies on the availability of high-quality training data and concentrates on the engineering issues to improve the performance of learners and taggers [13-25]. Building a high-quality training corpus is a huge enterprise because it is typically hand-made and therefore extremely expensive and slow to produce. A frequent claim justifying poor performance or incomplete evaluation for POS taggers is the dearth of training data. In spite of this, it is surprising how little effort has been made towards automating the tedious and very expensive hand-annotation procedures underlying the construction or extension of a training corpus. The utility of a training corpus is a function not only of its correctness, but also of its size and diversity. Splitting a large training corpus into register-specific components

---

[1] We don't discuss here the training and the tagging engines, which are language-independent and obviously play a fundamental role in the process.

can be an effective strategy towards building a highly accurate combined language model, as we will show in Section 2.5.

2.1. Tagsets encoding

For computational reasons, it is useful to adopt an encoding convention for both lexical and corpus tagsets. We briefly present the encoding conventions used in the Multext-East lexical specifications (for a detailed presentation, the interested reader should consult the documentation available at http://nl.ijs.si/ME/V3/msd/).

The morpho-lexical descriptions, referred to as *MSD*s, are provided as strings, using a linear encoding. In this notation, the position in a string of characters corresponds to an attribute, and specific characters in each position indicate the value for the corresponding attribute. That is, the positions in a string of characters are numbered 0, 1, 2, etc., and are used in the following way (see Table 1):

- the character at position 0 encodes part-of-speech;
- each character at position 1, 2,...,n, encodes the value of one attribute (person, gender, number, etc.), using the one-character code;
- if an attribute does not apply, the corresponding position in the string contains the special marker '-' (hyphen).

Table 1. The Multilingual Multext-East Description Table for the Verb

Position	Attribute	Value	Code
0	POS	verb	V
1	Type	main	m
		auxiliary	a
		modal	o
		copula	c
	l.s.	base	b
2	Vform	indicative	i
		subjunctive	s
		imperative	m
		conditional	c
		infinitive	n
		participle	p
		gerund	g
		supine	u
	l.s.	transgress	t
	l.s.	quotative	q
3	Tense	present	p
		imperfect	i
		future	f
		past	s
	l.s.	pluperfect	l
	l.s.	aorist	a
4	Person	first	1
		second	2
		third	3
5	Number	singular	s
		plural	p
	l.s.	dual	d
6	Gender	masculine	m
		feminine	f
		neuter	n
7	Voice	active	a
		passive	p
8	Negative	no	n
		yes	y
9	Definite	no	n
		yes	y
	l.s.	short_art	s
	l.s.	ful_art	f
	l.s.	1s2s	2
10	Clitic	no	n
		yes	y
11	Case	nominative	n
		genitive	g
		dative	d
		accusative	a
		locative	l
		instrumental	i
		illative	x
		inessive	2
		elative	e
		translative	4
		abessive	5
12	Animate	no	n
		yes	y
13	Clitic_s	no	n
		yes	y

The "does not apply" marker ('-') in the MSD encoding must be explained. Besides the basic meaning that the attribute is not valid for the language in question, it also indicates that a certain combination of other morpho-lexical attributes makes the current one irrelevant. For instance, non-finite verbal forms are not specified for Person.

The EAGLES recommendations (http://www.ilc.cnr.it/EAGLES96/morphsyn/morphsyn.html) provide another special attribute value, the dot ("."), for cases where an attribute can take any value in its domain. The 'any' value is especially relevant in situations where word-forms are underspecified for certain attributes but can be recovered from the immediate context (by grammatical rules such as agreement). By convention, trailing hyphens are not included in the MSDs. Such specifications provide a simple and relatively compact encoding, and are in intention similar to feature-structure encoding used in unification-based grammar formalisms.

As can be seen from Table 1, the MSD **Vmmp2s, will** be unambiguously interpreted as a Verb+Main+Imperative+Present+Second Person+Singular for any language.

In many languages, especially those with a productive inflectional morphology, the word-form is strongly marked for various feature-values, so one may take advantage of this observation in designing the reduced corpus tagset. We will call the tags in a reduced corpus tagset *c-tag*s. For instance, in Romanian, the suffix of a finite verb together with the information on person, almost always determine all the other feature values relevant for describing an occurrence of a main verb form. When this dependency is taken into account, almost all of the large number of Romanian verbal MSDs will be filtered out, leaving us with just three MSDs: Vm--1, Vm--2 and Vm—3, each of them subsuming several MSDs, as in the example below:

```
Vm--2 ⇒ {Vmii2s----y Vmip2p Vmip2s Vmsp2s----y Vmip2p----y Vmm-2p Vmm-2s
         Vmil2p----y Vmis2s----y Vmis2p Vmis2s Vmm-2p----y Vmii2p----y
         Vmip2s----y Vmsp2p----y Vmii2p Vmii2s Vmil2s----y Vmis2p----y
         Vmil2p Vmil2s Vmm-2s----y Vmsp2p Vmsp2s}
```

The set of MSDs subsumed by a c-tag is called its *MSD-coverage* denoted by `msd_cov(c-tag)`. Similar correspondences can be defined for any c-tag in the reduced corpus tagset. The set of these correspondences defines the mapping M between a corpus tagset and a lexical tagset. For reasons that will be discussed in the next section, a proper mapping between a lexical tagset and a corpus tagset should have the following properties:

- the set of *MSD-coverage*s for all c-tags represents a partition of MSD tagset
- for any MSD in the lexical tagset there exists a unique c-tag in the corpus tagset.

By definition, for any MSD there exists a unique c-tag that observes the properties above and for any c-tag there exists a unique MSD-coverage. The mapping M represents the essence of our tiered-tagging methodology.

As we will show, given a lexical tagset one could automatically build a corpus tagset and a mapping M between the two tagsets. If a training corpus is available and disambiguated in terms of lexical tags, the tiered tagging design methodology may generate various corpus tagsets, optimized according to different criteria. The discussion that follows concentrates on Romanian but similar issues arise and must be resolved when dealing with other languages.

2.2. The Lexical Tagset Design: A Case Study on Romanian

An EAGLES-compliant MSD word-form lexicon was built within the MULTEXT-EAST joint project within the Copernicus Program. A lexicon entry has the following structure:

`word-form` <TAB> `lemma` <TAB> `MSD`

where `word-form` represents an inflected form of the `lemma`, characterized by a combination of feature values encoded by `MSD` code. According to this representation, a word-form may appear in several entries, but with different MSDs or different lemmas. The set of MSDs with which a word-form occurs in the lexicon represents its *ambiguity class*. As an ambiguity class is common to many word-forms, another way of saying that the ambiguity class of word w_k is A_m, is to say that (from the ambiguity resolution point of view) the word w_k belongs to the ambiguity class A_m.

When the word-form is identical to the lemma, then an equal sign is written in the lemma field of the entry ('='). The attributes and most of the values of the attributes were chosen considering only word-level encoding. As a result, values involving compounding, such as compound tenses, though familiar from grammar textbooks, were not chosen for the MULTEXT-EAST encoding.

The initial specifications of the Romanian lexical tagset [26] took into account all the morpho-lexical features used by the traditional lexicography. However, during the development phase, we decided to exploit some regular syncretic features (gender and case) which eliminated a lot of representation redundancy and proved to be highly beneficial for the statistics-based tagging. We decided to use two special cases (*direct* and *oblique*) to deal with the nominative-accusative and genitive-dative syncretism, and to eliminate neuter gender from the lexicon encoding. Another feature which we discarded was *animacy* which is required for the vocative case. However, as vocative case has a distinctive inflectional suffix (also, in normative writing, an exclamation point is required after a vocative), and given that metaphoric vocatives are very frequent (not only in poetic or literary texts), we found the *animacy* feature a source of statistical noise (there are no distributional differences between animate and inanimate noun phrases) and, therefore, we ignored it.

With redundancy eliminated, the word-form lexicon size decreased more than fourfold. Similarly the size of the lexical tagset decreased by more than a half. While any shallow parser can usually make the finer-grained case distinction and needs no further comment, eliminating neuter gender from the lexicon encoding requires explanation. Romanian grammar books traditionally distinguish three genders: masculine, feminine and neuter. However there are few reasons – if any – to retain the neuter gender and not use a simpler dual gender system. From the inflectional point of view, neuter nouns/adjectives behave in singular as masculine nouns/adjectives and in plural as feminine ones. Since there is no intrinsic semantic feature specific to neuter nouns (inanimacy is by no means specific to neuter nouns; plenty of feminine and masculine nouns denote inanimate things) preserving the three-valued gender distinction creates more problems than it solves. At the lookup level, considering only gender, any adjective would be two-way ambiguous (masculine/neuter in singular and feminine/neuter in plural). However, it is worth mentioning that if needed, the neuter nouns or adjectives can be easily identified: those nouns/adjectives that are tagged with masculine gender in singular and with feminine gender in plural are what the traditional

Romanian linguistics calls neuter nouns/adjectives. This position has recently found adherents among theoretical linguists as well. For instance, in [27] neuter nouns are considered to be underspecified for gender in their lexical entries, having default rules assigning masculine gender for occurrences in singular and feminine gender for occurrences in plural.

For the description of the current Romanian word-form lexicon (more then one million word-forms, distributed among 869 ambiguity classes) the lexical tagset uses 614 MSD codes. This tagset is still too large because it requires very large training corpora for overcoming data sparseness. The need to overcome data sparseness stems from the necessity to ensure that all the relevant sequences of tags are seen a reasonable number of times, thus allowing the learning algorithms to estimate (as reliably as possible) word distributions and build robust language models. Fallback solutions for dealing with unseen events are approximations that significantly weaken the robustness of a language model and affect prediction accuracy. For instance in a trigram-based language model, an upper limit of the search space for the language model would be proportional to N^3 with N denoting the cardinality of the tagset. Manually annotating a corpus containing (at least several occurrences of) all the legal trigrams using a tagset larger than a few hundreds of tags is practically impossible.

In order to cope with the inherent problems raised by large tagsets one possible solution is to apply a tiered tagging methodology.

2.3. Corpus Tagset Design and Tiered Tagging

Tiered tagging (TT) is a very effective technique [28] which allows accurate morpho-lexical tagging with large lexicon tagsets and requires reasonable amounts of training data. The basic idea is using a hidden tagset, for which training data is sufficient, for tagging proper and including a post-processing phase for transforming the tags from the hidden tagset into the more informative tags from the lexicon tagset. As a result, for a small price in tagging accuracy (as compared to the direct reduced tagset approach), and with practically no changes to computational resources, it is possible to tag a text with a large tagset by using language models built for reduced tagsets. Consequently, for building high quality language models, training corpora of moderate size would suffice.

In most cases, the word-form and the associated MSD taken together contain redundant information. This means that the word-form and several attribute-value pairs from the corresponding MSD (called *the determinant* in our approach) uniquely determine the rest of the attribute-value pairs (*the dependent*). By dropping the dependent attributes, provided this does not reduce the cardinality of *ambiguity classes* (see [28]), several initial tags are merged into fewer and more general tags. This way the cardinality of the tagset is reduced. As a result, the tagging accuracy improves even with limited training data. Since the attributes and their values depend on the grammar category of the word-forms we will have different determinants and dependents for each part of speech. Attributes such as part of speech (the attribute at position 0 in the MSD encoding) and *orth*, whose value is the given word form, are included in every determinant. Unfortunately, there is no unique solution for finding the rest of the attributes in the determinants of an MSD encoding. One can identify the smallest set of determinant attributes for each part of speech but using the smallest determinant (and implicitly the smallest corpus tagset) does not necessarily ensure the best tagging accuracy.

A corpus tagset (Ctag-set) whose c-tags contain only determinant feature values is called a *baseline Ctag-set*. Any further elimination of attributes of the baseline Ctag-set will cause information loss. Further reduction of the baseline tagset can be beneficial if information from eliminated attributes can be recovered by post-tagging processing. The tagset resulting from such further reduction is called a *proper Ctag-set.*

The abovementioned relation M between the MSD-set and the Ctag-set is encoded in a mapping table that for each MSD specifies the corresponding c-tag and for each c-tag the set of MSDs (its msd-coverage) that are mapped onto it. The post-processor that deterministically replaces a c-tag with one or more MSDs, is essentially a database look-up procedure. The operation can be formally represented as an intersection of the *ambiguity class of the word w,* referred to as *AMB(w)*, and the msd-coverage of the c-tag assigned to the word *w*. If the hidden tagset used is a *baseline Ctag-set* this intersection always results in a single MSD. In other words, full recovery of the information is strictly deterministic. For the general case of a *proper Ctag-set*, the intersection leaves a few tokens ambiguous between 2 (seldom, 3) MSDs. These tokens are typically the difficult cases for statistical disambiguation.

The core algorithm is based on the property of *Ctag-set recoverability* described by the equation Eq.(1). We use the following notation: W_i, represents a word, T_i represents a c-tag assigned to W_i, MSD_k represents a tag from the lexical tagset, $AMB(W_k)$ represents the ambiguity class of the word W_k in terms of MSDs (as encoded in the lexicon Lex) and $|X|$ represents the cardinality of the set X.

$$\forall\ Ti \in \text{Ctag-set, msd-coverage } (Ti)=\{MSD1\ldots MSDk\}\subset \text{MSD-tagset},$$
$$\forall W_k \in Lex\ \&\ AMB(W_k)=\{MSD_{k1}\ldots MSD_{kn}\}\subset \text{MSD-tagset} \Rightarrow$$
$$\left|\text{msd-coverage}(T_i)\bigcap AMB(W_k)\right| = \begin{cases} 1 & \text{for} > 90\% \text{ cases} \\ >1 & \text{for} < 10\% \text{ cases} \end{cases} \tag{1}$$

Once Ctag-set has been selected, the designer accounts for the few remaining ambiguities after the c-tags are replaced with the corresponding MSDs. In the original implementation of the TT framework, the remaining ambiguities were dealt with by a set of simple hand-written contextual rules. For Romanian, we used 18 regular expression rules. Depending on the specific case of ambiguity, these rules inspect left, right or both contexts within a limited distance of a disambiguating tag or word-form (in our experiment the maximum span is 4). The success rate of this second phase is almost 99%. The rule that takes care of the gender, number and case agreement between a determiner and the element it modifies by solving the residual ambiguity between possessive pronouns and possessive determiners is as follows:

```
Ps|Ds
    {Ds.αβδ:(-1 Ncαβδy)|(-1 Af. αβδy)|(-1 Mo.αβδy)|(-2 Af.αβδn and –1 Ts)|
        (-2 Ncαβδn and –1 Ts)|(-2 Np and –1 Ts)|(-2 D..αβδ and –1 Ts)
    Ps.αβδ: true}
```

In English, the rule can be glossed as:

Choose the determiner interpretation if any of the conditions a) to g) is true:
  a) the previous word is tagged definite common Noun
  b) the previous word is tagged definite Adjective

c) the previous word is tagged definite ordinal Numeral
d) the previous two words are tagged indefinite Adjective and possessive Article
e) the previous two words are tagged indefinite Noun and possessive Article
f) the previous two words are tagged proper Noun and possessive Article
g) the previous two words are tagged Determiner and possessive Article.
Otherwise, choose the pronoun interpretation.

In the above rule $\alpha\beta\delta$ denotes values for gender, number and case respectively. In Romanian, these values are usually realized using a single affix.

In [29] we discuss our experimentation with TT and its evaluation for Romanian, where the initial lexicon tagset contained over 1,000 tags while the hidden tagset contained only 92 (plus 10 punctuation tags). Even more spectacular results were obtained for Hungarian, a very different language [30], [31], [32]. Hinrichs and Trushkina [33] report very promising results for the use of TT for German.

The hand-written recovery rules for the proper Ctag-set are the single language-dependent component in the tiered-tagging engine. Another inconvenience was related to the words not included in the tagger's lexicon. Although our tagger assigns any unknown word a c-tag, the transformation of this c-tag into an appropriate MSD is impossible, because, as can be seen from equation Eq.(1), this process is based on lexicon look-up. These limitations have been recently eliminated in a new implementation of the tiered tagger, called METT [34]. METT is a tiered tagging system that uses a maximum entropy (ME) approach to automatically induce the mappings between the Ctag-set and the MSD-set. This method requires a training corpus tagged twice: the first time with MSDs and the second time with c-tags. As we mentioned before, transforming an MSD-annotated corpus into its proper Ctag-set variant can be carried out deterministically. Once this precondition is fulfilled, METT learns non-lexicalized probabilistic mappings from Ctag-set to MSD-set. Therefore it is able to assign a contextually adequate MSD to a c-tag labeling an out-of-lexicon word.

2.3.1. Automatic Construction of an Optimal Baseline Ctag-set

Eliminating redundancy from a tagset encoding may dramatically reduce its cardinality without information loss (in the sense that if some information is left out it could be deterministically restored when or if needed). This problem has been previously addressed in [17] but in that approach a greedy algorithm is proposed as the solution. In this section we present a significantly improved algorithm for automatic construction of an optimal Ctag-set, originally proposed in [35], which outperforms our initial tagset designing system and is fully automatic. In the previous approach, the decision which ambiguities are allowed to remain in the Ctag-set relies exclusively on the MSD lexicon and does not take into account the occurrence frequency of the words that might remain ambiguous after the computation described in Eq. (1). In the present algorithm the frequency of words in the corpus is a significant design parameter. More precisely, instead of counting how many words in the dictionary will be partially disambiguated using a hidden tagset we compute a score for the ambiguity classes based on their frequency in the corpus. If further reducing a baseline tagset creates ambiguity in the recovery process for a number of ambiguity classes and these classes correspond to very rare words, then the reduction should be considered practically harmless even without recovering rules.

The best strategy in using the algorithm is to first build an optimal baseline Ctag-set, with the designer determining the criteria for optimality. From the baseline tagset, a corpus linguist may further reduce the tagsets taking into account the distributional properties of the language in question. As any further reduction of the baseline tagsets leads to information loss, adequate recovering rules should be designed for ensuring the final tagging in terms of lexicon encoding.

For our experiments we used the *1984* Multext-East parallel corpus and the associated word-forms lexicons [36]. These resources were produced in the Multext-East and Concede European projects. The tagset design algorithm takes as input a word-form lexicon and a corpus encoded according to XCES-specifications used by the Multext-East consortium.

Since for the generating the baseline Ctag-sets, no expert language knowledge is required, we ran the algorithm with the ambiguity *threshold* set to 0 (see below) and generated the baseline Ctag-sets for English and five East-European languages – Czech, Estonian, Hungarian, Romanian and Slovene. In order to find the best baseline tagset (the one ensuring the best tagging results), each generated tagset is used for building a language model and tagging unseen data (see the next section for details). We used a ten-fold validation procedure (using for training 9/10 of the corpus and the remaining 1/10 of the corpus for evaluation and averaging the accuracy results).

2.3.2. The Algorithm

The following definitions are used in describing the algorithm:

T_i = A c-tag

$S_{AC}(AMB_i)$ $=\Sigma_{w\in AMB_i} RF(w) \leq$ *threshold*: the frequency score of an ambiguity class AMB_i where:

RF(w) is the relative frequency in a training corpus of the word *w* characterized by the ambiguity class AMB_i and ***threshold*** is a designer parameter (a null value corresponds to the baseline tagset); we compute these scores only for AMBs characterizing the words whose c-tags might not be fully recoverable by the procedure described in Eq.(1);

$f_{AC}(T_i)$ $=\{(AMB_{ik},S_{AC}(AMB_{ik})|AMB_{ik}\cap$msd-coverage$(T_i)\neq\varnothing\}$is the set of pairs of ambiguity classes and their scores so that each AMB contains at least one MSD in msd-coverage(T_i);

pen(T_i,AMB_j)= $S_{AC}(AMB_j)$ if card $|AMB_j\cap$ msd-coverage $(T_i)|>1$ and 0 otherwise; this is a penalty for a c-tag labeling any words characterized by AMB_i which cannot be deterministically converted into an unique MSD. We should note that the same c-tag labeling a word characterized by a different AMB_j might be deterministically recoverable to the appropriate MSD.

PEN(T_i) = $\Sigma(pen(T_i,AMB_j)|AMB_j \in f_{AC}(T_i))$

DTR = $\{A_{Pi}\}$ = a determinant set of attributes: P is a part of speech; the index *i* represents the attribute at position *i* in the MULTEXT-East encoding of P; for instance, A_{V4} represents the *PERSON* attribute of the verb. The attributes in DTR are not subject to elimination in the baseline tagset generation. Because the search space of the algorithm is structured according to the determinant attributes for each part of speech, the running time significantly decreases as DTRs become larger.

POS(code)=the part of speech in a MSD or a c-tag code.

The input data for the algorithm is the word-form lexicon (MSD encoded) and the corpus (disambiguated in terms of MSDs). The output is a baseline Ctag-set. The CTAGSET-DESIGN algorithm is a trial and error procedure that generates all possible baseline tagsets and with each of them constructs language models which are used in the tagging of unseen texts. The central part of the algorithm is the procedure CORE, briefly commented in the description below.

```
procedure CTAGSET-DESIGN (Lex, corpus;Ctag-set) is:
 MSD-set = GET-MSD-SET (Lex)
 AMB = GET-AMB-CLASSES (Lex)
 DTR = {POS(MSD_i)}, i=1..|MSD-set|
 MATR = GET-ALL-ATTRIBUTES (MSD-set)
 T= {} ; a temporary Ctag-set
 for each AMB_i in AMB
   execute COMPUTE-S_AC(corpus, AMB_i)
 end for
 while DTR ≠ MATR
   for each attribute A_i in MATR\ DTR
     D=DTR ∪ {A_i} ; temporary DTR
     T=T ∪ execute CORE ({(AMB_i , S_AC(AMB_i))^+})
   end for
   A_k = execute FIND-THE-BEST(T)
   DTR= DTR ∪ {A_k} & T={}
 end while
 Ctag-set=KEEP-ONLY-ATT-IN-DTR (MSD-set, DTR)
; attribute values not in DTR are converted into '+'(redundant) in all MSDs & duplicates are removed.
 end procedure
 procedure FIND-THE-BEST ({(ctagset, DTR)^+}; Attr) is:
 rez = {}
  for each ctagset in {(ctagset_i, DTR_i)^+}
   tmp-corpus = execute MSD2CTAG(corpus, ctagset_i)
   train = 9/10*tmp-corpus & test = tmp-corpus \ train
   LM = execute BUILD-LANGUAGE-MODEL(train)
   Prec = execute EVAL (tagger, LM, test)
   rez = rez ∪ {(|ctagset_i|, Prec_i, DTR_i)}
  end for
  Attr = LAST-ATTRIB-OF-DTR_i-WITH-MAX-PREC_i-IN(rez)
 end procedure
 procedure CORE ({(AMB_i, S_AC(AMB_i))^+},DTR;({(T_i, msd-coverage(T_i))^+}, DTR))
  T_i = MSD_i  i=1..|MSD-set|
  msd-coverage(T_i)={MSD_i} & AMB(T_i)=f_AC(T_i)
  TH = threshold & Ctag-set={T_i}
  {repeat until no attribute can be eliminated
      for each T_i in Ctag-set
       {START: for each attribute A_jk of T_i so that A_jk∉DTR
         if newT_i is obtained from T_i by deleting A_jk
         1) if newT_i ∉ Ctag-set then
               Ctag-set=(Ctag-set\{T_i})∪{newT_i} continue from START
         2) else if newT_i =T_n∈ Ctag-set then
             msd-coverage(newT_i)= msd-coverage(T_n)∪msd-coverage(T_i)
             AMB (newT_i) = AMB(T_n) ∪ AMB(T_i)
             if PEN(newT_i) = 0 then
              Ctag-set=(Ctag-set\{T_n,T_i})∪{newT_i} continue from START
            else
            3) if PEN(newT_i) ≤ THR then
                mctag=T_i & matrib=A_jk & TH=PEN(newT_i)  continue from START
       end for}
     end for}
    { 4) eliminate matrib from mctag and obtain newT_i
```

```
        for each Tn în Ctag-set so that Tn = newTi
          msd-coverage(newTi) = msd-coverage(Tn) ∪ msd-coverage(mctag)
          AMB (newTi) = AMB(Tn) ∪ AMB(mctag)
          Ctag-set=(Ctag-set\{mctag,Tn})∪{newTi}
          TH=threshold  } ;  closing 4)
    end repeat }
  end procedure
```

The procedures BUILD-LANGUAGE-MODEL and EVAL were not presented in detail, as they are standard procedures present in any tagging platform. All the other procedures not shown (COMPUTE-S_{AC}, KEEP-ONLY-ATT-IN-DTR, MSD2TAG, and LAST-ATTRIB-OF-DTR_I-WITH-MAX-$PREC_I$-IN) are simple transformation scripts.

The computation of the msd-coverage and AMB sets in step **2)** of the procedure CORE can lead to non-determinism in MSD recovery process (i.e. PEN(newT$_i$) $\neq 0$). Step **3)** recognizes the potential non-determinism and, if the generated ambiguity is acceptable, stores the dispensable attribute and the current c-tag eliminated in step **4)**.

In order to derive the optimal Ctag-set one should be able to use a large training corpus (where all the MSDs defined in the lexicon are present) and to run the algorithm on all the possible DTRs. Unfortunately this was not the case for our multilingual data. The MSDs used in the *1984* corpus represent only a fraction of the MSDs present in the word-form lexicons of each language. Most of the ambiguous words in the corpus occur only with a subset of their ambiguity classes. It is not clear whether some of the morpho-lexical codes would occur in a larger corpus or whether they are theoretically possible interpretations that might not be found in a reasonably large corpus. We made a heuristic assumption that the unseen MSDs of an ambiguity class were rare events, so they were given a happax legomenon status in the computation of the scores $S_{AC}(AMB_j)$. Various other heuristics were used to make this algorithm more efficient. This was needed because generating of the baseline tagset takes a long time (for Slovene or Czech it required more than 80 hours).

2.3.3. Evaluation results

We performed experiments with six languages represented in the *1984* parallel corpus: Romanian (RO), Slovene (SI), Hungarian (HU), English (EN), Czech (CZ) and Estonian (ET). For each language we computed three baseline tagsets: the minimal one (smallest-sized DTR), the best performing one (the one which yielded the best precision in tagging) and the Ctag-set with the precision comparable to the MSD tagset. We considered two scenarios, sc1 and sc2, differing in whether the tagger had to deal with unknown words; in both scenarios, the ambiguity classes were computed from the large word-form lexicons created during the Multext-East project.

In sc1 the tagger lexicon was generated from the training corpus; words that appeared only in the test part of the corpus were unknown to the tagger;

In sc2) the unigram lexicon was computed from the entire corpus AND the word-form lexicon (with the entries not appearing in the corpus been given a lexical probability corresponding to a single occurrence); in this scenario, the tagger faced no unknown words.

The results are summarized in Table 2. In accordance with [37] we agree that "it is not unreasonable to assume that a larger dictionary exists, which can help to obtain a list of possible tags for each word-form in the text data". Therefore we consider the sc2 to be more relevant than sc1.

Table 2. Optimal baseline tagsets for 6 languages

Lang.	MSD-set		Minimal Ctag-		Best prec. Ctag-set		Ctag-set with prec. close to MSD	
	No.	Prec.	No.	Prec.	No.	Prec.	No.	Prec.
RO^{sc1}	615	95.8	56	95.1	174	96.0	81	95.8
RO^{sc2}	615	97.5	56	96.9	205	97.8	78	97.6
SI^{sc1}	2083	90.3	385	89.7	691	90.9	585	90.4
SI^{sc2}	2083	92.3	404	91.6	774	93.0	688	92.5
HU^{sc1}	618	94.4	44	94.7	84	95.0	44	94.7
HU^{sc2}	618	96.6	128	96.6	428	96.7	112	96.6
EN^{sc1}	133	95.5	45	95.5	95	95.8	52	95.6
EN^{sc2}	133	95.9	45	95.9	61	96.3	45	95.9
CZ^{sc1}	1428	89.0	291	88.9	735	90.2	319	89.2
CZ^{sc2}	1428	91.8	301	91.0	761	92.5	333	91.8
ET^{sc1}	639	93.0	208	92.8	355	93.5	246	93.1
ET^{sc2}	639	93.4	111	92.8	467	93.8	276	93.5

The algorithm is implemented in Perl. Brants' TnT trigram HMM tagger [25] was the model for our tagger included in the TTL platform [11] which was used for the evaluation of the generated baseline tagsets. However, the algorithm is tagger- and method-independent (it can be used in HMM, ME, rule-based and other approaches), given the compatibility of the input/output format. The programs and the baseline tagsets can be freely obtained from https://nlp.racai.ro/resources, on a research free license.

The following observations can be made concerning the results in Table 2:

- the tagging accuracy with the "Best precision Ctag-set" for Romanian was only 0.65% inferior to the tagging precision reported in [29] where the hidden tagset (92 c-tags) was complemented by 18 recovery rules;
- for all languages the "Best precision Ctag-set" (scenario 2) is much smaller than the MSD tagset, it is fully recoverable to the MSD annotation and it always outperforms the MSD tagset; it seems unreasonable to use the MSD-set when significantly smaller tagsets in a tiered tagging approach would ensure the same information content in the final results;
- using the baseline Ctag-sets instead of MSD-sets in language modeling should result in more reliable language models since the data sparseness effect is significantly diminished; the small differences in precision shown in Table 2 between tagging with the MSD-set and any baseline Ctag-set should not be misleading: it is very likely that the difference in performance will be much larger on different register texts (with the Ctag-sets always performing better);
- remember that the tagsets produced by the algorithm represent a baseline; to take full advantage of the power of the tiered tagging approach, one should proceed further with the reduction of the baseline tagset towards the hidden tagset. The way our algorithm is implemented suggests that the best approach in designing the hidden tagset is to use as DTRs the attributes retained in the "Minimal Ctag-set". The threshold parameter (procedure CORE) which controls the frequency of words that are not fully disambiguated in the tagged text should be empirically determined. To obtain the hidden tagset mentioned in [29] we used a threshold of 0.027.

There are several applications for which knowing just the part of speech of a token (without any other attribute value) is sufficient. For such applications the desired tagset would contain about a dozen tags (most standardized morpho-lexical specifications distinguish 13-14 grammar categories). This situation is opposite to the one we discussed (having very large tagsets). Is the Ctag-set optimality issue relevant for such a shallow tagset? In [29] we described the following experiment: in our reference training corpora all the MSDs were replaced by their corresponding grammar category (position 0 in the Multext-East linear encoding, see Table 2). Thus, the tagset in the training corpora was reduced to 14 tags. We built language models from these new "training corpora" and used them in tagging a variety of texts. The average tagging accuracy was never higher than 93%. When the same texts were tagged with the language models build from the reference training corpora, annotated with the optimal Ctag-set; and when all the c-tag attributes in the final tagging were removed (that is, the texts were tagged with only 14 tags) the tagging accuracy was never below 99% (with an average accuracy of 99.35%). So, the answer to the last question is a definite yes!

2.4. Tagset Mapping and Improvement of Statistical Training Data

In this section we address another important issue concerning training data for statistical tagging, namely deriving mapping systems for unrelated tagsets used in existing training corpora (*gold standards*) for a specific language. There are many reasons one should address this problem, some of which are given below:

- training corpora are extremely valuable resources and, whenever possible, should be reused; however, usually, hand-annotated data is limited both in coverage and in size and therefore, merging various available resources could improve both the coverage and the robustness of the language models derived from the resulting training corpus;
- since gold standards are, in most cases, developed by different groups, with different aims, it is very likely that data annotation schemata or interpretations are not compatible, which creates a serious problem for any data merging initiative;
- for tagging unseen data, the features and their values used in one tagset could be better predictors than those used in another tagset;
- tagset mappings might reveal some unsystematic errors still present in the gold standards.

The method discussed in the previous section was designed for minimizing the tagsets by eliminating feature-value redundancy and finding a mapping between the lexical tagset and the corpus tagset, with the latter subsuming the former. In this section, we are instead dealing with completely unrelated tagsets [38]. Although the experiments were focused on morpho-lexical (POS) tagging, the method is applicable to other types of tagging as well.

For the experiments reported herein, we used the English component of the *1984* MULTEXT-EAST reference multilingual corpus and a comparable-size subset of the SemCor2.0 corpus (http://www.cs.unt.edu/~rada/downloads.html#semcor).

Let us introduce some definitions which will be used in the discussion that follows:

- $A_{GS}(X)$ denotes the *gold standard corpus A* which is tagged in terms of the *X tagset* and by $B_{GS}(Y)$ the *gold standard corpus B* which is tagged in terms of the *Y tagset*.
- The *direct tagging* (DT) is the usual process of tagging, where a language model learned from a gold standard corpus $A_{GS}(X)$ is used in POS-tagging of a different corpus B: $A_{GS}(X) + B \rightarrow B_{DT}(X)$
- The *biased tagging* (BT) is the tagging process of the the same corpus $A_{GS}(X)$ used for language model learning: $A_{GS}(X) + A \rightarrow A_{BT}(X)$. This process is useful for validating hand-annotated data. With a consistently tagged gold standard, the biased tagging is expected to be almost identical to the one in the gold standard [39]. We will use this observation to evaluate the gold standard improvements after applying our method.
- The *cross-tagging* (CT) is a method that, given two reference corpora, $A_{GS}(X)$ and $B_{GS}(Y)$, each tagged with different tagsets, produces the two corpora tagged with the other one's tagset, using a mapping system between the two tagsets: $A_{GS}(X)+A_{DT}(Y)+B_{GS}(Y)+B_{DT}(X) \rightarrow A_{CT}(Y)+B_{CT}(X)$.

Cross-tagging is a stochastic process which uses both language models learned from the reference corpora involved. We claim that the cross-tagged versions $A_{CT}(Y)$, $B_{CT}(X)$ will be more accurate than the ones obtained by direct tagging, $A_{DT}(Y)$, $B_{DT}(X)$.

The cross-tagging works with both the gold standard and the direct-tagged versions of the two corpora and involves two main steps: a) building a mapping system between the two tagsets and b) improving the direct-tagged versions using this mapping system. The overall system architecture is shown in Figure 1.

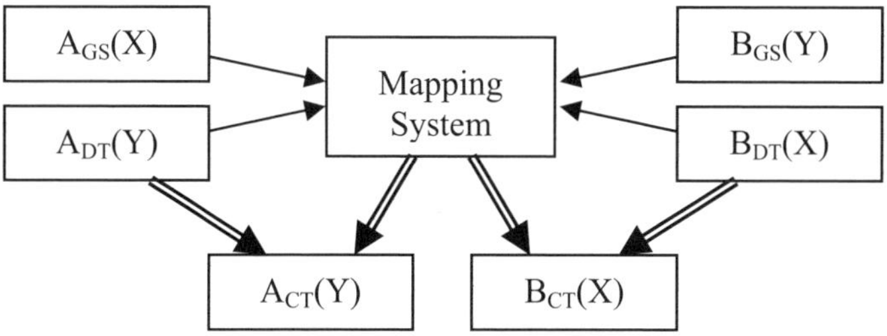

Figure 1. System Architecture

From the two versions of each corpus <$A_{GS}(X)$,$A_{DT}(Y)$> and <$B_{GS}(Y)$,$B_{DT}(X)$> tagged with the two tagsets (X and Y), we will extract two *corpus-specific mappings* <$M_A(X, Y)$> and < $M_B(X, Y)$>. Merging the two corpus-specific mappings there will result in a corpus-neutral, *global mapping* between the two considered tagsets M(X, Y).

2.4.1. Corpus-Specific Mappings

Let $X = \{x_1, x_2, \ldots, x_n\}$ and $Y = \{y_1, y_2, \ldots, y_m\}$ be the two tagsets. For a corpus tagged with both X and Y tagsets, we can build a *contingency table* (Table 3). For each tag $x \in X$, we define a subset of Y, $Y_x \subseteq Y$, that has the property that for any $y_j \in Y_x$ and for any $y_k \in Y - Y_x$, the probability of x conditioned by y_j is significantly higher than the probability of x conditioned by y_k. We say that x *is preferred* by tags in Y_x, or conversely, that tags in Y_x *prefer* x.

Table 3. The <X,Y> Contingency Table

	y_1	y_2	y_m	
x_1	N_{11}	N_{12}	N_{1m}	N_{x1}
x_2	N_{21}	N_{22}	N_{2m}	N_{x2}
…	…	…	…	…
x_n	N_{n1}	N_{n2}	N_{nm}	N_{xn}
	N_{y1}	N_{y2}	N_{ym}	N

The symbols have the following meanings:

N_{ij} – number of tokens tagged both with x_i and y_j
N_{xi} – number of tokens tagged with x_i
N_{yj} – number of tokens tagged with y_j
N – the total number of tokens in the corpus

Let $PSet(x_i)$ be the set of probabilities of $x_i \in X$, conditioned by each $y \in Y$:
$PSet(x_i) = \{p(x_i|y_j) \mid y_j \in Y\}$, where $p(x_i|y_j) = p(x_i,y_j) / p(y_j) \cong N_{ij} / N_{yj}$

Now, finding the values in $PSet(x_i)$ that are significantly higher than others means dividing $PSet(x_i)$ in two clusters. The most significant cluster (MSC), i.e. the cluster containing the greater values, will give us Y_x: $Y_x = \{y \in Y \mid p(x|y) \in MSC(P(x))\}$

A number of clustering algorithms could be used. We chose an algorithm of the single-link type, based on the raw distance between the values. This type of algorithm offers fast top-down processing (remember that we only need two final clusters) – sort the values in descending order, find the greatest distance between two consecutive values and split the values at that point. If more than one such greatest distance exists, the one between the smaller values is chosen to split on. The elements N_{ij} of the contingency table define a sparse matrix, with most of the values to cluster being zero. However, at least one value will be non-zero. Thus the most significant cluster will never contain zeroes, but it may contain all the non-zero values.

Let us consider the fragment of the contingency table presented in Table 4. According to the definitions above, we can deduce the following:

$PSet(x_1) = \{0.8, 0.05, 1\}$; $MSC(P(x_1))=\{0.8, 1\}$ $\Rightarrow Y_{x1}=\{y_1, y_3\}$

Table 4. A Contingency Table Example

	y_1	y_2	y_3	
x_1	80	50	5	135
…	…	…	…	…
	100	1000	5	1105

The preference relation is a first-level filtering of the tag mappings for which insufficient evidence is provided by the gold standard corpora. This filtering would eliminate several actual wrong mappings (not all of them) but also could remove correct mappings that occurred much less frequently than others. We will address this issue in the next section.

A *partial mapping* from X to Y (denoted PM_{*X}) is defined as the set of tag pairs $(x,y) \in X \times Y$ for which y prefers x. Similarly a partial mapping from Y to X (denoted by PM_{*Y}) can be defined. These partial mappings are corpus specific since they are constructed from a corpus where each token is assigned two tags, the first one from the X tagset and the second one from the Y tagset. They can be expressed as follows (the asterisk index is a place-holder for the corpus name from which the partial mapping was extracted):

$PM_{*X}(X, Y) = \{(x, y) \in X \times Y \mid y \in Y_x\}$

$PM_{*Y}(X, Y) = \{(x, y) \in X \times Y \mid x \in X_y\}$

The two partial mappings for a given corpus are merged into one corpus specific-mapping. So for our two corpora A and B we will construct the following two corpus specific-mappings:

$M_A(X, Y) = PM_{AX}(X, Y) \cup PM_{AY}(X, Y)$
$M_B(X, Y) = PM_{BX}(X, Y) \cup PM_{BY}(X, Y)$

2.4.2. The Global Mapping

The two corpus-specific mappings may be further combined into a single global mapping. We must filter out all the false positives the corpus-specific mappings might contain, while reducing the false negatives as much as possible. For this purpose, we used the following combining formula:
$M(X, Y) = M_A(X, Y) \cap M_B(X, Y)$

The global mapping contains all the tag pairs for which one of the tags prefers the other, in both corpora. As this condition is a very strong one, several potentially correct mappings will be left out from M(X, Y) either because of insufficient data, or because of idiosyncratic behavior of some lexical items. To correct this problem the global mapping is supplemented with the token mappings.

2.4.3. The Token Mapings

The global mapping expresses the preferences from one tag to another in a non-lexicalized way and is used as a back-off mechanism when the more precise lexicalized mapping is not possible. The data structures for lexicalized mappings are called *token mappings*. They are built only for token types, common to both corpora (except for hapax legomena).

The token types that occur only in one corpus will be mapped via the global mapping. The global mapping is also used for dealing with token types occurring in one corpus in contexts dissimilar to any context of occurrence in the other corpus.

For each common token type, we first build a *provisional token mapping* in the same way we built the global mapping, that is, build contingency tables, extract partial mappings from them, and then merge those partial mappings.

Example: The token type *will* has the contingency tables shown in Table 5.

Table 5. The tagging of token ***will*** in the *1984* corpus and a fragment of the *SemCor* corpus

1984 corpus

will	MD	VB	NN	
VMOD	170	1	1	172
NN	2	1	4	7
	172	2	5	179

SemCor corpus

will	VMOD	NN	
MD	236	1	237
VB	28	0	28
NN	0	4	4
	264	5	269

The tags have the following meanings: VMOD, MD – modal verb; NN (both tagsets) – noun; VB – verb, base form. Each table has its rows marked with the tags from the gold standard version and its columns with the tags of the direct-tagged version. The provisional token mapping extracted from these tables is:

$M_{will}(1984, SemCor) = \{(VMOD, MD), (NN, NN)\}$

It can be observed that the tag VB of the SemCor tagset remained unmapped.

A consistently tagged corpus assumes that a word occurring in similar contexts should be identically tagged. We say that a tag marks the class of contexts in which a word was systematically labeled by it.

If a word *w* of a two-way tagged corpus is tagged by the pair <x,y> and this pair belongs to $M_w(X,Y)$, this means that there are contexts marked by x similar to some contexts marked by y. If <x,y> is not in $M_w(X,Y)$, two situations are possible:

- either x or y (or both) are unmapped.
- both x and y are mapped to some other tags

In the next subsection we discuss the first case. The second case will be addressed in Section 2.4.5.

2.4.4. Unmapped Tags

A tag unmapped for a specific token type may mean one of two things: either none of the contexts it marks is observed in the other corpus, or the tag is wrongly assigned for that particular token type. The second possibility brings up one of the goals of this section, that is, to improve the quality of the gold standards.

If we decide that the unmapped tag was incorrectly assigned to the current token, the only thing to do is to trust the direct tagging and leave the tag unmapped.

In order to decide when it is likely to have a new context and when it is a wrong assignment, we relied on empirical observations leading to the conclusion that the more frequently the token type appears in the other corpus, the less likely is for a tag that is unmapped at token level to mark a new context. Unmapped tags assigned to tokens with frequencies below empirically set thresholds (see [38]) may signal the occurrence of the respective tokens in new contexts. If this is true, these tags will be mapped using the global map. To find out whether the new context hypothesis is acceptable, we use a heuristic based on the notion of *tag sympathy*.

Given a tagged corpus, we define the *sympathy between two tags* x_1 and x_2, of the same tagset, written $S(x_1,x_2)$, as the number of token types having at least one occurrence tagged x_1 and at least one occurrence tagged x_2. By definition, the sympathy of a tag with itself is infinite. The relation of sympathy is symmetrical.

During direct tagging, tokens are usually tagged only with tags from the ambiguity classes learnt from the gold standard corpus. Therefore, if a specific token appears in a context unseen during the language model construction, it will be inevitably incorrectly tagged during direct tagging. This error would show up because this tag, *x*, and the one in the gold standard, *y*, are very likely not to be mapped to each other in the mapping of the current token. If y is not mapped at all in the token's mapping, the algorithm checks if the tags mapped to y in the global mapping are sympathetic with any tag in the ambiguity class of the token type in question.

Some examples of highly sympathetic morphological categories for English are: nouns and base form verbs, past tense verbs and past participle verbs, adjectives and adverbs, nouns and adjectives, nouns and present participle verbs, adverbs and prepositions.

Example: Token Mapping Based on Tag Sympathy. The token type *behind* has the contingency tables shown in Table 6.

Table 6. Contingency tables of *behind* for the *1984* corpus and a fragment of the SemCor corpus

1984 corpus	
behind	IN
PREP	41
ADVE	9
	50

Part of *SemCor* corpus	
behind	PREP
IN	5
	5

The provisional token mapping is: M_{behind}(1984, SemCor) = {(PREP, IN)}

There is one unmapped tag: ADVE. The global mapping M contains two mappings for ADVE: M(ADVE)={RB, RBR}

The sympathy values are S(RB, IN) = 59, S(RBR, IN)=0

The sympathy relation being relevant only for the first pair, the token mapping for *behind* will become: M_{behind}(1984, SemCor) = {(PREP, IN), (ADVE, RB)}

This new mapping will allow for automatic correction of the direct tagging of various occurrences of the token *behind.*

We described the construction of the mapping data structures, composed of one global mapping and many token mappings. We now move on to the second step of the cross-tagging process, discussing how the mapping data structures are used.

2.4.5. Improving the Direct-Tagged Versions of Two Corpora

To improve the direct-tagged version of a corpus, we go through two stages: identifying the errors and correcting them. Obviously, not all errors can be identified and not all the changes are correct, but the overall accuracy will nevertheless be improved. In the next section we describe how candidate errors are spotted.

2.4.5.1. Error Identification

We have two direct-tagged corpora, $A_{DT}(Y)$ and $B_{DT}(X)$. They are treated independently, so we will further discuss only one of them, let it be $A_{DT}(Y)$. For each token of this corpus, we must decide if it was correctly tagged. Suppose the token w_k is tagged x in $A_{GS}(X)$ and y in $A_{DT}(Y)$. If the token type of that token, let it be w, has a token mapping, then it is used, otherwise, the global mapping is used. Let M_c be the chosen mapping.

If x is not mapped in M_c, or if $(x,y) \in M_c$, no action is taken. In the latter case, the direct tagging is in full agreement with the mapping. In the former, the direct tagging is considered correct as there is no reason to believe otherwise.

If x is mapped, but not to y, then y is considered incorrectly assigned and is replaced by the set of tags that are mapped to x in M_c.

At this point, each token in the corpus may have one or more tags assigned to it. This version is called the *star version* of the corpus A tagged with the tagset Y, written as A*(Y),. In the next section we show how we disambiguate the tokens having more than one tag in the star versions of the corpora.

2.4.5.2. The Algorithm for Choosing the Right Tag

Tag selection is carried out by retagging the star version of the corpus. The procedure is independent for each of the two corpora so that we describe it only for one of them. The retagging process is stochastic and based on trigrams. The language model is learned from the gold standard. We build a Markov model that has bigrams as states and emits tokens each time it leaves a state. To find the most likely path through the states of the Markov model, we used the Viterbi algorithm, with the restriction that the only tags available for a token are those assigned to that token in the star version of the corpus. This means that at any given moment only a limited number of states are available for selection.

The lexical probabilities used by the Viterbi algorithm have the form $p(w_k|y_i)$, where w_k is a token and y_i a tag. For $<w_k,y_i>$ pairs unseen in the training data[2], the most likelihood estimation (MLE) procedure would assign null probabilities ($p(w_k,y_i)=0$ and therefore $p(w_k|y_i)=0$). We smoothed the $p(w_k,x_i)$ probabilities using the Good-Turing estimation, as described in [40].

The probability mass reserved for the unseen token-tag pairs (let it be p_0) must somehow be distributed among these pairs. We constructed the set UTT of all unseen token-tag pairs. Let T(y) be the number of token types tagged y. The probability p(w,y), $<w,y>\in UTT$, that a token w might be tagged with the tag y was considered to be directly proportional to T(y), that is:

$$p(w, y) / T(y) = u = \text{constant} \tag{2}$$

Now p_0 can be written as follows:

$$p_0 = \sum_k \sum_i p(w_k, y_i), \text{ where } <w_k,y_i> \in UTT \tag{3}$$

In UTT all N(y) pairs of the type $\{<w_1,y>, <w_2,y> \dots <w_{N(y)},y>\}$ are considered to be of equal probability, u*T(y). It follows that:

$$p_0 = \sum_i N(y_i)\cdot u \cdot T(y_i) = u \cdot \sum_i N(y_i)\cdot T(y_i) \tag{4}$$

The lexical probabilities for unseen token-tag pairs can now be written as:

$$\text{for any } <w,y_i> \in UTT, \quad p(w,y_i) = \frac{p_0 \cdot T(y_i)}{\sum_i N(y_i)\cdot T(y_i)} \tag{5}$$

The contextual probabilities are obtained by linear interpolation of unigram, bigram, and trigram probabilities, that is:

$$p(y_i|y_1,\dots,y_{i-1}) = \lambda_1 p(y_i) + \lambda_2 p(y_i|y_{i-1}) + \lambda_3 p(y_i|y_{i-2},y_{i-1}) \text{ and } \lambda_1 + \lambda_2 + \lambda_3 = 1.$$

We estimated the values for the coefficients for each combination of unigram, bigram and trigram in the corpus. As a general rule, we considered that the greater the observed frequency of an n-gram and the fewer (n+1)-grams beginning with that n-gram, the more reliable such an (n+1)-gram is.

We first estimated λ_3. Let $F(y_{i-2},y_{i-1})$ be the number of occurrences for the bigram $y_{i-2}y_{i-1}$ in the training data. Let $N_3(y_{i-2},y_{i-1})$ be the number of distinct trigrams beginning

---

[2] Out of a very large number of unseen pairs in the gold standard, only those prescribed by the M_c-based replacements in the *star version* of the direct-tagged corpus are considered.

with that bigram. Then the average number of occurrences for a trigram beginning with y_{i-2},y_{i-1} is: $F_3(y_{i-2}, y_{i-1}, \bullet) = F(y_{i-2}, y_{i-1}) / N_3(y_{i-2}, y_{i-1})$.

Let $F_{3\max} = \max_i F_3(y_{i-2}, y_{i-1}, \bullet)$. We took λ_3 to be: $\lambda_3 = \log(F_3(y_{i-2}, y_{i-1}))/\log(F_{3\max})$.

Similarly λ_2 is computed as: $\lambda_2 = (1 - \lambda_3) \log(F_2(y_{i-1})) / \log(F_{2\max})$ and $\lambda_1 = 1-\lambda_2-\lambda_3$.

We have now completely defined the retagging algorithm and with it the entire cross-tagging method. Does it improve the performance of the direct tagging? Our experiments show that it does.

2.4.6. Experiments and Evaluation

We used two English language corpora as gold standards. The *1984* corpus, with approximately 120,000 tokens, contains the George Orwell's novel. It was automatically tagged but it was thoroughly human-validated and corrected. The tagset used in this corpus is the Multext-East (MTE) tagset. The second corpus was a fragment of the tagged SemCor corpus, using the Penn tagset, of about the same length, referred to as SemCorP (partial).

2.4.6.1. Experiment 1

After cross-tagging the two corpora, we compared the results with the direct-tagged versions: 1984_{DT}(Penn) against 1984_{CT}(Penn) and $SemCorP_{DT}$(MTE) against $SemCorP_{CT}$(MTE). There were 6,391 differences for the *1984* corpus and 11,006 for the SemCorP corpus. As we did not have human-validated versions of the two corpora, tagged with each other's tagset, we randomly selected a sample of one hundred differences for each corpus and manually analyzed them. The result of this analysis is shown in Table 7.

Table 7. Cross-tagging results

	Correct CTtags	Correct DTtags
100 differences in 1984(Penn)	69	31
100 differences in SemCorP(MTE)	59	41

Overall, cross-tagging is shown to be more accurate than direct tagging. However, as one can see from Table 7, the accuracy gain is more significant for the *1984* corpus than for SemCorP. Since the language model built from the *1984* corpus (used for direct tagging of SemCorP) is more accurate than the language model built from SemCorP (used for direct tagging of *1984*), there were many more errors in 1984(Penn) than in SemCorP(MTE). The cross-tagging approach described in this paper has the ability to overcome some inconsistencies encoded in the supporting language models.

2.4.6.2. Experiment 2

We decided to improve the POS-tagging of the entire SemCor corpus. First, to keep track of the improvements of the corpus annotation, we computed the identity score between the original and the biased-tagged versions. Let S^0(Penn) be the SemCor corpus in its original form, and S^0_{BT}(Penn) its biased tagged version.

Identity-score(S^0(Penn), S^0_{BT}(Penn)) = 93.81%

By cross-tagging the results of the first experiment, we obtained the double cross-tagged version of SemCor(Penn) which we denote as S^1(Penn).

Identity-score(S^0(Penn), S^1(Penn)) = 96.4%

These scores were unexpectedly low and after a brief analysis we observed some tokenization inconsistencies in the original SemCor, which we normalized. For instance, opening and closing double quotes were not systematically distinguished; so we converted all the instances of " and " into the DBLQ character. Another example of inconsistency referred to various formulas denoted in SemCor sometimes by a single token **f and sometimes by a sequence of three tokens *, *, f. In the normalized version of the SemCor only the first type of tokenization was preserved. Let S^2(Penn) denote the normalized version of S^1(Penn).

Identity-score(S^2(Penn), S^2_{BT}(Penn)) = 97.41%

As one can see, the double cross-tagging and the normalization process resulted in a more consistent language model (the BT identity score improved with 3.6%).

At this point, we analyzed the tokens that introduce the most differences. For each such token, we identified the patterns corresponding to each of their tags and subsequently corrected the tagging to match these patterns. The tokens considered in this stage were: *am*, *are*, *is*, *was*, *were*, and *that*. Let S^3 be this new corpus version.

Identity-score(S^3(Penn), S^3_{BT}(Penn)) = 97.61%

Finally, analyzing the remaining differences, we notices very frequent errors in tagging the grammatical number for nouns and incorrectly tagging common nouns as proper nouns and vice versa. We used regular expressions to make the necessary corrections and thus obtained a new version S^4(Penn) of SemCor.

Identity-score(S^4(Penn), S^4_{BT}(Penn)) = 98.08%

Continuing the biased correction/evaluation cycle would probably further improve the identity score, but the distinction between correct and wrong tags becomes less and less clear-cut. The overall improvement of the biased evaluation score (4.27%) and the observed difference types suggested that the POS tagging of the SemCor corpus reached a level of accuracy sufficient for making it a reliable training corpus.

Table 8. The most frequent differences between the double-cross tagging and the original tagging in SemCor

Double Cross-Tagging Tag	Token	Original Tag	Frequency
TO	to	VB	1910
VBN	been	VB	674
IN	in	RB	655
IN	in	VB	646
IN	of	RB	478
IN	on	VB	381
IN	for	VB	334
IN	with	VB	324
RBR	more	RB	314
DT	the	RB	306

To assess the improvements in S^4(Penn) over the normalized version of the initial SemCor corpus we extracted the differences among the two versions. The 57,905 differences were sorted by frequency and categorized into 10,216 difference types, with frequencies ranging from 1,910 down to 1. The 10 most frequent difference types are shown in Table 8.

The first 200 types, with frequencies ranging from 1910 to 40 and accounting for 25,136 differences, were carefully evaluated. The results of this evaluation are shown in Table 9.

Table 9. The most frequent 200 difference types among the initial and final versions of the SemCor corpus

# of differences	Correct Double Cross-Tagging	Correct Original tagging
25136	21224 (84.44%)	3912 (15.56%)

The experiments showed that the cross-tagging is useful for several purposes. The direct tagging of a corpus can be improved. Two tagsets can be compared from a distributional point of view. Errors in the training data can be spotted and corrected. Successively applying the method for different pairs of corpora tagged with different tagsets permits the construction of a much larger corpus, reliably tagged in parallel with all the different tagsets.

The mapping system between two tagsets may prove useful in itself. It is composed of a global mapping, as well as of many token mappings, showing the way in which contexts marked by certain tags in one tagset overlap with contexts marked by tags of the other tagset. Furthermore, the mapping system can be applied not only to POS tags, but to other types of tags as well.

2.5. Tagging with Combined Classifiers

In the previous sections we discussed a design methodology for adequate tagsets, a strategy for coping with vary large tagsets, methods for integrating training data annotated with different tagsets. We showed how gold standard annotations can be further improved. We argued that all these methodologies and associated algorithms are language independent, or at least applicable to a large number of languages. Let us then assume that we have already created improved training corpora, tagged them using adequate tagsets and developed robust and broad-coverage language models. The next issue is improving statistical tagging beyond the current state of the art. We believe that one way of doing it is to combine the outputs of various morpho-lexical classifiers. This approach presupposes the ability to decide, in case of disagreements, which tagging is the correct one. Running different classifiers either will require a parallel processing environment or, alternatively, will result in a longer processing time.

2.5.1. Combined classifier methods

It has been proved for AI classification problems that using multiple classifiers (of comparative competence and not making the same mistakes) and an intelligent conflict resolution procedure can systematically lead to better results [41]. Since, as we showed previously, the tagging may be regarded as a classification problem, it is not surprising that this idea has been exploited for morpho-lexical disambiguation [13], [29], [42], [43] etc. Most of the attempts to improve tagging performance consisted in combining learning methods and problem solvers (that is, combining taggers trained on the same data).

Another way of approaching classifier combination is to use one tagger (ideally the best one) with various language models learned from training data from different registers. These combined classifier approaches are called *combined taggers* and *combined register data* methods, respectively. Irrespective of a specific approach, it is important that the classifiers to be combined be of comparable accuracy, i.e. statistically they should be indiscernible (this condition can be tested using McNamer's test, [41]) and, equally important, they should make complementary errors, i.e. the errors made by one classifier should not be identical to (or a subset of) the errors made by the other. An easy evaluation of the latter combination condition for two taggers A and B can be obtained by the COMP measure [43]:

$COMP(A,B)=(1- N_{COMMON}/N_A) * 100$,

where N_{COMMON} represents the number of cases in which both taggers are wrong and N_A stands for the number of cases in which tagger A is wrong. The COMP measure gives the percentage of cases in which tagger B is right when A made a wrong classification. If the two taggers made the same mistakes, or if errors made by tagger B were a superset of those made by A, then COMP(A,B) would be 0. Although the COMP measure is not symmetric, the assumption that A and B have comparable accuracy means that $N_A \approx N_B$ and consequently $COMP(A,B) \approx COMP(B, A)$.

A classifier based on combining multiple taggers can be intuitively described as follows. For k different POS-tagging systems and a training corpus, build k language models, one model per system. Then, given a new text T, run each trained tagging system on it and get k disambiguated versions of T, namely $T_1, T_2 \ldots T_i \ldots Tk$. In other words, each token in T is assigned k (not necessarily distinct) interpretations. Given that the tagging systems are different, it is very unlikely that the k versions of T are identical. However, as compared to a human-judged annotation, the probability that an arbitrary token from T is assigned the correct interpretation in at least one of the k versions of T is high (the better the individual taggers, the higher this probability). Let us call the hypothetical guesser of this correct tag an *oracle* (as in [43]). Implementing an oracle, i.e. automatically deciding which of the k interpretations is the correct one is hard to do. However, the oracle concept, as defined above, is very useful since its accuracy allows an estimation of the upper bound of correctness that can be reached by a given tagger combination.

The experiment described in [42] is a combined tagger model. The evaluation corpus is the LOB corpus. Four different taggers are used: a trigram HMM tagger [44], a memory-based tagger [22], a rule-based tagger [19] and a Maximum Entropy-based tagger [21]. Several decision-making procedures have been attempted, and when a pairwise voting strategy is used, the combined classifier system yields the result of 97.92% and outscores all the individual tagging systems. However, the oracle's accuracy for this experiment (99.22%) proves that investigation of the decision-making procedure should continue.

An almost identical position and similar results are presented in [43]. That experiment is based on the Penn Treebank Wall Street Journal corpus and uses a HMM trigram tagger, a rule-based tagger [19] and a Maximum Entropy-based tagger [21]. The expected accuracy of the oracle is 98.59%, and using the "pick-up tagger" combination method, the overall system accuracy was 97.2%.

Although the idea of combining taggers is very simple and intuitive it does not make full use of the potential power of the combined classifier paradigm. This is because the main reason for different behavior of the taggers stems from the different modeling of the same data. The different errors are said to result from algorithmic biases. A complementary approach [29] is to use only one tagger T (this may be any tagger) but trained on different-register texts, resulting in different language models (LM1, LM2…). A new text (unseen, from an unknown register) is independently tagged with the same tagger but using different LMs. Beside the fact that this approach is easier to implement than a tagger combination, any differences among the multiple classifiers created by the same tagger can be ascribed only to the linguistic data used in language modeling (linguistic variance). While in the multiple tagger approach it is very hard to judge the influence of the type of texts, in the multiple register approach text register identification is a by-product of the methodology. As our experiments have shown, when a new text belongs to a specific language register, that language register model never fails to provide the highest accuracy in tagging. *Therefore, it is reasonable to assume that when tagging a new text within a multiple register approach, if the final result is closer to the individual version generated by using the language model LM, then probably the new text belongs to the LM register, or is closer to that register.* Once a clue as to the type of text processed is obtained, stronger identification criteria could be used to validate this hypothesis.

With respect to experiments discussed in [29] we also found that splitting a multi-register training corpus into its components and applying multiple register combined classifier tagging leads to systematically better results than in the case of tagging with the language model learned from the complete, more balanced, training corpus.

It is not clear what kind of classifier combination is the most beneficial for morpho-lexical tagging. Intuitively, though, it is clear that while technological bias could be better controlled, linguistic variance is much more difficult to deal with. Comparing individual tagger performance to the final result of a tagger combination, can suggest whether one of the taggers is more appropriate for a particular language (and data type). Adopting this tagger as the basis for the multiple-register combination might be the solution of choice.

Whichever approach is pursued, its success is conditioned by the combination algorithm (conflict resolution).

2.5.2. An effective combination method for multiple classifiers

One of the most widely used combination methods, and the simplest to implement, is majority voting, choosing the tag that was proposed by the majority of the classifiers. This method can be refined by considering weighting the votes in accordance with the overall accuracy of the individual classifiers. [42] and [43] describe other simple decision methods. In what follows we describe a method, which is different in that it takes into account the "competence" of the classifiers at the level of individual tag assignment. This method exploits the observation that although the combined classifiers have comparable accuracy (a combination condition) they could assign some tags more reliably than others. The key data structure for this combination method is called credibility profile, and we construct one such profile for each classifier.

2.5.3. Credibility Profile

Let us use the following notation:

$P(X_i)$ = the probability of correct tag assignment, i.e. when a lexical item should be tagged with X_i it is indeed tagged with X_i

$Q(X_j|X_i)$ = the probability that a lexical token which should have been tagged with X_j is incorrectly tagged with X_i

A credibility profile characterizing the classifier C_i has the following structure:

$$\mathrm{PROFILE}(C_i)= \{< X_1{:}P_1\ (X_m{:}Q_{m1}....X_k{:}Q_{k1}) > < X_2{:}P_2\ (X_{q2}{:}Q_{q2}....Q_{i2}{:}P_{i2}) > .... < X_n{:}P_n\ (X_s{:}Q_{sn}....Q_{jn}{:}P_{jn}) >\}.$$

The pair X_r:P_r in PROFILE(C_i) encodes the expected correctness (P_r) of the tag X_r when it is assigned by the classifier C_i while the list CL-X_r=(X_α:$Q_{\alpha r}$....X_α:$Q_{\beta r}$) represents the confusion set of the classifier C_i, for the tag X_r. Having a reference corpus GS, after tagging it with the C_i classifier, one can easily obtain (e.g. by using MLE - most likelihood estimation) the profile of the respective classifier:

P_r= P(X_r) = # of tokens correctly tagged with X_r /# of tokens tagged with X_r

Q_{ir}=Q(X_i|X_r) = # of tokens incorrectly tagged by the C_i with X_r instead of X_i/# of tokens in the GS tagged with X_r

If a tag X_α does not appear in the X_r-confusion set of the classifier C_i, we assume that the probability of C_i mistagging one token with X_r when it should be tagged with X_α is 0.

When the classifier C_i labels a token by X_r, we know that on average it is right in P(X_r) situations, but it can also incorrectly assign this tag instead of the one in its X_r-confusion set. The confidence in the C_i's proposed tag X_r is defined as follows:

$$\text{CONFIDENCE}(C_i, X_r) = P(X_r) - \sum_{Xj \in CL-Xr} Q^k(X_j \mid X_r) \quad (6)$$

The classifier that assigns the highest confidence tag to the current word W_k decides what tag will be assigned to the word W_k. A further refinement of the CONFIDENCE function is making it dependent on the decisions of the other classifiers. The basic idea is that the penalty (Q(X_1|X_r)+...+ Q(X_k|X_r)) in Eq. (6) is selective: unless X_j is not proposed by any competing classifier, the corresponding Q(X_j|X_r) is not added to the penalty value. This means that the CONFIDENCE score of a tag, X_r proposed by a classifier C_i is penalized only if at least one other classifier C_j proposes a tag which is in the X_r-confusion set of the classifier C_i.

Let $\beta_p(X_j)$ be a binary function defined as follows: if X_j is a tag proposed by a competitor classifier C_p and X_j is in the confusion list of the X_r-confusion set of the classifier C_i, then $\beta_p(X_j)$=1, otherwise $\beta_p(X_j)$=0. If more competing classifiers (say p of them) agree on a tag which appears in the X_a-confusion set of the classifier C_i, the penalty is increased correspondingly.

$$\arg\max_k \text{CONFIDENCE}(C_k, X_r) = P^k(X_r) - \sum_{Xj \in CL-Xa} Q^k(X_j \mid X_r) * \sum_p \beta_p(X_j) \quad (7)$$

In our earlier experiments (see [29]) we showed that the multiple register combination based on CONFIDENCE evaluation score ensured a very high accuracy (98,62%) for tagging unseen Romanian texts.

It is worth mentioning that when good-quality individual classifiers are used, their agreement score is usually very high (in our experiments it was 96,7%), and most of the errors relate to the words on which the classifiers disagreed. As the cases of full agreement on a wrong tag were very rare (less than 0.6% in our experiments), just looking at the disagreement among various classifiers (be they based on different taggers or on different training data), makes the validation and correction of a corpus tagging a manageable task for a human expert.

The CONFIDENCE combiner is very simple to implement and given that data needed for making a decision (Credibility profiles, Confidences, etc) is computed before tagging a new text and given that the additional runtime processing is required only for a small percentage of the tagged texts, namely for non-unanimously selected tags (as mentioned before, less than 3.3% of the total number of processed words), the extra time needed is negligible as compared to the proper tagging procedure.

3. Lemmatization

Lemmatization is the process of text normalization according to which each word-form is associated with its *lemma*. This normalization identifies and strips off the grammatical suffixes of an inflected word-form (potentially adding a specific lemma suffix). A lemma is a base-form representative for an entire family of inflected word-forms, called a paradigmatic family. The lemma, or the head-word of a dictionary entry (as it is referred to in lexicographic studies), is characterized by a standard feature-value combination (e.g. infinitive for verbs, singular & indefinite & nominative for nouns and adjectives) and therefore can be regarded as a privileged word-form of a *paradigmatic family*. Lemmas may have their own specific endings. For instance, in Romanian all the verbal lemmas end in one of the letters *a*, *e*, *i* or *î*, most feminine noun or adjective lemmas end in *ă* or *e*, while the vast majority of masculine noun or adjective lemmas have an empty suffix (but may be affected by the final consonant alternation: e.g. *brazi/brad* (pines/pine); *bărbați/bărbat* (men/man); *obraji/obraz* (cheeks/cheek) etc.).

Lemmatization is frequently associated with the process of morphological analysis, but it is concerned only with the inflectional morphology. The general case of morphological analysis may include derivational processes, especially relevant for agglutinative languages. Additionally, given that an inflected form may have multiple interpretations, the lemmatization must decide, based on the context of a word-form occurrence, which of the possible analyses is applicable in the given context.

As for other NLP processing steps, the lexicon plays an essential role in the implementation of a lemmatization program. In Sections 2.1 and 2.2 we presented the standardized morpho-lexical encoding recommendations issued by EAGLES and observed in the implementation of Multext-East word-form lexicons. With such a lexicon, lemmatization is most often a look-up procedure, with practically no computational cost. However, one word-form be may be associated with two or more lemmas (this phenomenon is known as *homography*). Part-of-speech information, provided by the preceding tagging step, is the discriminatory element in most of these cases. Yet, it may happen that a word-form even if correctly tagged may be lemmatized in different ways. Usually, such cases are solved probabilistically or heuristically (most often using the heuristic of "one lemma per discourse"). In Romanian this rarely happens, (e.g. the plural, indefinite, neuter, common noun "*capete*" could be lemmatized either as *capăt* (extremity, end) or as *cap* (head)) but in other languages this kind of lemmatization ambiguity might be more frequent requiring more fine-grained (semantic) analysis.

It has been observed that for any lexicon, irrespective its coverage, text processing of arbitrary texts will involve dealing with unknown words. Therefore, the treatment of *out-of-lexicon words* (OLW), is the real challenge for lemmatization. The size and coverage of a lexicon cannot guarantee that all the words in an arbitrary text will be lemmatized using a simple look-up procedure. Yet, the larger the word-form lexicon, the fewer OLWs occur in a new text. Their percentage might be small enough that even if their lemmatization was wrong, the overall lemmatization accuracy and processing time would not be significantly affected[3].

The most frequent approach to lemmatization of unknown words is based on a retrograde analysis of the word endings. If a *paradigmatic morphology* model [45] is available, then all the legal grammatical suffixes are known and already associated with the grammatical information useful for the lemmatization purposes. We showed in [46] that a language independent paradigmatic morphology analyser/generator can be automatically constructed from examples. The typical data structure used for suffix analysis of unknown words is a trie (a tree with its nodes representing letters of legal suffixes, associated with morpho-lexical information pertaining to the respective suffix) which can be extremely efficiently compiled into a finite-state transducer [47], [48], [49]. Another approach is using the information already available in the word-form lexicon (assuming it is available) to induce rules for suffix-stripping and lemma reconstruction. The general form of such a rule is as follows:

If a word-form has a suffix S that is characteristic for the grammar class C, remove S and add the suffix S' describing a lemma form for the class C.

Such an approach was adopted, among many others, in [11], [51], [52], [53], [54] etc. With many competing applicable rules, as in a standard morphological analysis process, a decision procedure is required to select the most plausible lemma among the possible analyses. The lemmatizer described in [11] implemented the choice function as a four-gram letter Markov model, trained on lemmas in the word-form dictionary. It is extremely fast but it fails whenever the lemma has an infix vowel alternation or a final consonant alternation. A better lemmatizer, developed for automatic acquisition of new lexical entries, taking into account these drawbacks is reported in [55].

4. Alignments

The notion of alignment is a general knowledge representation concept and it refers to establishing an equivalence mapping between entities of two or more sets of information representations. Equivalence criteria depend on the nature of the aligned entities, and the methodologies and techniques for alignment may vary significantly. For instance, ontology alignment is a very active research area in the Semantic Web community, aiming at merging partial (and sometimes contradictory) representations of the same reality. Alignment of multilingual semantic lexicons and thesauri is a primary concern for most NLP practitioners, and this endeavor is based on the commonly agreed assumption that basic meanings of words can be interlingually conceptualized. The alignment of parallel corpora is tremendously instrumental in multilingual lexicographic studies and in machine translation research and development.

Alignment of parallel texts relies on translation equivalence, i.e. cross-lingual meaning equivalence between pairs of text fragments belonging to the parallel texts. An alignment between a text and its translation makes explicit the textual units that

---

[3] With a one million word-form lexicon backing-up our tagging and lemmatization web services (http://nlp.racai.ro) the OLW percentage in more than 2G word texts that were processed was less than 2%, most of these OLW being spelling errors or foreign words. Moreover, for the majority of them (about 89%) the lemmas were correctly guessed.

encode the same meaning. Text alignment can de defined at various granularity levels (paragraph, sentence, phrase, word), the finer the granularity the harder the task.

A useful concept is that of *reification* (regarding or treating an abstraction as if it had a concrete or material existence). To reify an alignment means to attach to any pair of aligned entities a knowledge representation (in our case, a feature structure) based on which the quality of the considered pair can be judged independently of the other pairs. This conceptualization is very convenient in modeling the alignment process as a binary classification problem (good vs. bad pairs of aligned entities).

4.1. Sentence alignment

Good practices in human translation assume that the human translator observes the source text organization and preserves the number and order of chapters, sections and paragraphs. Such an assumption is not unnatural, being imposed by textual cohesion and coherence properties of a narrative text. One could easily argue (for instance in terms of rhetorical structure, illocutionary force, etc) that if the order of paragraphs in a translated text is changed, the newly obtained text is not any more a translation of the original source text. It is also assumed that all the information provided in the source text is present in its translation (nothing is omitted) and also that the translated text does not contain information not existing in the original (nothing has been added). Most sentence aligners available today are able to detect both omissions and deletions during translation process.

Sentence alignment is a prerequisite for any parallel corpus processing. It has been proved that very good results can be obtained with practically no prior knowledge about the languages in question. However, since sentence alignment errors may be detrimental to further processing, sentence alignment accuracy is a continuous concern for many NLP practitioners.

4.1.1. Related work

One of the best-known algorithms for aligning parallel corpora, CharAlign [56], is based on the lengths of sentences that are reciprocal translations. CharAlign represents a bitext in a bi-dimensional space such that all the characters in one part of the bitext are indexed on the X axis and all the characters of the other part are indexed on the Y-axis. If the position of the last character in the text represented on the X-axis is M and the position of the last character in the text represented on the Y-axis is N, then the segment that starts in origin (0,0) and ends in the point of co-ordinates (M,N) represents the *alignment line* of the bitext. The positions of the last letter of each sentence in both parts of the bitext are called *alignment positions*. By exploiting the intuition that long sentences tend to be translated by long sentences and short sentences are translated by short sentences, Gale and Church [55] made the empirical assumption that the ratio of character-based lengths of a source sentence and of its translation tend to be a constant. They converted the alignment problem into a dynamic programming one, namely finding the maximum number of alignment position pairs, so that they have a minimum dispersion with respect to the alignment line. It is amazing how well CharAlign works given that this simple algorithm uses no linguistic knowledge, being completely language independent. Its accuracy on various pairs of languages was systematically in the range of 90-93% (sometimes even better).

Kay and Röscheisen [57] implemented a sentence aligner that takes advantage of various lexical clues (numbers, dates, proper names, cognates) in judging the plausibility of an aligned sentence pair.

Chen [58] developed a method based on optimizing word translation probabilities that has better results than the sentence-length based approach, but it demands much more time to complete and requires more computing resources. Melamed [59] also developed a method based on word translation equivalence and geometrical mapping.

The abovementioned lexical approaches to sentence alignment, managed to improve the accuracy of sentence alignment by a few percentage points, to an average accuracy of 95-96%.

More recently, Moore [60] presented a three-stage hybrid approach. In the first stage, the algorithm uses length-based methods for sentence alignment. In the second stage, a translation equivalence table is estimated from the aligned corpus obtained during the first stage. The method used for translation equivalence estimation is based on IBM model 1 [61]. The final step uses a combination of length-based methods and word correspondence to find 1-1 sentence alignments. The aligner has an excellent precision (almost 100%) for one-to-one alignments because it was intended for acquisition of very accurate training data for machine translation experiments.

In what follows we describe a sentence aligner, inspired by Moore's aligner, almost as accurate, but working also for non-one-to-one alignments.

4.1.2. Sentence Alignment as a Classification Problem for Reified Linguistic Objects

An aligned sentence pair can be conveniently represented as a feature-structure object. The values of the features are scores characterizing the contribution of the respective features to the "goodness" of the alignment pair under consideration. The values of these features may be linearly interpolated to yield a figure of merit for a candidate pair of aligned sentences. A generative device produces a plausible candidate search space and a binary classification engine turns the alignment problem into a two-class classification task: discriminating between "good" and "bad" alignments. One of the best-performing formalisms for such a task is Vapnik's Support Vector Machine [62].

We used an open-source implementation of Support Vector Machine (SVM) training and classification - LIBSVM http://www.csie.ntu.edu.tw/~cjlin/libsvm [63] with default parameters (C-SVC classification and radial basis kernel function).

The aligner was tested on selected pairs of languages from the recently released 22-languages Acquis Communautaire parallel corpus [64] (http://wt.jrc.it/lt/acquis/).

The accuracy of the SVM model was evaluated using 10-fold cross-validation on five manually aligned files from the Acquis Communautaire corpus for the English-French, English-Italian, and English-Romanian language pairs. For each language pair we used approximately 1,000 sentence pairs, manually aligned. Since the SVM engines need both positive and negative examples, we generated an equal number of "bad" alignment examples from the 1,000 correct examples by replacing one sentence of a correctly aligned pair with another sentence in the three-sentence vicinity. That is to say that if the ith source sentence is aligned with the jth target sentence, we can generate 12 incorrect examples (i, j±1), (i, j±2), (i, j±3), (i±1, j), (i±2, j), and (i+3, j).

4.1.3. Sentence Alignment Classification Features

The performance of a SVM classifier increases considerably when it uses more highly discriminative features. Irrelevant features or features with less discriminative power negatively influence the accuracy of a SVM classifier. We conducted several experiments, starting with features suggested by researchers' intuition: position index of the two candidates, word length correlation, word rank correlation, number of translation equivalents they contain, etc. The best discriminating features and their discriminating accuracy when independently used are listed in the first column of Table 10. In what follows we briefly comment on each of the features (for additional details see [66]).

For each feature of a candidate sentence alignment pair (i,j), 2N+1 distinct values may be computed, with ±N being the span of the alignment vicinity. In fact, due to the symmetry of the sentence alignment relation, just N+1 values suffice with practically no loss of accuracy but with a significant gain in speed. The feature under consideration promotes the current alignment (i,j) only if the value corresponding to any other combination in the alignment vicinity is inferior to the value of the (i,j) pair. Otherwise, the feature under consideration reduces the confidence in the correctness of the (i,j) alignment candidate, thus indicating a wrong alignment.

As expected, the number of translation equivalents shared by a candidate alignment pair was the most discriminating factor. The translation equivalents were extracted using an EM algorithm similar to IBM-Model 1 but taking into account a frequency threshold (words occurring less than three times, were discarded) and a probability threshold (pairs of words with a the translation equivalence probability below 0,05 were discarded) and discarding null translation equivalents. By adding the translation equivalence probabilities for the respective pairs and normalizing the result by the average length of the sentences in the analyzed pair we obtain the sentence-pair translation equivalence score.

Given the expected monotonicity of aligned sentence numbers, we were surprised that the difference of the relative positions of the sentences was not a very good classification feature. Its classification accuracy was only 62% and therefore this attribute has been eliminated.

The sentence length feature has been evaluated both for words and for characters, and we found the word-based metrics a little more precise and also that using both features (word-based and character-based) did not improve the final result.

Word rank correlation feature was motivated by the intuition that words with a high occurrence in the source text tend to be translated with words with high occurrence in the target text. This feature can successfully replace the translation equivalence feature when a translation equivalence dictionary is not available.

Table 10. The most discriminative features used by the SVM classifier

Feature	Precision
Number of translation equivalents	98.47
Sentence length	96.77
Word rank correlation	94.86
Number of non-lexical tokens	93.00

The *non-lexical token correlation* in Table 10 refers to the number of non-lexical language-independent tokens, such as punctuation, dates, numbers and currency symbols contained in the two sentences of a candidate pair. After considering each feature independently, we evaluated their combinations.

Table 11. 10-fold cross validation precision of the SVM classifier using different combinations of features

Number of translation equivalents				x	**x**	x	x
Sentence length	x	x	**x**	x	**x**	x	x
Number of non-lexical tokens		x	**x**		**x**		x
Word rank correlation	x		**x**			x	x
Precision (%)	97.87	97.87	**98.32**	98.72	**98.78**	98.51	98.75

As building the translation equivalence table is by far the most time-consuming step during the alignment of a parallel corpus, the results in Table 11 outline the best results (in bold) without this step (**98.32%**) and with this step (**98.78%**). These results confirmed the intuition that word rank correlation could compensate for the lack of a translation equivalence table.

4.1.4. A typical scenario

Once an alignment gold standard has been created, the next step is to train the SVM engine for the alignment of the target parallel corpus. According to our experience, the gold standard would require about 1,000 aligned sentences (the more the better). Since the construction of the translation equivalence table relies on the existence of a sentence-aligned corpus, we build the SVM model in two steps. The features used in the first phase are word sentence length, the non-word sentence length and the representative word rank correlation scores, computed for the top 25% frequency tokens. With this preliminary SVM model we compute an initial corpus alignment. The most reliable sentence pairs (classified as "good", with a score higher than 0.9) are used to estimate the translation equivalence table. At this point we can build a new SVM model, trained on the gold standard, this time using all the four features. This model is used to perform the final corpus alignment.

The alignment process of the second phase has several stages and iterations. During the first stage, a list of sentence pair candidates for alignment is created and the SVM model is used to derive the probability estimates for these candidates being correct. The candidate pairs are formed in the following way: the ith sentence in the source language is paired with the jth presumably corresponding target sentence as well as with the neighboring sentences within the alignment vicinity, the span of which is document-specific. The index j of the presumably corresponding target sentence is selected so that the pair <i,j> is the closest pair to the main diagonal of the length bitext representation.

During the second stage, an EM algorithm re-estimates the sentence-pair probabilities in five iterations.

The third stage involves multiple iterations and thresholds. In one iteration step, the best-scored alignment is selected as a good alignment (only if it is above a pre-specified threshold) and the scores of the surrounding candidate pairs are modified as described below.

Let *(i, j)* be the sentence pair considered a good alignment; then

- the respective scores for candidates *(i-1, j-1)* and *(i+1, j+1)* are increased by a confidence bonus δ,

- the respective scores for candidates *(i-2, j-2)* and *(i+2, j+2)* are increased by δ/2,
- the respective scores for candidate alignments which intersect the correct alignment*(i, j)* are decreased by 0.1,
- the respective scores for candidates *(i, j-1)*, *(i, j+1)*, *(i-1, j)*, *(i+1, j)* are decreased by an amount inverse proportionate with their estimated probabilities; this will maintain the possibility for detecting 1-2 and 2-1 links; the correctness of this detection is directly influenced by the amount mentioned above,
- candidates *(i, n)* and *(m, j)* with $n \leq$ j-2, $n \geq$ j+2, $m \leq$ i-2, $m \geq$ i+2 are eliminated.

4.1.5. Evaluation

The evaluation of the aligner was carried out on 4 AcquisCom files (different from the ones used to evaluate precision of the SVM model). Each language pair (English-French, English-Italian, and English-Romanian) has approximately 1,000 sentence pairs and all of them were hand-validated.

Table 12. The evaluation of SVM sentence aligner against Moore's Sentence Aligner

Aligner&Language Pair	Precision	Recall	F-Measure
Moore En-It	**100,00**	97.76	98.86
SvmSent Align En-It	98.93	**98.99**	**98.96**
Moore En-Fr	**100,00**	98.62	99.30
SvmSent Align En-Fr	99.46	**99.60**	**99.53**
Moore En-Ro	**99.80**	93.93	96.78
SvmSent Align En-Ro	99.24	**99.04**	**99.14**

As can be seen from Table 12 our aligner does not improve on the precision of Moore's bilingual sentence aligner, but it has a very good recall for all evaluated language pairs and detects not only 1-1 alignments but many-to-many ones as well.

If the precision of a corpus alignment is critical (such as in building translation models, extracting translation dictionaries or other similar applications of machine learning techniques) Moore's aligner is probably the best public domain option. The omitted fragments of texts (due to non 1-1 alignments, or sentences inversions) are harmless in building statistical models. However, if the corpus alignment is necessary for human research (e.g. for cross-lingual or cross-cultural studies in Humanities and Social Sciences) leaving out unaligned fragments could be undesirable and a sentence aligner of the type presented in this section might be more appropriate.

4.2. Word Alignment

Word alignment is a significantly harder process than sentence alignment, in a large part because the ordering of words in a source sentence is not preserved in the target sentence. While this property was valid at the sentence alignment level by virtue of text cohesion and coherence requirements, it does not hold true at the sentence of word level, because word ordering is a language specific property and is governed by the syntax of the respective language. But this is not the only cause of difficulties in lexical alignment.

While the N-to-M alignment pairs at the sentence level are quite rare (usually less then 5% of the cases) and whenever this happens, N and, respectively, M aligned sentences are consecutive. In word alignment many-to-many alignments are more frequent and may involve non-consecutive words.

The high level of interest in word alignment has been generated by research and development in statistical machine translation [61], [67], [68], [69] etc. Similarly to many techniques used in data-driven NLP, word alignment methods are, to a large extent, language-independent. To evaluate them and further improve their performance, NAACL (2003) and ACL (2005) organized evaluation competitions on word alignment for languages with scarce resources, paired with English.

Word alignment is related to but not identical with extraction of bilingual lexicons from parallel corpora. The latter is a simpler task and usually of a higher accuracy than the former. Sacrificing recall, one could get almost 100% accurate translation lexicons. On the other hand, if a text is word-aligned, extraction of a bilingual lexicon is a free byproduct.

Most word aligners use a bilingual dictionary extraction process as a preliminary phase, with as high a precision as possible and construct the proper word alignment on the basis of this resource. By extracting the paired tokens from a word alignment, the precision of the initial translation lexicon is lowered, but its recall is significantly improved.

4.2.1. Hypotheses for bilingual dictionary extraction from parallel corpora

In general, one word in the first part of a bitext is translated by one word in the other part. If this statement, called the "*word to word mapping hypothesis*" were always true, the lexical alignment problem would have been significantly easier to solve. But it is clear that the "word to word mapping hypothesis" is not true. However, if the tokenization phase in a larger NLP chain is able to identify multiword expressions and mark them up as a single lexical token, one may alleviate this difficulty, assuming that proper segmentation of the two parts of a bitext would make the "*token to token mapping hypothesis*" a valid working assumption (at least in the majority of cases). We will generically refer to this mapping hypothesis the "*1:1 mapping hypothesis*" in order to cover both word-based and token-based mappings. Using the *1:1 mapping hypothesis* the problem of bilingual dictionary extraction becomes computationally much less expensive.

There are several other underlying assumptions one can consider for reducing the computational complexity of a bilingual dictionary extraction algorithm. None of them is true in general, but the situations where they do not hold are rare, so that ignoring the exceptions would not produce a significant number of errors and would not lead to losing too many useful translations. Moreover, these assumptions do not prevent the use of additional processing units for recovering some of the correct translations missed because they did not take into account these assumptions.

The assumptions we used in our basic bilingual dictionary extraction algorithm [70] are as follows:

- a lexical token in one half of the *translation unit* (TU) corresponds to at most one non-empty lexical unit in the other half of the TU; this is the 1:1 mapping assumption which underlines the work of many other researchers [57], [59], [71], [72], [73], [74] etc. However, remember that a lexical token could be a multi-word expression previously found and segmented by an adequate tokenizer;

- a polysemous lexical token, if used several times in the same TU, is used with the same meaning; this assumption is explicitly used also by [59] and implicitly by all the previously mentioned authors.
- a lexical token in one part of a TU can be aligned with a lexical token in the other part of the TU only if these tokens are of compatible types (part of speech); in most cases, compatibility reduces to the same part of speech, but it is also possible to define compatibility mappings (e.g., participles or gerunds in English are quite often translated as adjectives or nouns in Romanian and vice versa). This is essentially one very efficient way to cut the combinatorial complexity and postpone dealing with irregular part of speech alternations.
- although the word order is not an invariant of translation, it is not random either; when two or more candidate translation pairs are equally scored, the one containing tokens whose relative positions are closer are preferred. This preference is also used in [74].

4.2.2. A simple bilingual dictionary extraction algorithm

Our algorithm assumes that the parallel corpus is already sentence aligned, tagged and lemmatized in each part of the bitext. The first step is to compute a list of *translation equivalence candidates* (TECL). This list contains several sub-lists, one for each part of speech considered in the extraction procedure.

Each POS-specific sub-list contains several pairs of tokens <$token_S$ $token_T$> of the corresponding part of speech that appeared in the same TUs. Let TU^j be the jth translation unit. By collecting all the tokens of the same POS_k (in the order in which they appear in the text) and removing duplicates in each part of TU^j one builds the ordered sets $L^{Sj}{}_{POSk}$ and $L^{Tj}{}_{POSk}$. For each POS_i let $TU^j{}_{POSi}$ be defined as $L^{Sj}{}_{POSi} \otimes L^{Tj}{}_{POSi}$ (the Cartesian product of the two ordered sets). Then, CTU^j (correspondence in the jth translation unit) and the translation equivalence candidate list (for a bitext containing *n* translation units) are defined as follows:

$$CTU^j = \bigcup_{i=1}^{no.of.pos} TU^j_{POSi} \quad \& \quad TECL = \bigcup_{j=1}^{n} CTU^j \tag{8}$$

TECL contains a lot of noise and many translation equivalent candidates (TECs) are very improbable. In order to eliminate much of this noise, very unlikely candidate pairs are filtered out of TECL. The filtering process is based on calculating the degree of association between the tokens in a TEC.

Any filtering would eliminate many wrong TECs but also some good ones. The ratio between the number of good TECs rejected and the number of wrong TECs rejected is just one criterion we used in deciding which test to use and what should be the threshold score below which any TEC will be removed from TECL. After various empirical tests we decided to use the log-likelihood test with the threshold value of 9.

Our baseline algorithm is a very simple iterative algorithm, reasonably fast and very accurate[4]. At each iteration step, the pairs that pass the selection (see below) will be removed from TECL so that this list is shortened after each step and may eventually end up empty. For each POS, a $S_m * T_n$ contingency table (TBLk) is constructed on the basis of TECL, with S_m denoting the number of token types in the first part of the bitext and T_n the number of token types in the other part. Source token types index the rows of the table and target token types (of the same part of speech) index the columns. Each cell (i,j) contains the number of occurrences in TECL of the <T_{Si}, T_{Tj}> candidate pair:

$$n_{ij} = occ(T_{Si},T_{T_j});\ n_{i*} = \sum_{j=1}^{n} n_{ij}\ ;\ n_{*j} = \sum_{i=1}^{m} n_{ij}\ ;\ \text{and}\ n_{**} = \sum_{j=1}^{n}\left(\sum_{i=1}^{m} n_{ij}\right).$$

The selection condition is expressed by the equation:

$$TP^{k} = \{< T_{Si}\ T_{Tj} > \mid \forall p, q\ (n_{ij} \geq n_{iq}) \wedge (n_{ij} \geq n_{pj})\} \tag{9}$$

This is the key idea of the iterative extraction algorithm. It expresses the requirement that in order to select a TEC <T_{Si}, T_{Tj}> as a translation equivalence pair, the number of associations of T_{Si} with T_{Tj} must be higher than (or at least equal to) any other T_{Tp} ($p \neq j$). The opposite should also hold. All the pairs selected in TP^k are removed (the respective counts are substituted by zeroes). If T_{Si} is translated in more than one way (either because of having multiple meanings that are lexicalized in the second language by different words, or because of the target language using various synonyms for T_{Tj}) the rest of translations will be found in subsequent steps (if they are sufficiently frequent). The most used translation of a token T_{Si} will be found first.

One of the main deficiencies of this algorithm is that it is quite sensitive to what [59] calls indirect associations. If <T_{Si}, T_{Tj}> has a high association score and T_{Tj} collocates with T_{Tk}, it might very well happen that <T_{Si}, T_{Tk}> also gets a high association score. Although, as observed by Melamed, in general, indirect associations have lower scores than direct (correct) associations, they could receive higher scores than many correct pairs and this will not only generate wrong translation equivalents but will also eliminate several correct pairs from further considerations, thus lowering the procedure's recall. The algorithm has this deficiency because it looks at the association scores globally, and does not check within the TUs whether the tokens constituting the indirect association are still there. To reduce the influence of indirect associations, we modified the algorithm so that the maximum score is considered not globally but within each of the TUs. This brings the procedure closer to Melamed's competitive linking algorithm. The competing pairs are only TECs generated from the current TU and the one with the best score is the first one selected. Based on the 1:1 mapping hypothesis, any TEC containing one of the tokens in the winning pair is discarded. Then, the next best scored TEC in the current TU is selected and again the remaining pairs that include one of the two tokens in the selected pair are discarded. This way each TU unit is processed until no further TECs can be reliably extracted or TU is empty. This modification improves both the precision and recall in comparison with the initial algorithm. In accordance with the 1:1 mapping hypothesis, when two or

[4] The user may play with the precision-recall trade-off by setting the thresholds (minimal number of occurrences, log-likelihood) higher or lower.

more TEC pairs of the same TU share the same token and are equally scored, the algorithm has to make a decision to choose only one of them. We used two heuristics for this step: string similarity scoring and relative distance.

The similarity measure we used, COGN(T_S, T_T), is very similar to the XXDICE score described in [71]. If T_S is a string of *k* characters $\alpha_1\alpha_2 \ldots \alpha_k$ and T_T is a string of *m* characters $\beta_1\beta_2 \ldots \beta_m$ then we construct two new strings T'_S and T'_T by inserting, wherever necessary, special displacement characters into T_S and T_T. The displacement characters will cause T'_S and T'_T to have the same length p (max (k, m)≤p<k+m) and the maximum number of positional matches. Let $\delta(\alpha_i)$ be the number of displacement characters that immediately precedes the character α_i which matches the character β_i and $\delta(\beta_i)$ be the number of displacement characters that immediately precedes the character β_i which matches the character α_i. Let *q* be the number of matching characters. Using this notation, the COGN(T_S, T_T) similarity measure is defined by Eq.(10):

$$\mathrm{COGN}(T_S, T_T) = \begin{cases} \dfrac{\sum_{i=1}^{q} \dfrac{2}{1+|\delta(\alpha_i)-\delta(\beta_i)|}}{k+m} & \text{if } q > 2 \\ 0 & \text{if } q \le 2 \end{cases} \qquad (10)$$

The threshold for the COGN(T_S, T_T) was empirically set to 0.42. This value depends on the pair of languages in a particular bitext. The actual implementation of the COGN test includes a language-dependent normalization step that strips some suffixes, discards diacritics, reduces some consonant doubling, etc. The second filtering condition, DIST(T_S, T_T) is defined as follows:

if $((\langle T_S, T_T\rangle \in L^{Sj}_{posk} \otimes L^{Tj}_{posk})$&($T_S$ is the *n*-th element in L^{Sj}_{posk})&(T_T is the *m*-th element in L^{Tj}_{posk})) then DIST(T_S, T_T)=|n-m|.

The COGN(T_S, T_T) filter is stronger than DIST(T_S, T_T), so that the TEC with the highest similarity score is preferred. If the similarity score is irrelevant, the weaker filter DIST(T_S, T_T) gives priority to the pairs with the smallest relative distance between the constituent tokens. The bilingual dictionary extraction algorithm is sketched below (many bookkeeping details are omitted):

```
procedure BI-DICT-EXTR(bitext;dictionary) is:
    dictionary={};
    TECL(k)=build-cand(bitext);
    for each POS in TECL do
        for each TU^i_POS in TECL do
          finish=false;
          loop
            best_cand = get_the_highest_scored_pairs(TU^i_POS);
            conflicting_cand=select_conflicts(best_cand);
            non_conflicting_cand=best_cand\conflicting_cand;
            best_cand=conflicting_cand;
            if cardinal(best_cand)=0 then finish=true;
               else  if cardinal(best_cand)>1 then
                          best_card=filtered(best_cand);
                  endif;
                  best_pairs = non_conflicting_cand + best_cand
                  add(dictionary,best_pairs);
```

```
                    TU^i_POS=rem_pairs_with_tokens_in_best_pairs(TU^i_POS);
              endif;
           until {(TU^i_POS={})or(finish=true)}
         endfor
    endfor
    return dictionary
end

procedure filtered(best_cand) is:
    result = get_best_COGN_score(best_cand);
    if (cardinal(result)=0)&(non-hapax(best_cand)) then
         result = get_best_DIST_score(best_cand);
      else if cardinal(result)>1 then  result = get_best_DIST_score(best_cand);
          endif
    endif
    return result;
end
```

In [75] we showed that this simple algorithm could be further improved in several ways and that its precision for various Romanian-English bitexts could be as high as 95.28% (but a recall of 55.68% when all hapax legomena are ignored). The best compromise was found for a precision of 84.42% and a recall of 77.72%.

We presented one way of extracting translation dictionaries. The interested user may find alternative methods (conceptually not very different from ours) in [69], [71], [72], [74]. A very popular alternative is GIZA++ [67], [68] which has been successfully used by many researchers (including us) for various pairs of languages.

Translation dictionaries are the basic resources for word alignment and for building translation models. As mentioned above, one can derive better translation lexicons from word alignment links. If the alignment procedure is used just for the sake of extracting translation lexicons, the preparatory phase of bilingual dictionary extraction (as described in this section) will be set for the highest possible precision. The translation pairs found in this preliminary phase will be used for establishing so-called *anchor links* around which the rest of the alignment will be constructed.

4.3. Reified Word Alignment

A word alignment of a bitext is represented by a set of links between lexical tokens in the two corresponding parts of the parallel text. A standard alignment file, such as used in the alignment competitions [76], [77], is a vertical text, containing on each line a link specification:

<translation-unit ID><token-index for $lang_1$><token-index for $lang_2$><confidence>,

where <translation-unit ID> is the unique identifier of a pair of aligned sentences, <token-index for $lang_i$> is the index position of the aligned token in the sentence of language $lang_i$ of the current translation unit, while <confidence> is an optional specifier of the certainty of the link (with the value S(ure) or P(ossible)).

In our reified approach to word alignment [78] a link is associated with an attribute-value structure, containing sufficient information for a classifier to judge the "goodness" of a candidate link. The values of the attributes in the feature structure of a link (numeric values in the interval [0,1]) are interpolated in a confidence score, based on which the link is preserved or removed from the final word alignment.

The score of a candidate link (LS) between a source token α and a target token β is computed by a linear function of several feature scores [69].

$$LS(\alpha,\beta)=\sum_{i=1}^{n}\lambda_i * ScoreFeat_i\,;\sum_{i=1}^{n}\lambda_i=1 \qquad (11)$$

One of the major advantages of this representation is that it facilitates combining the results from different word aligners and thus increasing the accuracy of word alignment. In [78] we presented a high accuracy word aligner COWAL (the highest accuracy at the ACL 2005 shared track on word alignment [79]), which is a SVM classifier of the merged results provided by two different aligners, YAWA and MEBA. In this chapter, we will not describe the implementation details of YAWA and MEBA. Instead, we will discuss the features used for reification, how their values are computed and how the alignments are combined. It is sufficient to say that both YAWA and MEBA are iterative algorithms, language-independent but relying on pre-processing steps described in the previous sections (tokenization, tagging, lemmatization and optionally chunking). Both word aligners generate an alignment by incrementally adding new links to those created at the end of the previous stage. Existing links act as contextual restrictors for the new added links. From one phase to the other, new links are added with no deletions. This monotonic process requires a very high precision (at the price of a modest recall) for the first step, when the so called *anchor links* are created. The subsequent steps are responsible for significantly improving the recall and ensuring a higher F-measure. The aligners use different weights and different significance thresholds for each feature and each iteration. Each of the iterations can be configured to align different categories of tokens (named entities, dates and numbers, content words, functional words, punctuation) in the decreasing order of statistical evidence.

In all the steps, the candidates are considered if and only if they meet the minimum threshold restrictions.

4.3.1. Features of a word alignment link

We differentiate between *context-independent features* that refer only to the tokens of the current link (translation equivalence, part-of-speech affinity, cognates, etc.) and *context-dependent features* that refer to the properties of the current link with respect to the rest of links in a bitext (locality, number of traversed links, tokens index displacement, collocation). Also, we distinguish between bidirectional features (translation equivalence, part-of-speech affinity) and non-directional features (cognates, locality, number of traversed links, collocation, index displacement).

4.3.1.1. Translation equivalence

This feature may be used with two types of pre-processed data: lemmatized or non-lemmatized input. If the data is tagged and lemmatized, an algorithm such as the one described in Section 4.2.2 can compute the translation probabilities. This is the approach in the YAWA word aligner.

If tagging and lemmatization are not available, a good option is to use GIZA++ and to further filter the translation equivalence table by using a log likelihood threshold. However, if lemmatization and tagging are used, the translation equivalence table produced by GIZA++ is significantly improved due to a reduction in data sparseness. For instance, for highly inflectional languages (such as Romanian) the use of lemmas significantly reduces data sparseness. For languages with weak inflectional characteristics (such as English) the part of speech trailing most strongly contributes to the filtering of the search space. A further way of eliminating the noise created by GIZA++ is to filter out all the translation pairs below a LL-threshold. The MEBA word aligner takes this approach. We conducted various experiments and empirically set the value of this threshold to 6 on the basis of the estimated ratio between the number of false negatives and false positives. All the probability mass lost by this filtering was redistributed, in proportion to their initial probabilities, to the surviving translation equivalence candidates.

4.3.1.2. Translation equivalence entropy score

The translation equivalence relation is semantic and directly addresses the notion of word sense. One of the Zipf laws prescribes a skewed distribution of the senses of a word occurring several times in a coherent text.

We used this conjecture as a highly informative information source for the validity of a candidate link. The translation equivalence entropy score is a parameter which favors the words that have few high probability translations. For a word W having N translation equivalents, this parameter is computed by the equation Eq. (12):

$$ES(W) = 1 + \frac{\sum_{i=1}^{N} p(TR_i|W) * \log p(TR_i|W)}{\log N} \tag{12}$$

Since this feature is clearly sensitive to the order of the lexical items in a link $<\alpha,\beta>$, we compute an average value for the link: $0.5(ES(\alpha)+ES(\beta))$.

4.3.1.3. Part-of-speech affinity

In faithful translations, words tend to be translated by words of the same part of speech. When this is not the case, the differing parts of speech are not arbitrary.

The part of speech affinity can be easily computed from a translation equivalence table or directly from a gold standard word alignment. Obviously, this is a directional feature, so an averaging operation is necessary in order to ascribe this feature to a link:

$$PA = 0.5(p(POS_m^{L1}|POS_n^{L2}) + p(POS_n^{L2}|POS_m^{L1})) \tag{13}$$

4.3.1.4. Cognates

The similarity measure, $COGN(T_S, T_T)$, is implemented according to the equation Eq (10). Using the COGN feature as a filtering device is a heuristic based on the *cognate conjecture*, which says that when the two tokens of a translation pair are orthographically similar, they are very likely to have similar meanings (i.e. they are cognates). This feature is binary, and its value is 1 provided the COGN value is above a threshold whose value depends on the pair of languages in the bitext. For Romanian-English parallel texts we used a threshold of 0.42.

4.3.1.5. Obliqueness

Each token on both sides of a bi-text is characterized by a position index, computed as the ratio between the relative position in the sentence and the length of the sentence.

The absolute value of the difference between position indexes, subtracted from 1[5], yields the value of the link's "obliqueness".

$$OBL(SW_i, TW_j) = 1 - \left| \frac{i}{length(Sent_S)} - \frac{j}{length(Sent_T)} \right| \tag{14}$$

This feature is "context-free" as opposed to the locality feature described below.

4.3.1.6. Locality

Locality is a feature that estimates the degree to which the links are sticking together. Depending on the availability of pre-processing tools for a specific language pair, our aligners have three features to account for locality: (i) *weak locality*, (ii) *chunk-based locality* and (iii) *dependency-based* locality. The first feature is the least demanding one. The second requires that the texts in each part of the bitext be chunked, while the last one requires the words occurring in the two texts being dependency-linked. Currently, the chunking and dependency linking is available only for Romanian and English texts.

The value of the *weak locality* feature is derived from existing alignments in a window of k aligned token pairs centred on the candidate link. The window size is variable and proportional to the sentence length. If the relative positions of the tokens in these links are $<s_1\ t_1>, \ldots <s_k\ t_k>$ then the locality feature of the new link $<s_\alpha, t_\alpha>$ is defined by the following equation:

$$LOC = \frac{1}{k}\sum_{m=1}^{k} \frac{\min(|s_\alpha - s_m|, |t_\alpha - t_m|)}{\max(|s_\alpha - s_m|, |t_\alpha - t_m|)}) \tag{15}$$

If the new link starts with or ends in a token that is already linked, the index difference that would be null in the formula above is set to 1. This way, such candidate links would be given support by the LOC feature.

In the case of *chunk-based locality* the window span is given by the indices of the first and last tokens of the chunk. In our Romanian-English experiments, chunking is carried out using a set of regular expressions defined over the tagsets used in the target bitext. These simple chunkers recognize noun phrases, prepositional phrases, verbal and adjectival phrases of both languages. Chunk alignment is done on the basis of the anchor links produced in the first phase. The algorithm is simple: align two chunks $c(i)$ in the source language and $c(j)$ in the target language if $c(i)$ and $c(j)$ have the same type (noun phrase, prepositional phrase, verb phrase, adjectival phrase) and if there exist a link $\langle w(s), w(t)\rangle$ so that $w(s) \in c(i)$ then $w(t) \in c(j)$.

After chunk-to-chunk alignment, the LOC feature is computed within the span of aligned chunks. Given that the chunks contain few words, for the unaligned words instead of the LOC feature one can use very simple empirical rules such as: if *b* is aligned to *c* and *b* is preceded by *a*, link *a* to *c*, unless there exists a *d* in the same chunk with *c* and the POS category of *d* has a significant affinity with the category of *a*. The simplicity of these rules stems from the shallow structures of the chunks.

---

[5] This is to ensure that values close to 1 are "good" and those near 0 are "bad". This definition takes into account the relatively similar word order in English and Romanian.

Dependency-based locality uses the set of dependency links [80] of the tokens in a candidate link for computing the feature value. In this case, the LOC feature of a candidate link <s_{k+1}, t_{k+1}> is set to 1 or 0 according to the following rule:

```
if (between sk+1 and sα there is a (source language) dependency) and
   (between tk+1 and tβ there is also a (target language) dependency)
then LOC is 1 if  sα and tβ are aligned, and 0 otherwise.
```

Please note that if $t_{k+1} \equiv t_\beta$ a trivial dependency (identity) is considered and the LOC attribute of the link <s_{k+1}, t_{k+1}> is always set to 1.

4.3.1.7. Collocation

Monolingual collocation is an important clue for word alignment. If a source collocation is translated by a multiword sequence, the lexical cohesion of source words will often be also found in the corresponding translations. In this case the aligner has strong evidence for a many-to-many linking. When a source collocation is translated as a single word, this feature is a strong indication for a many-to-one linking.

For candidate filtering, bi-gram lists (of content words only) were built from each monolingual part of the training corpus, using the log-likelihood score with the threshold of 10 and minimum occurrence frequency of 3.

We used bi-grams list to annotate the chains of lexical dependencies among the content words. The value of the collocation feature is then computed similarly to the dependency-based locality feature. The algorithm searches for the links of the lexical dependencies around the candidate link.

4.3.2. Combining the reified word alignments

The alignments produced by MEBA were compared to the ones produced by YAWA and evaluated against the gold standard annotations used in the Word Alignment Shared Task (Romanian-English track) at HLT-NAACL 2003 [76] and merged with the GS annotations used for the shared track at ACL 2005 [77].

Given that the two aligners are based on different models and algorithms and that their F-measures are comparable, combining their results with expectations of an improved alignment was a natural thing to do. Moreover, by analyzing the alignment errors of each of the word aligners, we found that the number of common mistakes was small, so the preconditions for a successful combination were very good [41]. The Combined Word Aligner, **COWAL**, is a wrapper of the two aligners (YAWA and MEBA) merging the individual alignments and filtering the result. COWAL is modelled as a binary statistical classification problem (good/bad). As in the case of sentence alignment we used a SVM method for training and classification using the same LIBSVM package [63] and the features presented in Section 4.3. The links extracted from the gold standard alignment were used as positive examples. The same number of negative examples was extracted from the alignments produced by COWAL and MEBA where they differ from the gold standard. A number of automatically generated wrong alignments were also used.

We took part in the the Romanian-English track of the Shared Task on Word Alignment organized by the ACL 2005 Workshop on Building and Using Parallel Corpora: Data-driven Machine Translation and Beyond [77] with the two original aligners and the combined one (COWAL). Out of 37 competing systems, COWAL was rated the first, MEBA the 20th and TREQ-AL, an earlier version of YAWA, was rated the 21st. The utility of combining aligners was convincingly demonstrated by a significant 4% decrease in the alignment error rate (AER).

5. Conclusion

E-content is multi-lingual and multi-cultural and, ideally, its exploitation should be possible irrespective of the language in which a document – whether written or spoken – was posted in the cyberspace. This desideratum is still far away but during the last decade significant progress was made towards this goal. Standardization initiatives in the area of language resources, improvements of data-driven machine learning techniques, availability of massive amounts of linguistic data for more and more languages, and the improvement in computing and storage power of everyday computers have been among the technical enabling factors for this development. Cultural heritage preservation concerns of national and international authorities, as well as economic stimuli offered by new markets, both multi-lingual and multi-cultural, were catalysts for the research and development efforts in the field of cross-lingual and cross-cultural e-content processing.

The concept of *basic language resource and tool kit* (BLARK) emerged as a useful guide for languages with scarce resources, since it outlines and prioritizes the research and developments efforts towards ensuring a minimal level of linguistic processing for all languages. The quality and quantity of the basic language specific resources have a crucial impact on the range, coverage and utility of the deployed language-enabled applications. However, their development is slow, expensive and extremely time consuming. Several multilingual research studies and projects clearly demonstrated that many of the indispensable linguistic resources, can be developed by taking advantage of developments for other languages (wordnets, framenets, tree-banks, sense-annotated corpora, etc.). Annotation import is a very promising avenue for rapid prototyping of language resources with sophisticated meta-information mark-up such as: wordnet-based sense annotation, time-ML annotation, subcategorization frames, dependency parsing relations, anaphoric dependencies and other discourse relations, etc. Obviously, not any meta-information can be transferred equally accurately via word alignment techniques and therefore, human post-validation is often an obligatory requirement. Yet, in most cases, it is easier to correct partially valid annotations than to create them from scratch.

Of the processes and resources that must be included in any language's BLARK, we discussed tokenization, tagging, lemmatization, chunking, sentence alignment and word alignment. The design of tagsets and cleaning training data, the topics which we discussed in detail, are fundamental for the robustness and correctness of the BLARK processes we presented.

References

[1] European Commission. Language and Technology, Report of DGXIII to Commission of the European Communities, September (1992).

[2] European Commission. The Multilingual Information Society, Report of Commission of the European Communities, COM(95) 486/final, Brussels, November (1995).

[3] UNESCO. Multilingualism in an Information Society, International Symposium organized by EC/DGXIII, UNESCO and Ministry of Foreign Affairs of the French Government, Paris 4-6 December (1997).
[4] UNESCO. Promotion and Use of Multilingualism and Universal Access to Cyberspace, UNESCO 31st session, November (2001).
[5] S. Krauwer. The Basic Language Resource Kit (BLARK) as the First Milestone for the Language Resources Roadmap. In Proceedings of *SPECOM2003*, Moskow, October, (2003).
[6] H. Strik, W. Daelemans, ,D. Binnenpoorte, J. Sturm, F. Vrien, C. De Cucchiarini. Dutch Resources: From BLARK to Priority Lists. *Proceedings of ICSLP*, Denver, USA, (2002),. 1549-1552.
[7] E. Forsbom, B. Megyesi. Draft Questionnaire for the Swedish BLARK, presentation at BLARK/SNK workshop, January 28, GSLT retreat, Gullmarsstrand, Sweden, (2007).
[8] B. Maegaard, S., Krauwer, K.Choukri, L. Damsgaard Jørgensen. The BLARK concept and BLARK for Arabic. In *Proceedings of LREC*, Genoa, Italy, (2006), 773-778.
[9] D. Prys. The BLARK Matrix and its Relation to the Language Resources Situation for the Celtic Languages. In *Proceedings of SALTMIL Workshop on Minority Languages*, organized in conjunction with LREC, Genoa, Italy, (2006), 31-32.
[10] J. Guo. Critical Tokenization and its Properties. In *Computational Linguistics*, Vol. 23, no. 4, Association for Computational Linguistics,(1997), 569-596
[11] R. Ion. Automatic Semantic Disambiguation Methods. Applications for English and Romanian (in Romanian). Phd Thesis, Romanian Academy, (2007).
[12] A. Todiraşcu, C. Gledhill,D. Ştefănescu. Extracting Collocations in Context. In *Proceedings of the 3rd Language & Technology Conference: Human Language Technologies as a Challenge for Computer Science and Linguistics*, Poznań, Poland, October 5-7, (2007), 408-412.
[13] H. von Halteren. (ed.) Syntactic Wordclass Tagging. *Text, Speech and Language* book series, vol. 9, Kluver Academic Publishers, Dordrecht,/Boston/London, 1999.
[14] D. Elworthy. Tagset Design and Inflected Languages, *Proceedings of the ACL SIGDAT Workshop*, Dublin, (1995), (also available as cmp-lg archive 9504002).
[15] B. Merialdo. Tagging English text with a probabilistic model. *Computational Linguistics*, 20(2), (1994), 155–172.
[16] G. Tür, K. Oflazer. Tagging English by Path Voting Constraints. In *Proceedings of the COLING-ACL*, Montreal, Canada (1998), 1277-1281.
[17] T. Dunning. Accurate Methods for the Statistics of Surprise and Coincidence in *Computational Linguistics*19(1), (1993), 61-74.
[18] T. Brants. Tagset Reduction Without Information Loss. In *Proceedings of the 33rd Annual Meeting of the ACL*. Cambridge, MA, (1995), 287-289.
[19] E. Brill. Transformation-Based Error-Driven Learning and Natural Language Processing: A Case Study in Part of Speech Tagging. *Computational Linguistics,* 21(4), (1995), 543-565.
[20] S. Abney. Part-of-Speech Tagging and Partial Parsing. In Young, S., Bloothooft, G. (eds.) *Corpus Based Methods in Language and Speech Processing* Text, Speech and Language Technology Series, Kluwer Academic Publishers, (1997), 118-136.
[21] A. Rathaparkhi. A Maximum Entropy Part of Speech Tagger. *In Proceedings of EMNLP'96,* Philadelphia, Pennsylvania, (1996).
[22] W. Daelemans, J. Zavrel, P. Berck, S. Gillis. MBT: A Memory-Based Part-of-Speech Tagger Generator. In *Proceedings of 4th Workshop on Very Large Corpora,*Copenhagen, Denmark, (1996), 14-27.
[23] J. Hajič, ,H. Barbora. Tagging Inflective Languages: Prediction of Morphological Categories for a Rich, Structured Tagset. *In Proceedings of COLING-ACL'98,* Montreal, Canada, (1998), 483-490.
[24] D. Tufiş, O. Mason. Tagging Romanian Texts: a Case Study for QTAG, a Language Independent Probabilistic Tagger *In Proceedings of First International Conference on Language Resources and Evaluation,* Granada, Spain, (1998), 589-596.
[25] T. Brants. TnT – A Statistical Part-of-Speech Tagger. *In Proceedings of the 6th Applied NLP Conference*. Seattle, WA, (2000), 224-231.
[26] D. Tufiş, A. M. Barbu, V.Pătraşcu, G. Rotariu, C. Popescu. Corpora and Corpus-Based Morpho-Lexical Processing in D. Tufiş, P. Andersen (eds.) Recent Advances in Romanian Language Technology, Editura Academiei, (1997), 35-56.
[27] D. Farkas, D. Zec. Agreement and Pronominal Reference, in Gugliermo Cinque and Giuliana Giusti (eds.), *Advances in Romanian Linguistics*, John Benjamin Publishing Company, Amsterdam - Philadelphia, (1995).
[28] D. Tufiş Tiered Tagging and Combined Classifiers. In F. Jelinek, E. Nöth (eds) *Text, Speech and Dialogue*, Lecture Notes in Artificial Intelligence 1692, Springer, (1999), 28-33.
[29] D. Tufiş Using a Large Set of Eagles-compliant Morpho-lexical Descriptors as a Tagset for Probabilistic Tagging, Second *International Conference on Language Resources and Evaluation*, Athens May, (2000), 1105-1112.

[30] D. Tufiş, P. Dienes, C. Oravecz, T. Váradi. Principled Hidden Tagset Design for Tiered Tagging of Hungarian. Second *International Conference on Language Resources and Evaluation,* Athens, May, (2000), 1421-1428.
[31] T. Varadi. The Hungarian National Corpus. Proceedings of the Third *International Conference on Language Resources and Evaluation*, Las Palmas de Gran Canaria, Spain, May, (2002), 385-396.
[32] C. Oravecz, P. Dienes,. Efficient Stochastic Part-of-Speech tagging for Hungarian. Proceedings of the Third *International Conference on Language Resources and Evaluation*, Gran Canaria, Spain, May, (2002), 710-717.
[33] E. Hinrichs, J. Trushkina. Forging Agreement: Morphological Disambiguation of Noun Phrases. *Proceedings of the Workshop Treebanks and Linguistic Theories*, Sozopol, (2002), 78-95.
[34] A. Ceauşu. Maximum Entropy Tiered Tagging. In Proceedings of the Eleventh *ESSLLI Student Session*, ESSLLI (2006), 173-179.
[35] D. Tufiş, L. Dragomirescu. Tiered Tagging Revisited. *In Proceedings of the 4th LREC Conference.* Lisbon, Portugal, (2004), 39-42.
[36] T. Erjavec. MULTEXT-East Version 3: Multilingual Morphosyntactic Specifications, Lexicons and Corpora. In: Proceedings of the Fourth *International Conference on Language Resources and Evaluation*, LREC'04, (2004), 1535 - 1538.
[37] J. Hajic. Morphological Tagging: Data vs. Dictionaries. In *Proceedings of the ANLP/NAACL*, Seatle, (2000).
[38] F. Pîrvan, D. Tufiş Tagsets Mapping and Statistical Training Data Cleaning-up. In *Proceedings of the 5th International Conference on Language Resources and Evaluation*, Genoa, Italy, 22-28 May (2006), 385-390.
[39] D. Tufiş, E. Irimia. RoCo_News - A Hand Validated Journalistic Corpus of Romanian. In Proceedings of the 5th *International Conference on Language Resources and Evaluation*, Genoa, Italy, 22-28 May, (2006), 869-872.
[40] W. A. Gale, G. Sampson. Good-Turing Frequency Estimation Without Tears. *In Journal of Quantitative Linguistics*, 2/3, (1995), 217-237.
[41] T. Dietterich. Machine Learning Research: Four Current Directions, *In AI Magazine*, Winter, (1997), 97-136.
[42] H.v. Halteren, J. Zavrel, W. Daelemans, Improving Data Driven Wordclass Tagging by System Combination *In Proceedings of COLING-ACL'98,* Montreal, Canada, (1998), 491-497.
[43] E. Brill, J. Wu, Classifier Combination for Improved Lexical Disambiguation *In Proceedings of COLING-ACL'98* Montreal, Canada, (1998), 191-195.
[44] R. Steetskamp. An implementation of a probabilistic tagger Master's Thesis, TOSCA Research Group, University of Nijmegen, (1995).
[45] D. Tufiş. It would be Much Easier if WENT Were GOED. In Proceedings of the fourth *Conference of European Chapter of the Association for Computational Linguistics*, Manchester, England, (1989), 145 - 152.
[46] D. Tufiş. Paradigmatic Morphology Learning, in *Computers and Artificial Intelligence.* Volume 9 , Issue 3, (1990), 273 - 290
[47] K. Beesley, L. Karttunen. Finite State Morphology, *CLSI* publications, (2003), http://www.stanford.edu /~laurik/fsmbook/home.html.
[48] L. Karttunen, J. P. Chanod, G. Grefenstette, A. Schiller. Regular expressions for language engineering. *Natural Language Engineering*, 2(4), (1996), 305.328.
[49] M. Silberztein. Intex: An fst toolbox. *Theoretical Computer Science*, 231(1), (2000), 33.46.
[50] S. Džeroski, T. Erjavec. 'Learning to Lemmatise Slovene Words'. In: J.Cussens and S. Džeroski (eds.): *Learning Language in Logic*, No. 1925 in Lecture Notes in Artificial Intelligence. Berlin: Springer, (2000), 69-88.
[51] O. Perera, R. Witte, R. A Self-Learning Context-Aware Lemmatizer for German. In Proceedings of *Human Language Technology Conference and Conference on Empirical Methods in Natural Language Processing* (HLT/EMNLP), Vancouver, October 2005, pp. 636–643.
[52] T. M. Miangah. Automatic lemmatization of Persian words. In *Journal of Quantitative Linguistics*, Vol. 13, Issue 1 (2006), 1-15.
[53] G. Chrupala. Simple Data-Driven Context-Sensitive Lemmatization. In Proceedings of *SEPLN*, Revista nº 37, septiembre (2006), 121-130.
[54] J. Plisson, N. Lavrac, D. Mladenic. A rule based approach to word lemmatization. In Proceedings of *IS2004* Volume 3, (2004), 83-86.
[55] D. Tufiş, R. Ion,E. Irimia, A. Ceauşu. Unsupervised Lexical Acquisition for Part of Speech Tagging. In Proceedings of the 6th *International Conference on Language Resources and Evaluation* (LREC), Marrakech, Marroco, (2008).

[56] W. A. Gale, K.W. Church. A Program for Aligning Sentences in Bilingual Corpora. In *Computational Linguistics*, 19(1), (1993), 75-102.

[57] M. Kay, M., M. Röscheisen. Text-Translation Alignment. In *Computational Linguistics*, 19(1), 121-142.

[58] S. F. Chen. Aligning Sentences in Bilingual Corpora Using Lexical Information. In *Proceedings of the 31st Annual Meeting of the Association for Computational Linguistics,* Columbus, Ohio, (1993), 9-16.

[59] D. Melamed. Bitext Maps and Alignment via Pattern Recognition, In *Computational Linguistics* 25(1), (1999), 107-130.

[60] R. Moore. Fast and Accurate Sentence Alignment of Bilingual Corpora in Machine Translation: From Research to Real Users. In Proceedings of the *5th Conference of the Association for Machine Translation in the Americas*, Tiburon, California), Springer-Verlag, Heidelberg, Germany, (2002), 135-244.

[61] P. Brown, S. A. Della Pietra, V. J. Della Pietra, R. L. Mercer. The mathematics of statistical machine translation: parameter estimation in *Computational Linguistics*19(2), (1993), 263-311.

[62] V. Vapnik. *The Nature of Statistical Learning Theory*, Springer, 1995.

[63] R. Fan, P-H Chen, C-J Lin. Working set selection using the second order information for training SVM. Technical report, Department of Computer Science, National Taiwan University, (2005), (www.csie.ntu.edu.tw/~cjlin/papers/ quadworkset.pdf).

[64] R. Steinberger, B. Pouliquen, A. Widiger, C. Ignat, T. Erjavec, D. Tufiş. The JRC-Acquis: A multilingual aligned parallel corpus with 20+ languages. In Proceedings of the 5th *International Conference on Language Resources and Evaluation*, Genoa, Italy, 22-28 May, (2006), 2142-2147.

[65] D. Tufiş, R. Ion, A. Ceauşu, D. Stefănescu. Combined Aligners. In *Proceeding of the ACL2005 Workshop on Building and Using Parallel Corpora: Data-driven Machine Translation and Beyond.* June, 2005, *Ann Arbor, Michigan, June,* Association for Computational Linguistics, (2005),107-110.

[66] A. Ceauşu, D. Ştefănescu, D. Tufiş. Acquis Communautaire Sentence Alignment using Support Vector Machines. In Proceedings of the 5th *International Conference on Language Resources and Evaluation* Genoa, Italy, 22-28 May, (2006), 2134-2137.

[67] F. J. Och, H. Ney. Improved Statistical Alignment Models. In *Proceedings of the 38th Conference of ACL*, Hong Kong, (2000), 440-447.

[68] F. J. Och, H. Ney. A Systematic Comparison of Various Statistical Alignment Models, *Computational Linguistics*, 29(1), (2003),19-51.

[69] J. Tiedemann. Combining clues for word alignment. In *Proceedings of the 10th EACL*, Budapest, Hungary, (2003), 339–346.

[70] D. Tufiş. A cheap and fast way to build useful translation lexicons. In *Proceedings of COLING2002,* Taipei, China, (2002).1030-1036.

[71] C. Brew, D. McKelvie. Word-pair extraction for lexicography, (1996), http://www.ltg.ed.ac.uk/ ~chrisbr/papers/nemplap96.

[72] D. Hiemstra. Deriving a bilingual lexicon for cross language information retrieval. In *Proceedings of Gronics,* (1997), 21-26.

[73] J. Tiedemann. Extraction of Translation Equivalents from Parallel Corpora, In *Proceedings of the 11th Nordic Conference on Computational Linguistics*, Center for Sprogteknologi, Copenhagen, (1998), http://stp.ling.uu.se/~joerg/.

[74] L. Ahrenberg, M. Andersson, M. Merkel. A knowledge-lite approach to word alignment, in J. Véronis (ed) *Parallel Text Processing*, Kluwer Academic Publishers, (2000), 97-116.

[75] D. Tufiş, A. M. Barbu, R. Ion. Extracting Multilingual Lexicons from Parallel Corpora, *Computers and the Humanities*, Volume 38, Issue 2, May, (2004), 163 – 189.

[76] R. Mihalcea, T. Pedersen. An Evaluation Exercise for Word Alignment. *Proceedings of the HLT-NAACL 2003 Workshop: Building and Using Parallel Texts Data Driven Machine Translation and Beyond.* Edmonton, Canada, (2003), 1–10.

[77] J. Martin, R. Mihalcea, T. Pedersen. Word Alignment for Languages with Scarce Resources. In *Proceeding of the ACL2005 Workshop on Building and Using Parallel Corpora: Data-driven Machine Translation and Beyond.* June, Ann Arbor, Michigan, June, Association for Computational Linguistics, (2005), 65–74.

[78] D. Tufiş, R. Ion, A. Ceauşu, D. Ştefănescu. Improved Lexical Alignment by Combining Multiple Reified Alignments. In *Proceedings of the 11th Conference of the European Chapter of the Association for Computational Linguistics* (EACL2006), Trento, Italy, (2006), 153-160.

[79] D. Tufiş, R. Ion, A. Ceauşu, D. Stefănescu. Combined Aligners. In *Proceeding of the ACL2005 Workshop on Building and Using Parallel Corpora: Data-driven Machine Translation and Beyond.* June, Ann Arbor, Michigan, June, Association for Computational Linguistics, 2005, 107-110.

[80] R. Ion, D. Tufiş. Meaning Affinity Models. In E. Agirre, L. Màrquez and R Wicentowski (eds.): *Proceedings of the Fourth International Workshop on Semantic Evaluations* (SemEval-2007), Prague, Czech Republic, ACL2007, June, (2007), 282-287.

Language Engineering for Lesser-Studied Languages
S. Nirenburg (Ed.)
IOS Press, 2009

doi:10.3233/978-1-58603-954-7-51

Treebanking in VIT: from Phrase Structure to Dependency Representation

Rodolfo DELMONTE
University Ca' Foscari
Computational Linguistics Laboratory
Department of Language Sciences

Abstract: In this chapter, we are dealing with treebanks and their applications. We describe VIT (Venice Italian Treebank), focusing on the syntactic-semantic features of the treebank that are partly dependent on the adopted tagset, partly on the reference linguistic theory, and, lastly - as in every treebank - on the chosen language: Italian. By discussing examples taken from treebanks available in other languages, we show the theoretical and practical differences and motivations that underlie our approach. Finally, we discuss the quantitative analysis of the data of our treebank and compare them to other treebanks. In general, we try to substantiate the claim that treebanking grammars or parsers strongly depend on the chosen treebank; and eventually this process seems to depend both on factors such as the adopted linguistic framework for structural description and, ultimately, the described language.

Keywords: Treebanks, syntactic representation, dependency structure, conversion algorithms, machine learning from treebanks, probabilistic parsing from treebanks.

1. Introduction

In this chapter we will be dealing with treebanks and their applications. The questions that we ask ourselves are the following ones: What is a Treebank? Which treebanks are there? Where are they: what languages do the address? What dimensions and scope do they have? Do they reflect written or spoken language? What types of linguistic representation do they use? What are their companion tools?

Treebanks have become valuable resources for natural language processing (NLP) in recent years. A treebank is a collection of syntactically annotated sentences in which the annotation has been manually checked so that the treebank can serve as a training corpus for natural language parsers, as a repository for linguistic research, or as an evaluation corpus for NLP systems. In this chapter, we give an overview of the annotation formats in different treebanks (e.g. the English Penn Treebank (PT), the German TIGER treebank, the Venice Italian Treebank (VIT), etc.); introduce important tools for treebank creation (tree editors), consistency checking and treebank searches; and look into the many usages of treebanks ranging from machine learning to system evaluation.

Creating a treebank from scratch is a hard task for a less studied language that usually lacks digital resources such as corpora over which tagging has been carried out and checked manually. As will be argued in the sections below, this cannot be accomplished using freely available tools because they would require a tagged corpus. The suggestion is that of using a Finite State Automaton to produce the rule set needed incrementally. One typical such tool for tagging is Brill's TBT (Transformation-Based PoS Tagging) [1] or its corresponding Prolog version TnT [2].

Uses for a treebank range from parser evaluation and training to parallel tfor machine translation to result validation and grammar construction/induction in theoretical linguistics.

2. Determining Factors in Treebank Construction

The following is a list of factors that are of fundamental importance in deciding how a treebank and its underlying corpus should be organized. These factors are at the same time conditions of well-formedness of a treebank and may constitute an obstacle against the usability of the same treebank for machine learning purposes. We believe that a treebank should be endowed with:

- Representativeness in terms of text genres
- Representativeness in terms of linguistic theory adherence
- Coherence in allowing Syntactic-Semantic Mapping
- Ability to highlight distinctive linguistic features of the chosen language.

Each factor can impact negatively on the linguistic texture of a treebank, and may undermine its utility as a general linguistic reference point for studies of the chosen language. More specifically, we assume that the above factors would have to be determined on the basis of the following choices:

- Corpus (balanced) and representative of 6 or 7 different text genres vs. unbalanced/mono genre
- Strictly adherent to linguistic principles vs. loosely/non adherent (e.g. more hierarchical vs. less hierarchical)
- Constituency/Dependency/Functional structures are semantically coherent vs. incoherent
- Language chosen is highly canonical and regular vs. almost free word order language.

The final item is clearly inherent in the language chosen and not to be attributed to responsibilities of the annotators. However, as will be shown and discussed at length below, it may turn out to be the main factor in determining the feasibility of the treebank for grammar induction and probabilistic parsing.

2.1. Existing Treebanks and their main features

The main treebanks and related tools available at the time of writing are listed in Appendix 1. They have been subdivided into 6 categories:

1. Feature Structure or Dependency Representation.
2. Phrase Structure Representation.
3. Spoken Transcribed and Discourse Treebanks.
4. Tools.
5. Other resources based on treebanks.
6. Generic websites for corpora.

Section 3 will present in detail work carried out on the Italian treebank, which deals basically with syntactic representations. At this point, we briefly comment on the underlying problems of annotation and focus on discourse and semantic representation.

2.1.1. Annotating Discourse and Semantic Structure

Treebank annotation is usually carried out semi-automatically, but in the case of discourse and semantic representation it is usually manual. Manual annotation is inherently an error-prone process, so there is a need for very careful postprocessing and validation. We assume that beside syntactic trees, there are also two other similar types of hierarchical representation: semantic – which I will not discuss here - and discourse trees. What do these trees represent? Depending on the theory behind them, discourse structure can either be used to represent information about dependencies between units at the level of sentence or clause; or it is established on the basis of rhetorical relations, textual semantically founded discourse dependence, and eventually on the basis of communicative functions.

Linguistic items relevant for the markup of discourse structure are all related to the notion of "coherence" and "cohesion". They are:

- anaphoric relations;
- referring expressions of other types;
- discourse markers.

As to theories supporting discourse and semantic representation we may assume the following are relevant:

- Intention driven [3]
    - Motivation for DS found in the intention behind the utterances
    - Discourse segments related by Dominance and Precedence
    - Tree structure constrains accessibility of referents
- Text Based [4]
    - Motivation for DS found in the text
    - Discourse segments related on the basis of surface cues such as discourse markers
    - Relations between discourse segments labeled (e.g., elaboration, cause, contrast, etc.) from a finite – but potentially very large – set of DRs
- Discourse Information [5]
    - Dialogue Tagging, intention based
    - Motivation for DS found in communicative functions
    - Segment labeled on basis of communicative intention
    - Restricted to three levels:
        - moves, speech acts;
        - games, goals;
        - transactions, topics (these latter representations are not properly trees).

2.2. The theoretical framework

Schematically speaking, in the X-bar theory [6] (we refer here to the standard variety presented in LFG theory) each head – Preposition, Verb, Noun, Adjective and ADVerbial - is provided with a bar in hierarchical order: in this way the node on which a head depends is numbered starting from 0 and the subsequent dominant nodes have a bar, two bars and if necessary other bars (even though a two-bar projection is universally considered to be the maximum level). The hierarchical organization of the theory is reflected in the following abstract rewrite rules, where X is used instead of one of the heads (P,A,V,N,ADV), and there is an additional functional level, CP, based on Complementizer. The preterminal C0 thus corresponds to X0, Xbar is another term for X1, and XP stands for X2:

2.2.1. The theoretical schema of X-bar rules

CP	--> Spec, Cbar
Spec	--> C0
C0	--> Complementizer
Cbar	--> Adjuncts, XP
XP	--> Spec / Xbar
Spec	--> (Subject) NP
Xbar	--> X0 / Complements / Adjuncts
X0	--> Verb / Adjective / Noun / Adverb / Preposition

Spec (Specifier) is a nonterminal including constituents preceding the Head, usually modifiers or intensifiers. At sentence level, Spec contains the Subject NP for SVO languages. This rule schema is, however, too weak to be of use for practical purposes in a real corpus annotation task, because it conflates all sentence types into one single label CP. So we operated a series of tuning and specialization operations on the X-bar schema while at the same time trying not to betray its basic underlying principle, which is the requirement that each constituent or higher projection should have only one single head.

Some decisions were due to the need to include under the same constituent label linguistic material belonging to the specifier, which in our representation is a positional variant: i.e. all constituents coming before the head are in the specifier of that constituent. Our first choice had to do with the internal organization of the specifier of NP that, in the case of non-phrasal constituents, can consist of one or more linguistic elements belonging to different minor syntactic categories, as follows:

NP Spec -->Determiners, Quantifiers, Intensifiers
Verb Complex --> auxiliary verbs, modals, clitics, negatives, adverbials (including PPs), Verb

The choice to have a Spec structure was too difficult an option to pursue because it introduced an additional level of structure which was not easy to formalize in real texts, so we decided to leave minor non-semantic constituents that stood before the head in an atomic form, unless they required a structure of their own, which is the case with some quantifiers. Besides, semantic heads such as adjectives and adverbs always have their own constituent structure. As to the verb complex, it contained a number of atomic minor categories to which we did not want to give a separate structure if not required specifically, again in case we had a PP or an ADVerbial preceded by a modifier. So, tensed verb takes a separate structure we have called IBAR – or IR_INFL ("unreal" verb) when the verb is either in future, conditional or subjunctive form – and that can consist of more elements added to the constituency level of the tensed verb, as shown below. In view of the above, we came up with the following, less generic, X-bar schema (cf. [7]):

```
CP          --> SpecCP, Cbar
SpecCP      --> Adjuncts / Fronted Complements /
                Focused Arguments / Dislocated Constituents
Cbar        --> C1 / IP
Cbar        --> C0 / CP
C0          --> Complementizer
C1          --> Wh+ word
IP          --> SpecIP / Xbar / Complements / Adjuncts /
                Dislocated Constituents
SpecIP      --> (Subject) NP
Complements --> COMPlementTransitive / COMPlementINtransitive /
                COMPlementCopulative / COMPlementPASsive
Xbar        --> VerbalComplex
Spec        --> Adverbials / Quantified Structures / Preposed Constituents
```

Here the symbol IP appears, where I stands for Inflection of the Inflected or tensed Verb. However, it is apparent that the rules must be specialized: Cbar in the case of wh+ words can never precede a CP, i.e. a subordinate clause starting with a subordinating conjunction. On the other hand, when a complementizer is instantiated, CP may appear.

2.3. Syntactic Constituency Annotation

In the final analysis, what we wanted to preserve was the semantic transparency of the constituency representation in order to facilitate the syntax-semantics mapping if needed. In particular we wanted the Clause or IP to remain the semantically transparent syntactic nucleus corresponding to a Semantic Proposition with PAS (Predicate Argument Structures). For that purpose, we introduced a distinction between Tensed and Untensed Clauses, where the latter need their unexpressed Subject to be bound to some Controller in the matrix clause. Untensed clauses are Participials, Infinitivals and Gerundives which lack an expressed NP Subject universally. For that reason, linguistic theories have introduced he notion of Big PRO, as representing the unexpressed Subject of these clauses. A big PRO needs a controller – a grammatically or lexically assigned antecedent – in order for the clause to be semantically consistent. It is called controller (and not antecedent) because the syntactic structure licenses its structural location in a specific domain. In the case of arbitrary or generic reading, big PROs may also end up without a specific controller. Antecedents are only those specified by rules of pronominal binding or anaphora resolution.

We were also obliged to introduce a special constituency label due to the specific features of the corpus we analyzed: in particular, texts are full of fragments or sequences of constituents that do not contain a verb but still constitute a sentence.

Other specialized structures will be discussed further on, but at this point it is important to note that our representation does not employ a VP structure level: in fact, we preferred to analyze verbal groups as positioned on the same level as S, where there will also be a NP-Subject, if it is syntactically expressed. We also decided to introduce a label for each of the three main lexical types specifying the syntactic category of the verbal governor – the main lexical verb – to the complement structure which would thus be subcategorized according to different types of complements, among which we introduced features for voice and diathesis, to indicate the complements of a passive verb – COMPPAS, in order to allow an easy automatic conversion in case of the presence of an adjunct containing an agent in SPDA (Prepositional Phrase headed by preposition BY/DA) form. By doing this, VIT partially followed the German Treebank NEGRA [8], as it did with respect to specializing major non-terminal constituents, as discussed in the sections below. While on the contrary PennTrebank (hence PT as a whole) [9] differs for a less detailed and more skeletal choice, as specified in PT guidelines:

> "Our approach to developing the syntactic tagset was highly pragmatic and strongly influenced by the need to create a large body of annotated material given limited human resources. The original design of the Treebank called for a level of syntactic analysis comparable to the skeletal analysis used by the Lancaster Treebank... no forced distinction between arguments and adjuncts. A skeletal syntactic context-free representation (parsing)." (p. 23)

We show two examples below of how a structure in PT could be represented using our rule schema:

(1) In exchange offers that expired Friday, holders of each $1,000 of notes will receive $250 face amount of Series A 7.5% senior secured convertible notes due Jan. 15, 1995, and 200 common shares.

```
(
 (S (PP-LOC In
      (NP (NP exchange offers)
                 (SBAR (WHNP-1 that)
                      (S (NP-SBJ *T*-1)
                           (VP expired
                      (NP-TMP Friday))))))
  ,
  (NP-SBJ (NP holders)
       (PP of
          (NP (NP each $ 1,000 *U*)
             (PP of
               (NP notes)))))
  (VP will
     (VP receive
       (NP (NP (NP (ADJP $ 250 *U*) face amount)
                (PP of
                   (NP (NP Series A
                              (ADJP 7.5 %)  senior secured convertible notes)
                (ADJP due
                   (NP-TMP (NP Jan. 15)
                                                  ,
                                  (NP 1995))))))
                                  and
          (NP 200 common shares))))
  .)
 )
```

As can be seen, the sentence S begins with an Adjunct PP – an adjunct NP would have been treated the same way – which is then followed by the NP subject at the same level. In our representation, the adjunct would have been positioned higher, under CP:

```
(
 (CP (PP-LOC In
      (NP (NP exchange) offers
           (CP (WHNP-1 that)
                     (S (IBAR expired)
                         (COMPIN (NP-TMP Friday))))))
   ,
   (S
      (NP-SBJ (NP holders
           (PP of
            (NP (QP each) $ 1,000 *U*
             (PP of
              (NP notes))))))
      (IBAR will receive)
      (COMPT (COORD
           (NP (NP (ADJP $ 250 *U*)
                face amount
                 (PP of
                   (NP (NP Series A
                          (ADJP 7.5 %)
                            (ADJP senior secured convertible)
                      notes)
                     (ADJP due
                      (NP-TMP (NP Jan. 15)
                                                ,
                                   (NP 1995))))))
                                   and
                (NP 200 common shares)))))
.)
```

Also notice that we add an abstract COORD node that in this case is headed by the conjunction AND, and in other cases will be headed by punctuation marks.

An interesting question is posed by the role played by auxiliaries in case they are separated from the main verb by the NP Subject, as happens in English and Italian with Aux-To-Comp structures – shown and discussed below in Section 3. The NEGRA treebank has solved this problem by inserting a special label at the S and VP level as follows:

```
(
 (S  (S-MO
     (VMFIN-HD Mögen)
     (NP-SB
           (NN-NK Puristen)
              (NP-GR
               (PIDAT-NK aller)
               (NN-NK Musikbereiche) ))
     (ADV-MO auch)
     (VP-OC
           (NP-OA (ART-NK die)
                      (NN-NK Nase) )
            (VVINF-HD rümpfen) ))
   ($, ,)
   (NP-SB (ART-NK die)
           (NN-NK Zukunft)
               (NP-GR (ART-NK der)
                         (NN-NK Musik) ))
   (VVFIN-HD liegt)
   (PP-MO (APPR-AC für)
           (PIDAT-NK viele)
           (ADJA-NK junge)
```

```
            (NN-NK Komponisten) )
    (PP-MO
            (APPRART-AC im)
            (NN-NK Crossover-Stil)
                    ))
  ($. .) )
```

A more specialized inventory of constituents was chosen also in view of facilitating additional projects devoted to conversion into dependency structure which will be illustrated in Section 3 below. It also simplifies searching and allows for better specification of the structure to be searched. In particular, having a specialized node for tensed clauses, which is different from the one assigned to untensed ones, allows for better treatment of this constituent, which, as will be shown in Section 3 below, allows for some of its specific properties to be easily detected. Moreover, the assumption that the tensed verb complex – IBAR/IR_INFL - is the sentence head allows for a much easier treatment in the LPCFG (Lexicalized Probabilistic Context-Free Grammars) schema, where the head of the VP is also the head of S. In VIT the tensed verb does not have to be extracted from a substructure because it is already at the S level. In PT, the head, by contrast, could be the leaf of many different VP nodes depending on how many auxiliaries or modals precede the main lexical verb. In our case, for every operation of conversion in dependency structure, the number of levels to keep under control is lower when the task of detecting Head-root and Head-dependent relations.

Adding a VP node that encompasses the Verbal complex and its complement was not a difficult task to carry out. We have then produced a script that enables the transformation of the entire VIT without a VP node into a version that has it, but only in those cases where it is allowed by the grammar. In this way we successfully removed all those instances where the verbal group IBAR/IR_INFL is followed by linguistic material belonging to the S level, such as phrasal conjunctions, PP adjuncts or parenthetical structures. By doing this we were able to identify about 1,000 clauses out of the total 16,000 where the VP node has not been added by the script.

The following section describes work carried out to produce an algorithm for the automatic conversion of VIT, which uses traditionally bracketed syntactic constituency structures, into a linear word-based head-dependent representation enriched with grammatical relations, morphological features and lemmata. We are also still trying to produce a machine learning parsing algorithm that performs better than the current results (which are at present are slightly below 70%).

3. A Case Study: VIT, The Venice Italian Treebank

The VIT Corpus consists of 60,000 words of transcribed spoken text and of 270,000 words of written text. In this chapter we will restrict our description to the characteristics of written texts of our Treebank.

The first version of the Treebank was created in the years 1985-88 with the contribution of Roberto Dolci, Giuliana Giusti, Anna Cardinaletti, Laura Brugè, Paola Merlo who also all collaborated on the creation of the first Italian subcategorized frequency lexicon where the first 4,000 words in the frequency list of LIF were chosen. These procedures had been promoted by means of a research program financed by Digital Equipment Corporation (DEC) that was interested in building an Italian version of its voice synthetizer DECTalk, i.e. a system of vocal automatic synthesis from a written text in Italian based on the one realized for American English. To this end, it was necessary to recreate the same linguistic tools of the original version: that is a robust syntactic parser for unrestricted text [10], a morphological analyser [11] and a lexicon that could work with unrestricted Italian texts without vocabulary limitations. The treebank created at that time was only in paper form, because of the lack of other samples available worldwide – the one created by the University of Pennsylvania was a work-in-progress – and also for the lack of adequate software to produce annotation interactively and consistently.

The paper documents – that are still kept in the Laboratory of Computational Linguistics where they were produced – were used for the creation of a probabilistic context-free grammar of Italian, i.e. a list of all the rewriting rules produced by manual annotation and for every different rule the frequency value of the rule itself in the corpus. The chosen corpus consisted of 40.000 words taken from newspaper or magazine articles pertaining to politics, economics, current events and burocratic language: the texts were digitized and available on mainframe computers, but not annotated as for PoS. This phase of the work is documented in a paper [10]. Work for the creation of the treebank was then discontinually carried on reusing the above-mentioned texts and gradually expanding the corpus. This went on until the approval of the national project SI-TAL in 1998 which was also the right prompt to achieve a normalization of the overall syntactic annotation [12,13,14]. The current treebank uses those texts and others elaborated for the national project SI-TAL and the projects AVIP/API/IPAR as well as texts annotated on a number of internal project - as for instance one with IRST concerned with literary Italian texts.

The creation of a treebank is the last step in a long and elaborated process during which the original text undergoes a total transformation. The texts have been digitized and, if necessary, corrected – in case of orthographic or other sorts of errors, which have been removed in order to avoid unwanted and malformed syntactic structures. Subsequently, by employing the suite of automatic annotation programs by Delmonte et al. [15, 16, 17, 18], we proceeded to the tokenization of the texts, providing each word with a line or record and one or more indexes – in case the word was an amalgam or a cliticized verb. In this stage, we verified that those words consisting of a combination of letters and digits, letters and graphical signs, dates, formulas and other orthographic combinations that are not simple sequences of characters had been transformed appropriately and that no word of the original text had gone missing during the process.

From the resulting tokenized text we moved on to the creation of Multiwords – more on this topic in Section 3.3 below. This operation is accomplished using a specialized lexicon which has been created on purpose and in which one could add other forms or idiomatic expressions that have to be analyzed syntactically as one word because they constitute a single meaning and no semantic decomposition would be allowed. Inflected versions of each multiword had to be listed if needed.

At this stage of the work, we also created a lexicon specialized to particular domains. This has been done for use in the spoken Italian treebank based on a corpus of spontaneous dialogue from the national projects AVIP/API/IPAR [19, 20] where coding of semi-words, non-words and other forms of disfluencies has taken place; where possible, the specific lexicon also contained reference to the lemma of the word form.

Tagging is performed by assigning to each token previously found the tags or PoS labels on the basis of a wordform dictionary and of a morphological analyser that can proceed to do "guessing" in case the corresponding root cannot be found in the root dictionary. Guessing is done by decomposing a word in affixes, inflections and derivational ones, in order to identify an existing root; in lack of such information, a word will be classified with the temporary tag "npro" (proper noun) if uppercase or "fw" (foreign word) if lowercase. In this stage amalgamated words (e.g. DEL = Di/prep, lo/art_mas_sing), are split and two separate words are created; in addition to that, an image of the text in the form of sentences is created and these sentences will then be used for syntactic analysis which assumes the sentence as the ideal minimal span of text. As already stated above, all steps of morphological analysis and lemmatization together with the creation of specific lexica and treatment of multiwords have required one or more cycles of manual revision.

Tagging was completed by the semi-automatic phase of disambiguation, i.e. choice of single tag associated to every word according to context. The texts we analyzed showed an 1.9 ambiguity level: this means that every word was associated to almost two tags on average. To solve the problem of word disambiguation we used hybrid algorithms that are in part statistical and in part syntactic and converge in a program that has an interface for the annotator. The interface allows the annotator to take quick decisions as to which tag to assign in the current context even when the correct tag differs from the ones suggested by the automatic analysis. In this way, the annotator also takes care of those cases in which the system did not have enough lexical or morphological information to process the current word.

Eventually, parsing takes place. The results of automatic parsing are submitted to a manual check and in the end to the collation from a supervisor who is responsible of the eventual unification of the structural "variants" suggested by different annotators for the same structural type (two annotators were used for each input). This operation is critical and has required in some cases a total revision of some parts of the treebank itself, as has been the case with comparative and quantified structures in the project SI-TAL [21], some of which are illustrated below.

3.1. From Constituent Structure to Head-Dependent Functional Representation

This section describes work carried out to produce an algorithm for the automatic conversion of VIT, which uses traditionally bracketed syntactic constituency structures, into a linear word- and column-based head-dependent representation enriched with grammatical relations, morphological features and lemmata.

Dependency syntactic representation consists of lexical items – the actual words – linked by binary asymmetric relations called dependencies. As Lucien Tesnière formulated it [22]:

> La phrase est un ensemble organisé dont les èlèments constituants sont les mots. Tout mot qui fait partie d'une phrase cesse par lui-meme d'etre isolé comme dans le dictionnaire. Entre lui et ses voisins, l'esprit aperçoit des connexions, dont l'ensemble forme la charpent de la phrase. Les connexions structurals établissent entre les mots des rapports de dépendance. Chaque connexion unit en principe un terme supérieur à un terme inférieur. Le terme supérieur reçoit le nom de régissant. Le term inférieur reçoit le nom de subordonné. Ansi dans la phrase "Alfred parle" ... parle est le régissant et Alfred le subordonné.

If we try to compare types of information represented by the two theories we end with the following result:

- Phrase structure explicitely represent phrases (nonterminal nodes); structural categories (nonterminal labels) and possibly some functional categories (grammatical functions)
- Dependency structures explicitely represent head-dependent relations (direct arcs); functional categories (arc labels) and possibly some structural categories (POS).

The theoretical framework for the different versions of dependency grammar is represented, in addition to Tesnière's work, by Word Grammar (WG) [23, 24]; Functional Generative Description (FGD) [25]; Dependency Unification Grammar (DUG) [26]; Meaning Text Theory (MTT) [27]; Weighted Constraint Dependency Grammar (WCDG) [28, 29, 30]; Functional Dependency Grammar FDG [31, 32]; Topological/Extensible Dependency Grammar (T/XDG) [33].

We can briefly define dependency syntax to have to the following distinctive properties:

- It has direct encoding of predicate argument structure;
- dependency structure is independent of word order;
- for this reason, it is suitable for free word order languages (Latin, Walpiri, etc.)
- however, it has limited expressivity:
    - every projective dependency grammar has a strongly equivalent context-free grammar but not vice-versa;
    - it is impossible to distinguish between phrase modification and head modification in an unlabeled dependency structure.

To obviate to some of the deficiencies of the dependency model, we designed our conversion algorithm so that all the required linguistic information is supplied and present in the final representation, as discussed in the next section.

3.2. Conversion Algorithm for Head-Dependency Structures (AHDS)

Original sentence-based bracketed syntactic constituency structures are transformed into head-dependent, column-based functional representation using a pipeline of script algorithms. These scripts produce a certain number of intermediate files containing the Tokenization, the Head Table, and the Clause Level Head-Dependency Table (hence CLHDT). The final output is a file that contains the following items of linguistic information, in a column-based format:

id_num. word POS role id_head const. lemma [semantic/morphological features]

For example, the entry for the word competitività (competitiveness) will be as follows:
5 competitività N(noun) POBJ 4 SN competitività [sems=invar, mfeats=f]

In the Tokenization file VIT is represented as a list of words in the form of word-tag pairs. In addition, all multiword expressions have been relabeled into a set of "N" words preceding the head tagged as "MW". The Head Table defines what category can be head of a given constituent and specifies the possible dependents in the same structure. The Head Table differentiates dependents from heads and has been used together with the Tokenization file to produce the CLHDT file. The current Tokenization includes the label of the constituent to which the category belongs. It also differentiates between simple POS labels and labels with extended linguistic (syntactic, semantic, morphological) information.

The fully converted file also includes Grammatical Relation labels. In order to produce this output, we had to relabel NP SUBJects, OBJects and OBLiques appearing in a non-canonical position. A similar question is related to the more general need to tell apart arguments and adjuncts in ditransitive and intransitive constructions. In Italian, prepositional phrases can occur quite freely before or after another argument/adjunct of the same predicate. Our original strategy was to mark as OBLique the first PP under COMPIN, and PPby under COMPPAS (more on this in the next section). But it is impossible to mark ditransitive PP complements without subcategorization information or PPs marked as OBLiques without lexical information.

The solution to this problem was on the one hand the use of our general semantically labeled Italian lexicon which contains 17,000 verb entries together with a lexicon lookup algorithm, where each verb has been tagged with a specific subcategorization label and a further entry for prepositions for which it subcategorizes. The use of this lexicon has allowed the automatic labelling of PP arguments in canonical positions and reduced the task of distinguishing arguments from adjuncts to the manual labeling of arguments in non -positions.

On the other hand, as nominal heads were tagged with semantic labels, we proceeded to label possible adjuncts related to space and time. With verbs of movement, where the subcategorization frames required and the preposition heading the PP allowed it, we marked the PP as argument. We also relabeled as arguments all those PPs that were listed in the subcategorization frames of Ditransitives, again where the preposition allowed it.

We organized our work into a pipeline of intermediate steps that incrementally carrie out the full conversion task. In this way we also managed to check for consistency at different levels of representation.

3.3. Tagging and Multiwords

Checking consistency at the level of categories or parts of speech, was done with during the first step, tokenization. At this stage, we had to check for consistency with multiwords as they were encoded in the current version of VIT. The lack of this important annotation caused serious problems in the PennTreebank where the this problem was solved by assigning two different tags to the same word: e.g. the word "New" is tagged NNP and not JJ if it is followed by another NNP – "York" for example – to convey the fact that "New" has to be interpreted as part of the proper name "New York". However this has no justification from a semantic point of view: "New York," as a geographical proper name needs both words in order to access its referent, not just one. But all words that encode their meaning using more than one word form will not be captured as such in PT.

The initial conversion script takes the parenthesized VIT as input file and creates a treebank version with indices without words and then the complete head table where every constituent is associated to its head with a word id(entifier). For this purpose we differentiate nonterminal symbols from terminal ones and assign incremental indices to the latter.

As shown in Table 2, we eventually produce a vertically-arranged version which contains PoS labels and their fully specified meaning, followed by label of the constituent in which the word was contained. In addition, PoS labels have been commented and whenever possible, morphological features have been added.

3.3.1. Head-constituent relations

As a second step in our work we produced the table of head-constituent relations according to the rules formulated below. At this step we made sure that no category was left without a function: it could either be a dependent or a head. No dangling categories are allowed. We discovered that in the case of comparative constructions there was a need to separate the head of the phrase from the second term of comparison which did not have any specific constituent label. Working at constituent level, we had to introduce a new constituent label SC for comparative nominal structures, a label that is also used for quantified headed constructions. The relevant rules are specified in the table below. The head extraction process was carried on the basis of a set of head rules – some of which are presented below - according to Collins' model for English [35]. *Direction* specifies whether search starts from the right or from the left end of the child list dominated by the node in the *Non-terminal* column. *Priority* gives a priority ranking, with priority decreasing when moving down the list:

Constituent Non-terminal	Direction	Priority list
AUXTOC	Right	ause, auag,aueir,ausai,vsup
SN	Right	n,npro,nt,nh,nf,np,nc,sect,fw,relq,relin,relob,rel,pron, per_cent,int,abbr,num,deit,date,poss,agn,doll,sv2,f2,sa, coord
SAVV		part,partd,avvl,avv,int,rel,coord,fw,neg,f2
SA	Right	ag,agn,abbr,dim,poss,neg,num,coord,ppre,ppas,fw,star,f2
IBAR	Right	vin,viin,vit,vgt,vgin,vgc,vppt,vppin,vppc,vcir,vcl,vcg,vc, vgprog,vgsf,virin,vt,virt,vprc,vprin,vprogir,vprog,vprt,vsf ,vsupir, vsup,vci,coord

Table 1. Head-Constituent relations

3.4. Clause Level Head-Dependency Table (CLHDT)

The third step in our work was the creation of the CLHDT which contains a column where word numbers indicate the dependency or head relation, with the root of each clause bearing a distinctive dash, to indicate its role, as shown in Table 3. Rules for head-dependent relations are formulated below.

3.4.1. Rules for Head-Dependent Relations

At first we formulated a set of general rules as follows:

- Heads with no constituent – or dangling heads - are not allowed.
- Constituents with no heads are not allowed.

Coordinate structures are assigned an abstract head: they can have conjunctions, punctuation or nil as their heads. Conjunctions are a thorny question to deal with: in dependency grammars they are not treated as heads. However, we interpret this as a simple case of functional head government, similar to a complementizer heading its complement clause in a complex declarative structure. Punctuation plays an important role in parsing and in general it constitutes a prosodically marked non-linguistic item. This is very clear in transcribed spoken corpora where all pauses had to be turned into appropriate punctuation, as we had to do in our work on Italian Spontaneous Speech Corpora [20]. This is why we treat all "meaningful" punctuation marks in a similar fashion. Punctuation marks – dashes, quotations, parentheses, angled brackets, etc. – that may introduce parentheticals, direct speech or reported direct speech are treated as functional heads. Other punctuation marks like commas introduced just to mark a pause and play no additional structural role are left interspersed in the text, similarly to what is done in PT.

To better grasp the role of each constituent and its head in the conversion task, we divided up constituents into three main categories according to their function and semantic import. We converted our non-generic X-bar scheme into a set of constituent labels that were required to help to distinguish functional types as well as structural and semantic types. For these reasons, our typology of sentential constituents differentiates between:

- simple declarative clauses (F)
- complex declarative clauses (CP)
- subordinate clauses (FS)
- coordinate clauses (FC)
- complement clauses (FAC)
- relative clauses (F2)
- nonfinite tense clauses (SV2-SV3-SV5)
- interrogative clauses (FINT, CP_INT)
- direct (reported) speech (DIRSP)
- parenthetical, appositive and vocative (FP)
- stylistically marked utterances (literary and bureaucratic) (TOPF)
- fragments (including lists, elliptical phrases, etc.) (F3)

#ID=sent_00002	
F Sentence	**IBAR Verbal group (tensed verb)**
COORD Coordinate structure for constituents	**CONG Conjunction**
SN Nominal phrase	**N Noun**
SN Nominal phrase	**N Noun**
SPD Prepositional phrase with preposition DI	**PD Preposition_di**
SN Nominal phrase	**N Noun**
SA Adjectival phrase	**AG Adjective**
IBAR Verbal group with tensed verb	**VC Verb_copulative**
COMPC Complements governed by Copulative Verbs	**SAVV Adverbial phrase**
SAVV Adverbial phrase	**AVV Adverb**
SN Nominal phrase	**N Noun**
SPD Prepositional phrase with preposition DI	**PARTD Preposition_di_plus_article**

Tab. 2 Local Heads/Constituents Relations

3.5. Rules for Grammatical Relation Labels

The final step in the overall treebank conversion consists of assigning Grammatical Relation labels/roles. In a language like English, which imposes a strict position for SUBJect NP and OBJect NP, the labeling is quite straightforward. The same applies also to French, and German, which in addition has case markings to supplement constituent scrambling, i.e. the possibility to scramble OBJect and Indirect OBJect in a specific syntactic area.

In opposition to these and other similar languages, which are prevalent in Western language typology, Italian is an almost "free word-order" language. In Italian, non-canonical positions would indicate the presence of marked constructions – which might be intonationally marked – containing linguistic information that is "new", "emphasized" or otherwise non-thematic. Italian also allows free omission of a SUBJect pronoun whenever it stands for a discourse topic. Italian also has lexically empty non-semantic expletive SUBJects for impersonal constructions, weather verbs etc. This makes automatic labeling of complements or arguments vs. adjuncts quite difficult, if attempted directly on the basis of constituent labels without help from any additional (lexical) information.

We thus started to relabel non-canonical SUBJect and OBJect NPs, with the goal of eventually relabeling all non-canonical arguments. However, we realized that we could maintain a distinction between SUBJect and complements in general, where the former can be regarded as an EXTernal argument, receiving no specific information at syntactic level from the governing predicate to which they are related. Arguments that are complements are, in contrast, strictly INTernal and are directly governed by predicates, whether the latter are Verbs, ADJectives or Nouns. Prepositions constitute a special case in that they govern PPs which are exocentric constituents and are easily relatable to the NP head they govern. However, it must be possible to relate PPs to their governing predicate, which may or may not subcategorize for them, according to Preposition type.

We thus produced rules for specific labeling and rules for default labeling. Default labeling is a generic complement label that may undergo a modification in the second phase. Specific labeling will remain the same.

The process included the following steps. First, we manually listed all s_dis (preposed subject under CP), s_foc (focalized object/subject in inverted position, no clitic), s_top (topicalized subject/object to the right, with clitic) and ldc (left dislocated complement, usually SA/SQ/SN/SP/SPD/SPDA) structures.

Second, we compared all verbs to a list of verbs with their subcategorization properties marked and assigned the OBL role to prepositions heading an oblique constituent. Next, we assigned a semantic role to the head of every constituent according to the following rules (the list is incomplete):

Constituent	Dependency	Role
CCONG/ CONGF/ CONJL CCOM/ CONG	Always	CONG
SN/SQ	Governed by F	SUBJ
	Root of a sentence without a verb	SUBJ
	Governed by COMPT	OBJ
	Governed by COMPIN	ADJ
	Governed by COMPC	NCOMP
	Governed by F2	BINDER
	Headed by NT	ADJT
	Governed by SP/SPD/SPDA	
	Headed by NP (noun proper geographic)	POBJ-LOC
	Otherwise	POBJ

Table 3: Role assignment rule table

Table 4 illustrates the conversion process that uses the new labels on a sample sentence.

#ID=sent_01144					
0	restano	VIN(verb_intrans_tensed)	IBAR	-	CL(main)
1	valide	AG(adjective)	ACOMP	0	SA
2	le	ART(article)	SN	3	SN
3	multe	N(noun)	S_TOP	0	SN
4	già	AVV(adverb)	ADJM	3	SAVV
5	irrogate	PPAS(past_participle_absolute)	MOD	3	SV3
6	','	PUNT(sentence_internal)	SN	3	SN
7	per	P(preposition)	ADJ	3	SP
8	le	ART(article)	SN	9	SN
9	quali	REL(relative)	BINDER	7	SN
10	pende	VIN(verb_intrans_tensed)	IBAR	3	IBAR
11	il	ART(article)	SN	12	SN
12	giudizio	N(noun)	S_TOP	10	SN
13	davanti_al	PHP(preposition_locution)	MOD	12	SP
14	Tar	NPRO(noun_proper_institution)	POBJ	13	SN
15	'.'	PUNTO(sentence_final)	F	0	F

Table 4. Full conversion from phrase structure to dependency structure

The resulting treebank has 10,607 constituents with a subject role, 3,423 of which have been assigned manually because they are in a non-canonical position. Among the 7,184 SUBJ labels that were automatically identified, 46 constituents should have been assigned a different function, which means that we reached the precision of 0.99. On the other hand, 218 constituents should bear a SUBJ label instead of their actual label, which means that the value for recall is 0.97.

4. A Quantitative Study of VIT

In this section, we introduce and discuss the quantitative data related to the written portion of VIT and the constituents present in the 10,200 utterances of its Treebank. In particular, we focus on structures that are interesting from a parsing point of view and are called "stylistic" structures.

In a recent paper [34], Corazza et al. use a portion of VIT – 90,000 tokens produced in the SI-TAL project – to test the possibility of training a probabilistic statistical parser using the procedures already tested by Collins [35] and Bikel [36] for PT. The Corazza et al. study yielded less than 70% accuracy, so the question is whether this poor performance might be due to intrinsic difficulties presented by the structure of the Italian language, to the different linguistic theory that has been adopted (cf. the lack of a VP node) or to the different tagset adopted, more detailed than the one used in PT (see also [37, 38] for a discussion of the general problem of parser and treebank evaluation

Commenting on the seminal work on probabilistic parsers by Collins, Bikel states that the creation of a language model must be preceded by an important phase of preprocessing. In other words, language models must be developed on the basis of treebank data that is not "raw" but rather modified for this specific purpose. Collins' aim was to capture the greatest amount of regularities using the smallest number of parameters.

Probabilities are associated with lexicalized structural relations (structures where the head of the constituent to encode is present) to help with decisions about the choice of arguments vs. adjuncts, levels of attachment of a modifier and other similarly important matters that are difficult to capture using only tags. For this purpose, it was necessary to modify the treebank by marking complements, sentences with null or inverse subjects, and so on.

The preprocessing task accomplished by Corazza et al. is summarized below and is actually restricted to the use of lemmas in place of word forms as heads of lexicalized constituents:

> "As a starting point, we considered Model 2 of Collins' parser [35], as implemented by Dan Bikel [36], as its results on the WSJ are at the state-of-the-art. This model applies to lexicalized grammars approaches traditionally considered for probabilistic context-free grammars (PCFGs). Each parse tree is represented as the sequence of decisions corresponding to the head-centered, top-down derivation of the tree. Probabilities for each decision are conditioned on the lexical head. Adaptation of Collins' parser to Italian included the identification of rules for finding lexical heads in ISST data, the selection of a lower threshold for unknown words (as the amount of available data is much lower), and the use of lemmas instead of word forms (useful because Italian has a richer morphology than English; their use provides a non negligible improvement). At least at the beginning, we did not aim to introduce language-dependent adaptations. For this reason no tree transformation (analogous to the ones introduced by Collins for WSJ) has been applied to ISST."(p.4)

After a series of tests using two different parsers, researchers have come to the conclusion that

> "These preliminary results... confirm that performance on Italian is substantially lower than on English. This result seems to suggest that the differences in performance between the English and Italian treebanks are independent of the adopted parser... our hypothesis is that the gap in performance between the two languages can be due to two different causes: intrinsic differences between the two languages or differences between the annotation policies adopted in the two treebanks."(p.5-6)

Information theory-oriented analysis of the results of this experimentation led to a conclusion that the difference in performance is not due to the number of rules (and, therefore, the type of annotation introduced). The main reason is that structural relations among the rules are unpredictable:

> "First of all, it is interesting to note how the same coverage on rules results in the Italian corpus in a sensibly lower coverage on sentences (26.62% vs. 36.28%). This discrepancy suggests that missing rules are less concentrated in the same sentences, and that, in general, they tend to be less correlated the one with the other. This would not be contradicted by a lower entropy, as the entropy does not make any hypothesis on the correlation between rules, but only on the likelihood of the correct derivation. This could be a first aspect making the ISST task more difficult than the WSJ one. In fact, the choice of the rules to introduce at each step is easier if they are highly correlated with the ones already introduced."(p. 9).

4.1. Regularity and Discontinuity in Language and Its Representation

The above experiments leads to a number of conclusions. Intuitively, it appears that the better the structural regularity of a language or its representation, the higher the quality of statistical modeling. At the same time, in a language where many phenomena occur only once or just a few times (in technical terms, languages that feature many hapax, bis- or tris- legomena), creating a a good statistical model is less probabile due to sparseness of evidence. Linguistically speaking, this could be explained by the grammar of the language separating into core and periphery, as made manifest by quantitative analysis, see also [39]. To train a statistical parser one needs a great number of canonical structures belonging to the core grammar. One has to accurately account for the structures that compose the core grammar, while the ones that belong to the periphery can be amended *ad hoc*. Note that Collins has not introduced corrections in the original treebank used for training the parser. The errors of a statistical parser trained on a treebank must therefore be ascribed to the linguistic framework chosen by the annotators and hence to the language, see also [40; 41].

The summary quantitative data reported in Table 5 shows that over half of the Italian sentences (9,800 out of 19,099) do *not* have a lexically expressed subject in a canonical position, which makes determining the SN subject a highly unpredictable undertaking. The situation with PT is completely different. For instance, there are 4,647 sentences in PT that have been classified as topicalized structure (S-TPC) which includes argument preposing, direct reported speech, etc. Moreover there are 2,587 sentences with an inverse structure, classified as SINV, only 827 of which are also TPC. SINV sentences typically have the subject in post-verbal position.

For PT it made sense to correct the problem at the pre-processing phase, as was done by Collins (see also comments by Bikel). In our case this issue is certainly more complicated. In fact, the SN subject can be realized in four different ways: it can be lexically omitted, it can be found in an inverted position in the COMP constituents where complements are placed, or it can be found in dislocated position on the left or on the right of the sentence to which it is related, at CP level. In a preliminary annotation we counted over 3,000 cases of lexically expressed subject in non-canonical positions. There were also about 6,000 cases of omitted subject to be taken into account. All such sentences must be dealt with in different ways during the creation of the model.

If one considers that in PT there are 93,532 sentence structures – identifiable using the regular expression "(S (" – 38,600, or 41% of which are complex sentences, the cases of non-canonical SUBJect occur in only about 1% of the cases. By contrast, in VIT the same phenomenon has a much higher incidence: over 27% for non-canonical structures, and over 50% for the omitted or unexpressed subject. Table 5 also takes into consideration the annotation of complements in non-canonical positions.

Treebanks Vs. Non-canonical Structures	Non-canonical Structures (TU)	Structures with Non-Canonical Subject (TS)	Total (TU) Utterances	Total (TS) Simple Sentences	Totale Complex Sentences
VIT	3719	9800	10,200	19,099	6782
Percentage	27.43%	51.31%	63.75%		66.5%
PT	7234	2587	55,600	93,532	38,600
Percentage	13.01%	0.27%	59.44%		69.4%

Table 5. Comparison of non-canonical Structures in VIT and in PTB where we differentiate TU (total utterances) and TS(total simple sentences)

Table 6 shows absolute values for all non-canonical structures we relabeled in VIT. There were 7,172 canonical lexically expressed SUBJects out of the 10,100 total expressed SUBJects, which means that non-canonical subjects constituted 1/3 of all expressed SUBJects. Subject NPs positioned to the right of the governing verb were labeled S_TOP. Subject NPs positioned to the left of the governing verb but separated from it by a heavy or parenthetical complement were labeled as S_DIS. S_FOC was the label used for subjects in inverted postverbal positions in presentational structures. Finally LDC is the label for left dislocated complements with or without a doubling clitic.

LDC (left dislocated complements)	**S_DIS** (dislocated subject)	**S_TOP** (topicalized subject)	**S_FOC** (Focalized Subject)	**Total Non-Canonical**
251	**1037**	**2165**	**266**	**3719**

Table 6. Non-canonical Structures in VIT

5. Ambiguity and Discontinuity in VIT

In this section we briefly discuss some of the more interesting structures contained in VIT with respect to two important questions of ambiguity and discontinuity in Italian (see [42]). The most ambiguous structures are those involving adjectives. As mentioned above, adjectives in Italian may be positioned before or after the noun they modify almost freely for most lexical classes. Only a few classes must occur in a predicative position and a very small number of adjectives must be placed in front of the noun they modify when used attributively. A count of functional conversions of adjectival structures in VIT is as follows: there are 1,296 Complement APs (ACOMP), 18,748 Modifiers (MOD), 324 Adjuncts (ADJ) and 2,001 COORDinate APs.

5.1. Ambiguous Predicative Adjective Phrases (SAs)

Postnominal adjectives constitute the most challenging type since they may be considered as either post- or premodifiers of a nominal head. Even though postnominal non-adjacent SA occur in only 5.34% of the cases, they need to be identified by the parser. In the examples below we show that this process requires not only feature matching but also knowledge of adjectival lexical class. For every example from VIT we report the relevant portion of structure and a literal translation on the line below, preceded by a slash.

(1) sn-[art-i, n-posti,
spd-[partd-della, sn-[n-dotazione, sa-[ag-organica_aggiuntiva]]],
sa-[ag-disponibili, sp-[p-a,
/the posts of the pool organic additive available to

Syntactic ambiguity arises and agreement checking is not enough even though in some cases it may solve the attachment preferences for the predicative vs. the attributive reading.

(2) sn-[sa-[ag-significativi], n-ritardi]],
sn-[sa-[ag-profonde], n-trasformazioni],
ibar-[vt-investono],
/significative delays profound transformations affect

Several adjectival structures may appear consecutively and modify different heads as in:

(3) sn-[art-il, n-totale,
spd-[partd-dei, sn-[n-posti,
spd-[partd-della, sn-[n-dotazione, sa-[ag-organica]]],
ag-vacanti], sa-[ag-disponibili
/the total of the posts of the pool organic additive vacant available

where "vacanti" modifies the local head "posti", as well as "disponibili" which governs a complement. By contrast, in the example below, "maggiori" is not attached to the a possible previous head "orientamenti", but to a following one as the structure indicates,

(4) ibar-[vin-darebbe],
compin-[sp-[in-anche, part-agli,
sn-[n-orientamenti, spd-[pd-di, sn-[n-democrazia, sa-[ag-laica]]]]],
sn-[sa-[ag-maggiori
/would give also to the viewpoints of democracy laic main

5.2 Sentence Complement

Another interesting phenomenon relating to adjectival phrases is their ability to head sentential complements. In copulative constructions the adjectives are nominalized, as in the following:

(5) f-[sn-[art-il,
sa-[ag-bello]],
ibar-[vc-è],
compc-[fac-[pk-che]
/the beatiful is that

5.3 Difficult Problems: Quantification

Structures with quantifiers appearing in quantifier and comparative phrases pose special representation problems. Let's consider some examples.

(6) sq-[in-molto, q-più, coord-[sa-[ag-efficace, punt-,, ag-controllabile, cong-e, ag-democratico]],
sc-[ccom-di,
f2-[sq-[relq-quanto],
cp-[savv-[avv-oggi],
f-[ibar-[neg-non, vcir-sia]
/much more effective , controllable and democratic of how much today not be

(6) illustrates the case of coordinate adjectival phrases governed by the quantifier operator PIU'.

(7) cp-[sc-[ccom-tanto, sq-[q-più],
f-[ibar-[vc-sono], compc-[sa-[ag-lunghi]]],
sc-[ccom-tanto, sq-[q-maggiore],
f-[ibar-[vc-è],
compc-[sn-[art-la, n-soddisfazione, sa-[ag-finale]
/much more are long much higher is the satisfaction final

(7) illustrates comparative structures at the sentence level. By contrast, illustrates a case of quantification in a relative construction.

(8) cp-[
cp-[sa-[ag-generali],
sp-[p-per, f2-[relq-quanto,
f-[ir_infl-[vcir-siano]]]]], punt-,,
f-[sn-[art-le, n-regole], ibar-[vt-investono
/general for as much as be the rules involve

5.4 Fronted Prepositional Phrases (SPs) in Participials

Another interesting construction in Italian is the possibility to have fronted PP complements in participials. This structure may cause ambiguity and problems of attachment, as shown in the examples below.

(9) sp-[p-in,
sn-[n-base, sp-[part-al,
sn-[n-punteggio,
sv3-[sp-[p-ad, sn-[pron-essi]],
ppas-attribuito, compin-[sp-[p-con,
/on the basis of the scoring to them attributed with

In (9), "ad essi" could be regarded as a modifier of the noun "punteggio", whereas it is in reality a complement of "attribuito" which follows rather than precedes it.

(10) sp-[p-a,
coord-[sn-[sa-[ag-singoli], n-plessi], cong-o, sn-[n-distretti],
sv3-[sp-[p-in, sn-[pron-essi]], ppas-compresi, punto-.]]]]]]]]
/to single groups or districts in them comprised

The structure in (10) is more complex. Such structures can also be found in the literary style, as in (11).

(11) spd-[partd-della,
sn-[n-cortesia,
sv3-[sp-[p-in, sq-[q-più, pd-di, sn-[art-un_, n-occasione]]],
vppt-dimostrata,
compin-[coord-[sp-[p-a, sn-[pron-me]],
/of the courtesy in more than one occasion demonstrated to me

5.5 Subject Inversion and Focus Fronted APs

Other non-canonical structures subject-inverted clauses, focus-inverted APs and structures with left clitic dislocation with resumptive pronouns. Subject inversion in post-verbal position is very frequent construction, typically linked to the presence of an unaccusative verb governor, as in (12).

(12) f-[ibar-[vc-diventa],
compc-[savv-[avv-così],
sa-[in-più, ag-acuta],
sn-[art-la, n-contraddizione], sp-[p-tra
/becomes so more acute the contradiction between

The same may take place with copulas, though subjects are typically positioned after the open adjectival phrase complement, asin (13).

(13) f-ibar-[vc-è],
compc-[sa-[ag-peculiare,
sp-[part-all, sn-[np-Italia]]],
sn-[art-l, n-esistenza, spd-[pd-di
/is peculiar to Italy the existence of

(14) illustrates a fronted AP.

(14) cp-[s_foc-[ag-Buono],
f3-[sn-[cong-anche, art-l, n-andamento,
spd-[partd-delle, sn-[n-vendite
/good also the behaviour of the sales

All these structures are quite peculiar to the Italian language and also belong stylistically to a certain domain (financial news) and the type of newspaper in which they appear.

5.6 Hanging Topic and Left Clitic Dislocation

Italian allows a portion of information at the front of the utterance to be referred to the next sentence (alternatively it may be left implicit, that is become elided). Reference is usually made with a clitic pronoun. When the material fronted is not separated by a comma, a pause, this becomes a case of left clitic dislocation, as in (15) and (16).

(15) cp-[ldc-[art-una, n-decisione, sa-[ag-importante]],
f-[sn-[nh-Ghitti],
ibar-[clitac-l, ausa-ha, vppt-riservata],
/a decision important Ghitti it has reserved

(16) cp-[ldc-[sa-[ag-altra], n-fonte,
spd-[pd-di, sn-[n-finanziamento]]],
f-[ibar-[vc-sarà],
compc-[sn-[art-il, n-trattamento
/other source of funding will be the treatment

Example (17) illustrates a hanging topic

(17) cp-[sn-[sa-[ag-brutta], n-faccenda], punt-,,
f-[sn-[art-i, n-sudditi],
ibar-[clit-si, vt-ribellano, punto-.]]
/bad story , the populace self rebel

5.7 Aux-to-Comp Structures

Aux-to-comp structures are also attested both in bureaucratic and literary genres.

(18) cp-[f-[sn-[art-La, n-perdita],
sp-[p-per, sn-[art-il, npro-Rolo]],
ibar-[vcir-sarebbe],
compc-[congf-però,
spd-[pd-di, sn-[in-circa, num-'30', num-miliardi]]]],

topf-[auxtoc-[auag-avendo],
f-[sn-[art-la, npro-Holding],
sv3-[vppt-incassato,
compt-[sn-[n-indennizzi,
sp-[p-per, sn-[num-'28',
num-miliardi]]]]]], punto-.]
/the loss for the Rolo would be then of about 30 billion having the Holding cashed payments for 28 billions

In (18) the gerundive auxiliary precedes the subject NP which, in turn, precedes the lexical verbal head in participial form. Examples (19) and (20) illustrate peculiarly Italian aux-to-comp structures that appear in literary texts.

(19) fc-[congf-e, punt-',',
topf-[auxtoc-[clit-si, aueir-fosse],
f-[sn-[pron-egli],
sv3-[vppin-trasferito, cong-pure,
compin-[sp-[part-nel,
sn-[sa-[in-più, ag-remoto], n-continente]]]]]
/and , self would be he moved also in the more remote continent

(20) cp-[sn-[topf-[auxtoc-[art-l, ausai-avere],
f-[sn-[art-il, n-figlio],
sv3-[vppt-abbandonato,
compt-[sn-[art-il, n-mare],
sp-[p-per, sn-[art-la, n-città]]]]]],
f-[ibar-[clitdat-le, ause-era, avv-sempre, vppt-sembrato]
/the have the son abandoned the sea for the city her was always seemed

Similarly to classical aux-to-comp cases, an auxiliary is present as structural indicator of the beginning of the construction. We introduced a new special constituent TOPF to cover the auxiliaries and sentences where the lexical verbal head has to be found in order to produce an adequate semantic interpretation.

5.8 (In)Direct Reported Speech

Some sentential structures are (or should be) marked by special punctuation to indicate reported direct or indirect speech. In all these sentences we have treated the governing sentence – which usually is marked off by commas or dashes – as a parenthetical. We briefly comment 4 types of constructions:

- parentheticals inserted between SUBJ and IBAR;
- parentheticals inserted between material in CP and F;
- free reported direct speech and then quoted direct speech;
- direct speech is ascribed to an anonymous speaker who is nevertheless mentioned.

(21) dirsp-[par-'',
cp-[sp-[p-a, sn-[sa-[dim-questo], n-punto]],
f-[sn-[art-la, n-data],
par-'',
fp-[punt-,, f-[ibar-[ausa-ha, vppt-detto],
compt-[sn-[npro-d_, npro-Alema],
savv-[avv-ieri], nt-sera]]], punt-,],
par-'', ibar-[vin-dipende],
/'' at this point the date '' , said D'Alema last night , '' depends

in (21) quotes separate the portions of the utterance that constitute reported direct speech. The difficulty is that the Subject NP "la data" (the date) is separated from the Main Verb by the parenthetical governing clause. (22) presents another example of the same phenomenon.

(22) dirsp-[par-",
cp-[sp-[p-in, sn-[sa-[dim-questo], n-libro]],
f-[sn-[nh-madre, npro-Teresa],
fp-[par--, f-[ibar-[vt-spiegano],
compt-[sp-[part-alla,
sn-[npro-Mondadori]]]], par--],
ir_infl-[vcir-darà],
/"in this book Mother Theresa -- explain at the Mondadori - will give

Punctation does not help much in (21) since the parenthetical is introduced without indicating the end of the reported direct speech segment.

5.9 Residual Problems: Relatives And Complement Clauses As Main Sentences

Italian allows free use of relative clauses and complement clauses with a complementizer as main clauses. This is due partly to residual influence of Latin. In any case, this can be regarded as a stylish way of organizing a text.

(23) cp-[f2-[rel-Che,
cp-[fp-[punt-,, f-[ibar-[vt-sostengono],
compt-[sp-[part-alla, sn-[npro-Farnesina]]]], punt-,],
f-[ibar-[neg-non, ausa-ha,
sp-[p-per, avvl-niente],
vppt-gradito],
compt-[sn-[art-l, n-operazione, n-by_pass]],
punto-.]]]]
/That , maintain at the Farnesina , not has in no case liked the operation by_pass .

This example has the additional problem of the presence of a parenthetical sentence that should indicate the presence of an Indirect Reported Speech structure. It is not easy to detect.

(24) cp-[fac-[pk-che, savv-[avv-poi],
f-[sn-[art-la, n-legge],
ibar-[neg-non, virin-riesca],
compin-[sv2-[pt-a, viin-funzionare]]]],
punt-,,
f-[ibar-[vc-è],
compc-[sn-[art-un, n-discorso, f2-[rel-che
/That then the law not manages to work , is a matter that

6. Preliminary Evaluation

In this section we present preliminary data made available by Alberto Lavelli (see [34]) who implemented Bikel's model and parser for using with the standard machine learning procedure of 10-Fold Cross Validation. The first table refers to the homogeneous subset of VIT composed of sentences from *Il Sole-24 Ore*, a financial newspaper.

Tables 7a and 7b present data related to the whole of VIT. As can be noticed, there is no remarkable difference in the overall performance results which are represented by the values associated to Bracketing Recall and Precision: both converge on the final value of 70%.

Comment	Data
Number of sentences	**10189**
Number of Error sentences	**12**
Number of Skip sentences	**0**
Number of Valid sentences	**10177**
Bracketing Recall	**68.61**
Bracketing Precision	**68.29**
Complete match	**8.70**
Average crossing	**3.25**
No crossing	**38.37**
2 or less crossing	**61.73**
Tagging accuracy	**96.65**

Table 7a. Statistical parsing on complete VIT

A slight improvement is obtained when sentence length is reduced,

Comment	Data
Sentence length	**<=40 --**
Number of sentences	**8519**
Number of Error sentences	**12**
Number of Skip sentences	**0**
Number of Valid sentences	**8507**
Bracketing Recall	**71.87**
Bracketing Precision	**71.58**
Complete match	**10.40**
Average crossing	**1.94**
No crossing	**45.47**
2 or less crossing	**71.72**
Tagging accuracy	**96.55**

Table 7b. Statistical parsing on complete VIT with sentence length limitation

VIT differs greatly from PT not only in the number of sentences and amount of data but also in the choice to include linguistic material of different nature. In VIT there are five different genres – news, bureaucratic prose, political prose, scientific prose and literary prose – while in PT only one is represented. Hence the greater homogeneity of PT relative to VIT.

The limited size of VIT makes it difficult, if not impossible, to use it as a Language Model in the construction of probabilistic grammars for Italian. Therefore it is necessary to introduce corrective elements in order to enable the learning phase to distinguish sentences of different types (subject in canonical preverbal position, subject in non-canonical post-verbal position, lexically unexpressed subject, left dislocated hanging topic subject – either separated from the verb by other complements or composed of a "heavy" SN followed by punctuation, right dislocated hanging topic subject separated from the verb by other complements, etc.). For this purpose we implemented Bikel's language model directly on VIT and from preliminary results we can safely say that the same poor performance of around 70% accuracy is reconfirmed. More experiments will be carried out to confirm the hypothesis in Corazza et al., even though from the data in our possession such a confirmation is very likely.

Eventually, for poorly canonical languages which in most cases are also richly inflected, the best solution to the production of a parser is that of using as much linguistic information as possible – subcategorized lexicon, hand-crafted grammar, list of critical multiwords for better disambiguation - and create a manually crafted symbolic parser. This could be in the standard format of RTNs (Recursive Transition Networks) or cascaded FSAs (Finite State Automata), in the vein of Context-Free Grammars which will generate a consistent but partially correct structural output. Then the manual work of linguistic annotators is mandatory to search for recurrent errors to improve the parser. Until a final state of the output is reached which does no longer lend itself to such improvements. At this point, the treebank can only be perfected manually.

References

[1] Brill, E.. 1995. Transformation-based error-driven learning and natural language processing: A case study in part-of-speech tagging. *Computational Linguistics* **21**, (1995), 543-565.

[2] Brants,T. TnT: A statistical part-of-speech tagger. ANLP 2000.

[3] Grosz B., Sidner C., Attention, Intentions, and the Structure of Discourse, *Computational Linguistics* **12** (3), (1986), 175-204.

[4] Mann, W.C. & Thompson, S.A., *Rhetorical Structure Theory: A theory of text organization*, Technical Report ISI/RS-87-190, ISI, 1987.

[5] Jean Carletta, Amy Isard, Stephen Isard, Jacqueline Kowtko, Gwyneth Doherty-Sneddon, and Anne Anderson, The reliability of a dialogue structure coding scheme. *Computational Linguistics* **23** (1), (1997), 13-32.

[6] Jackendoff, R., *X-Bar Syntax*, The MIT Press, Cambridge, MA., 1977.

[7] Delmonte, R., Strutture Sintattiche dall'Analisi Computazionale di Corpora di Italiano, in Anna Cardinaletti(a cura di), *Intorno all'Italiano Contemporaneo*, Franco Angeli, Milano, (2004), 187-220.

[8] **http://www.coli.uni-saarland.de/projekte/sfb378/negra-corpus/**

[9] Marcus M. et al., Building a Large Annotated Corpus of English: The PennTreebank, *Computational Linguistics*, **19**, 1993.

[10] Delmonte R., R.Dolci, Parsing Italian with a Context-Free Recognizer, *Annali di Ca' Foscari XXVIII*, **1-2**, (1989), 123-161.

]11] Delmonte R., E.Pianta, IMMORTALE - Analizzatore Morfologico, Tagger e Lemmatizzatore per l'Italiano, in *Atti V Convegno AI*IA "Cibernetica e Machine Learning"*, Napoli, (1996), 19-22

[12] Montemagni et al., The Italian Syntactic-Semantic Treebank: Architecture, Annotation, Tools and Evaluation, *LINC*, ACL, Luxembourg, (2000), 18-27.

[13] Montemagni, S. F. Barsotti, M. Battista, N. Calzolari, A. Lenci O. Corazzari, A. Zampolli, F. Fanciulli, M. Massetani, R. Basili R. Raffaelli, M.T. Pazienza, D. Saracino, F. Zanzotto, F. Pianesi N. Mana, and R. Delmonte, Building the Italian Syntactic-Semantic Treebank. In Anne Abeillé, (editor), *Building and Using syntactically annotated corpora*, Kluwer, Dordrecht, (2003), 189–210.

[14] Delmonte R. How to Annotate Linguistic Information in FILES and SCAT, in *Atti del Workshop "La Treebank Sintattico-Semantica dell'Italiano di SI-TAL*", Bari, (2001), 75-84.

[15] Delmonte R., E.Pianta,Tag Disambiguation in Italian, in *Proc. Treebank Workshop ATALA*, Paris, (1999), 43-49.

[16] Delmonte R,.Luminita Chiran, Ciprian Bacalu, Elementary Trees For Syntactic And Statistical Disambiguation, in *Proc. TAG+5*, Paris, (2000), 237-240.

[17] Delmonte R., From Shallow Parsing to Functional Structure, in *Atti del Workshop AI*IA - "Elaborazione del Linguaggio e Riconoscimento del Parlato"*, IRST Trento, (1999), 8-19.

[18] Delmonte R. Shallow Parsing And Functional Structure In Italian Corpora, LREC, Atene, (2000),113-119.

[19] Delmonte R., Parsing Spontaneous Speech, in Proc. EUROSPEECH2003, Pallotta Vincenzo, Popescu-Belis Andrei, Rajman Martin "Robust Methods in Processing of Natural Language Dialogues" , Genève, (2003), 1-6.

[20] Delmonte R., Antonella Bristot, Luminita Chiran, Ciprian Bacalu, Sara Tonelli, Parsing the Oral Cor-

pus AVIP/API, in Albano Leoni A., Cutugno F., Pettorino M., Savy R.(a cura di), *Atti del Convegno "Il Parlato Italiano"*, M.D'Auria Editore, **N08**, (2004), 1-20.
[21] Delmonte R., Bristot A., Tonelli S. VIT - Venice Italian Treebank: Syntactic and Quantitative Features, in K. De Smedt, Jan Hajic, Sandra Kübler(Eds.), *Proc. Sixth International Workshop on Treebanks and Linguistic Theories*, Nealt Proc. Series **Vol.1**, (2007), 43-54.
[22] Tesnière, Lucien *Éléments de syntaxe structurale*, Paris, Klincksieck, (1959).
[23] Hudson R. *Word Grammar*, Blackwell, London, (1984).
[24] Hudson R. *English Word Grammar*, Blackwell, London, (1990).
[25] Petr Sgall, Eva Hajiçova, and Jarmila Panevova, *The Meaning of the Sentence in Its Semantic and Pragmatic Aspects*, D. Reidel & Academia, Dordrecht & Prague, (1986).
[26] Hellwig, Peter, "Dependency unification grammar", *Proceedings COLING--86*, (1986), 195--198.
[27] Mel'cuk, I., *Dependency Syntax: Theory and Practice*, State University of New York Press, (1988).
[28] Maruyama, H. Structural disambiguation with constraint propagation. *Proceedings of the 28th Meeting of the Association for Computational Linguistics (ACL)*, Pittsburgh, PA, (1990), 31-38.
[29] Harper, M. P. and Helzerman, R. A., Extensions to constraint dependency parsing for spoken language processing, *Computer Speech and Language* **9**, (1995), 187-234.
[30] Menzel, W. and Schroeder, I., Decision procedures for dependency parsing using graded constraints. In Kahane, S. and Polguère, A. (eds), *Proceedings of the Workshop on Processing of Dependency-Based Grammars*, (1998), 78-87.
[31] Tapanainen, P. and Jaervinen, T., A non-projective dependency parser, *Proceedings of the 5th Conference on Applied Natural Language Processing*, (1997), 64-71.
[32] Jaervinen, T. and Tapanainen, P., Towards an implementable dependency grammar, in Kahane, S. and Polguère, A. (eds), *Proceedings of the Workshop on Processing of Dependency-Based Grammars*, (1998), 1-10.
[33] Duchier, D. and Debusmann, R., Topological dependency trees: A constraint-based account of linear precedence, *Proceedings of the 39th Annual Meeting of the Association for Computational Linguistics (ACL)*, (2001), 180-187.
[34] Corazza A., Lavelli A., Satta G., Zanoli R., Analyzing an Italian Treebank with State-of-the-Art Statistical Parsers, *Proceedings of the 3rd Workshop on Treebanks and Linguistic Theories (TLT-2004*), Tübingen, Germany, (2004), 39-50.
[35] Collins, Michael, A new statistical parser based on bigram lexical dependencies, *Proceedings of the 34th Annual Meeting of the Association for Computational Linguistics*, (1996), 184–191.
[36] Bikel, Daniel M., Intricacies of Collins' parsing model. *Computational Linguistics*, **30** (4), (2003), 479-511.
[37] Black, E. , S. Abney, D. Flickinger, C. Gdaniec, R. Grishman, P. Harrison, D. Hindle, R. Ingria, F. Jelinek, J. Klavans, M. Liberman, M. Marcus, S. Roukos, B. Santorini, and T. Strzalkowski: A Procedure for Quantitatively Comparing the Syntactic Coverage of English Grammars, *Proceedings of the DARPA Speech and Natural Language Workshop*, (1991), 306-311.
[38] Carroll, J., T. Briscoe, A. Sanfilippo, Parser Evaluation: a Survey and a New Proposal, *Proceedings of the [First] International Conference on Language Resources and Evaluation*, (1998), 447-454.
[39] Gildea D. 2001. Corpus variation and parser performance. In *Proceedings of the 2001 Conference on Empirical Methods in Natural Language Processing (EMNLP 2001)*, (2001), Pittsburgh, PA, 167–202.
[40] Musillo G. & Khalil Sima'an, Towards comparing parsers from different linguistic frameworks. An information theoretic approach. In *Proceedings of the LREC-2002 workshop Beyond PARSEVAL. Towards Improved Evaluation Measures for Parsing Systems*, Las Palmas, Spain, (2002), 44-51.
[41] Nivre, Joakim , Koenraad de Smedt and Martin Volk: *Treebanking in Northern Europe: A White Paper*, Nordisk Sprogteknologi. Nordic Language Technology. Årbog for Nordisk Sprogteknologisk Forskningsprogram 2000-2004. Editor: Henrik Holmboe. Copenhagen. 2005.
[42] Rizzi L., *Issues in Italian Syntax*, Foris Publications, Dordrecht, 1982.

APPENDIX I

In this appendix we list website links related to Treebanks and tools. In a final section we list links for computational linguistics and generic corpora websites.

1. Feature Structure or Dependency Representation

Parc 700 Dependency Bank
700 sentences from section 23 of the Upenn Wall Street Journal Treebank
http://www2.parc.com/isl/groups/nltt/fsbank/
Prague Arabic Dependency Treebank
100,000 words approximately
http://ufal.mff.cuni.cz/padt
Prague Dependency Treebank
1,5 million words
3 layers of annotation: morphological, syntactic, tectogrammatical
http://ufal.mff.cuni.cz/pdt2.0/
Danish Dependency Treebank
5,500 trees approximately
http://www.id.cbs.dk/˜mtk/treebank/
Bosque, Floresta sinta(c)tica
10,000 trees approximately
http://acdc.linguateca.pt/treebank/info_floresta_English_html
French Functional Treebank
abeille@linguist.jussieu.fr
http://www.llf.cnrs.fr/Gens/Abeille/French-Treebank-fr.php
LinGO Redwoods
20,000 utterances (as for Fifth Growth)
http://lingo.stanford.edu/redwoods/
http://wiki.delph-in.net/moin/RedwoodsTop

2. Phrase Structure Representation

Penn Treebank
1 million words
dependency rules available for conversiion
http://www.cis.upenn.edu/˜treebank/home.html
ICE – International Corpus of English
2million words tagged and parsed
http://www.ucl.ac.uk/english-usage/ice/
BulTreeBank
14,000 sentences
dependency version available
http://www.bultreebank.org/
Penn Chinese Treebank
40,000 sentences
http://www.cis.upenn.edu/˜chinese/ctb.html
Sinica Treebank
61,000 sentences
http://godel.iis.sinica.edu.tw/CKIP/engversion/treebank.htm
Alpino Treebank for Dutch
150,000 words
http://www.let.rug.nl/vannoord/trees
TIGER/NEGRA
50,000/20,000 sentences
Dependency version available
http://www.ims.uni-struttgart.de/projekte/TIGER/TIGERCorpus
http://www.coli.uni-saarland.de/projekte/sfb378/negra-corpus/
TueBa-D/Z
22,000 sentences
Dependency version available
http://www.sfs.uni-tuebingen.de/en_tuebadz.shtml
TueBa-J/S
18,000 sentences
Dependency version available
http://www.sfs.uni-tuebingen.de/en_tuebajs.shtml
Cast3LB
18,000 sentences
Dependency version available
http://www.dlsi.ua.es/projectes/3lb/index_en.html
SUSANNE
Subset of Brown Corpus made up of 130,000 words
http://www.grsampson.net/Resources.html

3. Spoken Transcribed and Discourse Treebanks

Maptask
128 dialogues turned into 2597 files
there are similar efforts for other languages: Portuguese, Swedish, Dutch, Japanese
http://www.hcrc.ed.ac.uk/maptask/
PDTB – Penn Discourse TreeBank
Penn Treebank turned into Discourse Relation Treebank
http://www.seas.upenn.edu/~pdtb/
DGB – Discourse GraphBank
3110 sentences containing 8910 relations and clause pairs - 73Kwords
http://www.ldc.upenn.edu/Catalog/CatalogEntry.jsp?catalogId=LDC2005T08
RSTDT – Rhetorical Structure Theory Discourse Treebank
Lynn Carlson, Daniel Marcu, and Mary Ellen Okurowski
http://www.ldc.upenn.edu/Catalog/CatalogEntry.jsp?catalogId=LDC2002T07
Talbanken05
300,000 words
http://w3.msi.vxu.se/˜nivre/research/Talbanken05.html

Dependency version available
API-AVIP-IPAR - treebank
60,000 words - 5000 dialogue turns
http://www.cirass.unina.it/
CLIPS corpus
100 hours of spoken dialogues - phonetically annotated
http://www.clips.unina.it/
LIP corpus
500.000 tokens, 57 hours of spoken dialogues fully tagged and lemmatized
http://languageserver.uni-graz.at/badip/badip/20_corpusLip.php
CHRISTINE
80500 words
http://www.grsampson.net/RChristine.html

4. Tools

@annotate
http://www.coli.uni-saarland.de/projects/sfb378/negra-corpus/annotate.html
Ananas
http://www.atilf.fr/ananas/
BulTreebank Project
http://www.bultreebank.org
CLaRK System
http://www.bultreebank.org/clark/
DTAG Treebank Tool
http://www.isv.cbs.dk/~mbk/dtag/
KPML development environment
http://www.fb10.uni-bremen.de/anglistik/langpro/kpml/README.html
LTChunk Systemic Coder
http://www.ltg.ed.ac.uk/~mikheev/tagger_demo.html
LBIS Coder
http://www.brain.riken.jp/labs/mns/sugimoto/LBISST/english.html
MMAX
http://www.eml-research.de/english/research/nlp/download/mmax.php
Poliqarp
http://poliqarp.sourceforge.net/
RST Tool for annotating with RST relations by Marcu
http://www.isi.edu/~marcu/software.html
SALSA
http://www.coli.uni-saarland.de/projects/salsa/
UAM Corpus Tool
http://www.wagsoft.com/CorpusTool/
SysFan tool
http://minerva.ling.mq.edu.au/
TnT tagger
http://www.coli.uni-saarland.de/~thorsten/tnt/
Wordfreak
http://wordfreak.sourceforge.net/
FreeLing
http://garraf.epsevg.upc.es/freeling/

5. Other resources based on treebanks

ACE project: PropBank/VerbNet/FrameNet
http://verbs.colorado.edu/~mpalmer/projects/ace.html
FrameNet
http://framenet.icsi.berkeley.edu/
NomBank
http://nlp.cs.nyu.edu/meyers/NomBank.html
NomLex
http://nlp.cs.nyu.edu/nomlex/index.html
ComLex
http://nlp.cs.nyu.edu/comlex/index.html

6. Generic website for corpora and other linguistic resources

http://www.corpus-linguistics.com/html/nav/main.html
http://www.ai.mit.edu/projects/iiip/nlp.html
http://billposer.org/Linguistics/Computation/Resources.html
http://nlp.stanford.edu/links/linguistics.html
http://www.bmanuel.org/
http://www.bmanuel.org/clr/clr2_tt.html
http://www.glue.umd.edu/~dlrg/clir/arabic.html
http://www.ims.uni-stuttgart.de/info/FTPServer.html
http://www.lai.com/mtct.html
http://www.aclweb.org/index.php?option=com_content&task=view&id=31&Itemid=31

Language Engineering for Lesser-Studied Languages
S. Nirenburg (Ed.)
IOS Press, 2009

doi:10.3233/978-1-58603-954-7-81

Developing Proper Name Recognition, Translation and Matching Capabilities for Low- and Middle-Density Languages

Marjorie MCSHANE[1]

Institute for Language and Information Technologies
University of Maryland Baltimore County

Abstract. This article discusses methods for developing proper name recognition, translation and cross-linguistic matching capabilities for any language or combination of languages in a short amount of time, with relatively minimal work by native speaker informants. Unlike much work on proper name recognition, this work is grounded in knowledge-based rather than stochastic methods, and it extends to multi-lingual and multi-script name processing.

Keywords. low-density languages, proper name recognition, preprocessing

1. Introduction

The recognition of proper names is a basic need of natural language processing (NLP) systems. It is typically handled during the first stage of processing, known as preprocessing. Other phenomena commonly bundled into preprocessing include the determination of word and sentence boundaries, the recognition of dates and numbers, the stripping of metadata and non-textual content (as when processing Web pages), and so on. Recognizing proper names is important for systems that involve syntactic parsing and/or semantic analysis because proper names are not listed in typical lexicons (if they are listed at all, it is in gazetteers or onomastica) and multi-word proper names behave as a single constituent: for example, in the sentence *The Duke of Wellington crossed the Strait of Dover*, *the Duke of Wellington* functions as the subject and *the Strait of Dover* functions as the direct object.

Recognizing proper names is only one of many possible needs of NLP applications. In addition, an application might need to translate proper names, extract information about particular people, places, etc., from texts written in different languages and scripts, or help someone who heard a proper name in speech – but does not know for certain how to write it – look it up in some knowledge base.

This article describes two systems that were designed to treat different aspects of proper name processing. Like all systems, their specific features derive from a combination of their goals, the knowledge and computing resources available, the manpower devoted to their development, and theoretical and practical preferences of

---

[1] Department of Computer Science and Electrical Engineering, ITE 325, 1000 Hilltop Circle, Baltimore, Maryland, 21250, USA; E-mail: marge@umbc.edu.

developers. However, despite these idiosyncrasies, the conceptual substrate and lessons learned are quite generalizable to work on proper names in any language for any application.

The article is organized as follows. Section 2 describes the so-called "named entity recognition task" and overviews selected approaches and systems developed to carry it out. Section 3 describes the Boas II knowledge elicitation system, which elicits knowledge about proper names from speakers of any language and automatically converts that knowledge into a proper name recognition engine. Section 4 describes the GeoMatch geographical entity recognition and matching system, whose goal is to expand the data and enhance the search capabilities of an existing geographical database in order to make it more useful for multilingual applications. Section 5 concludes the paper.

2. The "Named Entity Recognition" Task

The automatic recognition of so-called "named entities" – which include proper names, numbers and dates – attracted much attention in response to the Named Entity Task of the Message Understanding Conferences, or MUCs (Chinchor 1997) [4]. This series of conferences, held from 1987 to 1997, were evaluation exercises in which participants competed in knowledge extraction tasks as well as a number of specialized subtasks, like reference resolution and named entity extraction. Participants were provided with descriptions of each task, the necessary output format for their systems, and an annotated corpus that could be used for training. Prior to corpus annotation, precise annotation guidelines had to be developed for each subtask. These guidelines are instructive as they elucidate the complexity of what might, at first blush, seem like straightforward phenomena. Taking proper names as an example, the MUC-7 task definition states that family names like *the Kennedys* are not to be tagged, nor are diseases, prizes, etc., named after people: *Alzheimer's, the Nobel prize*. Titles like *Mr.* and *President* are not to be tagged as part of the name, but appositives like *Jr.* and *III* ("the third") are. For place names, compound place names like *Moscow, Russia* are to be tagged as separate entities and adjectival forms of locations are not to be tagged at all: *American companies*. These decisions and many others like them are typically not universally agreed upon but rather reflect necessary compromises influenced by issues such as how difficult it will be to train annotators to follow the conventions and how useful the final corpus will be for a wide variety of NLP practitioners.

The rules of the game for the MUC competitions significantly affected the methods selected by participants: since participants were provided with large annotated corpora, stochastic approaches were favored. However, annotating corpora is expensive: it has been reported that tagging 100,000 words for syntactic features requires at least 33 hours by trained taggers (Bikel, Schwartz, and Weischedel 1999); and 100,000 words isn't even very much for stochastic training. Therefore, the predominance of stochastic systems over pattern-matching (i.e., knowledge-based) ones must be interpreted in context: if a similar competition were launched on low-density languages with no corpora provided, the research efforts in the field might well have taken a different turn.

Both stochastic and pattern-matching methods have produced good results from the best systems: in the 90's as the F-score, which is calculated as a combination of recall and precision.[2] However, both approaches generally require (a) a significant amount of static knowledge and (b) morphological and/or syntactic processors, making them not entirely applicable to low- and middle-density languages. Consider the knowledge needs of some noteworthy systems:

- BBN's IdentiFinder [3] uses a hidden Markov model and a minimum of 100,000 words of training data to learn to carry out named entity recognition for a language. However it performs much better with a million words of training data, which would require months of manual annotation. IdentiFinder uses bigrams rather than trigrams because using trigrams would require "exponentially more training data".
- An experiment in the supervised learning of named entity recognition for Greek involved bootstrapping from English [9]. The Greek resources needed to exploit this bootstrapping methodology include a tokenizer, a sentence splitter, a part-of-speech tagger, a gazetteer, a named-entity parser, a large hand-tagged corpus and, of course, an English system to bootstrap from.
- Another bootstrapping experiment involved Catalan, which is syntactically and lexically close to Spanish. Developers concluded that it is better to use bootstrapping from a similar language than stochastic methods applied to a small tagged corpus for the target language [10]. Of course, this methodology assumes that there exists another "less low density" language for which named entity recognition capabilities already exist.
- The named entity recognition system developed by Mikheev et al. [18] differs from most other systems in its relatively minimal reliance on gazetteers (static lists of named entities). The pitfalls of relying too heavily on gazetteers are well known and include: a) the impossibility of exhaustively listing all named entities; b) the overlap between, e.g., *Washington* as a place and as a person; and c) the fact that a given proper-name string, like *Adam Kluver*, could be a personal name, part of an organization name, part of a place name, etc. This system uses rule-based grammars, statistical models, a tagged corpus and a small inventory of names to learn to recognize named entities.
- The named entity recognition systems configured by NYU for successive MUCs reveal an interesting historical progression. For the first five MUCs, NYU used full syntactic and semantic analysis – based on a large grammar and lexicon of English – to support a pattern-matching approach; but all of this machinery did not produce the particularly good results. So for MUC-6 [7] they cut back on the processing and concentrated on specifics of the named entity recognition task, utilizing only a gazetteer, various specialized dictionaries, scenario-specific terms (each MUC covered a specific domain), a part-of-speech tagger, and task-specific noun phrase rules. Of course, even having cut back their resource requirements to this degree, the resources involved still surpass those likely to be available for low-density languages.
- SPARSER [11] is a high-quality pattern-matching-based named entity recognition system that relies on both internal and external evidence when analyzing named entities (internal evidence is evidence from within the

[2] The metrics "recall" and "precision" were, by the way, originally invented for the MUC conferences.

sequence of words and characters that comprise the name, whereas external evidence comes from the context adjacent to the name). The required resources include: a lexicalized grammar; a closed-class lexicon (a lexicon of "minor" parts of speech that cannot productively be added to over time); an open-class lexicon (a lexicon of nouns, verbs, adjectives and adverbs that can be added to over time as new phenomena arise in the world); a gazetteer; lists of trigger words; and a "moderately complex control structure that permits a deterministic parse and monotonoic semantic interpretation". SPARSER has been used in two domains: job changing and corporate joint ventures. The development of knowledge resources has focused on these domains.

- Another successful pattern matcher for English is LaSIE [22]. LaSIE is an all-purpose language processor that includes syntactic, semantic and discourse processing, and relies on an ontology to support semantic interpretation. Named entity recognition in LaSIE employs gazetteers, trigger words, a proper name grammar consisting of 177 rules, 100 Sentence Grammar rules from Penn TreeBank-II, and a parse of the whole text that results in a discourse interpretation. The Discourse Interpreter carries out coreference resolution and makes certain inferences about the semantic type of entities.

The common property of all the diverse systems mentioned above is their reliance on a significant amount of pre-prepared data and/or programs – which is natural for systems that target languages that have long been the object of NLP. However, if one needs to develop named-entity recognition capabilities for low-density languages, the cost and feasibility of all prerequisites must be considered.

Here we will explore how to develop systems that are, at base, language independent and can be readily configured to cover any language. Some such approaches already exist but, unlike our approach, they take a stochastic rather than a pattern-matching approach. For example, SRA's RoboTag [1] is a tagging tool and machine learner applicable to any language. Prerequisites for its use are a preprocessor, a morphological analyzer and a lexicon for the given language. Its goal is to allow the end user to build a tagging system for a language by providing examples of what should be tagged rather than requiring the user to learn a pattern language. Another stochastically oriented system that can be applied to any language – and, indeed, was configured to target low-density languages – is the Hopkins named-entity recognition system [6]. Developers sought to "build a maximally language-independent system for both named-entity identification and classification, using minimal information about the source language". Their algorithm begins with seed names for each class, learns contextual patterns that are indicative for those classes, then iteratively learns new class members and word-internal morphological rules. The system can work on both small and large corpora with more or less informant input. One can imagine that this system might productively be combined with the more knowledge-based systems described here such that the stochastic and knowledge-based methods are exploited to their best advantage.

3. Boas II: Proper Name Recognition via Expectation-Driven Knowledge Elicitation

Boas II is an environment that supports the configuration of proper name recognition capabilities for any language. It requires no external resources or processors, and only minimal development time by a speaker of the given language. The methodology, which we call expectation-driven knowledge elicitation, follows that of the original Boas system [12] – [17], [19]. First we will briefly describe Boas, for which Boas II serves as a task-specific supplement.

3.1. The Boas Precedent

Boas is a knowledge-elicitation system that guides linguistically naïve speakers of any alphabetic language (L) through the process of providing machine-tractable information about L. Although Boas was originally intended to support the automatic ramping up of L-to-English machine translation (MT) systems, the elicited knowledge could be used for any application.[3]

The requirements of the system, which oriented its development, were as follows. The knowledge elicited needed to cover ecology/preprocessing (writing system, orthographic conventions, punctuation, etc.), morphology, syntax and lexicon. The system had to be language-independent and applicable to any alphabetic language, with no language-specific adjustments or retrofitting; in other words, all phenomena from all natural languages had to be provided for (to the extent feasible) and the collected information had to be automatically convertible into processing resources. In addition, the system had to be accessible to an untrained user, which meant that the methodological initiative and a large degree of the responsibility for coverage had to rest with the system itself. Since the technological solution to the above requirements had to be practical, the informant's time had to be used efficiently. To enhance the utility of the system in practical applications, the target knowledge elicitation time was set at six months, which could be increased or decreased as resources permitted. The common working language of the interface was English, which not only permitted some degree of English-orientation in the knowledge-elicitation process (e.g., using English seed lexicons to drive lexical acquisition), but also facilitated the preparation of a vast apparatus of training and reference materials, which amount to an on-line introduction to descriptive linguistics. In essence, Boas was designed to act like a field linguist, but whereas a field linguist can describe a language using any expressive means, Boas had to represent the accumulated knowledge in a machine-tractable, structured fashion; and whereas field linguists often focus on idiosyncratic ("linguistically interesting") properties of a language, Boas had to concentrate on the most basic, most widespread phenomena.

The overarching approach to developing Boas was to compile an inventory of cross-linguistically attested parameters, values and realizations that describe languages in general. The parameters represent categories of phenomena that need to be covered in the description of L, the values represent choices that orient what might be included in the description of that phenomenon for L, and the realization options suggest the

[3] Restricting the system to alphabetic languages that have distinct word boundaries was a programmatic decision. This approach to KE could, however, be extended to non-alphabetic languages as well.

kinds of questions that must be asked to gather the relevant information. Users of Boas, therefore, needed to complete what might be described as a "smart" multiple-choice exam: the choices were prepared beforehand but the path through the elicitation process depended on which choices were made. In addition, the option to provide a new value (a new type of realization of any of the phenomena) was always open, since we knew beforehand that it would be practically impossible to achieve complete cross-linguistic adequacy in our recorded realizations. A sample of the parameters, values and realizations used in Boas is shown in Table 1. The first block illustrates inflection, the second closed-class meanings, the third, ecology and the fourth, syntax.

Table 1. Sample parameters, values and means of their realization in Boas.

Class	Parameter	Values	Means of Realization
Inflection	Case Relations	nominative, accusative, dative, instrumental, abessive, etc.	flective morphology, agglutinating morphology, isolating morphology, prepositions, postpositions, etc.
	Number	singular, plural, dual, trial, paucal	flective morphology, agglutinating morphology, isolating morphology, particles, etc.
	Tense	present, past, future, timeless	flective morphology, agglutinating morphology, isolating morphology, etc.
Closed-class meanings	Possession	+/-	case-marking, closed-class affix, word or phrase, word order, etc.
	Spatial Relations	above, below, through, etc.	word, phrase, preposition or postposition, case-marking
Ecology	Expression of Numbers	integers, decimals, percentages, fractions, etc.	numerals in L, digits, punctuation marks (commas, periods, percent signs, etc.) or a lack thereof in various places
	Sentence Boundary	declarative, interrogative, imperative, etc.	period, question mark(s), exclamation point(s), ellipsis, etc.
Syntax	Grammatical Role	subjectness, direct-objecness, indirect-objectness, etc.	case-marking, word order, particles, etc.
	Agreement (for pairs of elements)	+/- person, +/- number, +/- case, etc.	flective, agglutinating or isolating inflectional markers

Boas was implemented as a prototype system and used by developers in a number of applications. It is not a commercial product and is not distributable. However, sufficient details of the system are available in the papers referred to above to permit reimplementation.

3.2. Boas II: Overview and Goals

Like Boas, Boas II is a language-independent system whose resident knowledge includes cross-linguistically attested expectations about linguistic phenomena. In the case of Boas II, the purview is proper names. The system guides users through the process of providing language-specific information about proper names that is then used to automatically configure a proper name recognizer. For reasons associated with the funder's preferences, Boas II places primary emphasis on names of people, but also covers names of companies, institutions, buildings, locations, geographical names and events (e.g., World War II). Like Boas, Boas II was developed as a prototype system and is not distributable. For that reason – and because this article seeks to describe not specific systems but approaches to treating low-density languages – we will not focus on details of implementation but, rather, on the content of and rationale behind the system. Interested readers can find details about our implementation in McShane et al. 2005.

Boas II takes a pattern-matching approach to proper name recognition. An important aspect of the work is compiling inventories of named entity components (e.g., personal names, family names) by means of iterative corpus-based methods. These inventories both support higher-level corpus work and improve the overall functioning of the named entity recognizer. As explained above, compiling inventories does not solve all problems of proper name recognition; however, it does help a great deal. Although Boas II does not employ machine learning, the knowledge acquired during use of this system could support stochastic methods. For example, the Hopkins team (Cucerzan and Yarowsky 1999; cf. above) reports that "F-measure increases roughly logarithmically with the total length of the seed wordlists in the range 40-300", meaning that the larger the available inventories of elements, the better the results. Since Boas II is strong on inventory building, its output could be input to something like the Hopkins' system.

Like the original Boas, Boas II elicits only that information that can be immediately exploited by the system. It does not elicit interesting factoids about name use in different languages that have more sociolinguistic interest than computational linguistic import – at least given the current state of the art. For example, some of the cross-linguistic aspects of proper name usage that we learned from responses to a survey conducted through the Linguist List are:[4]

- Afghans generally do not have a surname, but they do have two personal names, the latter of which is often mistakenly taken to be a surname by Westerners (though a reanalysis of the status of the second name has come about, at least for many Afghans who have contacts with the west);
- Brazilian children have a compound surname consisting of their mother's surname followed by their father's surname; so Elisa Wamierbon Pinchemel is the child of Augusto Pinchemel and Elisa Wamierbon;
- Brazilian children tend to have 2 or 3 personal names and tend to be called by the second or third of them;
- In Serbo-Croatian, following the personal name is a patronymic, but it can be either a special form of the patronymic or the base form of the father's name;

---

[4] Thanks to the many respondents to this survey, whose observations are cited here and below.

- In Swahili, parents' names change after a child is born: the mother is called Mama-wa <Mama-ya, Mama> + son's personal name, and the father is called Baba-wa <Baba-ya, Baba> + son's Personal name for father.

Some such information could be important if an NLP system attempted to carry out reasoning based on cross-referencing family members: e.g., a system might use a patronymic to link a particular real-world son to his father. However, if a system that advanced were developed for a language, the elicitation of such coreference-based information – which is difficult to render using pre-defined parameters and values – could be carried out independently.

3.3. Creating Pattern Inventory for People's Names

In this section, we describe the subtasks of the Boas II system. We omit certain pedagogical materials used to initiate readers into the goals of the system, since that information has already been provided above. Most of the subtasks can be completed in any order, with the exception of certain self-evident prerequisites: e.g., you cannot create patterns of components until you have selected an inventory of components to participate in those patterns.

3.3.1. Basic inventory of components

In this subtask, the user is presented with a list of category names from which he chooses the ones relevant for L. The inventory and examples, minus the checkboxes used in the interface, are shown in Table 2.

Table 2. Components of people's names.

Category Name	Example
Personal	John
Family	Smith
Tribal	Abnaki
Patronymic	Ivanovich
Matronymic	Espinosa
Middle	Ann
Title	Mr., Mrs.
SocialRole	Professor, Dr.
Descriptor	III, Jr.
Particle	von, de
Initial	A.
Comma	(John Smith, DDS)
Article	the, 'la'/'en' (Catalan) (the Duke of Marlborough; the Greens; also used before names in Modern Greek)
Preposition	of (the Duke of Marlborough)
TerritorialDesignation	Marlborough (John, Duke of Marlborough)
TermOfRespect	e.g., 'Mother' in Bahasa Indonesian can be used as a sign of respect, with no kinship implied or the necessity that the addressee be older than the speaker: e.g., Mother Susan, for a woman named Susan
TribalParticle	Al (Al Ghamdi in Arabic)
Caste	Pico Iyer ('Iyer' is the caste name for Saivite Brahmins)
SocialRelation	this category includes, but is not limited to, kinship terms (cf. TermOfRespect above); e.g., Arabic 'abu' "father of"; 'ibn' "son of"; also servant of, etc.

FormerNameIndicator	e.g., Alice Smith nee Johnson
Called	German 'gen.', as in Theo Vennemann gen. Nierfeld
WordForFamily	familia (e.g., la familia [Husband'sFirst Surname] in Castillian Spanish)
HistoricalFamily	In Westphalia, the typical means of calling Theo Schulte might be Winter's Theo, since the old family name or name of the estate was Winter
Pangilan	A shortened name but, unlike nicknames as English speakers understand them, these are (e.g., in Javanese)
Conjunction	e.g., i 'and' in Catalan can be used between surnames (Antoni Badia i Margarit, where Badia and Margarit are Family names)

The interface explains to users that we have tried to use maximally uncontroversial labels for categories of names, but no labeling system is perfect. Users can accept our labels or they can use their own labels. However, if they do the latter, they will not be able to take advantage of the previously prepared syntactic patterns that use our labeling conventions (cf. Section 3.3.2). In other words, there is a practical advantage to accepting our label "personal", but if a user strongly prefers the label "given" or "first", he can use it; he will simply have to create by hand all of the syntactic patterns in which it participates.

3.3.2. Basic syntactic patterns

The user is presented with the subset of patterns from our inventory of common syntactic patterns that contain the components selected for L. For example, if Personal, Initial and Family are all selected by the user, then the patterns he will see will include Personal Family (*Robert Jones*), Personal Initial Family (*Robert T. Jones*), Personal (*Robert*), Family (*Jones*). The full inventory of patterns is shown in Table 3. The basic syntactic patterns do not include iteration of elements, information about which is elicited later. Examples are missing in cases for which "native" illustrations were not readily available, although the patterns were attested by speakers of some language.

Table 3. Inventory of syntactic patterns for people's names.

Pattern	**Example**
Personal Family	Howard Jones
Personal Tribal	~
Personal Caste	Pico Iyer (Tamil)
Family Personal	Li Bai (Chinese)
Initial Family	H. Jones
Initial Tribal	~
Family Initial	Li B.
Personal Initial Family	Howard P. Jones
Personal Initial Tribal	~
Family Personal Initial	~
Personal Middle Family	Howard Paul Jones
Personal Middle Tribal	~
Family Personal Middle	~
Personal Patronymic Family	Ivan Pavlovich Belyj (Russian)
Personal Patronymic Matronymic	found in Spanish[5]

[5] One can also interpret such names as Personal Family Family. In this system, doubled family names are elicited later. The only reason to split patronymics from matronymics is in case they belong to different stored inventories of names.

Initial Initial Family	H. P. Jones
Initial Initial Tribal	~
Family Initial Initial	~
Initial Middle Family	H. Paul Jones
Initial Middle Tribal	~
Family Initial Middle	~
Title Family	Mr. Jones
Title Personal Family	Mr. Howard Jones
Title Initial Family	Mr: H. Jones
Title Personal Initial Family	Mr. Howard H. Jones
Title Personal Middle Family	Mr. Howard Paul Jones
Title Initial Initial Family	Mr. H. P. Jones
Title Initial Middle Family	Mr. H. Paul Jones
SocialRole Family	Mr. Jones
SocialRole Personal Family	Mr. Howard Jones
SocialRole Initial Family	Mr. H. Jones
SocialRole Personal Initial Family	Mr. Howard H. Jones
SocialRole Personal Middle Family	Mr. Howard Paul Jones
SocialRole Initial Initial Family	Mr. H. P. Jones
SocialRole Initial Middle Family	Mr. H. Paul Jones
Personal Family Comma Descriptor	Howard Jones, Jr.
Initial Family Comma Descriptor	H. Jones, Jr.
Personal Initial Family Comma Descriptor	Howard P. Jones, Jr.
Personal Middle Family Comma Descriptor	Howard Paul Jones, Jr.
Initial Initial Family Comma Descriptor	H. P. Jones, Jr.
Initial Middle Family Comma Descriptor	H. Paul Jones, Jr.
Title Personal Family Comma Descriptor	Mr. Howard Jones, Jr.
Title Initial Family Comma Descriptor	Mr. H. Jones, Jr.
Title Personal Initial Family Comma Descriptor	Mr. Howard H. Jones, Jr.
Title Personal Middle Family Comma Descriptor	Mr. Howard Paul Jones, Jr.
Title Initial Initial Family Comma Descriptor	Mr. H. P. Jones, Jr.
Title Initial Middle Family Comma Descriptor	Mr. H. Paul Jones, Jr.
SocialRole Personal Family Comma Descriptor	Mr. Howard Jones, Jr.
SocialRole Initial Family Comma Descriptor	Dr. H. Jones, Jr.
SocialRole Personal Initial Family Comma Descriptor	Dr. Howard H. Jones, Jr.
SocialRole Personal Middle Family Comma Descriptor	Dr. Howard Paul Jones, Jr.
SocialRole Initial Initial Family Comma Descriptor	Dr. H. P. Jones, Jr.
SocialRole Initial Middle Family Comma Descriptor	Dr. H. Paul Jones, Jr.
Personal Family Descriptor	Howard Jones Jr.
Initial Family Descriptor	H. Jones Jr.
Personal Initial Family Descriptor	Howard P. Jones Jr.
Personal Middle Family Descriptor	Howard Paul Jones Jr.
Initial Initial Family Descriptor	H. P. Jones Jr.
Initial Middle Family Descriptor	H. Paul Jones Jr.
Title Family Descriptor	Mr. Jones Jr.
Title Personal Family Descriptor	Mr. Howard Jones Jr.
Title Initial Family Descriptor	Mr. H. Jones Jr.
Title Personal Initial Family Descriptor	Mr. Howard H. Jones Jr.
Title Personal Middle Family Descriptor	Mr. Howard Paul Jones Jr.
Title Initial Initial Family Descriptor	Mr. H. P. Jones Jr.
Title Initial Middle Family Descriptor	Mr. H. Paul Jones Jr.
SocialRole Personal Family Descriptor	Dr. Howard Jones Jr.
SocialRole Initial Family Descriptor	Dr. H. Jones Jr.
SocialRole Personal Initial Family Descriptor	Dr. Howard H. Jones Jr.
SocialRole Personal Middle Family Descriptor	Dr. Howard Paul Jones Jr.
SocialRole Initial Initial Family Descriptor	Dr. H. P. Jones Jr.
SocialRole Initial Middle Family Descriptor	Dr. H. Paul Jones Jr.
Title Personal Patronymic Family	Gospodin Ivan Pavlovich Belyj (Russian)

SocialRole Personal Patronymic Family	Profesor Ivan Pavlovich Belyj (Russian)
Article Family	The Greens; la Badia (Catalan – fem. sg.)
Article Personal Family	la Antoni Badia (Catalan)
Personal Comma SocialRole Preposition Family	John, Duke of Marlborough
TribalParticle Tribal	Al Ghamdi (Arabic)
SocialRole Personal Family Preposition TerritorialDesignation	Lord Stewart Sutherland of Houndwood
SocialRole Family Preposition TerritorialDesignation	Lord Sutherland of Houndwood
Personal Comma SocialRole Preposition TerritorialDesignation	John, Duke of Marlborough
Personal Comma SocialRole Family Preposition TerritorialDesignation	Stewart, Lord Sutherland of Houndwood
TerritorialDesignation Initial Personal	Vilayanur S. Ramachandran (Tamil)
TerritorialDesignation Personal Personal	Attipat Krishnaswami Ramanujan (Tamil)
Personal SocialRelation Personal	Ali b. Abu-Talib (Ali son of Abu-Talib); A'ishah b. Abu-Bakr (A'ishah daughter of Abu-Bakr) (Arabic)
SocialRelation Personal	Umm Habibah (mother of Habibah)
Personal Family FormerNameIndicator Family	Jane Smith nee Johnson
Personal Initial Family FormerNameIndicator Family	Jane R. Smith nee Johnson
Personal Middle Family FormerNameIndicator Family	Jane Ruth Smith nee Johnson
Initial Middle Family FormerNameIndicator Family	J. Ruth Smith nee Johnson
Personal Family Called Family	Theo Vennemann gen. Nierfeld (German)
Title Personal	Dr. Abdullah (Arabic)
Personal SocialRole Particle Family Called Family	Bruno Baron von Freytag gen. Löringhoff (German)
Article Title Preposition Surname	la Señora de [Husband's First Surname] (Spanish)
Article Family WordForFamily	The Cook Family
Article WordForFamily Family	la familia [Husband'sFirst Surname] (Spanish)
HistoricalFamily Personal	Winter's Theo (German in Westphalia)
Title Pangilan	(Javanese)
SocialRelation Pangilan	(Javanese)
Personal Family Conjunction Family	Antoni Badia i Margarit (Catalan)
Article Personal	la Antoni (Catalan)
Article Personal Family Conjunction Family	la Antoni Badia i Margarit (Catalan; less common)
Article Family Conjunction Family	la Badia i Margarit (Catalan)
Personal Patronymic	Ivan Pavlovich (Russian)
Patronymic	Pavlovich (Russian; colloq.)
TermOfRespect Personal	Mother Susan (Bahasa Indonesia)
Personal	Mary
Personal Middle	Mary Elizabeth

3.3.3. Additional Components and Syntactic Patterns

The user is then presented with his or her current inventory of personal name components and permitted to supplement it, if necessary, either with completely new elements or by preferred names for elements that were included in the initial inventory. If any new elements are provided, the current inventory of syntactic patterns is displayed to the user and he is asked to supplement it to account for the new elements.

3.3.4. Iteration of components

Iteration of name components is a common phenomenon: e.g., German permits multiple titles, as in *Dr. Dr. Mueller*; personal names in French (not to mention English) often contain two elements: *Jean Claude, Mary Beth*; multiple descriptors are used in many languages, as in *John Smith, MD, PhD*. In this task, the user is asked to indicate which name components can iterate, how many times (2-4 are elicited directly; if more, the user must manually enter the relevant patterns), and what punctuation can intervene between iterated components (e.g., dash, space).

3.3.5. Inventories of titles, professions, etc.

The user is asked to translate whichever elements from our resident list of titles and professions might be useful for proper noun recognition in L. For convenience, we loosely group the list according to the categories Titles, General Professional, Military, Royalty, Political, Business, Medical, Academic, Entertainment/Communication, Family Role, Legal Role and Other. We do not provide these lists in full for reasons of space.

3.3.6. Compiling Inventories of components

The user is asked to provide a seed inventory of examples for each type of name component: e.g., if he were configuring a system for English, he might add the following components to the categories "personal" and "family":

> Personal: Ann, Mary, Susan, Keith, Albert, …
> Family: Jones, Smith, Harris, McDuff, …

These seed lists, along with the seed list of titles described in Section 3.3.5, will be used as heuristics during later corpus work. If inventories of such elements are available externally, they can be imported using Boas II's import function.

In the current implementation, a word that explicitly belongs to one category will be blocked from matching another category: e.g., if *Mr.* is listed as a Title, it will not match the Family name slot in a pattern. If a given entity can belong to more than one category – e.g., *Washington* can be a TerritorialDesignation, a Personal name or a Family name – it must be listed explicitly in each category. Although the decision to permit strings to belong to only one category unless otherwise indicated can lead to some missed matches (e.g., if *Washington* were listed as a Family name, the string *Washington Erving* would not be properly analyzed), we have found it a more practical solution than permitting the extensive false positives encountered when not using such a filter.

The processing of eliciting inventories of category members also includes the option of compiling a stop list: that is, entities that should not be matched in any corpus searches. This stop list will be very helpful for people's names, since one would not expect words like *house* or *dog*, even if capitalized, to be part of a person's name. However, if a user will be covering, for example, company names, he or she must be careful not to overpopulate the stop list: e.g., if *dog* is in the stop list, the system will not find *Happy Dog Dog Food Company*. Eliciting different stop lists for different types of named entities is not part of this version of the system, though it would be a useful future enhancement.

3.3.7. Nicknames

The user is given the option of providing nickname equivalents for the current inventory of Personal names, since such correspondences can be important for systems that carry out coreference resolution for named entities. When searching the corpus for named entities, the system interprets nicknames the same as full personal names, and includes nicknames as entries in the list of personal names. The correspondences between full names and nicknames is, however, stored should that information be useful for an application.

3.3.8. Punctuation

An inventory of punctuation marks that occur outside of personal names is elicited (those that occur inside of names were elicited earlier and incorporated into the syntactic patterns). This inventory is used for parsing corpora: for example, if a period is a name-external punctuation mark, then the text string *Ann. Bill* will be understood as containing two different names, not a single proper name. Recall that Boas II does not require any prerequisite technologies – it answers for all its own prerequisites; therefore, the understanding of punctuation, which would be an aspect of preprocessing in an end application, must be handled explicitly.

3.3.9. Morphological forms

The user is asked if components of names can occur in non-base morphological forms, like the plural or in a case that is different from that of the citation form. The answer to this question will alert developers to the need to incorporate external morphological analysis, as could be carried out, for example, by the type of analyzer automatically generated by the original Boas system. Morphological analysis is particularly important for flective languages, like Russian, for which a given proper name can have a dozen inflectional forms.

3.3.10. Capitalization

The user is asked if capitalization can aid in the detection of proper names. Note, however, that even if capitalization is generally a strong heuristic for a proper names, like it is in English, capitalization conventions are often not followed in informal genres, like email and blogs. Therefore, even if capitalization is a heuristic in a language, the user is asked before each run of the proper name recognizer whether or not he wants capitalization to be considered as a heuristic.

3.3.11. Heuristics for components

The user is asked to provide prefixes and/or suffixes that suggest that a given string represents a certain type of personal name component. For example, the suffix *-ovich* in

Russian strongly suggests a patronymic. As with capitalization, this heuristic can either be used or ignored during any given run of the proper name recognizer.

3.4. Treating Proper Names Not Referring to People

In this section, the user provides pattern-matching knowledge for proper names that refer to entities other than people: bodies of water, buildings, geological entities, publications, company names and proper-noun events (e.g., *World War II; the Sydney Olympics*). The knowledge elicitation process is the same for all these subtypes of entities. We will use bodies of water for illustration.

The user is presented with a list of types of bodies of water in English and asked (a) to provide translations, as applicable, into L; (b) to add L variants of any other keywords (like *lake* and *river*) that indicate bodies of water; (c) to select from among three syntactic patterns in which "body of water keywords" can participate:

1. word* + body of water keyword (e.g., *Amazon River*)
2. body of water keyword + word* (e.g., *Lake Michigan*)
3. body of water keyword + preposition/postposition/particle + word*
   (*Gulf of Mexico*)

Word* indicates one or more proper-noun words. If pattern 3 is selected, then the applicable prepositions, postpositions or particles are elicited. The elicitation of these patterns is not as fine-grained as for people's names, which, as mentioned earlier, reflects the stated goals of the funder. Enhancements to this thread of knowledge elicitation would include providing more patterns to select from, especially for company names since, as [6] shows, the variety of patterns for company names is rich indeed. In Boas II, knowledge about proper names that do not refer to people is used primarily to block false positives when searching for people's names.

3.5. Corpus Work

Using just the knowledge requested above, which might take a user between 30 minutes and two hours to provide, Boas II can automatically configure a proper name recognition system. However, the quality will probably not be very good from the outset because listing is not easy: if one is asked to list 50 kinds of dogs, he might get stuck at 12, whereas if he sees a list of words, he can easily pick out which ones are dogs. The same is true of patterns of proper names: it is likely that the user will have forgotten some the first time round, and it is likely that the inclusion of certain stop words into the stop words list will significantly improve results. For this reason, we use iterative corpus-based methods to help users to improve the system.

3.5.1. Upload/select corpus

The user uploads one or more corpora, following the instructions to convert them into UTF-8 encoding, then selects one to work with. This assumes, of course, that some electronic text is available, thus justifying the configuration of a proper name recognition tool to begin with.

3.5.2. Preparing to search

The user is asked to select one syntactic pattern at a time from the inventory he created earlier. This pattern is searched for in the selected corpus, with matches being returned for the user's approval or rejection. When the user accepts a candidate, all components of it that are not already part of the respective inventory are recorded. For example, if the user agrees that *Polly Jones* represents the pattern Personal Family, and if *Polly* is not yet in the list of Personal names for English (but *Jones* is in the list of Family names), *Polly* will automatically be added to the inventory of personal names, and Polly Jones will be added to the inventory of complex known entities – another part of the growing knowledge base of Boas II.

Patterns are searched for individually precisely in order to permit components of approved candidates to be automatically added to the respective inventories. This would not be possible if one searched simultaneously for different patterns, like Title Surname and Personal Surname, since the system would not know if the first string of an approved entity were a Title or a Personal name. (Another implementation option would have been to permit searching for multiple patterns at one time; however, the necessity of individually labeling each element of approved candidates would have been, we hypothesized, too time-consuming. Yet another, more expensive, implementation option would have been to permit both search options, with each option being employed by users as they chose.) The inventory of patterns presented includes any necessary expansions based on component iteration. So, if a user indicated that Personal Patronymic Family was a valid pattern, and also indicated that Family names could be iterated twice with either a hyphen or a white space between them, the inventory of patterns would be expanded to include Personal Patronymic Family-Family and Personal Patronymic Family Family.

Since selecting good search strategies is important for making Boas II robust with a minimum of user effort, we carefully explain the ramifications of various search strategies to users. As an example of the pedagogical aspect of Boas II, we provide this explanation in full.

The next step in this process has two goals:

1. to test how well the system can find named entities in a corpus of {Language}, and
2. to increase the inventories of each type of named entity component to improve search results with each iteration of this process.

The process will go as follows.

1. From the list of valid syntactic structures for names in {Language}, you will choose a pattern you want the system to search for in the corpus. E.g., **Title Personal Family**. The reason we are having you choose one pattern at a time is so that automatic (therefore fast) labeling of components can be carried out.

2. The system will carry out the search and present you with candidate names, e.g.,

Mr.	Tom	Smith
Ms.	Judy	Garland

3. You will accept or reject each as a valid representative of **this pattern**. Any candidate that you accept will automatically have its component parts labeled according to the original search pattern, and those components will be automatically added to the relevant name component list. So, if you are searching for "Title + Family" and the system returns "Mrs. Mary" (which is actually Title + Personal), you should reject that candidate; otherwise, the name "Mary" would be incorrectly added to the list of valid Family names for English.
4. Then you will launch another search, choosing a different pattern to search for: e.g., **Personal Patronymic Family**. You will keep repeating this process until the system is finding most of the relevant syntactic patterns for names and the system's inventory of elements belonging to each name components is quite large, or until you run out of time.

At any time you can return to the pages that elicit components of named entities or patterns using them, should you find that some components or patterns are missing. You can also manually add to the inventories of components (like Family names) or to the stop list at any time.

The most important aspect of this process is **figuring out a good strategy** for searching – we'll try to help. The worst case would be to start out searching for, say, a Family name used alone because if {Language} uses capitalization like English does, every single capitalized word – including the first word of every sentence – will be selected as a candidate; and if {Language} doesn't use capitalization, every single word in general will be selected (after all, how can the system know something is *not* a Family name?). A better strategy is to start from the most restricted types of patterns, like those that use titles or contain many components.

3.5.3. Launch search

To launch a search, the user selects one of the syntactic patterns he has already established for L and indicates whether he wants any heuristics to be attached to any of the components. For example, if the language is Ukrainian, and if the user correctly indicated that the pattern "Personal Family" was permitted. He can then say:

1. whether each component must be capitalized (yes)
2. whether only known instances of components should be sought (this depends upon his goal; if, for example, he wants to extend the inventory of known Family names without finding too many false positives, he might want to accept only 'known' Personal names)
3. whether affixation heuristics should be used (probably not, but possibly yes, depending on how large the corpus is and the user's particular goals).

Figure 1 shows the results of one search in Ukrainian; the actual text is less important than the look and feel of the process.

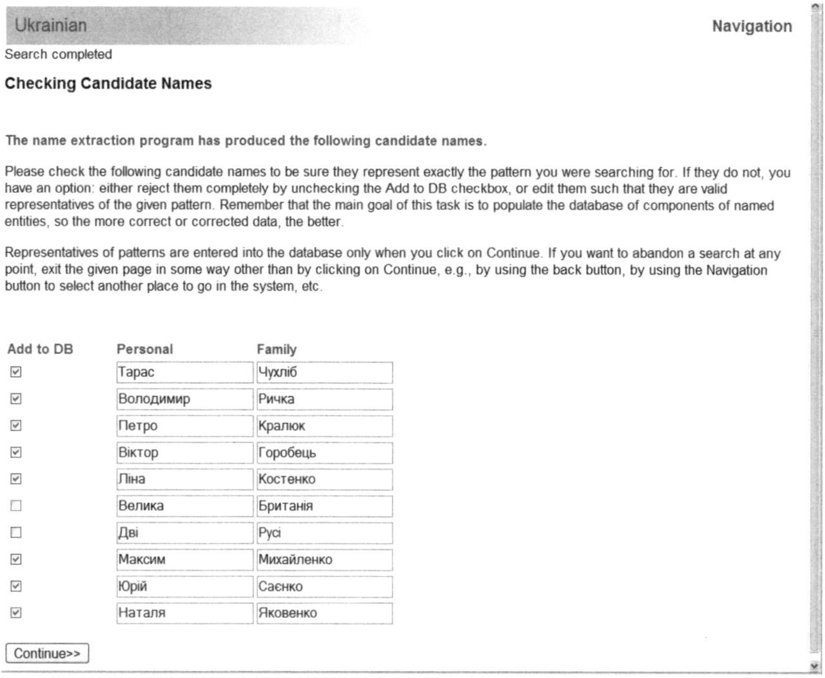

Figure 1. First page of results of a search for the pattern Personal Family in Ukrainian.

The user can review the results, unchecking any that do not represent the pattern in question. For orientation, the first of the rejected entities refers to *Great Britain.*

3.6. Informant Time Needed

Developing proper name recognition capabilities for a language using Boas II is intended to take from several hours to several days, depending on the desired quality and coverage of the system as well as the named-entity identification heuristics of the given language We expect the lower boundary of useful elicitation time to be about two hours, during which time the informant would indicate basic components of proper names, the syntactic patterns in which they participate, and some detection heuristics (e.g., capitalization, morphological triggers); he would also build seed lists of components. In this very fast ramp-up scenario, only very small inventories of components would be compiled.

The amount of informant time necessary to ramp up a system of a given quality will depend, among other things, upon the following.

- **Language typology.** Languages with few proper name heuristics – like those that lack capitalization or that use capitalization for every noun (like German) – will require large inventories of name components before good results are achieved. We cannot suggest any magic bullets for proper name recognition in such languages, as we do not believe any such exist. By contrast, languages in which titles commonly introduce names, or in which morphological forms strongly suggest certain types of components (e.g., a given suffix is only used in patronymics), will permit better results with smaller inventories of components.

- **The size and coverage of inventories built by the informant.** The inventories of named entity components act as both positive and negative heuristics for entity recognition. As such, the bigger the inventory, the better the results.
- **What resources are already available.** As part of the Boas II project, we compiled inventories of personal and family names for many languages, which can be exploited by informants for those languages. More such lists might be available on the Web or in other machine-readable resources. In fact, even print resources – like phone books – could be helpful for creating lists, despite the time needed to scan or even type in the entities. In addition, stop lists – like the words in a basic dictionary – are very useful. Any on-line lexicon that can be formatted into a list of head words can be imported into Boas II and used as a blocking heuristic (e.g., capitalized *And* at the beginning of a sentence is certainly not part of a proper name in English).
- **The breadth of the system.** Any subset of named entities can be the focus of a system built with Boas II: e.g., one could build only a person identifier, in which all elicitation tasks not related to people could be skipped.
- **How easily one can find or build a corpus.** Corpus-based elicitation methods are used to drive the compilation of inventories of named entity components as well as to help informants to recall patterns that might not have come to mind in the initial elicitation of patterns; however, the corpus must be built outside of the system and uploaded.

3.7. Recap of Boas II

Let us reconsider the status and potential contribution of a system like Boas II. Such a system can be put in front of a speaker of any alphabetic language, who will be lead through a process of knowledge elicitation for which the system itself takes much of the initiative for what work is carried out and how it is carried out. When a relatively small amount of information has been provided about a language, the system automatically configures a proper name recognition system, which can then be improved through iterative corpus-oriented trial and error. The important point for NLP developers involved with low- and middle-density languages is that the same system can be used for any language, and no external resources (apart from a corpus) or external processors are required.

4. GeoMatch: Multilingual Processing of Place Names

As we have just seen, lists of proper names are a very useful resource for the task of proper name recognition. While such lists can never be expected to contain *all* proper names, they can provide a simple and accurate means of detecting and categorizing many proper names.

If we extend proper name processing to cross-linguistic applications, it would be very useful to have a cross-indexed multi-lingual, multi-script database of proper names. That is, is would be useful to be able to look up how the capital of Russia is rendered in every language using both that language's native script and any other scripts that one might expect to encounter. The system we describe in this section, called GeoMatch, takes a step toward building just such a resource. It is not yet a knowledge elicitation system like Boas or Boas II, but the approaches developed for the initial subset of languages could easily be applied to other languages using Boas-like methodologies. Like Boas and Boas II, GeoMatch was implemented as a proof-of-concept system. Unlike the other systems, it builds upon an existing knowledge resource called the Geographic Names Database (GNDB).

The GNDB contains approximately 5.5 million geographic names and 4.0 million features, covering all countries of the world. For the most part, the names in GNDB are in the native language of the country where they are located: for example, names in Russia are in Russian. However, **all names are rendered as Latin strings** – they are not in the original script of the given language. So, for example, the Russian city known in English as Krasnodar will be listed as *Krasnodar*, which is the transliteration of the native Cyrillic *Краснодар*; and the Russian city known in English as Moscow will be listed as *Moskva*, which is the transliteration of the Cyrillic *Москва*. These examples highlight a noteworthy point about the cross-lingual rendering of names: in some cases, as with Krasnodar, proper names are *transliterated* between languages using rule-based correspondences (which may or may not be univocal), whereas in other cases, as with Moscow, they are *translated* idiosyncratically. We will continue differentiate between *transliteration* and *translation* based on whether the process is productive and rule-driven or idiosyncratic.

The GNDB was developed over decades, largely manually, and before the time when non-English language support in computers was readily available. As such, there are no companion databases that contain the "original" native script versions of entities. GNDB is currently available both as a search function over the Web and as text files for those wishing to incorporate its contents into computer systems (http://gnswww.nga.mil/geonames/GNS/index.jsp).

The specific goals of the GeoMatch project were to make the GNDB more useful as a resource (a) for people searching it over the Internet, and (b) for multi-lingual text processing applications. We were asked to approach this project using knowledge-based rather than stochastic methods because the results of prior attempts to use fuzzy-matching to improve searches for Arabic place names were deemed to be of insufficient quality.

The exclusive use of Latin script in the database leads to certain deficiencies, whether the GNDB is used in the Internet search application or is incorporated into an NLP system. For example, there are often many ways to transliterate a non-Latin string into Latin script and only one of them is recorded in the GNDB, meaning that if a person or system uses another, the entity will not be found. For example, in Russian, when the vowel *a* follows a palatalized consonant it is written as *я*, which has three canonical transliterations into English – *ya* (popular), *ja* (scholarly), *ia* (Library of Congress); GNDB uses only the first. Moreover, as discussed above, names are not always transliterated between languages, they can also be translated, in which case the cross-linguistic forms can be very different. So, ideally, a repository of geographical names would include the rendering of each geographical name in each language and script, and robust transliteration engines would permit users to search for strings using various search strategies.

Covering the geographical entities in every country using every language and script was out of scope for this exploratory project, so three languages and their respective country databases were selected: Russian/Russia, Ukrainian/Ukraine, Polish/Poland. As will be shown, the algorithms developed for these can be applied directly to more languages and country databases, providing the potential to turn the already information-packed GNDB into an even more robust resource to support NLP and geographic research needs.

4.1. The Seed Database

The data in the GNDB cover all countries of the world and are freely available as text files, divided by country, with no licensing requirements or restrictions. The data include both linguistic and extra-linguistic information, totaling 25 fields.[6] The fields of particular interest for language processing are:

UFI	unique feature identifier – uniquely identifies the entity using a six-digit number
UNI	unique name identifier – uniquely identifies a given string (which can be used to identify more than one place) using a six-digit number
FC	feature classification – identifies the general type of the entity (e.g., populated place, vegetation, hydrographic) using one of nine (multi-)letter codes
DSG	feature designation code – identifies the specific type of the entity (e.g., populated place, river, canal) using over 500 multi-letter codes; many DSGs can be realized in language as keywords, with the DSG-keyword associations being central to our linguistic processing[7]
LC	language code – indicates the language of the given database entry; the field is rarely filled in even if the given entity is not in the native language of the country (an instance of a knowledge gap in the resource); most database entities, however, are in the language of the given country
Generic	indicates the keyword, if any, in the string; the field is rarely filled in, even for entities that contain a keyword (another knowledge gap)
Full_Name	the full name of the entity, written in Latin script and including diacritics, if applicable
Full_Name_ND	the full name of the entity, written in Latin without diacritics, typed using QWERTY, the visible English keyboard

The combination of UFI (the actual place) and UNI (the string that renders it) uniquely identifies each database entry.

[6] The full inventory of DSG codes is available at http://gnswww.nga.mil/geonames/Desig_Code/Desig_Code_Help.jsp

[7] In some cases, we have found more than one keyword corresponding to a given DSG; in others, we have not yet found any keywords for a given DSG. Our inventory of keywords reflects analysis of the data in the GNDB as well as dictionary searches.

The GeoMatch work comprises two parts: enhancing the content of the databases and improving the search capabilities. Each is discussed in turn.

4.2. Database Enhancement

The process of enhancing the databases for Russia, Ukraine and Poland is shown in Figure 1, each step of which is briefly described below.

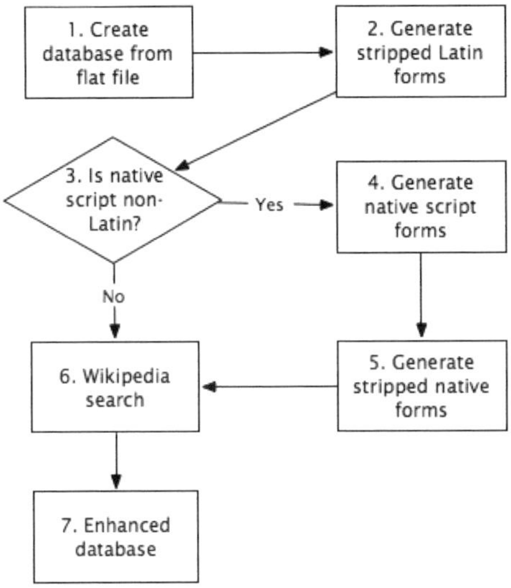

Figure 2. The algorithm for enhancing the GNDB.

Step 1. Although the GNDB exists as a database for use by the Internet search application, the database itself is not publicly distributed. Instead, flat files containing its data are distributed. The first step, therefore, is to create a database for each country from the corresponding flat file that can be downloaded from the Internet.

Step 2. This step is devoted to keyword recognition. We define keywords as strings like *mountain* and *river* that are the part of a proper name that identifies the type of entity: e.g., *Mississippi River* is a river. We call proper names stripped of their keywords "stripped" forms.

It is important to recognize keywords, and to recognize the stripped forms of proper names, for the following reasons:

- Entities that can include keywords sometimes appear in the GNDB with their keyword and sometimes without their keyword: for example, what we know in English as *Lake Baikal* might have appeared as *Ozero Baikal* (where 'ozero' means 'lake') or just as Baikal. Whereas the lack of an overt keyword might seem like an oversight, it actually might not have been because the acquirers of the GNDB unfailingly indicated the nature of the entity by selecting the relevant feature designation code, like LK for lake. So entering Baikal [DSG: LK] says, unambiguously, that this is a lake; entering it as Ozero Baikal is perfectly fine, but not strictly necessary. However, if a person or NLP system wanted to find namely the string *Ozero Baikal*, Baikal would not be a match.

- If an entity is recorded in GNDB with a keyword, sometimes the keyword is in the native language (e.g., Russian for the Russia database), and sometimes it is in English, German or some other language. For example, the database might contain *Lake Baikal* rather than *Ozero Baikal*. In this case, the keyword must be understood as being separate from the actual "proper name" part of the string.
- When a user is searching the database, he can either include or not include a keyword or DSG code. That is, he might type in *Baikal* and indicate that the DSG code is LK; or he might type in *Lake Baikal* and expect the system to understand that he wants only lakes named Baikal. No matter how the user types in the entity and how the entity happened to be entered into the GNDB originally, we want the desired correspondences to be found.

In order to support fast keyword processing at runtime, we supplemented the GNDB by what we call Stripped_Latin forms, which correspond to the Full_Form and Full_Form_ND fields except without the keywords. Whenever a search string is entered, it is parsed and only the proper name parts, minus the keywords, are searched for in the "stripped" columns of the database.

Automatically identifying keywords is not trivial: e.g., 'lake' in *Lake Louise* is not a keyword (this is a city) but 'lake' in *Lake Baikal* is (this is a lake). Our keyword stripping algorithm relies on two types of information to determine whether what looks like a keyword is actually functioning as one: the feature designation (DSG) of the entity and the inventory of keywords and their corresponding DSGs that we compiled into a new Keywords-database.

The Keywords-database covers several hundred keywords in four languages (Russian, Ukrainian, Polish and English) and includes all possible variants of each language's keywords, like every reasonable transliteration of Russian and Ukrainian keywords into Latin script. It also includes a smattering of keywords from other languages, like German and Czech, that were used occasionally in the databases. Creating this inventory was labor-intensive because, as mentioned above, the Generic field is most often empty in the original data; and even when a keyword string is identified, all of its "meaningful" DSG correspondences must be detected: e.g., the keyword 'sea' might be used as a keyword relating to entities of type BAY and LK (lake), but certainly not entities of type PPL (populated place).

The keyword stripping algorithm is as follows:

1. If the entity is composed of only 1 word, there is no keyword.
2. If the entity is composed of >1 word, search the Keywords-database for any of the component words, considering any matches potential keywords. Keywords in all languages are considered since English and German keywords are common in all files, Russian keywords are common in the Ukraine file, etc.
3. If there is > 1 potential keyword
   And if one is at the beginning of the string and the other is at the end of the string,
   Then the first one is the candidate keyword.
   Else the last one is the candidate keyword.
4. If the any of the DSGs of the candidate keyword, as recorded in the Keywords-database, matches the DSG of the entity in question, the candidate

keyword is considered an actual keyword and is stripped; else nothing is stripped.

This algorithm has been shown to work robustly for the languages in question. If this approach is expanded to other languages, two modifications might be necessary: the number of languages in which potential keywords are sought (step 2) should be restricted to avoid false positives (e.g., one might not want to look for Chinese keywords in the Russian database), and expectations regarding the linear ordering of keywords in multiple-candidate scenarios (step 3) must be parameterized.

The only errors so far in the stripping process have been due to the failure to include some keyword in the Keywords-database or the omission of a necessary DSG association for a keyword (e.g., the keyword 'river' is used for entities described as STM (stream), not only RV (river)).

Steps 3-4. The next step was to generate exactly one Cyrillic rendering of each Latin string in the Russia and Ukraine databases because Russian and Ukrainian are written in Cyrillic, making the Cyrillic forms the true native forms. In the general case, it would have been impossible to do this because there are several ways that certain Cyrillic characters can be rendered into Latin and, when converting the Latin back into Cyrillic, some ambiguities arise. However, the nature of the original GNDB data helps significantly because a single transliteration convention was largely used throughout (despite some inconsistencies that must be expected in a resource of this size). Therefore, we created a transliteration engine that take the GNDB Latin forms and posits a single Cyrillic variant for each one. Despite a few errors associated with unforeseen letter combinations, which could fixed globally, the results were quite good. There were, however, some residual ambiguities that would have had to have been fixed manually: e.g., the Latin apostrophe can indicate either an apostrophe or a soft sign in Ukrainian, with context providing little power of disambiguation. We did not carry out such manual correction.

All transliteration in this system is carried out using the same engine, whether the transliteration is used for database population or for processing search strings in the ways discussed below. The input to the transliteration engine is a table of correspondences between letters and letter combinations in a source language and a target language. There are no language specific rules and no contextual rules, apart from the ability to indicate the beginning of a string and the end of a string. In addition, longer input strings are selected over shorter strings. As in Boas and Boas II, we intentionally kept the implementation language-neutral so that the component resources could be applied to any alphabetic language.

An example of a row in the English-to-Russian table is as follows. This says that the Latin letters yy at the end of a word ($) are to be rendered as Cyrillic ый.

yy$ ый

For the task of populating the Russia and Ukraine databases with a single Cyrillic variant for each entity, we used special one-to-one transliteration tables, whereas for the search application described below we used one-to-many tables. (Details on this are below.)

Prior to transliterating the entities in the Full_Form field into Cyrillic, we stripped any non-native keywords from them since, e.g., an English or a German keyword used in a supposedly Russian string should not be transliterated.

Step 5. The same as Step 2 except that Cyrillic keywords are stripped rather than Latin ones.

Step 6. The objective of this task is to mine Wikipedia (a) to attest our posited Cyrillic variants of geographical names and (b) to extract multilingual variants of found names. We save extracted multi-lingual variants to a Wikipedia Database that was cross-indexed with our linguistically embellished GNDB using the entity's unique combination of UFI and UNI values.

Our search and extraction engine mimics the search function in Wikipedia, leveraging the fact that the Web address for each entry is predictable based on the head entry (i.e., the head word or phrase for the entry). Each head entry is stored on the page using a strict naming convention: e.g., Krasnodar in English, Spanish and Russian is found at:

http://**en**.wikipedia.org/wiki/**Krasnodar**
http://**es**.wikipedia.org/wiki/**Krasnodar**
http://**ru**.wikipedia.org/wiki/**Краснодар**

The links to related pages in other languages are encoded in a highly structured manner, making them readily detected automatically. The links to the Spanish and Russian pages for Krasnodar from the English page are:

<li class="interwiki-es">
<a href="http://es.wikipedia.org/wiki/Krasnodar">Español</a></li>

<li class="interwiki-ru">
<a href="http://ru.wikipedia.org/wiki/%D0%9A%D1%80%D0%B0
%D1%81%D0%BD%D0%BE%D0%B4%D0%B0%D1%80">
Русский</a></li>

Since the Russian string for Krasnodar requires non-ASCII characters, it is encoded using percent-escape notation, in which each character is represented by a pair of percent-escapes (e.g., Cyrillic *а* is represented as %D0%B0). Percent-escape notation permits UTF-8 characters to appear in Web addresses (see [8] for a concise overview and [2] for a more in-depth treatment).

Our engine creates a list of Web addresses to search for from our inventory of geographical entities: if a Web page for the given address exists, then the engine follows the links to corresponding pages in other languages, opening up each page and searching for the "meta" tag with the first parameter-value pair *name = "keywords"*. The first value for the parameter *content* within that same tag is always the headword as rendered in the given language. In the underlying html for the Spanish of our Krasnodar example, the tag looks as follows:

<meta name="keywords" **content="Краснодар**,Нетребко,
Анна Юрьевна,Бондарь Александр,[…] " />

Our engine currently does only light parsing of the input data, as by inserting underscores between multi-word entities and removing parentheses. We did not download Wikipedia prior to carrying out our experiments, although in retrospect that would have been well advised.

Step 7. The final enhanced database contains, in addition to the 25 original fields: (a) a **Native** field containing Cyrillic variants for Russia and Ukraine; (b) a **Stripped_Latin** field containing the Full_Form (in Latin) without keywords; (c) a **Stripped_Bare** field containing the Full_Form_ND (diacritic-free Latin) without keywords; (d) a **Stripped_Native** field containing the Cyrillic form without keywords; (e) a new **Keywords-database** that includes multi-lingual keywords with their DSG correspondences; and (f) a new **Wikipedia-database** that includes the multi-lingual variants of all found entities along with their language attributions and explicit link (via UFI/UNI) to their original database anchor.

4.3. The Search Interface

The application we used to test the utility of our database supplementation and multi-lingual transliteration engine is a search engine that is similar to the one that currently accesses the GNDB but contains additional search features. The interface is shown in Figure 3.

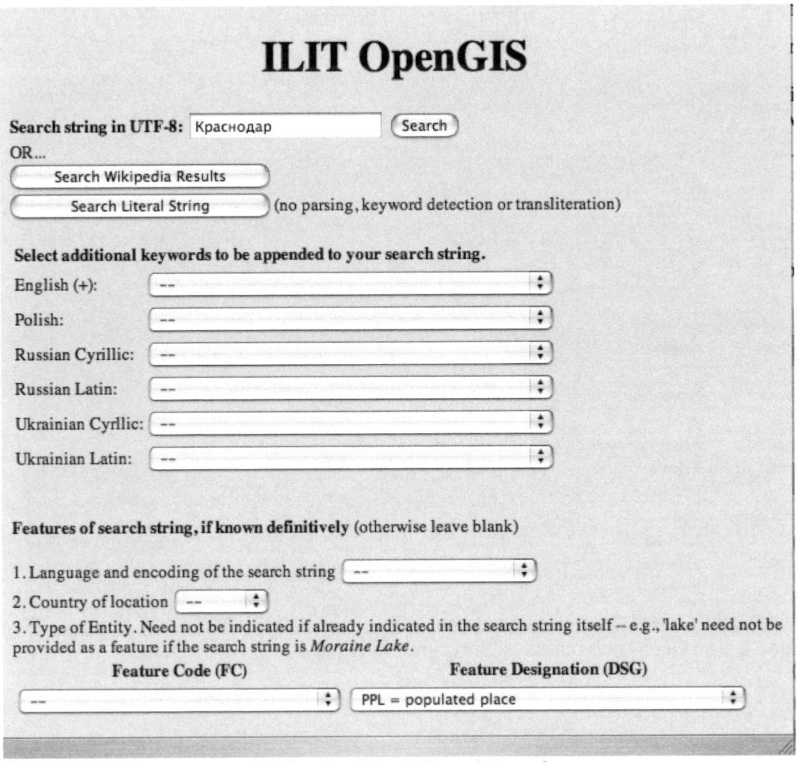

Figure 3. The GeoMatch Search Interface.

A search string can be in entered in any language and script as long as it is in UTF-8 encoding. In the figure, the search string is in Russian. There are three search buttons, all of which return a select inventory of properties of the entity, drawn from the GNDB, as well as any multi-lingual variants found in Wikipedia.

Search	Searches the Russia, Ukraine and Polish databases using the main search algorithm, described below.
Search Wikipedia Results	Searches the Wikipedia database for strings in other languages.
Search Literal String	Searches the Russia, Ukraine and Poland databases on the string literally as typed, with no transliteration or keyword processing.

The output of the search in Figure 3 is shown in Figure 4. The Wikipedia results are below the main database information. In this prototype, we display only a subset of features for each entity (due to screen real estate), and we permit the user to constrain the search using only select features (e.g., DSG but not latitude or longitude); however, it would be trivial to expand the display and feature selection to include all features.

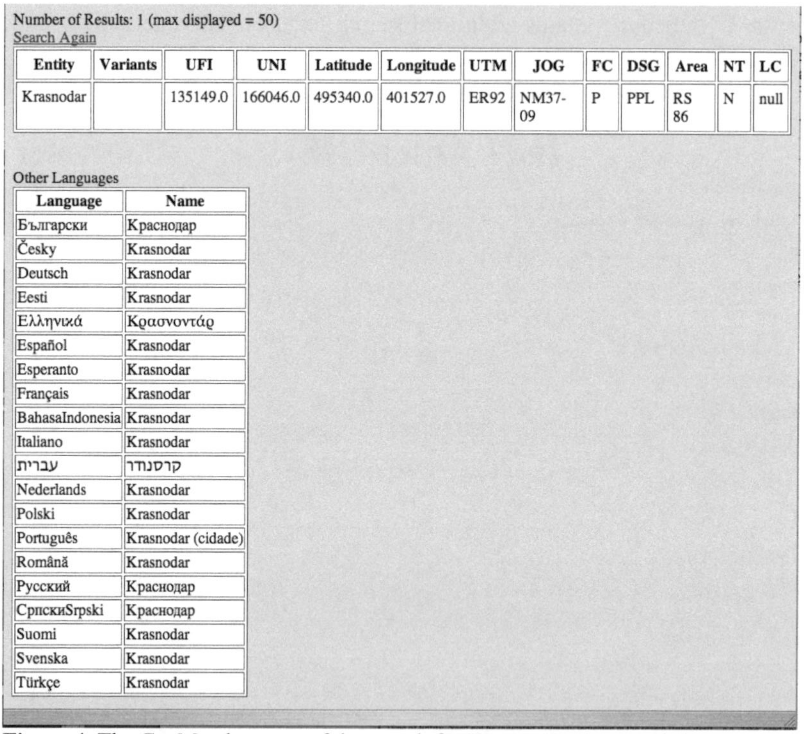

Number of Results: 1 (max displayed = 50)
Search Again

Entity	Variants	UFI	UNI	Latitude	Longitude	UTM	JOG	FC	DSG	Area	NT	LC
Krasnodar		135149.0	166046.0	495340.0	401527.0	ER92	NM37-09	P	PPL	RS 86	N	null

Other Languages

Language	Name
Български	Краснодар
Česky	Krasnodar
Deutsch	Krasnodar
Eesti	Krasnodar
Ελληνικά	Κρασνοντάρ
Español	Krasnodar
Esperanto	Krasnodar
Français	Krasnodar
BahasaIndonesia	Krasnodar
Italiano	Krasnodar
עברית	קרסנודר
Nederlands	Krasnodar
Polski	Krasnodar
Português	Krasnodar (cidade)
Română	Krasnodar
Русский	Краснодар
СрпскиSrpski	Краснодар
Suomi	Krasnodar
Svenska	Krasnodar
Türkçe	Krasnodar

Figure 4. The GeoMatch output of the search for Краснодар (Krasnodar).

4.4. The Main Search Strategy

In describing the search algorithms, we first concentrate on the main Search function, which targets the three databases and four languages (including English) treated in this system. When launching a search, the user may choose to specify values for any of the following features. None are required and if none are entered, all relevant algorithms are called in turn.

1. The language and script of the search string: *English; Polish, Latin; Polish, Extended Latin; Russian, Cyrillic; Russian, Latin; Ukrainian Cyrillic; Ukrainian, Latin.*
2. The location of the entity: Russia, Poland or Ukraine.
3. The feature specification (FS), which can be one of 9 values.
4. The feature designation (DSG), which can be one of over 500 values.

The user can insert keywords into the search string by selecting them from the menu of keywords for each language/script combination. For the Russian Latin and Ukrainian Latin keywords, only one of the many transliterations understood by the system is listed. Typing in a keyword is equivalent to selecting the associated feature designation code (DSG).

A flowchart for the main search strategy is presented in Figure 5.

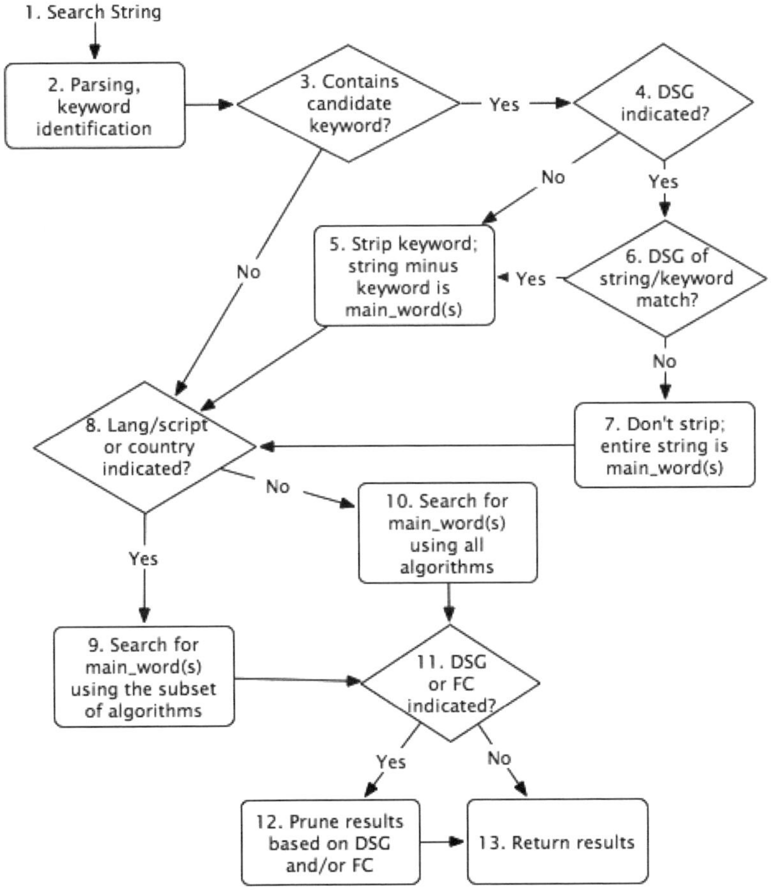

Figure 5. The main search strategy.

Step 1. The search string is input with optional feature selection.

Steps 2-7. The string is parsed and keyword identification and stripping is carried out using the same methods as described in the database population task, Step 2.

Steps 8-10. The search algorithms are divided by language/script and country, with one algorithm devoted to each pair, making 21 algorithms in all. If either the language/script or the country is explicitly provided by the user, then the number of algorithms that have to be launched is decreased accordingly. If no features are provided, all algorithms are launched in turn and all results are returned.

Our search algorithms attempt to cover *any* reasonable transliteration of a string. We do, however, assume that when strings are transliterated into Latin, they will be transliterated by an English speaker; therefore, we use, for example, *v* to indicate phonetic [v], not *w*, as would be done by German speakers. Of course, Polish also uses *w* for [v], but this and other special Polish orthographic details are accounted for explicitly in our transliteration tables for language pairs that include Polish.

A thumbnail sketch of the main search algorithms for our countries and languages of interest is below, divided into conceptual classes. Recall the contents of the following fields that we have added to the original database:

Stripped_Native: Cyrillic forms with keywords stripped
Stripped_Latin: Latin (with diacritics) forms with keywords stripped
Stripped_Bare: Latin (without diacritics) forms with keywords stripped

The following abbreviations are used in the algorithms: en (English); ru (Russian); uk (Ukrainian); pl (Polish).

The language of input is the native one for the country of location: Russian/Russia, Ukrainian/Ukraine, Polish/Poland.

For Russia and Ukraine

If the input is in Latin, transliterate using the en-ru or en-uk engine, then search in the Stripped_Native field. The reason we transliterate into Cyrillic rather than just searching for the Latin is that there are many possible Latin variants for many of the entities, and only one is recorded in the database. Rendering the string back into Cyrillic neutralizes this problem.

For Poland

Search the Stripped_Latin and/or Stripped_Bare fields; if the script was indicated by the user (Extended Latin or Basic Latin) only one of these fields need be searched.

The language of input is not the native one for the country of location.

Transliterate the input into the native language using the appropriate transliteration engine(s). This can comprise one or two stages of transliteration. For example,

<u>One-stage transliteration:</u> The string is in Cyrillic Ukrainian but the place is located in Russia. Use the uk-ru engine to generate a Cyrillic Russian variant and search for it in the Stripped_Native field of the Russia database.

<u>Two-stage transliteration</u>: The string is in Ukrainian Latin but the place is in Russia. Use the en-uk engine to generate a Cyrillic Ukrainian variant, then use the uk-ru engine on that output to generate a Cyrillic Russian

variant. Search for the Cyrillic Russian variant in the Stripped_Native field of the Russia database.

An important aspect of our transliteration strategy is to permit many different transliterations of certain letters and letter combinations. This reflects the fact that: (a) a user might be searching for something heard, not written, in which case he will render it phonetically, and (b) a user cannot be expected to always follow canonical transliteration schemes, which can never be agreed upon anyway.

Consider the following Polish place names and how they might sound to a speaker of English [ ] or Russian { }.

Bóbrka [Bubrka] {Бубрка}
Bartężek [Bartenzhek / Bartezhek] {Бартенжек / Бартежек}
Bądze [Bondze] {Бондзе}

If the user were conveying these place name based on what he heard, he would likely use the search strings above. However if he saw the name in print, he might decide simply to ignore the diacritics, ending up with a different inventory of search strings. For this reason, our transliteration tables contain many target possibilities for many of the source letters and letter combinations: e.g., Polish *ó* can be rendered as English *u* or *o*, and as Russian *y* or *o*; similarly, Polish *ą* can be rendered as English *on, om* or *o*, and as Russian *ом, он* or *о*.

Consider the following example of 2-stage transliteration. Russian Latin input is used to search for the Polish place name *Byczoń*. This ends with a palatalized *n,* which can be represented in Russian Latin as *n'* and in Russian Cyrillic as *нь*. However, it is common to leave out the apostrophe indicating palatalization when using Russian Latin (and many English speakers do not hear the palatalization to begin with), which means that Russian Latin *n* can be intended to mean either a palatalized (*нь*) or an unpalatalized (*н*) letter.

The algorithm called when a Russian Latin string is used to search for a place in Poland is first to transliterate from Russian Latin to Russian Cyrillic, then to transliterate from Russian Cyrillic to Polish. The possibility that palatalization will not be indicated in the original Latin string must be handled either in the Russian Latin to Russian Cyrillic transliteration, in which case every *n* can mean *н* or *нь*, or in the Russian Cyrillic to Polish transliteration, in which case every *н* must be understood as either *n* or *ń*. Clearly, if we insisted that people input every string "correctly", we could circumvent some such problems; however, this would be unrealistic and not in the service of users. In short, extensive system testing suggested the need for far more transliteration correspondences than those that would reflect typical, canonical transliteration schemes.

The reason why our search application does not suffer from a one-to-many transliteration scheme is that there is no need for exactly one ouput from the transliteration engine: all of the generated strings can be searched for the in database and typically only one of them is found. Many generated candidates represent impossible strings in the target language, which could be filtered out by language-specific contextual rules that we did not, however, develop for this prototype. If the approach were expanded to many more languages and countries, however, we might need to prune the output results in order to not generate false positives. In our testing so far we have not had problems with false positives, and even if we did, this search application has a person as the end user, and that person could filter out the false positives using the inventory of features returned for each hit. Here we touch on an important aspect of this – or any – application: it must be catered to what it is supposed to do, with development efforts targeted at namely those goals. For this application, robustly finding matches in the database is more important than generating a single answer for multi-stage transliteration.

Steps 11-12. If the FC or DSG features are provided, these are used to prune the search results. They could alternatively have been used to constrain the search at the outset.

4.5. Additional Search Strategies

The two additional search buttons permit searching the Wikipedia-database directly and searching the main database without keyword processing or transliteration. The latter is a slower search in which all relevant fields are searched: Full_Name, Full_Name_ND, Stripped_Latin, Stripped_Bare and, for Russia and Ukraine, Native and Native_Stripped. One situation in which the latter search strategy might be useful is the following: A user knows that his search string includes a word that looks like a keyword but is not; however, he cannot block keyword interpretation by entering the entity's correct DSG because he does not know it. In this case, seeking an exact string match is a better search strategy.

4.6. New Possibilities Provided by the GeoMatch Search Strategy

Using the GeoMatch search strategy a user has the following search support not provided by the GEOnet Names Server (GNS):

- He can provide a search string in one language for an entity located in a place having a different native language.
- He can provide a search string that contains the main search word(s) in one language/script and a keyword in another language/script and still have the appropriate keyword interpretation carried out.
- He can provide search strings in any language, even those not explicitly targeted in this application, since the Wikipedia-database results cover a wide range of languages.
- He can receive not only the geographical information from the original GNDB but also multi-lingual variants and their language attributions.
- He can constrain the search not only using the seed database features but also using language and script.

4.7. Evaluation

We attempted to evaluate GeoMatch by randomly selecting entities from each country database and searching for them using all possible language/script combinations; however, the results were not indicative of the progress made due to the nature of the data and the scope of the project. GeoMatch was a small prototype project aimed at developing algorithms, not cleaning databases. As with any large databases, those for

Russia, Ukraine and Poland presented challenges related to inconsistency and underspecification of data. For example:

- Although the Full_Form fields are supposed to contain strings in the language of the given country (albeit in Latin), strings in many other languages and scripts are scattered throughout, not indicated as such using the available Language Code (LC) field
- Compiling the inventory of keywords and their DSG correspondences was a big job, and we still have not achieved complete coverage (especially in terms of finding all "meaningful" DSG correspondences for each keyword)
- There are some outstanding errors in our initial one-to-one Cyrillic transliteration for population of the Native field that can only be hand corrected due to actual ambiguities.

Using less formal, glass-box evaluation methods, we became convinced that the algorithms show a lot of promise and that proof of concept was achieved. However, further evaluation will need to wait for a continuation of the project, when the abovementioned trivial but evaluation-affecting problems have been resolved.

As concerns the evaluation of the Wikipedia aspect of the work, numerically, the results might seem like a drop in the bucket, with around 1 in 25 being found. For each hit, a subset of the languages represented in Wikipedia provided a variant. However, it is important to note that most geographical entities that have multi-lingual *translations* (which are idiosyncratic) rather than *transliterations* (which follow rules) are the historically more important, well-known places (like *Moscow*), which are likely to be accounted for in Wikipedia, making the Wikipedia supplements extremely valuable. Moreover, the Wikipedia results show proof of concept that using on-line resources either to gather or to vet posited variants is realistic and useful.

However, even when an entity is found in Wikipedia, that is not a guarantee that it refers to the intended place. It is possible that translation/transliteration decisions will be different for different types of proper names that are rendered identically in English. Table 4 shows an example from Russian, in which the English string *Jordan* is translated/transliterated in three different ways for different types of entities.

Table 4. Various renderings of *Jordan* in Russian.

English	*Gloss*	*Russian (Cyrillic)*	*Russian (back transliterated)*
Jordan	a country	Иордания	Iordanija
Jordan	a river	Иордан	Iordan
Jordan	a person	Джордан	Dzhordan

We provide back transliterations in column 4, using one of the many Russian-English transliteration schemes, simply to orient readers not familiar with Cyrillic as to the type of morphological and phonetic distinctions being conveyed. This particular example will not prove problematic for our current engine because our current engine only accepts exact matches of Wikipedia head entries, and the head entries differ for each of the entities, as shown in Table 5.

Table 5. Wikipedia head entries that include the word *Jordan.*

English, as in Wikipedia	*Russian (Cyrillic), as in Wikipedia*	*Russian (back transliterated)*
Jordan	Иордания	Iordanija
Jordan River	Иордан (река)	Iordan (reka)
Neil Jordan	Джордан, Нил	Dzhordan, Nil

However, we can imagine that there could be cases in which identical head entries – be they composed of a single word or multiple words – could have different renderings in a given language when referring to different types of entities. In addition, this problem will be met with more frequently when expand our Wikipedia matches to include substrings: for example, if Wikipedia did not have an entry for *Jordan* but did have an entry for *Jordan River*, our engine could hypothesize that the rendering of *Jordan* would be the same when used independently as when used in collocation *Jordan River*. While this strategy will very often work, it clearly will not always work and will require external attestation, as by corpus search.

The second problem is that authors of Wikipedia pages do not always precisely agree as to how to represent the head entries. Table 5 shows two such cases: the Russian equivalent of *Jordan River* has the word for 'river' in parentheses, and the Russian equivalent of Neil Jordan has the first and last names reversed with a comma in between. Another example is that the English entry for *Los Angeles* uses the head entry *Los Angeles, California* whereas the Russian equivalent just lists the name of the city, *Лос-Анджелес*, without the state. Parsing and semantic analysis of the head entries in each of the linked languages would be the optimal method of detecting such lacks of parallelism. The algorithms for such parsing and analysis are certainly less complex than those needed for the typical unconstrained named entity recognition task, in which detecting the span of the named entity in open text and determining its semantic class (e.g., person vs. organization) are central. The work needed to clean the results of the Wikipedia extraction task is, therefore, more a matter of development than research, since the parser and semantic analyzer for each language need to be parameterized to include the correct inventory of generic terms (not only for geographic entities), relevant word order constraints, and perhaps a search of other named entities in the language to detect things like the state 'California' being appended to the city 'Los Angeles' in the example above.

We did not attempt to vet place names using a traditional Web search engine – something that certainly could have been done. However, vetting variants that way would not have provided cross-linguistic variants, so finding entities in Wikepedia would be preferable.

As concerns comparing GeoMatch with other systems, the best locus of comparison is NewsExplorer (http://press.jrc.it/NewsExplorer/home/en/latest.html). NewsExplorer clusters around 15,000 news articles a day in 40 languages, extracting and matching up named entities across languages and using them to populate a large multi-lingual database [20], [21]. Although this system is very relevant to the work reported here, it does not supercede this work for three reasons. First, the NewsExplorer database is not publicly available, though some search functions are. Second, the reported methods are not sufficiently detailed to make them truly reproducible: e.g., only 9 of 30 "substitution rules" that were found useful for transliteration tasks are described. Third, the system does not solve several kinds of problems that our development efforts are seeking to address. For example, the methods implemented by NewsExplorer require that the search string be a multi-word entity in order to cut down on spurious results; however, many (perhaps, even, the majority of) geographical entities are single-word entities. So the goals pursued by GeoMatch and NewsExplorer are quite similar, but different methods are employed that exploit different available resources and processors.

4.8. How to Extend the Coverage of the GeoMatch System

Knowledge-based systems that cover only a subset of a larger problem bear the burden of proof that they can be expanded to cover the whole problem space in finite time and with finite resources. Let us consider the ideal for the environment under discussion here and how the work already accomplished will support that.

1. The geographical databases for all countries of the world should be automatically provided with a reasonably confident native-script variant that could be validated over time using digital resources. Our current transliteration engine can accept transliteration tables for any language pairs as long as they are in UTF-8. (Recall that it requires no language-specific rules.) Since the original Latinization of place names used when building the GNS resource was supposed to have been done using a single transliteration system for each language, there should not be too much spurious ambiguity. Relatively fast analysis of the output of automatic transliteration can be followed either by improvement of the transliteration tables and rerunning of the data, or by global changes to the transliterated variants to correct recurring problems. Idiosyncratic aspects will naturally need to be hand corrected.
2. Attested multi-lingual variants for entities in all countries should be extracted from resources like Wikipedia and stored as a database supplement. The success of this task, of course, depends entirely on what the world community decides to enter into Wikipedia or what can be found on sites reporting news, current events, etc.
3. An inventory of keywords in all languages, along with their valid DSG associations, should be compiled. Although creating a full inventory of keywords that might represent the hundreds of DSGs would take some time, particularly as one might have to be a specialist to tell them apart, covering the most prominent 100 or so would be very fast for a native speaker. Such an inventory could be expanded over time.
4. The keyword stripping algorithm should be amended, if necessary, to cover language-specific orderings of "meaningful" keywords (e.g., in the string *River ABC Meadow*, would River or Meadow be the keyword for the given language?).
5. Multi-lingual access to any of the country databases should be supported so that a user could, e.g., type in a string in Bulgarian when looking for a place name in Turkey. This task is the most complex, but it seems that the complexity could be moderated using the notion of Language Hubs, which would be not unlike airport hubs: just as one does not need to be able to fly directly from every city to every city, one does not need to have a transliteration engine from every language to every language. Certain languages could act as hubs, permitting "translation passage" to and from a large number of languages, not unlike what is done linguistically at the United

Nations. A given language might have access to one hub (e.g., R3) or more than one hub (e.g., A2).

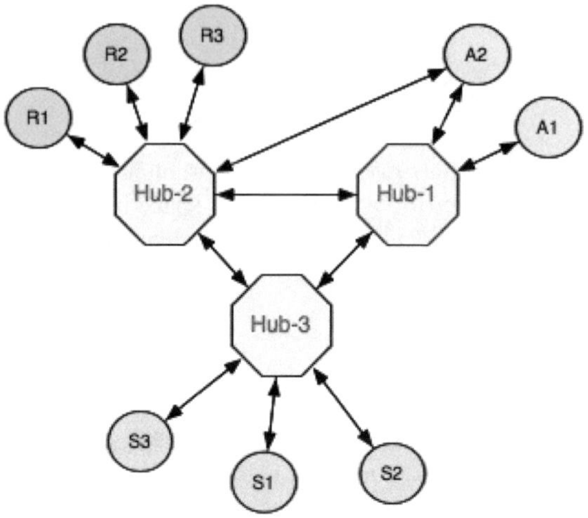

Figure 6. Using language hubs to expand GeoMatch.

Language hubs should be chosen with practical considerations in mind like the level of international prominence, how closely the spelling in the language reflects the phonetics, and how many other languages might readily feed into the given hub. Of course, this is simply a preliminary suggestion, the details of which would require further study.

5. Final Thoughts

The systems described above, Boas II and GeoMatch, seek to support proper name recognition for a wide variety of languages. Boas II provides the infrastructure to quickly ramp up a proper name recognizer for any language with no external resources needed. GeoMatch serves as an example of how an available knowledge base that was not initially developed to serve NLP can be expanded and leveraged to support multi-lingual language processing. These enabling technologies could be exploited in applications ranging from question answering to machine translation to the automatic generation of object or event profiles through the mining of multi-lingual text sources. For the purposes of this volume, the import of these systems lies in the fact that are as applicable for low- and middle-density languages as they are for high-density languages.

Acknowledgements

This work was supported by two grants from the United States Department of Defense.

References Cited

[1] Bennett, Scott W., Aone, Chinatsu Aone and Lovell, Craig. 1997. Learning to tag multilingual texts through observation. *Proceedings of the Second Conference on Empirical Methods in Natural Language Processing.*

[2] Berners-Lee, T., Fielding, R & Masinter. L 2005. Uniform Resource Identifier (URI): Generic Syntax. The Internet Society. Available at http://www.gbiv.com/protocols/uri/rfc/rfc3986.html.

[3] Bickel, Daniel M., Richard Schwartz and Ralph M. Weischedel. 1999. An algorithm that learns what's in a name. *Machine Learning* 34(1-3): 211-231.

[4] Chinchor, Nancy. 1997. MUC-7 Named Entity Recognition Task Definition. Version 3.5, September 17, 1997. Available at http://www-nlpir.nist.gov/related_projects/muc/proceedings/ne_task.html.

[5] Coates-Stephens S. 1993. *The Analysis and Acquisition of Proper Names for the Understanding of Free Text.* Hingham, MA: Kluwer Academic Publishers.

[6] Cucerzan, Silviu and David Yarowsky. 1999. Language independent named entity recognition combining morphological and contextual evidence. *Proceedings, 1999 Joint SIGDAT Conference on Empirical Methods in NLP and Very Large Corpora*, pp. 90-99.

[7] Grishman, Ralph. 1995. Where's the syntax? The New York University MUC-6 System. *Proceedings of the Sixth Message Understanding Conference.*

[8] Ishida, R. 2006. An Introduction to Multilingual Web Addresses. W3C Architecture Domain. Available at http://www.w3.org/International/articles/idn-and-iri/.

[9] Karkaletsis, Vangelis, Georgios Paliouras, Georgios Petasis, Natasa Manousopoulou, Constantine D. Spyropoulos. 1999. Named-Entity recognition from Greek and English texts. *Journal of Intelligent and Robotic Systems* 26 (2): 123-135.

[10] Màrquez, Lluís, Adrià de Gispert, Xavier Carreras, and Lluís Padró. 2003. Low-cost named entity classification for Catalan: Exploiting multilingual resources and unlabeled data. *Proceedings of the ACL 2003 Workshop on Multilingual and Mixed-language Named Entity Recognition*, pp. 25-32.

[11] McDonald, D. 1996. Internal and external evidence in the identification and semantic categorization of proper names. In B. Boguraev and J. Pustejovsky, editors, *Corpus Processing for Lexical Acquisition*, pp. 21-39.

[12] McShane, Marjorie, Sergei Nirenburg and Ron Zacharski. Mood and modality: Out of theory and into the fray. 2004. *Natural Language Engineering* 19(1): 57-89.

[13] McShane, Marjorie and Sergei Nirenburg. 2003. Blasting open a choice space: Learning inflectional morphology for NLP. *Computational Intelligence* 19(2): 111-135.

[14] McShane, Marjorie and Sergei Nirenburg. 2003. Parameterizing and eliciting text elements across languages for use in natural language processing systems. *Machine Translation* 18(2): 129-165.

[15] McShane, Marjorie, Sergei Nirenburg, Jim Cowie and Ron Zacharski. 2002. Embedding knowledge elicitation and MT systems within a single architecture. *Machine Translation* 17(4):271-305.

[16] McShane, Marjorie and Ron Zacharski. 2005. User-extensible on-line lexicons for language learning. Working Paper #05-05, Institute for Language and Information Technologies, University of Maryland Baltimore County.
Available at http://ilit.umbc.edu/ILIT_Working_Papers/ILIT_WP_05-05_Boas_Lexicons.pdf.

[17] McShane, Marjorie, Ron Zacharski, Sergei Nirenburg, Stephen Beale. 2005. The Boas II Named Entity Elicitation System. Working Paper 08-05, Institute of Language and Information Technologies, University of Maryland Baltimore County.
Available at http://ilit.umbc.edu/ILIT_Working_Papers/ILIT_WP_08-05_Boas_II.pdf.

[18] Mikheev, Andrei, Marc Moens and Claire Grover. 1999. Named entity recognition without gazetteers. *Proceedings of EACL '99.*

[19] Nirenburg, S. 1998. Project Boas: "A linguist in the box" as a multi-purpose language resource. *Proceedings of the First International Conference on Language Resources and Evaluation*, Granada, Spain.

[20] Pouliquen, B, Steinberger, R, Ignat, C. & de Groeve, T. 2004. Geographical Information Recognition and Visualisation in Texts Written in Various Languages. *Proceedings of the 19th Annual ACM Symposium on Applied Computing (SAC'2004), Special Track on Information Access and Retrieval (SAC-IAR),* vol. 2, pp. 1051-1058. Nicosia, Cyprus, 14 - 17 March 2004.

[21] Pouliquen, B., Steinberger, R, Ignat, C., Temnikova, I, Widiger, A, Zaghouani, W & Zizka, J. 2005. Multilingual person name recognition and transliteration. *Journal CORELA - Cognition, Représentation, Langage.*

[22] Wakao, T., R. Gaizauskas and Y. Wilks. 1996. Evaluation of an algorithm for the recognition and classification of proper names. *Proceedings of COLING-96.*

Language Engineering for Lesser-Studied Languages
S. Nirenburg (Ed.)
IOS Press, 2009

doi:10.3233/978-1-58603-954-7-117

Bi- and Multilingual Electronic Dictionaries: Their Design and Application to Low- and Middle-Density Languages*

Ivan A DERZHANSKI[1]
Department of Mathematical Linguistics, Institute of Mathematics and Informatics, Bulgarian Academy of Sciences

Abstract. This paper covers the fundamentals of the design, implementation and use of bi- and multilingual electronic dictionaries. I also touch upon the Bulgarian experience, past and present, in creating electronic dictionaries, as well as specialised tools for their development, within several international projects.

Keywords. electronic dictionaries, bilingual dictionaries, multilingual dictionaries, low- and middle-density languages

> Almansor was expected, on entering, to give the Oriental salutation of peace, which the professor responded to with great solemnity. He would then motion to the young man to seat himself by his side, and begin a mixture of Persian, Arabic, Coptic and other languages, under the belief that it was a learned Oriental conversation. Near him would be standing one of his servants, holding a large book. This was a dictionary, and when the old gentleman was at a loss for a word, he would make a sign to his slave, hastily open the volume, find what he wanted, and continue his conversation.
>
> —Wilhelm Hauff, 'The History of Almansor'
> (translated by Herbert Pelham Curtis)

Introduction

Lexicography is one of the oldest branches of linguistics, whose history, according to a widespread view, begins with dictionaries of Sumerian and Akkadian compiled as early as 2600 BCE. It is also one of the branches best visible to the general public, since few products of linguistic research are so widely known and used as dictionaries. Therefore it has a prominent place among the linguistic disciplines.

The relations of lexicography and linguistic theory are manifold. On one hand, lexicography *requires* linguistic theory as a source of analysis and methodology; but it also serves as a touchstone, because what can be represented in the dictionary must have been studied, understood and formalised to a sufficient extent. On the other hand, lexicography *supports* linguistic theory by recording its results in a tangible and intuitive form and by providing material for further research in the form of integrated

* Several sources were used when writing this essay, most extensively [1–3].

[1] Institute of Mathematics and Informatics, Bulgarian Academy of Sciences, bl. 8 Acad G Bonchev St, 1113 Sofia, Bulgaria, email ‹iad58g@gmail.com›.

information about linguistic objects. This is especially important when dealing with a language that has not been the object of much scientific scrutiny.

The advent of computer technology in the late 20th century has brought forth a new kind of reference resource – the electronic dictionary – and it is growing in popularity rapidly as the information technologies permeate linguistic research and everyday life. It differs from the paper dictionary in medium, but also in other important ways. What is it really, and how is it designed and created?

1. Lexicography: an Overview

Since dictionaries of all kinds have some things in common, we shall discuss the concept of a dictionary and the typology of dictionaries before we get to the specific features of electronic bi- and multilingual dictionaries.

1.1. Dictionaries

A dictionary is a list of linguistic units (typically words or, less commonly, multi-word expressions) established in a language system as represented by the usage of a certain community.[2] Every linguistic unit listed in the dictionary is the **headword** of an **entry**, which also contains information on the headword, further subdivided into

- orthographic, including
  - another graphic presentation (in languages with more than one script),
  - hyphenation (if hard to predict),
- phonetic, including
  - standard pronunciation (ideally in full for every word if the orthography is not phonetic, otherwise for those parts that deviate from the rules),
  - recognised (acceptable, deprecated but known) variation,
- grammatical, including
  - part of speech and agreement class (e.g., gender),
  - valency and subcategorisation (case governed by a preposition, transitivity of a verb, regular co-occurrence with other words),
  - inflexional class (declension or conjugation),
  - a small selection of inflected forms serving to reconstruct the paradigm,
  - derived words,
- semantic, including
  - one or more definitions with comments and examples of use,
  - synonyms, antonyms, meronyms, hyponyms and hypernyms,
- stylistic (domain, register of usage, frequency, cultural notes),
- historical (date of first recorded use, date of last recorded use if obsolete),
- etymological (original form and meaning, language of origin and language whence borrowed if a loanword).

---

[2] In extreme cases this is a community of one, e.g., a single author. But it must be remembered that in all other cases the language system is heterogeneous to one degree or the other, and at the other extreme there are dictionaries which list headwords not of one, but of several related language systems, such as dialects (especially of unwritten languages with no single standard) or diachronic stages of the development of a language over an extended period, labelling each featured word as pertaining to some but not the others.

In most dictionaries the headword is presented in its **citation form**, conventionally chosen by the language's grammatical tradition and its speakers' intuition as the form of the lexeme or idiom that is least marked and best suited to represent it. Occasionally (in particular, but not exclusively, in dictionaries of Semitic languages) the headword is a root and the words derived from it are headwords of subentries. (This has a parallel in phraseological dictionaries, which frequently group idiomatic expressions on the basis of the most constant and prominent word in them, e.g., *(as) cross/sulky/surly as a bear with a sore head* and *catch the bear before you sell his skin* under **bear**; this makes lookup easier, because the beginning can vary, as in this example.) Non-citation forms (esp. suppletive or otherwise morphologically aberrant ones) may be listed as headwords with references to the main entry for the citation form as an aid to the user.

Some types of dictionaries define and describe the denoted entity or phenomenon instead of (or in addition to) the headword.

The information within the entry is arranged and ordered in a certain way designed to optimise the use of the dictionary. With the same purpose the definitions should comply with several other requirements:

- standardisation: like things should be rendered alike throughout the dictionary, so that each **lexicographic type** (group of words with shared linguistically relevant properties) is treated in a uniform manner,
- simplicity: the wording should be plain, precise and unambiguous,
- economy: if possible, the definition should be laconic rather than verbose,
- completeness: all relevant meanings and uses should be covered, and each word should be given an exhaustive **lexicographic portrait** (characterisation of its linguistically relevant properties which set it apart from the rest).

It should be kept in mind that complete coverage of a living language, although sometimes claimed by lexicographers, is unattainable. Therefore the choice of words and meanings that are featured necessarily reflects the lexicographer's standards and considerations, theoretical views and perhaps aesthetic, moral and ideological values, even if the dictionary strives to be descriptive rather than prescriptive (or proscriptive). Nearly all dictionaries limit their attention to what is deemed right, although some list frequently misspelt words, for example, with references to the correct spellings.[3]

The entries in the dictionary are nearly always put in a predetermined order, which enables conventional search for headwords. In the most common case the order is **semasiological**—in a canonical lexicographic order[4] by the orthographic representation (or occasionally the transcribed pronunciation) of the headword; entries in which these representations of the headwords coincide (i.e., homographs) are usually ordered as the same words would be in another dictionary of the same language, e.g., one using a different script (in a character dictionary of Japanese—as they would be in a phonetic dictionary), by part of speech or by frequency. In some dictionaries the arrangement is **onomasiological**—by subject matter, so that the user searches not for a form of representation but for a semantic field, then perhaps for a subfield, etc., and the emphasis is not on the definition of the concept but on its classification and position in

[3] For example, as pointed out in [4], a medical dictionary can usefully feature the frequent misspelling *flegmon* with a pointer to the correct *phlegmon*.

[4] That is, alphabetically if the script is an alphabet; if not, there are other strategies (there exist, for example, several popular schemes for ordering Chinese characters, all of which use the number of strokes and the lexicographic ordering of certain parts of the character).

a taxonomy.[5] Other types of specialised dictionaries arrange the material by **frequency** or in other less common ways.

In a folio edition there customarily are conventions regarding the use of various typefaces, capitalisation, special symbols and labels etc. to identify the various parts of the entry and kinds of information in it. The set of rules and methods used when composing the entries forms the **metalanguage** of the dictionary.

In most dictionaries the entries are supplemented by **auxiliary material** (front and back matter). Part of this material explains the purpose and specificity of the dictionary by telling the history of its compilation, naming the intended audience, the criteria for selecting the headwords and the sources of material. The rest, which facilitates the use of the dictionary, usually includes a list of abbreviations, annotation symbols and other conventions, an explanation of the ordering, a description of the structure of the entry, and sometimes a concise reference grammar, grammar tables, lists of special classes of lexical items (proper names, chemical elements, military ranks and the like), a corpus of sample texts (especially worthwhile for poorly documented languages), indices which enable search in non-canonical ways (e.g., an alphabetical index in a thesaurus, a character index in an alphabetical romanised dictionary of Chinese), etc.

1.2. Levels of the Dictionary's Structure

Several levels of structure are distinguished in the organisation of a dictionary.

The **macrostructure** (overall, vertical or paradigmatic organisation) of the dictionary defines its nature and purpose as well as its place within the general typology of dictionaries. It includes such features as the selection of headwords, the choice of illustrations, the ordering of the entries and the metalanguage. (The part of the macrostructure that concerns the division of the content into front, body and back matter is sometimes called the **megastructure**.)

The **mesostructure** (also called **mediostructure**) includes the relations between entries within the dictionary, e.g., derivation rules and cross-references, as well as relations between entries and other entities of the dictionary, such as the grammatical description or the sample texts.

The **microstructure** (internal, horizontal or syntagmatic organisation) determines the setup of the entry, the arrangement of the information within it, the hierarchy of meanings. This concerns both the ordering of the different kinds of information and the arrangement of like entities. It is customary, for example, for the various meaning of a word to compose a tree structure, where more closely related ones are grouped together, and for meanings of the same level to be listed with the more frequent or fundamental ones first and the metaphorical and less common ones last; this optimises the search time.[6]

---

[5] Dictionaries with semasiological and onomasiological ordering may be called respectively **reader's** and **writer's** or **decoding** and **encoding** dictionaries, because of what one needs to know in order to locate an entry and what one learns from it.

[6] Anticipating things somewhat, in a translating dictionary it can also guard the user against some of the most absurd errors: I have in my collection would-be Russian lists of ingredients of biscuits claiming to contain *милая* 'darling, sweetheart' or *студень* 'galantine' and instructions to *кильватер* 'wake (of a ship)' a jumper, these being legitimate translations of the English words *honey*, *jelly* and *wash*, only not the first ones; evidently the words were looked up in a way that ignored the ordering of the meanings in the dictionary.

1.3. Structure of the Dictionary Entry

A dictionary entry consists of two parts: a **register part** (on the left) and an **interpretation part** (on the right). The register part may consist of the headword alone, but other information can also be encoded there in a way that alters the graphic form of the headword but does not prevent the eye from recognising it[7]: for example,

- vowel length, stress or tone may be marked by a diacritic that is seldom or never used for this purpose in ordinary writing (in Russian dictionaries this is an acute accent over the stressed vowel, in German a dot underneath; English dictionaries often prefer a mark after the stressed syllable, as in **proˊgress**, and some dictionaries of Japanese place a superscript digit – the identifier of the accentuation pattern – at the end of the word, as in **ikebana**^{2} with high pitch on the *e*),
- a letter may be replaced by another to mark a peculiarity of pronunciation (in some dictionaries of Italian the letter **ſ** – not used in the current orthography – as a substitute for **s** indicates that the sound is voiced),
- an initial or final part which changes in inflexion may be separated from the rest of the word by a non-orthographic character such as a vertical line (Estonian **ve|si, -e, -tt, -tte**, indicating the fact that *vesi*, *vee*, *vett*, *vette* are the four fundamental case forms of the word meaning 'water'),
- words may be broken into syllables, likewise by a non-orthographic character such as a middle dot, to show how they can be hyphenated (**pro·gress** in British English dictionaries, **prog·ress** in American ones).

The register entry also may house a label (usually a Roman or subscript Arabic numeral) whereby to differentiate the headword from its homographs. Everything else is contained in the interpretation part.

1.4. Work on the Register

The register parts of all entries together form the **register** (or **lexicon**) of the dictionary; this is the set of all linguistic units covered.

The choice of the register is a crucial part of the creation of any dictionary. It is designed once at the beginning of the development of the dictionary and can be edited when the dictionary is updated.

Designing the register means choosing the lexical material which will be included in accordance with the design criteria (a frequency no less than a predetermined minimum, productive use in derivation, use in set expressions). Available dictionaries may be employed as sources of words. A corpus of texts may also serve as a source of material or as a measure of frequency. If the language is poorly documented, words are elicited from competent speakers; in this case, of course, the question of leaving out rare words doesn't arise.

Editing the register involves adding new entries (part of this activity may be made automatic if productive derivation is made into procedures), as well as eliminating obsolete words or meanings, arbitrary short-lived neologisms and detected non-words. It may be done as a response to changes in the language, the lexicographer's knowledge or the design policies.

---

[7] It may, however, be a major obstacle for OCR. This wasn't an issue when the technique was invented.

1.5. Grammatical Dictionaries

The dictionary and the grammar are mutually complementary, mutually indispensable components of the linguistic description. The division of information between them is not always obvious. In principle the grammar describes the general rules that apply to entire categories and classes and the dictionary concerns itself with the classification and description of individual words. Words which have exceptional morphology or are key constituents in idiomatic constructions are borderline: they are normally listed in the dictionary and also mentioned in the grammar. Since dictionary and the grammar have to refer to one another, it is crucial that they should use the same concepts and terms (which can't be taken for granted in practice).

A **grammatical dictionary** (*alias* **morphological dictionary**) aims to present comprehensively the lexicon of the language (or some section thereof), as a dictionary generally does, but places the emphasis on morphology rather than semantics, enabling the conversion 'word form ↔ lemma + grammatical meaning' in both directions (identifying the **lemma** – the lexical unit – and the grammatical form or, conversely, constructing a required form of a given word). Typically each entry refers the user to one or several tables containing paradigms or rules.

This process requires a formal model of morphology, i.e., a division of the set of words into non-intersecting paradigmatic classes with algorithmically described rules for derivation and inflexion. While perhaps dispensable for English, where storing all inflected forms of a word as a list is enough for many purposes, such a model is essential for inflecting or agglutinative languages with large paradigms.

1.6. Bilingual Dictionaries

Most of what was said so far applies to **bilingual dictionaries** as well, except that in them the key portion of the interpretation part of each entry is a translation counterpart. I stop short of saying 'translation equivalent', because it seldom is. Contrary to what is often assumed, the correspondence between words of different languages is typically not one-to-one but many-to-many, both because homonymy and polysemy are a fact of any language and, perhaps more importantly, because each language has its own way of categorising the world and singling out concepts that it lexicalises.[8]

Many design choices (concerning metalanguage, register and interpretations) in a bilingual dictionary depend on whether it is **passive** (reception-oriented) or **active** (production-oriented), i.e., which of the two languages the user is expected to be more familiar with.[9] In the former case the goal is to explain the meanings of a word of the **source language** to a reader more familiar with the **target language**, the translation counterparts being merely one way of doing so (an extended description of the meaning being another, indispensable if there is no counterpart[10]); if the corresponding words in the two languages are superficially similar, such a dictionary can afford to be very

[8] This applies first and foremost to all-purpose dictionaries. In the terminology of professional fields such as the natural sciences, whose development is an international enterprise, exact one-to-one correspondences (that is, translation equivalents) are the rule, not the exception.

[9] In spite of this dichotomy, most bilingual dictionaries aim to be both reception- and production-oriented due to practical considerations (having to do with efficiency of compilation and publication).

[10] This is the case with culture-specific concepts (natural entities from where the speakers of the source language live, artefacts or customs peculiar to their way of life), but not exclusively so: *serendipity* or *wishful thinking* are notoriously resistant to translation, although the concepts are of universal relevance.

laconic, or even leave out such words altogether. In the latter case it is assumed that the user knows the source language and can identify the relevant meaning, but doesn't know the translation and, if there are several possible candidates, shall need more help in choosing the most appropriate one among them, taking into account the pragmatic as well as the semantic context. In either case more information of all kinds (grammatical, stylistic etc.) should be given on the words of the less familiar language, whether they are headwords or interpretations. Among other things, these words are naturally deemed to be in greater need of illustration through examples of use, although those are always translated into the more familiar language except in some learner's dictionaries.

A bilingual dictionary is sometimes equipped with a reverse index which makes it possible to locate entries by translations contained in them rather than the headword.

1.7. Multilingual Dictionaries

An extension of bilingual dictionaries are **multilingual dictionaries**, which are usually organised in the same general way, but with translation counterparts in two or more languages, rather than one, listed in sequence in each entry.[11] A variant (more often chosen for specialised dictionaries, e.g., of the terminology of a certain field of human endeavour) consists of numbered lists of words; the user needs to locate the word in the list for the source language and then look up the same number in the list for the required target language.

Multilingual dictionaries save shelf space, as well as lookup time in the admittedly infrequent case that one really wants to know the counterparts of a word or expression in several other languages simultaneously, and also if one often needs to translate similar documents into different languages (a reasonably common situation, and bound to become more and more frequent in this age of global communication, especially in massively multilingual societies such as the European Union). Also, adding one more language to a multilingual dictionary tends to be less labour-intensive than creating a new bilingual dictionary, thus economically more viable for languages with relatively few speakers and learners.

On the other hand, the register of a bilingual dictionary depends to some extent on the target language (words of the source language are more likely to be included if their translation might be challenging), and in light of this the design of a dictionary with several target languages presents a serious problem for the lexicographer.

2. Electronic Lexicography

The expression **electronic dictionary** started life in the last quarter of the 20th century as a term for a specialised device—a handheld computer dedicated to storing a lexical data base and performing lookup in it. The term retains this meaning, but nowadays it is also – and increasingly often – used to denote a lexical data base with associated software capable to run on an all-purpose computer.

As classical lexicography is in a complex relationship with linguistic theory, so is electronic lexicography with computational linguistics, of which electronic dictionaries are a product whilst also serving as tools and feedstock for creating other products.

[11] Occasionally the term multilingual dictionary is applied to all dictionaries of two and more languages (including bilingual ones as well), implying an opposition 'mono- : multi-'; but this is not what is meant here.

```
<entry>
<hw>цел</hw>
<gen>ж.</gen>
<struc type="Sense" n="1">
<def>Това, към което е насочена някаква дейност, към което някой се
        стреми; умисъл, намерение.</def>
<eg><q>С каква цел отиваш в града?</q></eg>
<eg><q>Вървя без цел.</q></eg>
<eg><q>Постигнах целта си.</q></eg>
<eg><q>Целта оправдава средствата.</q></eg></struc>
<struc type="Sense" n="2">
<def>Предмет или точка, в която някой стреля, към която е насочено
        определено действие, движение, удар и под.; прицел.</def>
<eg><q>Улучих целта.</q></eg></struc>
<struc type="Phrases">
<struc type="Phrase" n="1"><orth>Имам (нямам) [за] цел.</orth>
<def>стремя се (не се стремя) към нещо.</def>
<eg><q>Нямам за цел да му навредя.</q></eg></struc>
<struc type="Phrase" n="2"><orth>Попадам в целта.</orth>
<def>улучвам, умервам.</def></struc>
</struc>
<etym><lang>нем.</lang>&gt;<lang>рус.</lang></etym>
</entry>
```

Figure 1. The CONCEDE dictionary of Bulgarian: A sample lexical entry.

2.1. Types of Electronic Dictionaries

Electronic (machine-readable) dictionaries are of two main types. (Actually, three if the dictionary scanned into an aggregate of page images, infinitely durable, compact and portable but offering no other advantages over the folio edition, is also counted as type zero.)

The first type is the electronic version (retyped manually, adapted from publisher's files or OCRed) of a traditional dictionary designed for human use, stored as a text file or a data base. In addition to faster lookup, such a dictionary contains the potential for diverse forms of search at least in the headwords if not the complete entries, and an interpretation obtained from it, although designed for human reading and understanding, can be copied and pasted into a document. An electronic edition may preserve the visual markup of the paper version or add a level of logical markup consisting of tags which identify the types of information in the several parts of the entry. Such a dictionary can be made available for lookup online or stored locally and linked into other programs, so that the user can call up an entry by choosing a word in a document open, e.g., in a browser or word processor.

As an example, Figure 1 presents the entry for the noun *цел* 'goal, target' taken from an electronic dictionary of Bulgarian developed within the project CONCEDE[12] on the basis of [5]. The entry includes the headword, its gender (*ж.* for *женски* 'feminine'; this also signals that the word is a noun, since only nouns have gender as a lexical feature), definitions of two major senses (1. 'what an activity is directed towards,

[12] The EU project CONCEDE (Consortium for Central European Dictionary Encoding, 1998–2000) developed lexical data bases for six Central and Eastern European languages (Bulgarian, Czech, Estonian, Hungarian, Roumanian and Slovene).

what someone strives for; design, intent' and 2. 'an object or point at which someone shoots, towards which is an action, movement, blow etc. is directed; sight') illustrated by examples, two set expressions (lit. 'have as a goal' and 'hit the target') with definitions and a sentence exemplifying the first one, as well as brief information on the etymology of the word (German by way of Russian). The markup reflects the logical structure of the entry; the tags ('orthographic representation', 'definition', 'example', 'quote') can be translated into various forms of typographic emphasis if the entry is displayed for human perusal, but they also make it possible for the required portion of the information to be chosen automatically.

The second type are computer dictionaries as components of various applications (search engines, part-of-speech taggers, grammar checkers, information extracting and question-answering systems, machine translation systems, etc.). The interpretation parts of the entries in these must comply with a more rigid format, so that they can be used by software; they must be simpler, but at the same time more comprehensive, than those in a dictionary exclusively intended for human use, and are even more of a proof of the adequacy of the theoretical foundations of the linguistic description. The amount of information in the entries depends on the type and purpose of the application.

2.2. Advantages of Electronic Dictionaries

Electronic dictionaries have several advantages over their conventional counterparts:

1. Size is not an issue. A digital dictionary has potential for infinite growth in depth and breadth: it needn't be small, medium or large by design. Also, more indices and a more voluminous corpus can be enclosed.
2. Many purposes can be served by a single reference work (with an explanatory dictionary, a grammatical dictionary, dictionaries of synonyms, antonyms, phraseology, etymology, etc., all in one integrated linguistic system).
3. The entries can include audio-, video- and other types of unprintable material, as well as hyperlinks to other entries and to information stored on remote computers and accessible through the 'Net, in addition to their conventional content.
4. A word can be looked up by typing or pasting it into a form or selecting it in a document and invoking the dictionary by keyboard or mouse action, which is significantly faster than leafing. In the same vein, several dictionaries can be united through a shared interface, so that when a search is initiated, the system chooses which dictionary to consult on the basis of such clues as the script, or looks up the word in all dictionaries and displays the results of all the searches simultaneously.
5. Flexible full-text search (using wildcards, a combination of parameters, etc.) and presentation of its results in a user-friendly form are easy to implement.
6. Digital grammatical dictionaries can implement inflexion at least partly as procedures for morphological analysis and generation which are run upon demand, rather than tables (saving space and minimising errors) or rules applied by the user (economising human effort).
7. Easy update is possible, which also implies that can be augmented and kept up-to-date by continued distributed collective effort under the guidance of a moderator (wiki-style).

The extensibility of the electronic dictionary means that the choice of register is not a permanent decision on its coverage. None the less this choice always affects the efficiency of the design and use of the dictionary. At the pilot stage, when the entries are few, the opportune selection of headwords can make up for their paucity and broaden the spectrum of experiments available to the designers. At the production stage the importance of the good choice of entries stems from the waning observability of the waxing register.

3. Bi- and Multilingual Electronic Dictionaries

As any electronic dictionary, an electronic bilingual or multilingual dictionary may be a digitalised edition of a conventional reference work, perhaps augmented by types of information specific to this medium (recorded pronunciations, hyperlinks, full-text search, etc.). Alternatively, it may be a system of monolingual dictionaries of different languages interlinked at the level of entries.

3.1. The First Strategy: a System of Multilingual Entries

Figure 2 shows two entries from a multilingual dictionary of the Bambara language (Mali) implemented in SIL International's lexicographic system Lexique Pro. Each entry in this dictionary contains a Bambara headword with part of speech marked, glosses of its various meanings in French and English and, for some words, glosses in German, the scientific name (of a plant or animal), information on the structure or origin of the word, a category (place in a taxonomy), collocations, synonyms or associated words (e.g., **turu** 'to plant' under **jiri** 'tree', **warijɛ** 'silver' under **sanu** 'gold') and examples of use along with French and English translations. There are also entries for derivational suffixes (e.g., **-nin** diminutive), because the morphological analyses of words that contain them are hyperlinked to them.

The interface provides a browsing window where the program can display the user's choice of an alphabetical list of Bambara headwords sorted from the beginning or the end or of French, English or German glosses, or the taxonomy as a set of tree structures with the Bambara words in the leaves; a search form (with the option of searching in Bambara fields only or in all languages); and a window for the results, where a chosen entry can be presented or the entire text of the dictionary displayed and scrolled, with all Bambara words provided with hyperlinks to their entries.

This dictionary is made for the learner of Bambara who already knows one of the other two (actually three in progress) languages. Contrariwise, other dictionaries may presume one language more familiar than the rest. Several popular references (Collins Multilingual Dictionary, ABBYY Lingvo Multilingual Version) are organised as suites of independent bilingual dictionaries from the native language of the prospective user (English and Russian, respectively) to several others and back. When the interface is made so that dictionaries can be changed quickly and easily in mid-lookup, such a suite creates much of the sensation of using a genuine multilingual dictionary, in which the various translations of a word or expression are combined in a single entry.

Ala

n.

• Dieu
God
Gott

From: arabe

Ala ka kuma
parole de Dieu
word of God

A bɛ Ala bolo.
C'est dans la main de Dieu.
It's in God's hands.

jirikunanin

n.

• nim, planté souvent pour donner de l'ombre
Neem tree, often planted for shade

Azadarichta indica

Morph.: **jiri-kuna-nin**
[lit. 'little bitter tree']

Category: Trees

Syn: **jirinin**$_1$

Figure 2. Two entries from the Lexique Pro dictionary of Bambara.

3.2. The Second Strategy: a System of Monolingual Dictionaries

The other possible way of envisaging a bilingual dictionary is as a pair of monolingual integrated linguistic systems linked by an interface which allows the user, after having located the required entry in the dictionary of one language, to move thence to the corresponding entry (or to one of several similar entries) in the dictionary of the other. This makes for a more balanced structure, as neither language is source or target by design, but becomes one or the other by virtue of the direction of the lookup. Such a bilingual linguistic system must be based on comparable monolingual corpora and a parallel bilingual corpus at the design stage, and may still be complemented by them as a ready-made product.

In the same line of thought a multilingual electronic dictionary can be envisaged as a set of pairs of bilingual dictionaries, so that there is no single default familiar or default unfamiliar language. But implementing it as such in practice is extravagant, because this requires $n \times (n-1)$ pairs of languages in an n-lingual dictionary. A more efficient solution is to use an **interlingua** – a pivot language – which reduces the number of pairs to $2n$ (from each target language to the interlingua and back). The translation is then not from source to target but from source through interlingua to target, although this obliquity must remain hidden from the user and, needless to say, must cause the least possible loss or distortion of meaning. The interlingua may be

- a subset of one of the featured languages,
- a natural language other than the featured languages,
- an artificial but speakable language (such as Esperanto),
- a semantic interlingua, whose words are references to an ontology of concepts.

An increasingly popular strategy for building a multilingual dictionary on the basis of an ontology is exemplified by the EuroWordNet system, an assembly of semantic networks for several European languages constructed upon a common ontology and equipped with an interlingual index. This strategy actually integrates a synonym and a

претовар|я, -иш *vp.* v. **претоварям**
претоп|я, -иш *vp.* v. **претапям, претопявам**
претопява|м, -ш *vi.* przetapiać; *przen.* asymilować
претор, -и *m hist.* **pretor** *m*
преториан|ец, -ци *m* pretorianin *m*
преториански *adi.* pretoriański
I преточ|а, -иш *vp.* v. **претакам**
II преточ|а, -иш *vp.* v. **II преточвам**
I преточвам v. **претакам**
II преточва|м, -ш *vi.* ostrzyć nadmiernie
претрайва|м, -ш *vi.* v. **претрая**
претра|я, -еш *vp. lud.* przetrwać
претрива|м, -ш *vi.* przecierać, przecinać, przepiłowywać;
    ~м праговете wycieram (obijam) cudze progi
претри|я, -еш *vp.* v. **претривам**

[b]претовар|я, -иш[/b] [i]vp.[/i] v. [b]претоварям[/b]
[b]претоп|я, -иш[/b] [i]vp.[/i] v. [b]претапям, претопявам[/b]
[b]претопява|м, -ш[/b] [i]vi.[/i] przetapiać; [i]przen.[/i] asymilować
[b]претор, -и[/b] [i]m[/i] [i]hist.[/i] [b]pretor[/b] [i]m[/i]
[b]преториан|ец, -ци[/b] [i]m[/i] pretorianin [i]m[/i]
[b]преториански[/b] [i]adi.[/i] pretoriański
[b]I преточ|а, -иш[/b] [i]vp.[/i] v. [b]претакам[/b]
[b]II преточ|а, -иш[/b] [i]vp.[/i] v. [b]II преточвам[/b]
[b]I преточвам[/b] v. [b]претакам[/b]
[b]II преточва|м, -ш[/b] [i]vi.[/i] [b]ostrzyć nadmiernie[/b]
[b]претрайва|м, -ш[/b] [i]vi.[/i] v. [b]претрая[/b]
[b]претра|я, -еш[/b] [i]vp.[/i] [i]lud.[/i] przetrwać
[b]претрива|м, -ш[/b] [i]vi.[/i] przecierać, przecinać, przepiłowywać;
    [b]~м праговете[/b] wycieram (obijam) cudze progi
[b]претри|я, -еш[/b] [i]vp.[/i] v. [b]претривам[/b]

Figure 3. The Bulgarian–Polish dictionary: an excerpt after OCR and proofreading (above) and after the first round of markup (below).

translation system: the lexical material in each network is structured in terms of **synsets** (sets of synonymous words), and the shared indexing permits transition from any synset to its counterparts in other languages.

3.3. A Case Study: Bulgarian–Polish Electronic Lexicography

The Department of Mathematical Linguistics of the Bulgarian Academy of Sciences Institute of Mathematics and Informatics is currently involved in the joint project 'Semantics and Contrastive Linguistics with a Focus on Multilingual Electronic Dictionaries' with the Institute of Slavic Studies of the Polish Academy of Sciences. The practical purpose of this project is to develop bilingual electronic resources for Bulgarian and Polish, including Bulgarian–Polish and Polish–Bulgarian digital dictionaries. It is anticipated that at a later stage multilingual electronic dictionaries will be created by adding Ukrainian, Lithuanian and other languages to the programme.

The first resource for developing the Bulgarian–Polish and Polish–Bulgarian dictionaries will be the most recent printed bilingual dictionaries ([6] and [7], each of a volume of approximately 60 000 words and of comparable coverage). They have been scanned and scheduled for OCR, proofreading and mark-up.

Figure 3 shows a sample excerpt from the Bulgarian–Polish dictionary [6] after OCR and proofreading and after the first round of markup, at which the formatting (boldface, italics) is replaced by tags. Subsequent rounds will structure the entries on the basis of the grammatical and stylistic annotation (which here consists of a mixture of abbreviated Latin and Polish words, as the folio edition is primarily meant for a Polish user) and translate the visual tags into logical ones ('grammatical info', 'usage info', etc.). Also, the marking of stress on all Bulgarian words (a casualty of the OCR) will be restored.

Unfortunately, these dictionaries were published two decades ago, and are already dated due to the changes in technology, economy and politics of this period, which have put a large number of expressions out of use and introduced an even larger number of new ones. Besides, many of the words in the dictionaries were arguably obsolete already at the time of publication, and there are even some of which it is questionable whether they ever existed or are artefacts of the compilation.

These circumstances (which make the work on the digital dictionaries all the more expedient) emphasise the significance of the second resource, a bilingual digital corpus of contemporary usage. This corpus will help to determine what words and meanings are actually in use and also (more importantly at the early stage of the work) to select those that are particularly frequent and therefore good candidates for use in a small-scale experimental version of the dictionary. It will be created within the project, with an initial size estimated at 300,000 word forms, taken partly from fiction texts and partly from non-fiction ones.

The fiction part will be composed of three sections: Bulgarian original texts and their translations into Polish, Polish original texts and their translations into Bulgarian, and texts translated from other languages into both Bulgarian and Polish. The texts from each of the first two sections can be expected to have a bias towards their original languages (that is, the originals will better represent the language they are in than the translations will), therefore a balance between them is very desirable. The third section should be neutral in this regard, but of a lesser comparative value, as two translations from a third language are predictably more distant from one another. An obvious problem with this part of the corpus is that most fiction that is readily available as machine-readable files (from publishers or on the internet) predates the two dictionaries.

The non-fiction texts will include documents of the European Union (this takes advantage of the fact that the EU, as a matter of policy, makes its entire documentation available in the official languages of all member states, including Polish and Bulgarian) and other material added depending on availability.

3.4. Adding Procedurality

An interesting question which arises in connexion of the creation of a bilingual digital dictionary is the representation of certain meanings which are frequently lexicalised in one language by means of derivational categories but are expressed by periphrasis in the other.

Let us consider mode of action[13] as an example. Mode of action, an aspectual derivational category which quantifies the event or specifies such features as

[13] This expression is a translation of the German term *Aktionsart*, the use of which for a derivationally motivated semantic classification of verbs recognised in particular in the Slavic languages and related to, but different from, aspect goes back to [8].

completion or recurrence, spatial orientation, intensity or degree of involvement of the arguments, is a morphosemantic trait shared by all Slavic languages, which also tend to agree on its actual realisation (prefixation, primarily: Polish **leżeć** 'lie, recline', **poleżeć** 'lie *for a while, briefly*'; Bulgarian **лежа** and **полежа** dto. respectively). However, its productivity varies from one language to the other. It is common knowledge that Bulgarian has made up for the simplification of its nominal morphology (the loss of morphological case) by enriching the derivational and inflexional morphology of its verb. Even a cursory look at a traditional Bulgarian–Polish dictionary[14] reveals large groups of entries where the most common expression of a certain mode of action in Polish is periphrastic, as with the attenuative or delimitative[15] in these examples:

погазва|м, -ш *vi.* deptać, brodzić *(trochę)*
погор|я, -иш *vp.* popalić się *(trochę, krótko)*; [...]
погъделичква|м, -ш *vi.* łaskotać, łechtać *(trochę, lekko)*
погълта|м, -ш *vp.* łyknąć *trochę*
погърмява|м, -ш *vi.* pogrzmiewać, grzmieć *od czasu do czasu*, [...]
подадва|м, -ш *vi. lud.* dawać *po trochę, od czasu do czasu*

('trample; burn; tickle; swallow; thunder; give *a little, occasionally*').

This happens particularly often as a result of polyprefixation (that is, derivation by adding a preverb – in this case **по-** – to an already prefixed verb), which is not alien to Polish (or any other Slavic language), but is particularly well developed in Bulgarian:

позагаз|я, -иш *vp.* zabrnąć, wpaść w ciężkie położenie *(trochę)*
позагатн|а, -еш *vp.* napomknąć, wspomnieć *mimochodem*
позагледа|м, -ш *vp.* spoglądnąć, spojrzeć, popatrzyć *(trochę, od czasu do czasu)*
понатежава|м, -ш *vi.* stawać się *trochę* cięższym, ciążyć *trochę*
понатисн|а, -еш *vp.* nacisnąć, przycisnąć *trochę*
понатовар|я, -иш *vp.* naładować *trochę*, obciążyć, obarczyć *trochę*

('get into trouble; hint; stare; weigh down; press; load *a little*').

In these entries the italicised adverbial modifiers render the meaning of the mode of action of the Bulgarian verb. It may also be a construction with the lexical meaning expressed as a gerund and the mode of action (here transgressive) as the main verb:

претъркаля|м, -ш *vp.* przetoczyć, *przesunąć* tocząc

('roll *over*, *shift* rolling'),

or the lexical meaning as a subordinate infinitive and the mode of action (definitive) as the main verb:

допушва|м, -ш *vi. kończyć* palić, dopalać np. papierosa
допява|м, -ш *vi.* dośpiewywać, *kończyć* śpiewać
доработва|м, -ш *vi. kończyć* pracować, *kończyć* opracowywać

('*finish* smoking; singing; working'),

---

[14] The sample entries here and henceforth are from [6].

[15] The classification of modes of action employed here follows [9]. The attenuative ('do with low intensity') mode of action and the delimitative ('do for a short time') naturally overlap to a certain extent.

or the lexical meaning as a *nomen actionis* and the mode of action (supergressive) as the main verb again:

> **надпива|м (се), -ш** *vi.* pić więcej od innych; *prześcigać (się) w* piciu
> **надплува|м, -ш** *vp. prześcignąć w* pływaniu
> **надпрепусква|м, -ш** *vi. prześcigać (się) w* szybkiej jeździe, biegu

('*outdo (one another) in* drinking; swimming; riding').

Since prefixation (including polyprefixation) is productive in Bulgarian and new lexical units with compositional, predictable meaning are created in the flow of discourse upon demand, listing them in the lexicon is an unviable task, as well as a highly redundant one, as the examples show. A more promising approach would be to add a certain amount of procedurality to the dictionary, that is, to allow unlisted words that appear to be derived according to productive patterns to be recognised and analysed automatically, and their translations into the other language generated to be at the same time. This would require an efficient way of encoding and handling the restrictions on the application of the patterns.

Similar techniques could be applied for the treatment of evaluatives (diminutives and augmentatives), words for females, abstract nouns and other productive derivatives in the bilingual digital dictionary.

References

[1] P.G.J. van Sterkenburg (ed.), *A Practical Guide to Lexicography*, John Benjamins, 2003.

[2] В.А. Широков, *Елементи лексикографії* ('Elements of Lexicography'), Kiev, 2005.

[3] I.A. Derzhanski, L. Dimitrova and E. Sendova, Electronic Lexicography and Its Applications: the Bulgarian Experience. In: В.А. Широков (ed.), *Прикладна лінгвістика та лінгвістичні технології* ('Applied Linguistics and Linguistic Technologies'), Kiev, 2007, 111–118.

[4] R.H. Baud, M. Nyström, L. Borin, R. Evans, S. Schulz and P. Zweigenbaum, Interchanging Lexical Information for a Multilingual Dictionary. In: AMIA 2005 Symposium Proceedings, 31–35.

[5] Д. Попов (ред.), Л. Андрейчин, Л. Георгиев, Ст. Илиев, Н. Костов, Ив. Леков, Ст. Стойков, Цв. Тодоров, *Български тълковен речник* ('A Bulgarian Explanatory Dictionary'), Sofia, 1994.

[6] F. Sławski, *Podręczny słownik bułgarsko–polski z suplementem* ('Bulgarian–Polish Desk Dictionary with Supplement'), Warsaw, 1987.

[7] S. Radewa, *Podręczny słownik polsko–bułgarski z suplementem* ('Polish–Bulgarian Desk Dictionary with Supplement'), Warsaw, 1988.

[8] S. Agrell, *Aspektänderung und Aktionsartbildung beim polnischen Zeitworte* ('Aspectual Change and Formation of Modes of Action in the Polish Verb'), Lund, 1908.

[9] К. Иванова, *Начини на глаголното действие в съвременния български език* ('Modes of Verbal Action in Modern Bulgarian'), Sofia, 1974.

B. Levels of Language Processing and Applications

Language Engineering for Lesser-Studied Languages
S. Nirenburg (Ed.)
IOS Press, 2009

doi:10.3233/978-1-58603-954-7-135

Computational Morphology for Lesser-studied Languages

Kemal OFLAZER [a,1]
[a] *Sabancı University*

Abstract. Many language processing tasks such as parsing or surface generation need to either extract and process the information encoded in the words or need to synthesize words from available semantic and syntactic information. This chapter presents an overview of the main concepts in building morphological processors for natural languages, based on the finite state approach – the state-of-the-art mature paradigm for describing and implementing such systems.

Keywords. Morphology, computational morphology, finite state morphology, two-level morphology, rewrite rules, replace rules, morphotactics, morphographemics

Introduction

Words in languages encode many pieces of syntactic and semantic information. Many language processing tasks such as parsing or surface generation need to either extract and process the information encoded in the words or need to synthesize words from available semantic and syntactic information. Computational morphology aims at developing formalisms and algorithms for the computational analysis and synthesis of word forms for use in language processing applications. Applications such as spelling checking and correction, stemming in document indexing etc., also rely on techniques in computational morphology especially for languages with rich morphology. *Morphological analysis* is the process of decomposing words into their constituents. Individual constituents of a word can be used to determine the necessary information about the word as a whole and how it needs to interpreted in the given context. Such information may range from basic part-of-speech information assigned from a fixed inventory of tags to structural information consisting of the relationships between components of the word further annotated with various features and their values. *Morphological generation* synthesizes words by making sure that the components making up a word are combined properly and their interactions are properly handled.

This chapter will present an overview of the techiques for developing finite state morphological processors that can be used in part-of-speech tagging, syntactic parsing, text–to–speech, spelling checking and correction, document indexing and retrieval. The purpose of this chapter, however, is not to provide a detailed coverage of various aspects of computational morphology; the reader is referred to several recent books covering

[1]Corresponding Author: Kemal Oflazer, Sabancı University, Orhanlı, Tuzla, Istanbul, 34956, Turkey; E-mail: oflazer@sabanciuniv.edu

this topic (see e.g., Sproat [7] for a quite comprehensive treatment of computational morphology and Beesley and Karttunen [2] for an excellent exposition of finite state morphology.)

The chapter starts with a brief overview of morphology and computational morphology and then presents an overviews of recent approaches to implementing morphological processors: two-level morphology and cascaded rule systems, as a mature state-of-the-art paradigms to implement wide-coverage morphological analysers.

1. Morphology

Morphology is the study of the structure of the words and how words are formed by combining smaller units of linguistic information called *morphemes*. We will briefly summarize some preliminary notions on morphology, based on the book by Sproat [7].

Morphemes can be classified into two groups depending on how they can occur: *free morphemes* can occur by themselves as a word while *bound morphemes* are not words in their own right but have to be attached in some way to a free morpheme. The way in which morphemes are combined and the information conveyed by the morphemes and by their combination differs from language to language. Languages can be loosely classified with the following characterizations:

1. *Isolating languages* are languages which do not allow any bound morphemes to attach to a word. Mandarin Chinese with some minor exceptions is a close example of such a language.
2. *Agglutinative languages* are languages in which bound morphemes are attached to a free morpheme like "beads on a string." Turkish, Finnish, Hungarian and Swahili are examples of such languages. In Turkish, e.g., each morpheme usually conveys one piece of morphological information such as tense, agreement, case, etc.
3. *Inflectional languages* are languages where a single bound morpheme (or closely united free and bound forms) simultaneously conveys multiple pieces of information. Latin is a classical example. In the Latin word "amō" (I love), the suffix +ō expresses 1st person singular agreement, present tense, active voice and indicative mood.
4. *Polysynthetic languages* are languages which use morphology to express certain elements (such as verbs and their complements) that often appear as separate words in other languages. Sproat [7] cites certain Eskimo languages as examples of this kind of a language.

Languages employ various kinds of morphological processes to "build" the words when they are to be used in context: e.g., in a sentence:

1. *Inflectional morphology* introduces relevant information to a word so that it can be used in the syntactic context properly. Such processes do not change the part-of-speech, but add information like person and number agreement, case, definiteness, tense, aspect, etc. For instance in order to use a verb with a third person singular subject in present tense, English syntax demands that the agreement morpheme `+s` be added, e.g. "comes".

2. *Derivational morphology* produces a new word usually of a different part-of-speech category by combining morphemes. The new word is said to be *derived* from the original word. For example, the noun "sleeplessness" involves two derivations: first we derive an adjective "sleepless" from the noun "sleep", and then we derive a new noun from this intermediate adjective to create a word denoting a concept that is in some way related to the concept denoted by the original adjective. A derivational process is never demanded by the syntactic context the word is to be used in.
3. *Compounding* is the concatenation of two or more free morphemes (usually nouns) to form a new word (usually with no or very minor changes in the words involved). Compounding may occur in different ways in different languages. The boundary between compound words and normal words is not very clear in languages like English where such forms can be written separately though conceptually they are considered as one unit, e.g. "firefighter" or "fire-fighter" is a compound word in English while the noun phrase "coffee pot" is an example where components are written separately. German is the prime example of productive use of compounding to create new words on the fly, a textbook example being "Lebensversicherungsgesellschaftsangesteller" [2] consisting of the words "Leben", "Versicherung", "Gesellschaft" and "Angesteller" with some glue in between.

Morphemes making up words can be combined together in a number of ways. In *purely concatenative* combination, the free and bound morphemes are just concatenated. *Prefixation* refers to a concatenative combination where the bound morpheme is affixed to the beginning of the free morpheme or a stem, while *suffixation* refers to a concatenative combination where the bound morpheme is affixed to the end of the free morpheme or a stem. In *infixation*, the bound morpheme is inserted to the stem it is attached to (e.g., "fumikas" ("to be strong") from "fikas" ("strong") in Bontoc, [7]). In *circumfixation*, part of the attached morpheme comes before the stem while another part goes after the stem. In German, e.g., the past participle of a verb such as "tauschen" ("to exchange") is indicated by "getauscht". Semitic languages such as Arabic and Hebrew use *root and pattern combination*, where a "root" consisting of just consonants is combined with a pattern and vowel alternations. For instance in Arabic, the root "ktb" (meaning the general concept of writing) can be combined with the template `CVCCVC` to derive new words such as "kattab" ("to cause to write") or "kuttib" ("to be caused to write"). *Reduplication* refers to duplicating (some part of) a word to convey morphological information. In Indonesian, e.g., total reduplication is used to mark plurals: "orang" ("man"), "orangorang" ("men") [7]. In *zero morphology*, derivation/inflection takes place without any additional morpheme. In English the verb "to second (a motion)" is derived from the ordinal "second". In *subtractive morphology*, part of the word form is removed to indicate a morphological feature. Sproat [7] gives the Muskogean language Koasati as an example of such a language, where a part of the form is removed to mark plural agreement.

[2] life insurance company employee

2. Computational morphology

Computational morphology studies the computational analysis and synthesis of word forms for eventual use in natural language processing applications. Almost all applications of computational analysis of word forms have been on written or orthographic forms of words where tokens are neatly delineated. Since the main theme in this book and the NATO ASI it is based on, is the processing of written language, we will from now on assume that we are dealing with written forms of words.

Morphological analysis breaks down a given word form into its morphological constituents, assigning suitable labels or tags to these constituents. Morphological analysis has analogous problems to all those in full-blown parsing albeit usually at a smaller scale. Words may be ambiguous in their part-of-speech and/or some additional features For example, in English, a word form such as "second" has six interpretations, though not all applications will need all distinctions to be made:

1)	second	Noun	*Every second is important.*
2)	second	Number	*She is the second person in line.*
3)	second	Verb (untensed)	*He decided to second the motion.*
4)	second	Verb (present tense)	*We all second this motion.*
5)	second	Verb (imperative)	*Second this motion!*
6)	second	Verb (subjunctive)	*I recommended that he second the motion.*

In a language like Turkish, whose morphology is more extensive, words may be divided up in a number of ways, e.g. a simple word like "koyun" may be decomposed into constituents in five ways:[3]

1)	koyun	Noun, singular, nominative case	*sheep*
2)	koy+un	Noun, singular, 2nd person singular possessive, nominative case	your bay
3)	koy+[n]un	Noun, singular, genitive case	of the vote
4)	koy+un	Verb, imperative	put !
5)	koyu+[u]n	Adjective (root), derived into Noun, singular, 2nd person singular possessive, nominative case	your dark (thing)

Computational morphology attempts to model and capture two main aspects of word formation: *morphophonology* or *morphographemics*, and *morphotactics*. Morphophonology and its counterpart for words in written form, morphographemics, refer to the changes in pronunciation and orthography that occur when morphemes are put together. For instance in English, when the derivational suffix *+ness* is affixed to the adjective stem *happy* to derive a noun, we get *happiness*. The word final *y* in the spelling of *happy* changes to an *i*. Similarly, in the present continuous form of the verb *stop*, we need to duplicate the last consonant of the root to get *stopping*. Turkish, for instance, has a process known as vowel harmony, which requires that vowels in affixed morphemes agree in various phonological features with the vowels in the root or the preceding morphemes. For instance, *+lar* in *pullar* (stamps) and *+ler* in *güller* (roses) both indicate plurality; the vowel *u* in the first word's root forces the vowel in the suffix to be an *a* in the former and the *ü* in the second word's root forces the vowel in the suffix to be an *e*.

[3]Morpheme boundaries have been marked with "+", while "[...]" denotes parts of morphemes deleted when they are combined with the root.

Words where such agreement is missing are considered to be ill-formed. Computational morphology develops formalisms for describing such changes, the contexts they occur in, and whether they are obligatory or optional (e.g., *modeling* and *modelling* are both valid forms.)

Morphotactics describes the structure of words, that is, how morphemes are combined to form words as demanded by the syntactic context and with the correct semantics (in the case of derivational morphology). The root words of a language are grouped into lexicons based on their part-of-speech and other criteria that determine their morphotactical behaviour. Similarly, the bound morpheme inventory of the language is also grouped into lexicons. If morphemes are combined using prefixation or suffixation, then the morphotactics of the language describes the proper ordering of the lexicons from which morphemes are chosen. Morphotactics in languages like Arabic require more elaborate combinations where roots consisting of just consonants are combined with a vocalisation template that describes how vowels and consonants are interdigitated to form the word with the right set of features.

Although, there have been numerous one-of-a-kind early systems that have been developed for morphological analysis, computational morphology, especially finite state morphology, has gained a substantial boost after Koskenniemmi's work [5] which introduced the *two-level morphology* approach. Later the publication of the seminal paper by by Kaplan and Kay [3] on the theoretical aspects of finite state calculus, and the recent book with the accompanying software by Beesley and Karttunen [2] established the finite state approach as the state-of-the-art paradigm in computational morphology.

In finite state morphology, both the morphotactics component and the morphographemic components can be implemented as finite state transducers: computational models that map between regular sets of strings. As shown in Figure 1, the morphographemics transducer maps from surface strings to lexical strings which consist of lexical morphemes and the lexicon transducer maps from lexical strings to feature representations.

As again depicted in Figure 1, the morphographemic finite state transducer and the morphographemic transducer can be combined using *composition* which produces a single transducer that can map from surface strings (e.g., `happiest`) to feature strings (e.g., `happy+Adj+Sup` denoting a superlative adjective with root *happy*). Since finite state transducers are reversible, the same transducer can also be used to map from feature strings to surface strings.

2.1. Morphotactics

In order to check if a given surface form corresponds to a properly constructed word in a language, one needs a model of the word structure. This model includes the root words for all relevant parts-of-speech in the language (nouns, adjectives, verbs, adverbs, connectives, pre/postpositions, exclamations, etc.), the affixes and the paradigms of how root words and affixes combine to create words.

Tools such as the Xerox finite state tools, provide finite state mechanisms for describing lexicons of root words and affixes and how they are combined. This approach makes the assumption that all morpheme combinations are essentially concatenative or can be 'faked' with concatenation. A typical lexicon specification looks like the following where root words with common properties are collected and linked to the proper suffix lexicons by continuations.

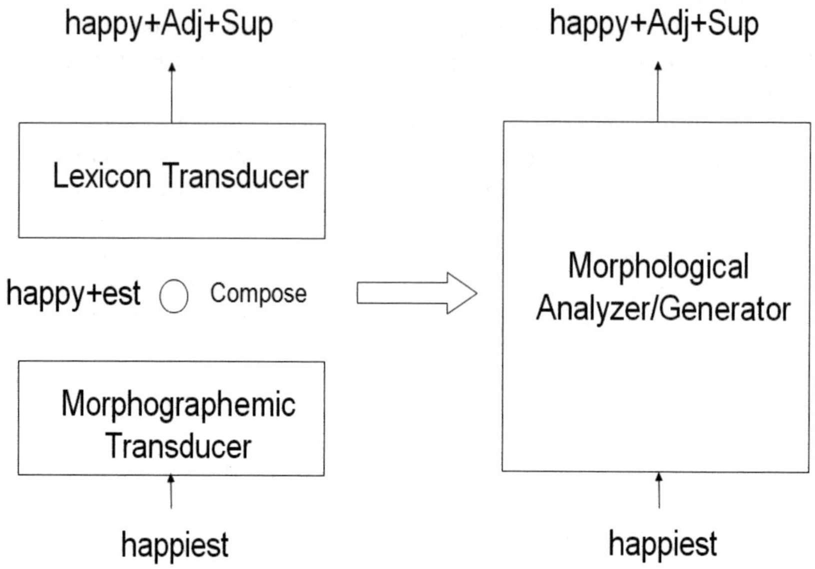

Figure 1. High-level architecture of a morphological analyzer

```
LEXICON ROOT
NOUNS;
REGULAR-VERBS;
IRREGULAR-VERBS;
ADJECTIVES;
....


LEXICON NOUNS
     abacus      NOUN-STEM;
     car         NOUN-STEM;
     table       NOUN-STEM;
     ....
     information+Noun+Sg:information End;
     ...
     zymurgy     NOUN-STEM;

LEXICON NOUN-STEM
     +Noun:0 NOUN-SUFFIXES

LEXICON NOUN-SUFFIXES
      +Sg:0      End;
      +Pl:+s       End;


LEXICON REGULAR-VERBS
      admire   REG-VERB-STEM;
      head     REG-VERB-STEM;
```

```
      ..
      zip       REG-VERB-STEM;


LEXICON IRREGULAR-VERBS
      ..

LEXICON ADJECTIVES
      ..

...

LEXICON REG-VERB-STEM
     +Verb:0 REG-VERB-SUFFIXES;

LEXICON REG-VERB-SUFFIXES
     +Pres+3sg:+s  End;
     +Past:+ed   End;
     +Part:+ed    End;
     +Cont:+ing  End;
```

Every lexicon entry consists of a pair of strings (written as one string when they are the same), which denote mappings between lexical word strings and feature strings. For example, in the `REGULAR-VERBS` lexicon, the string `admire` maps to `admire`, while in the lexicon `REG-VERB-SUFFIXES` `+ed` maps to either `+Past` or `+Part`, denoting verbal morphological features. One of these can be the empty string, denoted by `0`. For instance, in the lexicon `NOUN-SUFFIXES` the empty string is mapped to `+Sg`. These string-to-string mappings can be implemented by a finite state transducer [2,3]. This transducer maps from segmented lexical strings to feature strings. Figure 2 depicts what the internal structure of finite state lexicon transducer looks like.

2.2. *Morphographemics*

The morphographemic transducer generates all possible ways the input surface word can be segmented and "unmangled" as sanctioned by the graphemic conventions or morphophonological processes of the language as reflected to the orthography. However, the morphographemic transducer is oblivious to the lexicon; it does not really know about words and morphemes, but rather about what happens (possibly at the boundaries) when you combine them. This obliviousness is actually a good thing: languages easily import or generate new words, but not necessarily new morphographemic rules! (and usually there are a "small" number of rules.)

For instance, in English, there is a rule which inserts a *g* after a vowel followed by a *g* and before a vowel in a suffix: bra**gg**ed, flo**gg**ed. One wants these rules to also apply to new similar words coming to the lexicon: blo**gg**ed. So such rules are not lexically conditioned, i.e., they do not apply to specific words, but rather in specific narrow contexts.

There are two main approaches to implementing the morphographemic transducer:

1. Parallel Rule Transducers– Two-level morphology

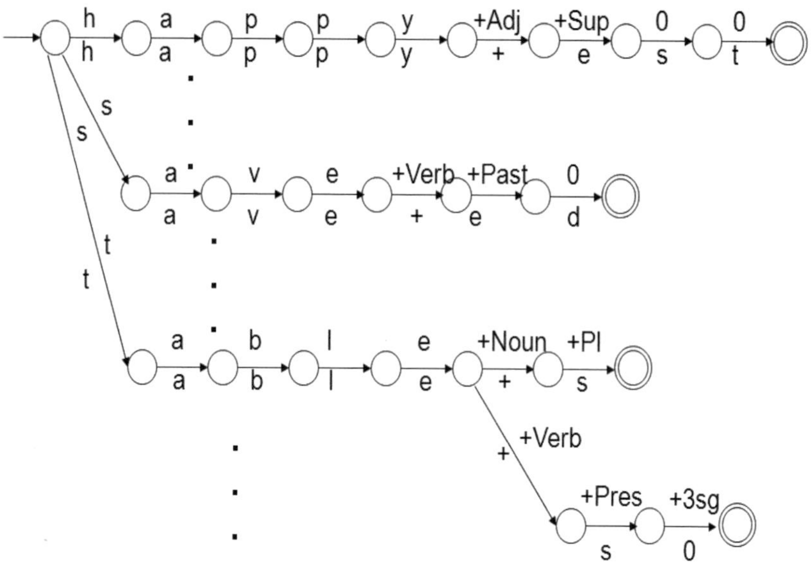

Figure 2. The internal structure of a lexicon transducer

2. Cascaded Replace Transducers

2.3. *Parallel Rule Transducers: Two-level morphology*

Two level morphology posits two distinct levels of representations for a word form: the *lexical level* refers to the abstract internal structure of the word consisting of the morphemes making up the word and the *surface level* refers to the orthographic representation of a word form as it appears in text. The morphemes in the lexical level representation are combined together according to language-specific combination rules, possibly undergoing changes along the way, resulting in the surface level representation. The changes that take place during this combination process are defined or constrained by language-specific rules. Such rules define the correspondence between the string of symbols making up the lexical level representation and the string of symbols making up the surface level representation. For instance, in English, the lexical form of the word "blemishes" can be represented as `blemish+s` indicating that the root word is `blemish` and the plural marker is the bound morpheme `+s` combined by concatenation denoted by the `+`. The English spelling rule of *epenthesis* requires that an `e` has to be inserted after a root ending with `sh` and before the morpheme `s`, resulting in `blemishes`. We textually represent this correspondence by aligning the lexical and surface characters that map to each other as shown below. In this example and in the examples to follow later the symbol `0` stands for the *null symbol* of zero length which never appears in any surface form when printed.

Lexical: `blemish+0s`
Surface: `blemish0es (blemishes)`

The changes are expressed by a set of *two-level rules* each of which describes one specific phenomenon (such as epenthesis above), along with the contexts the phenomenon occurs in and whether it is obligatory or optional.

Before we proceed further, some automata-theoretic background would be helpful. Let us consider a finite alphabet whose symbols are actually pairs of atomic symbols `l:s`, where `l` is a lexical symbol and `s` is a surface symbol. One can define regular languages over such pairs of symbols using regular expressions. For instance given the alphabet `A = {a:0, a:a, b:b, c:0, c:c}`, the regular expression `R = (b:b)*(a:0)(b:b)* (c:0)` describes a regular language containing strings like `b:b b:b b:b a:0 b:b b:b c:0`, where the first three `b:b` pairs match `(b:b)*` in the regular expression, `a:0` pair matches the expression `(a:0)`, the next two `b:b` pairs match the expression `(b:b)*` and finally the `c:0` pair matches the expression `(c:0)`. We can also view this string of pairs of lexical–surface symbols as a correspondence, showing the sequence of lexical and surface symbols separately:

Lexical: `bbbabbc`
Surface: `bbb0bb0` `(bbbbb)`

Such a regular expression can be converted into a finite-state recognizer over the same alphabet using standard techniques.

Another way to view this recognizer is as a *transducer* that maps between strings consisting of the lexical symbols and strings consisting of the surface symbols.[4] Thus, for the example above, the lexical string `bbbabbc` would be transduced to the surface string `bbbbb`, if the lexical level is treated as the input string and the surface level is treated as the output string. The transduction would be in the reverse direction if the roles of the levels are interchanged. On the other hand, the lexical string `bbabbbb` cannot be transduced because it is missing a `c` at the end and hence cannot lead the transducer to its final state.

In general, regular expressions are too low a notation to describe morphographemic changes or correspondences. Two-level morphology provides higher-level notational mechanisms for describing constraints on strings over an alphabet, called the *set of feasible pairs* in two-level terminology. The set of feasible pairs is the set of all possible lexical–surface pairs. Morphographemic changes are expressed by four kinds of rules that specify in which context and how morphographemic changes take place. The contexts are expressed by regular expressions (over the set of feasible pairs) and describe what comes on the left (`LC`, for left context) and on the right (`RC`, for right context), of a morphographemic change.

1. The *context restriction rule* `a:b => LC _ RC` states that a lexical `a` may be paired with a surface `b` only in the given context, i.e., `a:b` may only occur in this context (if it ever occurs in a string). In this case *the correspondence implies the context*. For instance in English, the `y:i` correspondence (in a word like *happiness*, is only allowed between a consonant (possibly followed by an optional morpheme boundary) and a morpheme boundary. This is expressed by a rule like `y:i => C (+:0) _ +:0` where `C` denotes a consonant.

[4]Such transducers are slightly different from the classical finite state transducers in that (i) they have final states just like finite state recognizers and (ii) a transduction is valid only when the input leads the transducer into one of the final states.

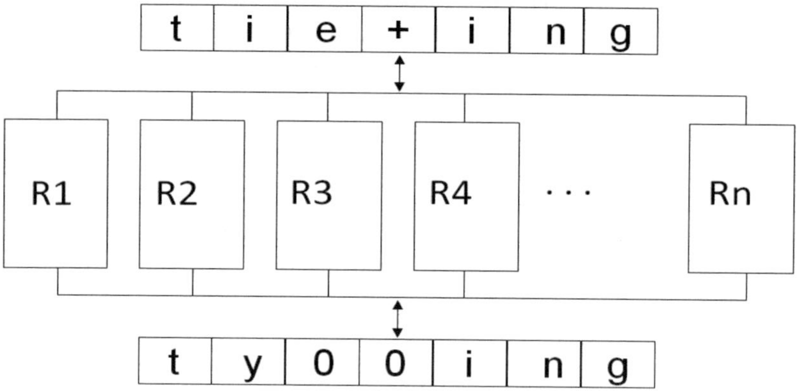

Figure 3. Parallel transducers in two-level morphology

2. The *surface coercion rule* `a:b <= LC _ RC` states that a lexical `a` *must be* paired with a surface `b` in the given context, i.e. no other pairs with `a` as its lexical symbol can appear in this context. In this case *the context implies the correspondence*. Note that `a:b` is not prohibited from occurring in other contexts. For instance in English, the `'` in a genitive suffix has to be deleted on the surface, if the previous consonant is an `s` that belongs to the plural morpheme. One would express this by a rule of the sort `s:0 <= +:0 (0:e) s +:0 ' _`. Note that there are other contexts where a `s` may be dropped, but no obligatorily.
3. The *composite rule* `a:b <=> LC _ RC` states that a lexical `a` must be paired with a surface `b` in the given context and this correspondence is valid only in the given context. This rule is the combination of the previous two rules. For instance, in English the i:y correspondence (as in *tie+ing* being *tying*), is valid only before a `e:0` correspondence followed by a morpheme boundary followed by an `i`, and futhermore in this context a lexical `i` *has* to be paired with a surface `y`. This is expressed by the composite rule `i:e <=> _ e:0 +:0 i`.
4. The *exclusion rule* `a:b /<= LC _ RC` states that lexical symbol `a` may not be paired with a surface symbol `b`, i.e. `a:b` cannot occur in this context. For instance, the tt y:i correspondence in the context restriction rule above cannot occur if the morpheme on the right hand side starts with an `i` or a `'` (the genitive marker). Thus a rule like `y:i /<= C (+:0) _ +:0 [ i | ']` prevent the context restriction rule from applying in situations like *try+ing* or *spy+'s*.

The constraints expressed by these rules are compiled into finite-state recognizers which operate in parallel on the lexical and surface symbol pairs as depicted in Figure 3. A given string of lexical–surface pairs is accepted by a collection of such recognizers if none of the individual recognizers ends up in a rejecting state.

We will illustrate the possibilities of this system with some examples for two-level rules and the corresponding recognizers.

Turkish Vowel Harmony Turkish has a phenomenon called *vowel harmony* where with some exceptions, the vowels in suffix morphemes have to agree in certain phonological features with the most recent vowel in the stem the morpheme is attached to. For instance, in its (considerably) simplified form, if the surface representation of the last vowel in the stem is a front vowel (one of “e”, “i”, “ö” or “ü” in Turkish), then an unrounded back vowel (which will be represented in the lexical representation by the symbol as `A`) in a lexical morpheme is resolved as “e” on the surface. Otherwise, if the last vowel is a back vowel (one of “a”, “ı”, “o” or “u”), then it is resolved as “a”. The following data exemplifies this phenomenon:

Lexical:	`masa+lAr`	`masa+Noun+Plu`
Surface:	`masa0lar`	`(masalar)`
Lexical:	`okul+lAr`	`okul+Noun+Plul`
Surface:	`okul0lar`	`(okullar)`
Lexical:	`ev+lAr`	`ev+Noun+Plu`
Surface:	`ev0ler`	`(evler)`
Lexical:	`gül+lAr`	`gül+Noun+Plu`
Surface:	`gül0ler`	`(güller)`

Thus, we have two feasible pairs in our set of feasible pairs with `A` as their lexical symbol: `A:a` and `A:e`. Let us also assume we have the additional feasible pairs `a:a, b:b, ..., z:z`, (called the default pairs), and `+:0` for morpheme boundaries. The rule

```
A:a   <=>  [ A:a | a:a | ı:ı | u:u | o:o ]
           [ b:b | c:c | ... | z:z ]* +:0
           [ b:b | c:c | ... | z:z ]* _
```

indicates the `A` should be paired only with an `a` in the left context comprising

1. a surface back vowel (indicated by the first set of alternatives following <=>),
2. followed by any number of feasible pairs of consonants pairing with themselves (indicated by the second set of alternatives)
3. followed by a morpheme boundary (`+:0`), and
4. followed by again any number of consonant pairs.

The right context is irrelevant as nothing after the morpheme vowel being resolved can affect the rule.

As such, the rule looks quite verbose and clumsy, but a little bit of additional notational convention leads to quite succinct rule descriptions. We define the following shortcuts:

- `@` acts as a wildcard, matching any symbol
- `Vback` indicates any surface back vowel
- `C` is the set of all surface consonants

So `@:Vback` would denote the set of feasible pairs whose surface symbol is a back vowel. With these conventions, we can write the rule above in a much shorter form:

```
A:a <=> @:Vback @:C* +:0 @:C* _
```

This rule handles the back vowel cases. To cover the complementary instance of this kind of vowel harmony, we have its companion rule which corresponds to the front vowel contexts.

```
A:e => @:Vfr @:C* +:0 @:C*_
```

where `Vfr` denotes the set of front vowels `{e,i,ö,ü}`.

Epenthesis in English For another example we look at the phenomenon of epenthesis in English, where an `e` is inserted on the surface. The phenomenon can be exemplified by the following data:

Lexical:	`fox+s`	`kiss+s`	`church+s`	`spy+s`
Surface:	`foxes`	`kisses`	`churches`	`spies`

The two-level rule describing epenthesis could be written as:

```
+:e <=> [ Csib | s h | c h | y:i | o ] _ s [+:@ | #]
```

where `Csib` stands for the sibilant consonants `{s, x, z}`. Note that, in this example, instead of using a `+:0` pair and a `0:e` pair, a single pair `+:e` has been used. The right context is such that either a further morpheme boundary or the end of a word may follow the `s`.

Clearly English has many more phenomena and the reader is referred to more detailed sources for these such as Ritchie *et al.* [6] or Karttunen and Wittenburg [4]. In addition, there are quite a number of other sources for information on writing two-level rules and one can refer to those for more comprehensive treatments of both general and language-specific phenomena (e.g. Antworth [1]).

A language will have few tens of such two-level rules. Each of these rules are compiled into finite state transducers and then intersected to create a one single transducer that accounts for all the rules. For a technical reason, these transducers have to map between equal-length lexical and surface strings (as in general finite state transducers are not closed under intersection). This is why `0`, the epsilon symbol has to be treated as a normal symbol in the rules and the corresponding transducers and once the transducers are intersected, additional transducers can replace these with actual epsilon.

2.4. *Cascaded Rules*

Cascaded rules provide another approach for implementing the morphographemics transducer. This approach is based on *replace rules* which define relations over two regular sets of strings. A replace rule relates a string in one regular language to all strings in the other regular language in which certain substrings have been replaced by some other substring. For example, the replace rule `a -> b` defines a relation in which a string in the input (upper) language is related to all strings in the output (lower) languages which are exactly like the input string except all *a*'s have been replaced by *b*'s: e.g., *aabc* is related to *bbbc*, *bcbb* is related to *bcbb* and *aaaa* is related to *bbbb*. One can also think of these rules in a "procedural", way as *transducing* an input string into 0 or more output string through replacement. The replacements can also be conditioned on left and right contexts in the input and output strings. For example, the rule `a -> b || c _ d` defines a replace rule in which only the *a*'s in the input upper string that occur after a *c* and before a *d* are replaced by *b*'s. Note that the lengths of output strings need not be the same as the length of input string: one can shorten or lengthen a string. For example, the rule `aab -> 0`[5] replaces every substring of *aab*'s by the empty string effectively

[5] We again use `0` to denote the empty string, commonly denoted by ϵ in standard automata theory books.

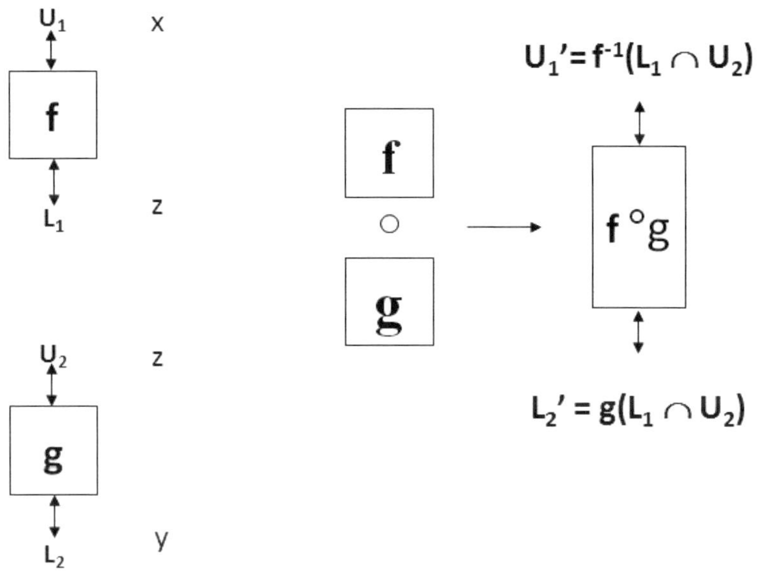

Figure 4. Composition of finite state transducers

shortening the input string. For a very thorough treatement of replace rules, please refer to seminal article by Kaplan and Kay [3].

Replace rules (with some technical restrictions on how overlapping contexts are interpreted) can be compiled into finite state transducers. The transducers defined by replace rules can also be combined by an operation of *composition*, the equivalent of relation/function composition in algebra. Figure 4 shows the composition of transducers. Transducer T_1 defines a relation R_1 between languages U_1 and U_1 and T_2 defines a relation R_2 between languages U_2 and U_2. The composed transducer T (on the right) defines the relation

$$R = R_1 \circ R_2 = \{(x, y) : x \in U_1, y \in L_2 \text{ and}$$
$$\exists z \in L_1 \cap U_2 \text{ such that } (x, z) \in R_1 \text{ and } (z, y) \in R_2\}$$

Note that with a "procedural" interpretation, the lower transducer "operates" on the "output" of the upper transducer, that is, the upper transducer feeds into the lower transducer. When multiple transducers are combined through compositions, such interactions have to be kept in mind as sometimes they may have unintended consequences. Note also that the composed transducer can be computed offline from the two component transducers. A typical cascaded rule system consists of a few tens of replace rules as depicted in Figure 5.

We will use the notation of the Xerox *xfst* regular expression language to describe a series of replace rule forms that are commonly used in building cascaded-rule morphographemic transducers. For more details on these and much more, refer to the book

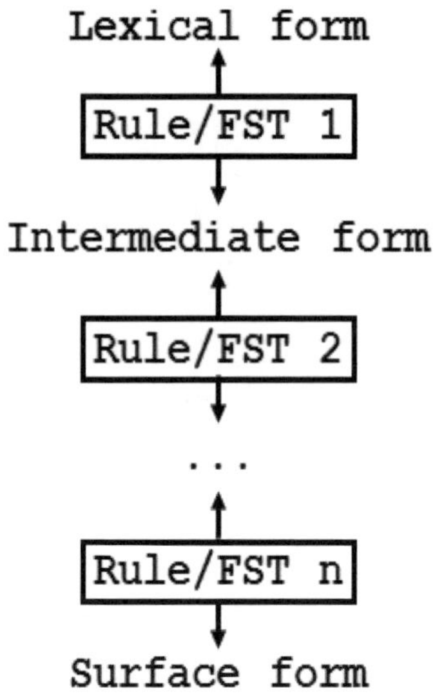

Figure 5. A cascade rule system organization

by Beesley and Karttunen [2]. Here A, B denote regular expressions that sets of strings describing the strings that are to be replaced and the target strings that replace them respectively. LC and RC denote regular expressions that describe the contexts in which the replacements are licensed.

- `A -> B || LC _ RC`: Replace strings matching the regular expression A by all strings matching regular expression B such that the string matching A on the upper side is preceded by a string matching LC and followed by a string matching RC; the contexts restrict the upper side.
- `A -> B // LC _ RC`: Replace strings matching the regular expression A by all strings matching regular expression B such that the string matching B on the lower side is preceded by a string matching LC and the string matching A on the upper side is followed by a string matching RC; the left context restricts the lower side and the right context restricts the upper side.
- `A -> B \\ LC _ RC`: Replace strings matching the regular expression A by all strings matching regular expression B such that the string matching A on the upper side is preceded by a string matching LC and the string matching B on the lower side is followed by a string matching RC; the left context restricts the upper side side and the right context restricts the lower side.
- `A -> B \/ LC _ RC`: Replace strings matching the regular expression A by all strings matching regular expression B such that the string matching B on the lower side is preceded by a string matching LC and followed by a string matching RC; the contexts restrict the lower side.

xfst allows such rules to be combined in various ways to achieve additional functionality: multiple rules can be applied to a string in parallel and they may have common or separate left and right contexts. For example,

```
A -> B, C -> D ||  LC _ RC
```

replaces A with B and C with D whenever either occurs in the context LC and RC. On the other hand, the rule

```
A - >B || LC1 _ RC1 ,, C - >D || LC2 _ RC2
```

replaces A with B in context $LC1$ and $RC1$, and C with D in context $LC2$ and $RC2$; all these replacements are done in parallel.

We will now demonstrate the use of these rules to describe several rules of Turkish morphographemics and combine them. Let use define the following sets of vowels and consonants for use in subsequent rules:

- A denotes the low unrounded vowels a and e
- H denotes the high vowels ı, i, u, and $ü$
- $VBack$ denotes the back vowels a, ı, o and u
- $VFront$ denotes the front vowels e, i, $ö$ and $ü$.
- $Vowel$ denotes all vowels – the union of $VBack$ and $VFront$
- $Consonant$ denotes all consonants

1) The first rule implements the following morphographemic rule:

> A vowel ending a stem is deleted if it is followed by the morpheme $+Hyor$: For example $ata + Hyor$ becomes $at + Hyor$

The rule `Vowel -> 0 || _ "+" H y o r` implements this. A vowel just before a morpheme boundary (indicated by + and escaped with " ") followed by the relevant (lexical) morpheme is replaced by `0` (ϵ) on the lower side.

2) The second rule implements the following morphographemic rule:

> A high vowel starting a morpheme is deleted if it is attached to a segment ending in a vowel. For example $masa + Hm$ becomes $masa + m$.

The rule `H -> 0 || Vowel  "+" _` implements this. Note that this is a more general version of the first rule. Since the replacements of the two rules are contradictory, the more specific rule takes precedence and is placed before the general rule in the cascade.

3) Implementing vowel harmony using cascaded replace rules is a bit tricky since classes of vowels depend on each other in a left-to-right fashion. Thus we can not place vowel harmony rules one after the other. For this reason we use parallel replace rules with the left context check on the lower side so that each rule has access to the output of the other parallel rules. We need 6 parallel rules, 2 to resolve A and 4 to resolve H:

```
A - >a // VBack Cons* "+" Cons* _ ,,
A -> e // VFront Cons* "+" Cons* _ ,,
H -> u // [o | u] Cons* "+" Cons* _ ,,
H -> ü // [ö | ü] Cons* "+" Cons* _ ,,
H -> ı // [a | ı] Cons* "+" Cons* _ ,,
```

```
H -> i // [e | i] Cons* "+" Cons* _
```

The important point to note in this set of parallel rules is that each rule applies independently in parallel, but they check their contexts on the lower side where all relevant vowels have been already resolved so that they can condition further vowels to the right.

4) The fourth rule is another parallel rule but this time the left context and the right context are shared between the replacements. It implements the following morphographemic rules involving the devoicing of certain consonants:

> *d*, *b*, and *c* are realized as *t*, *p* and *ç* respectively, either at the end of a word or after certain consonants.

The rule

```
d -> t, b-> p, c -> ç // [h | ç | ş | k | p | t | f | s ] "+" _
```

implements this. Again the left contexts have to be check on the lower side since a consonant that is modified can now condition the devoicing of another consonant to the right.

5) The fifth rule handles the following morphographemic rule

> Morpheme-initial *s*, *n*, *y* are deleted when they are preceded by a stem ending with a consonant.

The rule `[s|n|y] -> 0 || Consonant "+" _` implements this.

6) The last rule is a clean-up rule that removes the morpheme boundary symbol: `"+" -> 0.`

These rules are ordered and composed as shown in Figure 6 to obtain the morphographemics transducer which can then be combined with the lexicon transducer to build the morphological analyzer. Note that although we have designed the rules assuming that the replacements occur from upper-side to lower-side, the transductions also work in the reverse direction so that a given surface form can be transduced to possible lexical forms.

In this section, we have provided a glimpse of using replace rules for building a series of cascaded rules for building the morphographemics component. A full system for almost any language would require tens of rules that have to be carefully ordered to obtain the correct functionality. We again refer the reader to the book by Beesley and Karttunen [2] which has additional details and examples on transducers and replace rules.

3. Conclusions

Many natural language processing systems require that words in a natural language be properly identified and that the constituents of words be extracted to aid for further syntactic and semantic processing. Yet other natural language systems such as machine translation need to synthesize words from any available syntactic and semantic information. In this chapter we have presented a brief overview of finite state morphology, the state-of-the-art approach in computational morphology to construct such morphological processors. We have presented an overview of two-level morphology and cascaded rule

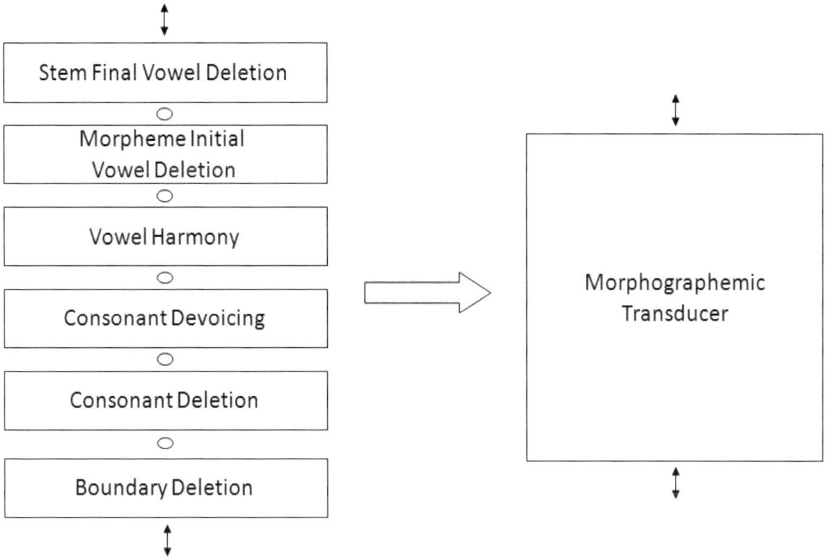

Figure 6. Combining the replace rules with composition

approaches to building the morphographemics component and combining it with a finite state model of the lexicon. We strongly suggest that the interested reader follow-up on the topic with the Beesley and Karttunen book [2] and experiment with the available software provided as a companion to build morphological processor for his/her language.

References

[1] Evan L. Antworth. *PC-KIMMO: A two-level processor for Morphological Analysis*. Summer Institute of Linguistics, Dallas, Texas, 1990.

[2] Kenneth R. Beesley and Lauri Karttunen. *Finite State Morphology*. CSLI Publications, Stanford University, 2003.

[3] Ronald M. Kaplan and Martin Kay. Regular models of phonological rule systems. *Computational Linguistics*, 20(3):331–378, September 1994.

[4] Lauri Karttunen and K. Wittenburg. A two-level morphological analysis of English. *Texas Linguistics Forum*, 22:217 – 228, 1983.

[5] Kimmo Koskenniemi. Two-level morphology: A general computational model for word form recognition and production. Publication No: 11, Department of General Linguistics, University of Helsinki, 1983.

[6] Graeme D. Ritchie, Graham J. Russell, Alan W. Black, and Stephen G. Pulman. *Computational Morphology*. ACL-MIT Series in Natural Language Processing. The MIT Press, 1992.

[7] Richard Sproat. *Morphology and Computation*. MIT Press, Cambridge, MA, 1992.

Language Engineering for Lesser-Studied Languages
S. Nirenburg (Ed.)
IOS Press, 2009

doi:10.3233/978-1-58603-954-7-153

Practical Syntactic Processing of Flexible Word Order Languages with Dynamic Syntax

David TUGWELL
School of Computer Science
University of St Andrews
Scotland, UK
dtugwell@gmail.com

Abstract. This paper presents an approach to the automatic syntactic processing of natural language based on the newly-emerging paradigm of Dynamic Syntax, and argues that this approach offers a number of practical advantages for this task. In particular, it is shown that is particularly suited to tackling the problems by languages displaying a relatively free constituent order, which is often the case for the lesser-studied low- and middle-density languages.

Dynamic Syntax relies on three assumptions, all of which run against the mainstream of generative orthodoxy. These are that the basis of grammar should be taken to be individual grammatical constructions, that it must rely on a rich representational semantics, and most radically that it should be a dynamic system building structure incrementally through the sentence, thus matching the time-flow of language interpretation.

The paper outlines the construction of a probabilistic syntactic model for English, and discusses how it may be extended and adapted for other languages.

Keywords. generative grammar, methodology, dynamic syntax, syntactic constructions, language modelling

Introduction

The many years since the founding of generative grammar have seen much debate on the nature of grammars, and many proposals for radically differing architectures for the models of grammar themselves, but even among the most sharply dissenting voices, there has been surprisingly little disagreement on basic assumptions about the methodology of the enterprise itself. There has been widespread concord that grammars are to be modelled using some form of syntactic structure, that this structure should be essentially static, abstracting away from the time-flow of language, that it should be largely autonomous, working independently of semantics, pragmatics or phonology, and finally that the grammar should be constructed in isolation from any use that may be made of it in processing.

In recent times, however, these assumptions have begun to come under challenge from a number of groups working within the generative paradigm itself. The first challenge is the constructionist argument that grammars should be based, like traditional descriptive grammars, on individual grammatical constructions, formed from a complex of syntactic, semantic, pragmatic and intonational constraints [14]. The second challenge is the argument that a detailed representational semantics has a large role to play in the way words can go together, with a corresponding simplification of the syntactic component itself [9]. Most radical of all is the claim that by overhauling our conception of what grammars are, and viewing them instead as dynamic systems that construct representations of meaning word-by-word through the sentence, we can build more faithful and explanatory models of the syntactic process [22].

In this paper I will firstly review the methodology adopted by the generative paradigm, re-examining old arguments and questioning old assumptions about the conclusions we should draw from them. In the next section of the paper I describe a specific architecture for a dynamic model of syntax and show how it can be used to tackle a range of constructions in English, as well as examples of flexible word order that have proved problematic to approaches based on constituency or dependency structures. In the final section I outline an implemented probabilistic dynamic model for English syntax, showing how it can be constructed and evaluated.

1. Generative Grammar

1.1. The Generative Enterprise

I will assume that in studying the syntax of natural languages we are essentially investigating the human linguistic capacity: the make-up and operation of some aspect of the human brain. This *conceptualist* approach is the dominant one in modern linguistics, established as such in [7], and places linguistics ultimately within the biological sciences.

I will further assume that we are attempting to investigate the process by which a sequence of words becomes associated with its possible meanings, and conversely the process by which some meaning can be expressed by some sequence of words. These are unobservable processes, unyielding to direct investigation, their operation hidden murkily inside a black box, as in this representation of the first of these processes, language interpretation.

WORD STRING ⇒ BLACK BOX ⇒ MEANING

I will take it that the enterprise of generative grammar is an attempt to investigate what is going on inside the box by constructing a formal model of it.

> Modelling becomes necessary whenever the object of a scientific discipline cannot be observed directly. The object is frequently compared then to a 'black box'.., of which one knows only what materials it takes as 'input' and what it

produces as 'output'... As it is impossible to dismount the 'black box' without interfering with its operation, the only way one can learn about its contents is by constructing a model on the basis of its input and output. One has to form a certain hypothesis on the possible structure of the 'black box', the object, and then realise it in the form of a logical apparatus capable of transforming certain materials in the same manner. If the logical apparatus indeed functions like the object, then it is considered an approximation, or a model of it... [1], p.89.

I quote at length as I feel it important that we continually bear in mind that the linguistic model itself is not the object of interest, it is merely a tool, a necessarily imperfect and limited one, but nevertheless a tool that we assume will allow us to discover insights into the human language capability itself. And this is what we may call the "generative assumption".

1.2. Constraints on the Model (1): Modularity

What goes on in the processor may be mired inside its black box, but nevertheless following the insightful observations and arguments in [7], it has long been established that the process must be composed of distinct modules. Following the arguments in the first chapter of each and every introduction to linguistics, we can conclude that the following examples show that a sentence can be:

(1) Grammatical but not processable: *The man the cat the dog the woman liked chased bit died.*

(2) Grammatical and processable, but apt to lead to processing failure at first pass: *The horse raced past the barn fell.*

(3) Grammatical and processable, without being interpretable as a possible scenario in the world: *Colourless green ideas sleep furiously.*

The natural conclusion to draw is that the process of mapping between strings of words and meanings must be **modular**. There must be something about the processor that places an absolute limit on memory, and a processing strategy which can be defeated even by grammatical sentences. There must also be some grammatical component, which is distinct from the processor that uses it, and also separate from our concepts about what are possible or anticipated situations in the world. This **grammatical competence**, identified with the the speaker's *knowledge of the language*, can then be seen as the proper object of the study of syntax, abstracting away from its use by the processor.[1] This is an important and valuable insight that cannot and should not be brushed aside.

The assumption that standardly follows, however, is that it is possible to construct a model of this competence component, a *generative grammar*, in isolation

[1] Unfortunately, another type of abstraction was bundled together with the idea of competence in [7], that of idealisation: "an ideal speaker-hearer, in a completely homogeneous speech community". This has led to a great deal of confusion. Such an idealisation would be natural to make in the modelling of any complex natural system and would apply just as well to a model of performance as to the grammatical competence component of that model. It is not a distinguishing feature of models of competence.

from its use in the wider processes of interpretation or production, and that this should be the path followed. And in investigating syntax, this is the assumption that has been made, and this is the path that has been followed, almost without exception, across the entire spectrum of generative approaches. However, for the assumption to be valid, for this competence component to be modellable, it needs to have some generally agreed input and output. Just because we know that the grammatical competence exists somewhere inside the black box, interacting with the processor, it does not mean that we are in a position to investigate it in isolation.

The standard assumption is that *grammaticality judgements* provide us with our necessary output conditions to assess the working of the model. But, as has been pointed out many times, the idea of people being able to provide such judgements is implausible:

> It does not make any sense to speak of grammaticality judgements given Chomsky's definitions, because people are incapable of judging grammaticality — it is not accessible to their intuitions. Linguists might construct arguments about the grammaticality of a sentence, but all a linguistically naive subject can do is judge its acceptability. [31], p.26.

All we can expect from people are reasonably uniform judgements about possible meanings of naturally-occurring sentences, for without such broad agreement language would not function. Trying to get a model of competence to match deviancy judgements people give for unnatural constructed sentences, judged without context, seems an approach doomed to failure, even though it represents standard practice in syntactic research. This is not only because these judgements are not reliable either between speakers, or as every syntactician knows from personal experience, by the same speaker, but also because it is impossible to know *a priori* to what extent processing factors and plausibility factors are at play in these judgements.[2]

We must conclude, therefore, that the question as to where the boundaries between the modules lie is not something open to direct observation, it is also hidden inside the black box. Although the modularity arguments show that a faithful model of the linguistic capacity must respect this modular structure, it is free to decide where these boundaries lie, and free to decide which resources belong to which modules and how the modules fit together.

1.3. Constraints on the Model (2): Incrementality

One additional piece of information that we have about the process of language understanding is that it is extremely fast, practically word by word. Numerous experiments have shown, and it is obvious through intuition, that we construct meaning incrementally, without waiting for the end of the sentence. Indeed the only way that users can identify the words of the sentence is by constructing an interpretation as quickly as possible and using this as a constraint on which words

[2] So this should not be entirely ruled out as one method of testing the plausibility of an overall processing model of comprehension, but not a competence grammar in isolation.

we might expect. It has also been shown that all types of semantic and pragmatic information are used in this construction of meaning.

Therefore, the competence grammar must be such that it can be used in the processing model to allow interpretation to take place in this fashion. It can be argued, however, that static syntactic structures typically place obstacles to a maximally incremental interpretation, as we can see by considering the incremental interpretation of the following sentences, bracketed according to some generic constituent structure.

(4) $[_S$ $[_{np}$ The dogs $]$ $[_{vp}$ barked $]$ $]$

(5) $[_S$ $[_{np}$ The dogs $]$ $[_{vp}$ $[_{vp}$ barked$]$ and $[_{vp}$ howled $]$ $]$ $]$

In (4), if we build the syntactic structure as quickly as the grammar allows, we can calculate when we get to the word *barked* that the subject of the VP that contains it is the NP headed by *dogs*. We can expect that language users could use this information to prefer *barked* over other potential candidates, such as *parked*, *sparked*, using their knowledge that dogs are typical barkers. Turning to (5), where *barked* is the first element of a coordinated VP, intuition would tell us that we would expect to make the same preference as soon as the word *barked* is reached. However, if they follow the grammar, it appears that users must wait until they have finished the coordinated VP *barked and howled*, before this can be combined with the NP subject and it can finally be established that *dog* is the subject of *bark*. To make matters worse, the VP may be indefinitely long: *the dogs barked, howled, woofed... and whined.*

So the assumption that the model is using a competence grammar based on such constituent structure[3] seems to be incompatible with the evidence of the incrementality of interpretation. Alternatively, we might argue that this competence grammar exists at some level inside the language faculty, but it is not being directly employed by the processor, which is perhaps using some dynamic reinterpretation of the grammar. But in this case it is hard to see what the role of the grammar is, if it is not used by the processor, and we would like to know what the actual grammar being used by the processor is like. A more straightforward conclusion is to insist that our grammar be compatible with use in an incremental model of interpretation and to accept that this is a hard constraint that the incrementality of interpretation places on it.

1.4. Evaluation of models

It was proposed above that "if the logical apparatus indeed functions like the object, then it is considered an approximation, or a model of it...". But how do we know if the model is "functioning like the object"? Or alternatively how do we know if one model is functioning more like the object than another? This is important not only if we want to compare two different models, but also if we want some metric to improve the model we have. This is not the hypothetical,

[3]It should be noted that the same problem will arise even with grammars with a considerably more flexible notion of constituent structure, such as the Categorial Grammar of [32], or indeed with dependency grammars, such as [19].

philosophical question posed in [7] of how we should choose between two models that functioned perfectly, but the practical one of how can we measure improvement in an actual, necessarily imperfect, model. It is difficult to overstate the importance of such an objective measure — without it we are condemned to subjective and partial evaluations, not knowing if seeming improvements in one area result in an overall improvement of the model or are accompanied by worse performance in another.

It was stated above that the model must match the input and output of the object of study, here taken to be the process of language interpretation. The input can be taken as a string of words and the output some representation of the meaning or meanings of that string. But representing meaning is fraught with problems as to precisely what we should include in the representation and how we should represent it. We therefore need a more objective and quantifiable method of evaluating the model.

When faced with the task of making objective assessments of the language abilities of students, language teachers will typically use a *cloze* test. In these tests subjects are given real texts with words blanked out and their task is to guess what the original words were. Perhaps surprisingly, scores on such a simple test are held to be a very reliable indicator of language ability:

> ..cloze testing is a good indicator of general linguistic ability, including the ability to use language appropriately according to particular linguistic and situational contexts. [18], p.17.

This technique for evaluating human performance has much in common with that for choosing the best probabilistic model of a language, or *language model*, as being the one that makes the best prediction of the next word in a text, that is the one that can achieve the lowest cross-entropy estimate.[4]

Such an idea is not without precedent in linguistics, indeed it takes us back to the founder of the transformational analysis of language, Zellig Harris, who introduced transformations in an attempt to capture the invariant collocational relationships between words and so predict whether a word would be more or less probable in a particular position.

> ... a central problem for a theory of language is determining the departures from equiprobability in the successive parts of utterances. [15], p.54.

If we accept the idea that the best model is the one making the best predictions for a missing word in a text, however, we should be careful not to apply it indiscriminately. It is still the case that the model has to satisfy the requirements of recognising and representing the accepted ambiguities of language, which rules out linguistically implausible models such as n-grams. However given any linguistically credible model, any improvement in the syntactic component should result in an improvement at the level of word prediction.[5]

---

[4]See [2] for discussion of this measure.

[5]Of course this is not to dispute that improved models of knowledge of the world and the processes of reasoning will also have an important impact, perhaps far outweighing that of a good syntax. The point is that given two models with identical non-syntactic aspects, the one with the better modelling of syntax will be a better predictor.

1.5. Summary

To sum up, our review of the methodology of generative grammar has established that to investigate the black box of the language faculty, we have to build a model of it, matching the input and output conditions; that this model is necessarily one of the language processor as a whole; that it should nevertheless contain distinct modules, including one we can identify as the competence grammar; that the grammar must be able to be used in incremental interpretation; that we can only evaluate the performance of the model as a whole, not any of its component modules, as they are not accessible to observation; that our best hope of objective quantitative evaluation of the model is in measuring its ability to predict words in a text.

In the next section of the paper I will introduce a model of the competence component of the grammar that is compatible with the methodology we have established.

2. The Foundations of a Compatible Model

2.1. Grammatical Constructions

The idea of grammatical constructions is by no means a new one. Traditional descriptive grammars list the constructions of the language — recurring patterns that learners cannot be expected to know either on the basis of other constructions in the language or from their abilities as language users — giving information about their meaning and context of use. The central insight of Construction Grammar[6] is that the entire grammar can be viewed as being formed of such constructions, defined as a form-meaning pair not predictable from its component parts, and that they range in their degree of productivity on a spectrum from non-productive forms such as morphemes and fixed idioms to freely productive syntactic constructions.

Constructions can be subject to syntactic, semantic, pragmatic and intonational constraints, thus challenging the principle of Autonomous Syntax of mainstream generative grammar. Furthermore, the Construction Grammar approach challenges the assumption that meanings of sentences are composed solely through the composition of meanings of the lexical items which they contain, as the construction itself makes a direct and consistent contribution to the meaning that is assembled.

One notable feature of Construction Grammar has been its emphasis on dealing, as much as possible, with the entire language and not just some "core" phenomena. This concern with achieving as wide as coverage as possible, with the frequent use of corpus evidence, ties in well with the methodological desire, as argued in the preceding chapter, to embed the grammar in a wide-coverage model that can be quantitatively evaluated.

From the perspective of language acquisition, it is argued by [34] that children essentially learn language construction by construction and use available evidence

[6] See [14] and [10]

to modify and constrain the conditions that apply to the use of the construction. Tomasello argues that such a construction-based approach can rely on general cognitive abilities and the unique human ability to comprehend intention, rather than on a self-contained "language instinct".

2.1.1. Russian Approximative Inversion Construction

For a particularly striking example of a grammatical construction we may look at approximative inversion in Russian, illustrated in (6).

(6) a. Ya videl sorok studentov
I saw forty students (= I saw forty students)
b. Ya videl studentov sorok
I saw students forty (= I saw *around* forty students)

It can be seen in (6b) that placing the numeral after the noun head, instead of the canonical position in front of it, gives rise to an obligatory approximate interpretation.[7] If we start from the assumption that the meaning of a sentence is composed from the meaning of the lexical items it contains, then the question arises: where does the approximate meaning come from? It would be missing a huge generalisation to suppose that each numeral in the language has an exact meaning and an approximate meaning, and that these appeared in different syntactic positions. It is surely much simpler to suppose that the approximate meaning must arise from and be part of the construction itself.

The meaning of this construction cannot be predicted and has to be learnt as a separate item in the language, in the same way as an item of vocabulary. It provides strong evidence that we cannot avoid recognising the existence of grammatical constructions and indeed suggests that we should take them as essential components of our grammar.

2.2. Conceptual Representation

The idea of using syntactic structure to characterise syntax has its roots in the immediate constituent analysis of the American structuralist school, where it was conceived as a way to describe the distribution of word types, without having to deal with problems of meaning.[8] While it is quite understandable why this approach was adopted, it subsequently became entrenched as a central assumption of mainstream generative grammar, leading directly to "syntactocentric" models of competence and the concept of Autonomous Syntax.

The opposing position, that generative grammar should be based on detailed representational semantic structure, was first proposed in [3]. At the same time, a parallel program of language analysis in Artificial Intelligence, using conceptual structures and semantic decomposition, was carried out under the label *semantic parsing* [30]. Subsequently, the assumption is readopted into the generative line by [20], where the importance to the grammar of such semantic primitives such as PATH and PLACE was recognised and argued convincingly. From the background

[7] For further details of this construction, see [11] and [26].
[8] See [24] for discussion of this point.

of a more mainstream syntactic approach, [13] also acknowledge the necessity for distinguishing a fine-grained palette of semantic objects such as *proposition, outcome, fact* and *soa* ("state of affairs") in order to make a precise characterisation of subcategorisation requirements.

To motivate the need to refer to semantic information in the grammar, we can consider the subcategorisation requirements of a verb like *put.* In textbooks this may be given, in its primary usage as in *put something somewhere*, as "V NP PP". However, the final "*somewhere*" argument may actually be realised by constituents with a number of different syntactic categories as shown in (7).

(7)	He put it	on the table [PP] there [AdvP] the same place he always puts it [NP] too high for anyone to reach [AP/AdvP]

If we were to increase the number of possible subcategorisation frames for this meaning of *put*, allowing these additional patterns, we would then quickly run into a problem of massive overgeneration of the grammar, making the sentences in (8) also grammatical.

(8)	*He put it	of the table [PP] then [AdvP] the same porridge [NP] too fast [AP/AdvP]

It is clear that the second external argument in this construction must be interpretable as a location.[9] This information must be found in the lexical entries for *on*, *there*, *place* and *high.*

It might be argued that this is not a problem for the competence grammar and that the sentences in (8) are actually grammatical, but bad because they violate selectional restrictions. As argued previously, we have no way of knowing the exact boundaries of the competence grammar, so it is not possible to prove or disprove this. All we can be satisfied with is if the model as a whole captures the requisite "departures from equiprobability", to use Harris's expression. However, allowing such sentences would create an huge amount of overgeneration in the grammar, which using semantic information would avoid.

Of course, it is quite possible to import this information into the syntax with a frame such as *V NP XP [locative]*, where the final argument is a constituent of any category having some feature *locative*, but this is simply smuggling semantic distinctions into the syntax itself.

> In a syntactocentric theory... every combinatorial aspect of semantics must be ultimately derived from syntactic combinatoriality. In other words, syntax must be at least as complex as semantics. On the other hand, if Conceptual Structure is an autonomous component, there is no need for every aspect of it to be mirrored in syntax.[9], p.19

[9]Furthermore, it should be interpreted as the location of the theme as a result of the action of putting, which is why *he put the moon under the table* is just as unlikely as *the moon is under the table.*

Furthermore, it soon becomes evident when we look outside syntax textbooks and look to cover the widest range of naturally-occurring language that the need for identifying such semantic objects as *frequency, duration, time, location* becomes of even greater importance.

One longstanding weakness of representative semantics of the kind described is the seeming arbitrariness of many of the distinctions that have to be made, for example, that of how many thematic roles should be identified. If we are in a position to make an objective evaluation of the system the grammar is a part of, however, we have a way of testing if different ways of dividing the semantic world have any impact on improved performance. The same point is made by Suppes:

> Beginning with a probabilistic grammar, we want to improve the probabilistic predictions by taking into account the postulated semantic structure. The test of the correctness of the semantic structure is then in terms of the additional predictions we can make." [33], p.392

2.3. Dynamic Syntax

The syntactic structure approach to modelling syntax abstracts away from the time-flow of language, so that one can build up structures from any point of the string, starting at the end or in the middle.

In a dynamic model of syntax, words are seen as performing transitions between successive states, which are typically taken to be the growing interpretation of the sentence.

$$S_0 \xrightarrow{w_1} S_1 \xrightarrow{w_2} S_2 \xrightarrow{w_3} S_3 \ldots\ldots\ldots S_{n-1} \xrightarrow{w_n} S_n$$

If we indeed take the states to represent the growing interpretation then there is clearly no limit on their size, and formally the model can be seen as a Markov model with a countably infinite number of states. The famous argument in [6] as to the insufficiency of finite-state Markov models for syntactic description does not apply to them.[10]

A dynamic model of the competence grammar was proposed in [16] and in the following decade there were a number of independent proposals for dynamic grammars. The approach of [27] was used primarily to solve long-standing problems of non-constituent coordination. [35] considers the dynamic analysis of a wide variety of syntactic phenomena from English and other languages. In the framework of [22], a decorated logical tree structure is built up word by word, and the approach is used to explore a number of problems in anaphora resolution, relative clause structures, and other phenomena.

Apart from these linguistic motivations, adopting a dynamic grammar is also likely to satisfy the constraint that it be directly employable in an incremental model of language understanding. The parser and the grammar must always be seen as being separate entities, but the more directly the parser is able to employ the grammar, all else being equal, the better.

---

[10]See [17] for a discussion of the formal power of incremental grammars and arguments for their "superior properties in terms of mathematical complexity".

3. The Proposed Model

3.1. Semantic Representation

Let us take (9) as an example sentence and first consider how we might wish to represent its meaning, which will be the output of our model of language interpretation.

(9) Bill went across the street.

Employing the analysis of [20] would give us the following conceptual structure, containing five conceptual constituents:

$$[_{Situation}\ \text{PAST}\ ([_{Event}\ \text{GO}\ ([_{Thing}\ \text{BILL}],[_{Path}\ \text{ACROSS}\ ([_{Thing}\ \text{STREET; DEF}])])])]$$

For our purposes it will be preferable to represent the information inherent in this structure in a distributed way, breaking it up into individual atoms of information. To do this we introduce variables for each of the constituents and represent the relations between them as functions, giving an unordered conjunction of information as in (9a).

situation(s) & past(s) & ⇒(s,e) & event(e) & go_v(e) & theme(e,x) & path(e,p) & male(x) & named(x,Bill) & singular(x) & path(p) & across_p(p) & theme(p,x1) & street_n(x1) & definite(x1) & singular(x1)

(9a) Semantic representation for *Bill went across the street*

Some minor details have been changed, but nothing substantial hinges on this and readers should feel free to substitute their semantic representation of choice, the only requirement being that it is represented as pieces of information about a collection of related semantic objects. The semantic representation could also be viewed as a logical form, annotated with extra information further identifying and expanding the entities.

The subscripts *_n, _v* and *_p* serve to distinguish the particular lexical entry, for example that it is the verb *go* that we are dealing with and not the noun *go*.[11] Also we have to introduce names for relations that are represented structurally in the Jackendoffian conceptual structure. The relation between the situation and the eventuality (here an event) that it contains is represented with the symbol ⇒ (to be read as "supports" or "contains"). Bill is the *theme* of the event *e* and the path "across the street" is the *path* of this event.[12]

[11] Similarly, in the case of homonyms with separate lexical entries, we should also distinguish in some way the particular entry we are referring to, for example the game *go* and a *go* on the roundabout.

[12] Here we use *path* in two distinct functions: as the name of a relation and as the type of a semantic constituent. It should also be made clear that the semantic labels *singular* and *past* are

Unlike the case in Jackendoff's conceptual structures, no attempt will be made here at lexical decomposition, in which *Bill crossed the street*, for example, would end up with a similar representation to (9a). Instead we will stick closely to the lexical items themselves.

3.2. Incremental derivation

Given that the representation in (9a) is the end state in the interpretation of sentence (9), the task of the dynamic grammar is to derive it word-by-word through a sequence of states. It is clear that we can only add the information provided by a particular word in the sentence when we reach the word. Let us then assume that the sequence of state in the derivation is represented in figure 1 and that in doing so we make the following assumptions.

1. Semantic constituents undergoing construction are placed on a *stack*, which is shown in the derivation diagram with its top to the right. So when the word *street* is added there are four constituents on the stack, the situation *s* being on the bottom and the definite entity *x1* on the top. In general, new constituents are placed on the stack and will be removed only when complete.
2. We start in State 0, ie. before the first word, with the situation *s* already in existence, although it contains no other information. This can be taken to mean that we have an expectation of a situation.[13]
3. Transitions between successive states in general only add information to the growing representation. The conjunction of information is implicit.
4. Transitions between successive states may take place with or without the consumption of a word from the input string. These transitions will be referred to as *lexical* and *postlexical* transitions, respectively.
5. The derivation diagram shows only the information *added* at each state, but of course previous information added at previous states still persists throughout the derivation, so the content of a constituent at any state is the totality of information that has been added to it up to that point.

To run through the derivation, transition 1 (that is, the transition from state 0 to state 1) is a lexical transition adding a new constituent x to the stack. Transition 2 is a postlexical transition that removes x from the stack and attaches it with the *syntactic relation* of *subject* to the situation *s*. We will use a small number of syntactic relations, such as *subject*, which do not contribute to the meaning of the expression, but have a structural role in the construction of the meaning. Transition 3 is a lexical transition where the word *went* adds the information to *s* that it is *past* and creates a new event *e* supported by the situation *s*, and which inherits its *subject* value. This is followed by a postlexical transition in which the subject is marked with the first thematic role *theme* of the verb *go*.

to be distinguished from properties of lexical entries, for example of *street* and *went* respectively. It might be clearer to employ distinct terms for the features of semantic constituents, such as *quantity* =*1* and *Time* = T_0, but as long as we bear the distinction in mind it should not lead to problems.

[13] Of course, this is assuming no previous context. In a dialogue, for example when beginning a reply to a question, the start state may already contain information.

State	Word	Constituent Stack ⟶			
0		s situation(s)			
1	**Bill**	s	**x** male(x), named(x,Bill), sg(x)		
2		s subject(s,x)			
3	**went**	s past(s), ⇒(s,e)	**e** event(e), go_v(e), subject(e,x)		
4		s	**e** theme(e,x)		
5	**across**	s	**e** path(e,p)	**p** path(p), across_p(p)	
6	**the**	s	**e**	**p**	**x1** definite(x1)
7	**street**	s	**e**	**p**	**x1** street_n(x1), sg(x1)
8		s	**e**	**p** theme(p,x1)	**x1**
9		s	**e**	**p**	
10		s	**e**		
11		s			

Figure 1. Incremental derivation of *Bill went across the street*

The derivation is effectively completed at transition 8 with the attachment of *x1* as the *theme* of the *path p*. The final three transitions successively remove the completed top constituent on the stack until only the single situation *s* remains and we can say the derivation is successful.

3.3. The grammar and the parser

The *construction stack* used in the derivation is to be identified with the *parse stack* typically used by a parser in the construction of the syntactic structure. This represents a fundamental redivision of resources between the parser and the grammar, bringing the stack structure into the grammar itself. As argued in the methodological discussion, we do not know *a priori* where we should draw the division between parser and grammar, just that such a division must exist. It can be argued that redefining the stack as a structure used by the grammar actually simplifies both the grammar and parser, in that the grammar can thus avoid having to use a separate level of syntactic structure as a framework to construct meaning, and the parser can simply use the structures and objects defined by the competence grammar itself, and is left with the sole task of choosing which path or paths to follow.

> "...considerations of parsimony in the theory of language evolution and language development... lead us to expect that... a close relation is likely to hold between the competence grammar and the structures dealt with by the psychological processor, and that it will incorporate the competence grammar in a modular fashion." [32], p.227.

3.4. The absence of syntactic structure

If we turn the derivation diagram on its side, we may be able to see in it the ghosts of syntactic structure. For example, the period when the constituent *x1* is on the stack corresponds to the input of the string "the street", and we might be tempted to refer to this span as an NP. Similarly, the path *p* is on the stack for the string *along the street*, corresponding to a standard PP, the event *e* corresponds to the sequence *went along the street*, a VP, and the whole situation s is on the stack for the whole sentence, an S. This correspondence is revealing, in that it illustrates how thinking of syntax in terms of syntactic constituency has seemed so plausible. However, these structures that we might be tempted to see in the derivation diagram are purely epiphenomenal – all that is used in the derivation is the information in the lexical entries for the words (which all theories must have), the growing semantic/conceptual representation (which is the output of the system) and the stack (which would be needed for parsing in any case). There is no need, and no place, for any further level of representation.

Furthermore, although in this simple English sentence the semantic constituents correspond to contiguous word strings, in general this is not necessarily the case. We may allow our transition rules to bring constituents back onto the stack at some later point in the derivation and add further information to them. Such an action will correspond to creating "discontinuous constituents", but since they are in any case phantom constituents, their discontinuity is not problematic.

So, the semantic representation is constructed not in a static way on a framework of syntactic structure, but incrementally using the parse stack. Is there a fundamental reason why this approach is doomed to failure?

> Should *all* syntactic structure be slashed away? Our goal, a theory of syntax with the minimal structure necessary to map between phonology and meaning leaves open the possibility that there is *no* syntax at all: that it is possible to map directly from phonological structure (including prosody) to meaning. ...we think it is unlikely." [9], p.20

The problem with the argument here is the equation of *syntax* with *syntactic structure*. The transition rules of the dynamic syntax are *syntactic* rules, but they operate by building *semantic* structure. They may refer to *syntactic* information about words, such as their wordclass and subcategorisation requirements, but this information stays in the lexicon and is not projected into a syntactic structure. It is clear that languages need syntax, but not clear that they need syntactic structure, indeed I have argued that any such apparent structures are purely epiphenomenal and can only serve as descriptions of strings of words that all add information to the same semantic constituent .

3.5. Transition Rules

To demonstrate the operation of the grammar, we have been effectively working in reverse, starting with the desired final interpretation and then positing a succession of states which will arrive at this interpretation. We now have to formulate the rules of the grammar that will allow this succession of states, that is we must formulate transition rules.

The general form of all rules may be represented as in (2):

Rules may set conditions on the lexical entry of the current word (in the case of *lexical* transition rules), on the current state of the interpretation **S** and specify what new information will be added to form the next state **S+1**.

As an example of a lexical transition, we might represent the rule that applied when we added a finite verb, such as *went* in (9), in the following manner:

Lex:	Conditions on lexical entry of input word
S:	Conditions on current state of interpretation
S+1:	Information added at next state of interpretation

Figure 2. General schema for transition rules

Lex:	verb(lex), finite(lex)
S:	situation(ac), subject(ac, X)
S+1:	$\Rightarrow$(ac,new), head(lex)(new), subject(new, X)

Figure 3. ADD FINITE VERB transition rule

Here we use the variable *lex* to refer to the lexical entry for the current word and introduce a variable *ac* (for *Active Constituent*) to refer to the *topmost element* on the stack. For the added information at the following state, we employ a variable *new* to refer to a newly-created constituent.[14] The variable **X** is used here to indicate not only that the Active Constituent must have a subject, but also that it will be identical to the subject of the new constituent at the next state.

Postlexical transition rules do not consume a word from the input string, but can apply at any time if the current state meets the conditions. As an example, figure (4) is a representation of the rule that performs transition 2 in the derivation, removing the Active Constituent from the stack and attaching it as the subject of the underlying situation.

S:	complete(ac), situation(subac)
S+1:	subject(subac, ac), nonstack(ac)

Figure 4. ADD SUBJECT transition rule

Here we use the variable *subac* to refer to the second-to-top constituent on the stack. Typically, lexical transition rules will impose conditions on the lexical entry and the Active Constituent, while postlexical transition rules will impose conditions on the Active Constituent and Sub-Active Constituent.[15] We are free to think of added information like *nonstack(ac)* as either a new piece of information about the interpretation, updating the previous information *stack(ac)*, or as an action to be performed, ie. *pop the stack.*

Returning to the derivation of our example (9), we can informally name the transition rule performing each transition to give figure 5.[16]

[14]For simplicity, I ignore here the way the tense of the finite verb supplies information about the *time* of the situation.

[15]Though this is by no means a stipulation of the grammar.

[16]In this and future derivations we simplify by omitting the variable name in features, and the first variable in relations, as this is always identical to the name of the constituent being constructed.

Word	Rule	Constituent Stack ⟶			
	initial	s situation			
Bill	*shift*	s	**x** male, named:Bill, sg		
	add-subject	s subject:x			
went	*finite-verb*	s past, ⇒e	**e** event, go_v, subject:x		
	active-voice	s	**e** theme:x		
across	*complement*	s	**e** path:p	**p** path, across_p	
the	*shift*	s	**e**	**p**	**x1** definite
street	*noun-head*	s	**e**	**p**	**x1** street_n, sg
	complement	s	**e**	**p** theme:x1	**x1**
	reduce	s	**e**	**p**	
	reduce	s	**e**		
	reduce	s			

Figure 5. Derivation of (9) showing transition rules

3.5.1. Transition rules as constructions

Transition rules in the model correspond broadly to grammatical constructions. Any identifiable construction should correspond to a single transition rule, a single learnable move. in the construction of meaning. Rules should be able to take account of semantic, pragmatic, phonological and intonational information, as well as syntactic information about the words involved.

3.6. Coordination

We previously used a coordination construction, (4) *the dogs barked and howled*, to argue against the plausibility of syntactic constituency, given that we know that *dogs* is the theme of *barked* before the coordinated VP can be completed. We shall now take a brief look, therefore, at treatment of coordination in the dynamic model and how we can be assured of incremental interpretation of the coordinate structure.

The derivation of i(4) is given in figure 6[17] and shows that interpretation of the initial string *the dogs barked* takes place incrementally, just as if it had occurred as a separate sentence, with *dogs* being attached immediately attached as the *theme* of *bark* as we required. The coordination itself is achieved by a new lexical transition rule applying at the word *and*. This creates a new conjoined object *s1*, which takes as values of the conjunction operator *&* the finished situation *s* and a new constituent *s2*. Crucially this second conjunct can share information from a previous state of the first conjunct. Here it shares the information in *s* at **State 3** that it is a *situation* and has *x* as its subject. This shared information is shaded in the diagram for illustrative purposes, but has the same status as any information in a constituent. The derivation can then continue with the finite verb *howled* using the transition rule already given.

[17] To save space, here and in subsequent derivations I omit the final transitions where completed constituents are simply reduced from the stack.

	s situation		
the	s	**x** definite	
dogs	s	**x** dog_n, pl	
	s subject:x		
barked	s past, ⇒e	**e** event, bark_v, subject:x	
	s	**e** theme:x	
	s		
and	**s1** &:[s,s2]	**s2** situation, subject:x	
howled	**s1**	**s2** past, ⇒e1	**e1** event, howl_v, subject:x
	s1	**s2**	**e1** theme:x

Figure 6. Derivation of *The dogs barked and howled*

The transition at *and* could alternatively have added to the new constituent *s2* the information present in *s* at **State 0**, ie. just designating it as an empty *situation*. This transition would be needed if the second conjunct was complete sentence as in *The dogs barked and the cats miaowed.*

This simple rule for coordination, in which the second conjunct shares information from some previous state of the first conjunct, is in reality forced on us by the incremental nature of the grammar. However, it has some very desirable consequences when we consider such long-standing coordination problems as non-constituent coordination (10) and the coordination of constituents of unlike syntactic categories (11).

(10) He took ⟨Jim to town today ⟩ and ⟨Jill to school yesterday⟩.

(11) He was ⟨talented⟩, but ⟨doing too little to justify his wage⟩.

Both of these cases follow from our single simple coordination rule without further stipulation. In (10) the second conjunct will share information up to and including the word *taking*, and can then proceed with the additional arguments and modifier. In (11), the second conjunct shares the information up to and was *was* and then continues with the progressive construction. Indeed, if these examples were not grammatical we would be faced with a tricky task of adding stipulations to rule them out. So, both for reasons of allowing incremental interpretation and closely fitting the data, it seems that the dynamic treatment of coordination may be on the right track.[18]

3.7. Wh-movement

So much syntactic argumentation in generative grammar has involved "movement" constructions that it will be instructive to demonstrate how the dynamic approach deals with it.

(12) Who did Bill like _ ?

[18] See [27] for extensive discussion of non-constituent coordination from the perspective of a dynamic grammar.

In (12) the problem for the dynamic approach is what to do with the semantic constituent formed by *who* until it can be attached as the theme of *like*. We have already seen one syntactic relation *subject* which holds a semantically unattached constituent in place. To deal with movement we introduce another syntactic relation *store*, which can hold a list of constituents (actually constituent addresses) rather than a single value.

	s situation	
who	s	**x** human, wh
did	s question, past, store:[x]	
Bill	s	**x1** male, named:Bill, sg
	s subject:x1	
like	s ⇒e, store:[]	**e** state, like_v, subject:x1, store:[x]
	s	**e** experiencer:x1
	s	**e** theme:x, store:[]

Figure 7. Who did Bill like?

There are two new transition rules needed here. First is the rule that applies at the auxiliary verb *was* taking the completed constituent x of the stack and putting its address in the *store* feature of the situation s. The conditions for this rule are sketched in figure 8.

Lex:	verb(lex), finite(lex), auxiliary(lex)
S:	wh(ac), situation(subac)
S+1:	question(subac), store(subac, ac), nonstack(ac)

Figure 8. INVERTED AUXILIARY transition rule

The second new rule is a postlexical transition rule that interprets an element on the store, ie. removing the top constituent on the store and attaching it with a thematic role. This is the last transition to apply here, attaching x as theme of the event e.[19]

Together with the treatment of coordination this analysis also predicts the pattern observed in [25]: p.490, that in *wh*-questions the fronted object cannot be shared, by itself, between the two conjuncts, as demonstrated in (13).

(13) *Which guy did Bill ignore __ and should Jill pay __ ?
(14) Which guy did Bill ignore __ and should Jill pay?

This follows automatically. When we get to the conjunction *and*, the grammar gives us the choice of either sharing the state of the situation before *which*, ie. an empty situation, in which case we get a normal yes-no question as the second conjunct, as in (14), or we can return to the state after *did* is added, in which case the situation already has a tense and the finite verb *should* cannot be added.[20]

[19] We also have to extend our rules for adding lexical verbs to make sure that the store value is inherited by the new constituent, as happens here at the word *like*.

[20] We could of course return to this state after *did* and continue instead with a subject and bare infinitival as in *which guy did Bill ignore __ and Jill pay __ ?*

3.7.1. Subject extraction

As mentioned above we must allow rules introducing complements to inherit the store feature, and doing so will allow indefinitely deep object extraction as in (15). However, it will not explain how extraction can take place out of subject position as in (16) (or rather, from a dynamic perspective, how a constituent in store can later become subject of an embedded clause).

(15) Who did he think (that) John said (that) he liked _ ?
(16) Who did he think (*that) _ had lied?

The only way to derive (16) is to introduce a postlexical transition which attaches a new *situation* complement, at the same time taking the constituent on top of the store and installing it as subject of the new situation.[21] This rule applies at transition 7 of the derivation in figure 9 to create the new situation *s1* with its subject *x*.

	s situation			
who	s	**x** human, wh		
did	s question, past, store:[x]			
he	s	**x1** male, sg		
	s subject:x1			
think	s $\Rightarrow$e, store:[]	**e** state, think_v, subject:x1, store:[x]		
	s	**e** experiencer:x1		
	s	**e** store:[], theme:s1	**s1** situation, subject:x	
had	s	**e**	**s1** past, perfect	
lied	s	**e**	**s1** $\Rightarrow$e1	**e1** event, lie_v, subject:x
	s	**e**	**s1**	**e1** agent:x

Figure 9. Who did he think had lied?

It is not a problem for the grammar that we have to posit a separate construction to allow the derivation, as the marked status of subject extraction is well-established, being disallowed in many languages and being acquired by children considerably later than object extraction. The need for a postlexical transition to perform subject extraction also has the immediate consequence that there will be no possibility of beginning the embedded clause with a complementizer, thus explaining the much-studied *that*-trace effect. This follows as the only function of the complementizer *that* is to create a new situation, but this has already been created by the postlexical subject-extraction transition.[22]

[21] We will in any case need a postlexical transition rule to introduce contact embedded clauses as in *He thinks he lied.*

[22] This explanation may be compared with the many to be found in the generative literature made in terms of suppositions about abstract properties of abstract syntactic structures. For example, one of two explanations of the phenomenon given in [8]: 'Suppose that the intermediate trace can only be governed from outside CP if it bears the same index as the head of CP (see clause (c) of Lasnik and Saito's definition, where an intervening CP blocks government). Suppose further that when the head of CP is empty, the element in the CP specifier assigns its index to the head of CP by a process of agreement. Then when *that* is present, the trace in the CP specifier will not be coindexed with the head of CP and as such will not be eligible for antecedent government from outside CP".

This subject extraction transition (or store-to-subject switching transition) also solves the puzzle of how the accusative form of relative pronouns can seemingly end up in subject position of embedded clauses, as in (17) (even, or perhaps particularly, when the writer uses *whom* in this construction colloquially). It also explains how the same constituent can be extracted out of both object and (embedded) subject position at the same time, as in (18), with no clash of case.

(17) Young Ferdinand, whom they suppose is drown'd. *Tempest III iii 92*

(18) The candidate who/whom he supported, but thought could not win.

In both cases, the derivation goes through because the constituent starts off as being in store, and therefore a non-subject form is used, and only later in the derivation is it reattached as a subject.

4. Dealing with more flexible word orders

4.1. Scrambling in the German Mittelfeld

Reape [28] presents the following example of a German subordinate clause, (19), with its typical verb-final word order. The ordering of the preverbal arguments, in what is known as the *Mittelfeld*, makes any kind of immediate constituent analysis exceedingly problematic, as each of the arguments is separated from its dependent-head by other constituents.

(19)	... daß	es	ihm	jemand	zu lesen	versprochen	hat.
	... that	it(acc)	him(dat)	someone(nom)	to read	promised	has
	... that someone promised him to read it.						

In fact, as Reape shows, the pre-verbal arguments may be arranged in any order.

(20)	...daß	es ihm jemand es jemand ihm ihm es jemand ihm jemand es jemand es ihm jemand ihm es	zu lesen versprochen hat.

Such arbitrary constituent orders pose obvious problems for approaches based on syntactic structures, whether based on syntactic dependencies or syntactic constituents, as it appears to be impossible to avoid crossing dependencies or discontinuous constituents. This has led leading researchers working in the HPSG paradigm to abandon the assumption that constituent structure determines word order at all. Instead they add an extra level of representation to capture the surface order of constituents: for Reape [28] this is "Word Order Domains" and for Kathol's "Linear Syntax" [21] it is "topological fields defined orthogonally to constituency".

From the perspective of Dynamic Syntax, however, there is no need to complicate the model by adding an extra level of representation. Indeed, because we have no representation of syntactic structure in the model no problem of "tangling" in this level can arise. Instead, figure 10 shows that a quite straightforward analysis is possible making use of the feature *store* that we introduced above for English.

dass	s situation	
es	s	**x** neuter, nom/acc, singular
	s store:[x]	
ihm	s	**x1** dat, masc, singular
	s store:[x,x1]	
jemand	s	**x2** nom, indef, human
	s store:[x,x1,x2]	
zu lesen	s	**e** event, inf, lesen_v, agent:α
	s store:[x1,x2]	**e** theme:x
versprochen	s	**e1** event, pp, versprechen_v, theme:e, agent:α
	s store:[x2]	**e1** benef:x1
hat	s pres, perf, $\Rightarrow$e1, subj:x2, store:[], α=x2	

Figure 10. ...daß es ihm jemand zu lesen versprochen hat.

In figure 10 as each element in the Mittelfeld is created there is no possibility of interpretation in the growing semantic structure and so it is taken off the stack and placed in the store. When we get to the infinitival *zu lesen* we are not in a position to identify the subject and hence the agent of the event and hence fill it with a placeholding variable α. We are, however, able to fill the *theme* role of the event with the stored entity x *es*, which is thus removed from the store. The event *e1* introduced at *versprechen* can take the infinitival event e as its *theme* and as it is a subject control verb its subject and agent must be the same as that of event e, ie. the placeholder α. The event *versprechen* can also fill its benefactive role with the dative *x1* and thus remove it from the store. Finally the finite verb *hat* takes the past participle event *e1* as its content and the remaining store element *x2* as its subject, which can now be resolved to replace the placeholder α as agents of the two events.[23]

We can thus argue that the basic architecture of the grammar is the same for English and German, which is surely a welcome conclusion. For English, however, the store is used less extensively and generally in a "last in first out" manner, exemplified in the well-known examples in (21).

(21) a. Which violin$_i$ is this sonata$_j$ hard to play $\_\__j$ on $\_\__i$?
b. *Which sonata$_i$ is this violin$_j$ hard to play $\_\__i$ on $\_\__j$?

Whereas, in the case of German, greater use is made of stored constituents and they can be accessed irrespective of their position on the store.

[23]It is perhaps possible that this element might be predicted to be agent of the events even before the finite verb is reached. This does not affect the argument for the advantage of the dynamic approach in this example however.

4.2. Scrambling in Czech

An even more extreme example of scrambling is presented by the following naturally-occurring Czech example (22)[24]:

(22) Za dnešní kríze by se lidem jako Petr kvúli jejich přímúm takový byt žádný majitel domu za tu cenu nemohl na tak dlouhou dobu snažit pronajímat.
{in today's crisis} *cond refl* {people-DAT like Petr} {because-of their income} {such apartment} {no owner house-GEN} {for that price} couldn't {for such long time} try let
In today's crisis no landlord would try to let such a flat to people like Petr for that rent for such a long period because of their income.

It will be apparent from perusal of the example that the complements and adjuncts of the event headed by *let* are not adjacent to it, occur in a seemingly arbitrary order, and are also interspersed with adjuncts of the matrix clause, making a representation of the VP headed by *let* highly problematic. Alternatively, in dependency terms, an analysis would involve a large number of crossing dependencies.

	s situation		
za dnešní kríze	s store:[x]	**x** [IN TODAY'S CRISIS]	
by	s conditional		
se	s refl		
lidem jako Petr	s store:[x,x1]	**x1** dat, [TO PEOPLE LIKE PETR]	
kvúli jejich přímúm	s store:[x,x1,x2]	**x2** [BECAUSE OF THEIR INCOME]	
takový byt	s store:[x,x1,x2,x3]	**x3** nom/acc, [SUCH A FLAT]	
žádný majitel domu	s store:[x,x1,x2,x3,x4]	**x4** nom, [NO LANDLORD]	
za tu cenu	s store:[x,x1,x2,x3,x4,x5]	**x5** [FOR THAT PRICE]	
nemohl	s neg, [CAN], sbj:x4, store:[x,x1,x2,x3,x5]		
	s mod:[x,x2] store:[x1,x3,x5]		
na tak dlouhou dobu	s store:[x1,x3,x5,x6]	**x6** [FOR SUCH A LONG TIME]	
snažit	s ⇒e	**e** event, refl, [TRY], agent:x4	
pronajímat	s	**e** theme:e1	**e1** event, [RENT], agent:x4
	s store:[x1,x5,x6]	**e**	**e1** theme:x3
	s store:[x5,x6]	**e**	**e1** benef:x1
	s store:[]	**e**	**e** mod:[x5,x6]

Figure 11. Schematic derivation of example (22)

Due to the inordinate length of the example, I will not present a word-by-word analysis but instead ignore the internal composition of the constituents, just looking at how the entities get to receive the correct interpretation. Figure 11 makes extensive use of the store in much the same way as we did for the German example above, with elements going onto the store when they are in no position

[24] A corpus example, due originally to Karel Oliva.

to receive an interpretation, and coming off the store when an opportunity for interpretation arises.[25] As was the case for German, there is no English-type restriction on what order the elements on the store are accessed.

Using the implementation of the English dynamic grammar described below, it is necessary only to modify a couple of transition rules to allow the grammar to find the correct analysis. These are first to modify the topicalization rule so instead of just one topic placed on the store as in English, we are allowed an arbitrary number of elements, and second to allow any element on store to be interpreted at any time and not just the topmost element. With these modifications, the rest of the grammar necessary for the analysis of this sentence and its English equivalent can be virtually identical.

5. Current Implementation

I have given in the previous section a series of syntactic analyses to suggest the attractions of the model in terms of elegance and explanatory power. In the first half of this paper, however, I argued that such piecemeal syntactic argumentation can at best be suggestive and does not replace the need for an objective, wholescale evaluation of the model. For this we need to embed the competence grammar in a processing model with the capacity to make predictions about likely strings of words. The grammar outlined in this paper has been developed in tandem with such a predictive probabilistic model of language interpretation and to conclude the paper I shall give an outline of the current state of this implementation, and discuss ways of moving towards the goal of a full integrated model.

5.1. Transition Rules

The core of the grammar is a set of around 150 lexical and 50 postlexical transition rules, specified as in the previous section with conditions on the present word (if lexical) and the present state and the resulting new information to be added to the interpretation to form the next state. These rules have been developed by hand in interaction with parsing corpus data. The lexical rules range from the very general and productive, such as ADD FINITE-VERB, to lexically specific rules for such words as *else*, *own* (as in *their own*), the floating quantifiers (em both, all, each) and others. The range of syntactic constructions covered presently includes *wh*-movement; finite, infinitival and reduced relative clauses; pied-piping; topicalization; gerundive and participal phrases; *it*-clefts; pseudoclefts; extraposition; *tough*-movement; slifting (*John, it seems, has left*); parasitic gaps; correlative comparatives; tag questions and many others. All of these constructions correspond to a single transition rule in the grammar.

[25]To save space, in this diagram I have collapsed the formation of the constituent and its being removed from the stack and place on the store into a single transition.

5.2. Semantic representation

The semantic representation employed is a somewhat simplified version of that given in the previous section, the simplifications resulting from the demands of wide-coverage. The present representation makes no distinction between states and events, and indeed collapses the situation and its contained eventuality (ie. state/ event) together, resulting in flatter representations. Such a simplification has practical advantages, for example it reduces the potential for modifier attachment amibiguities, but is hard to defend as being linguistically sufficient. There is also no distinction between the different thematic roles, with complements instead being marked simply as *argument-1*, *argument-2* and so forth. Both these simplifications are necessitated by the lack of a lexicon suitably marked-up with semantic information. In the longer term, it should be possible to automatically analyse corpora to build steadily richer semantic distinctions into the lexicon and hence into the semantic representations. As argued before, having a model open to objective evaluation gives us a way of calculating the improvement in performance that any refinement of semantic description might achieve.

5.3. World Knowledge

In addition to our knowledge of grammar, an important part of how we can predict words in sentences is our knowledge of likely scenarios in the world. As argued previously, we should be able to distinguish a noisy string of phonemes /*d o g z p a: k t*/ as *dogs barked*, rather than *dogs parked* or *dog sparked*, simply from our knowledge of the typical behaviour of dogs. This is where we might expect our computational model to be at an irretrievable disadvantage. However help is at hand. The system substitutes its lack of world knowledge by using information about grammatical relation frequencies automatically extracted from the 100-million word British National Corpus.[26] Using this information it is possible to calculate for a wide range of grammatical relations the Mutual Information score, a statistical measure for the chance of cooccurrence — a positive score indicating a positive correlation and a negative score a negative one.

If we consider the two following grammatical sentences: (23) seems intuitively to describe a much more likely scenario, and therefore to be much more likely to occur in a text, than (24).[27]

(23) The angry man walked quickly across the street.

(24) The vertebrate silence worries the legal sail

A look at the M.I. scores for grammatical relations identified in the two sentences, shown in the following table, shows that we are able to capture the difference between the two. The grammatical relations contained in (24), none

modifier, *man_n*, *angry_adj*	2.6
argument-1, *walk_v*, *man_n*	2.7
modifier, *walk_v*, *quickly_adv*	3.5
walk_v, *across_p*, *street_n*	3.4

modifier, *silence_n*, *vertebrate_adj*	-1.3
argument-1, *worry_v*, *silence_n*	-4.5
argument-2, *worry_v*, *sail_n*	-3.5
modifier, *sail_n*, *legal_adj*	-3.1

Figure 12. Relations in (23) and (24) with their Mutual Information (M.I.) scores

of which actually occurred in the 100 million word corpus, are estimated to be strongly negative, as opposed to the positive scores for (23).[28]

It should also be borne in mind, that adding these estimates of "likely scenarios" to our model does not compromise the modularity of the system. The modularity is still maintained, the competence grammar working independently of such collocational information, and we can investigate and modify each part of the system in turn.

5.4. Processing strategy

Using knowledge of the absolute frequency of individual words, the relative frequency of the differing lexical entries associated with those words, the frequency with which each transition rules applies, and the M.I. scores for grammatical relations outlined above, the system assigns a probability estimate for each state in the derivation. This allows the parser to rank the competing derivations in terms of likelihood, which is crucial when there may potentially be many thousands of possible competing derivations, which will often be the case with a wide-coverage system. In the current system, the parser employs the simple strategy of keeping only the top-ranked n sentences at each stage in the parse, this being known as n-best *beam search.*

With this probability estimate at each state in the derivation, the system can already provide a great deal of feedback in the development of the grammar itself. There is still some work to be done, however, principally in improving the robustness of the system, before we can achieve the methodological goal we set ourselves of calculating the truly objective measure of cross-entropy against a test corpus, that is how well it predicts the language in general.

6. Evaluation of the System

Here I set out two evaluation methodologies and discuss how the system performs. As the system and the syntax it embodies is still in an early period of development, evaluation is more important for development than for comparison with alternative approaches. However, it is also useful to show the potential of

[26] This work is described in [23].

[27] This is a translation of *Le silence vertébral indispose la voile licite*: Tesniere's precursor to Chomsky's *Colourless green ideas sleep furiously*. Chomsky's own example is quoted too often to fulfil its original function as a grammatical, but non-occurring sentence!

[28] Reassuringly, returning to our previous example, the M.I. score for *dog_n* as first argument of *bark_v* is 8.1, as opposed to -4.9 and -3.9 for *park_v* and *spark_v*, respectively. So in this case too corpus evidence provides a good substitute for knowledge of the world.

the dynamic approach and compare its performance with alternative established technologies

6.1. Part-of-Speech Tagging

One simple evaluation of the performance of the dynamic system is to compare how well it finds the correct part-of-speech for words in sentences from the BNC. This can then be compared with CLAWS4 tagging supplied with the corpus. CLAWS4 is a hybrid tagger employing additional stages of postprocessing with a template tagger and patching rules (described in [12]). It has been developed over a considerable period of time and going head to head with such an established system should provide a stiff test. To avoid issues arising from different divisions into wordclasses between the dynamic system and CLAWS4 and to reduce the amount of human evaluation required, we restricted the comparison to the case of deciding between verbs and nouns (VVB vs. NN1: eg. *dream*, and VVZ vs. NN2: eg. *dreams*). According to the documentation supplied with the BNC, these distinctions are the greatest sources of tagging errors in the corpus.[29] Here the choice is almost always clear-cut for a human annotator and the choice of the dynamic parser is simply taken as the corresponding lexeme in the derivation with the highest score. A random selection of sentences from the BNC was made: 307 containing words which could be both NN1 and VVB[30] and 206 containing words which could be NN2 and VVZ.[31] These sentences, with their CLAWS4 tags, were then checked by hand and errors noted.

The sentences were then given, without their tags, to the dynamic parser. If a derivation of the complete string was found, even if not a completed derivation, the lexeme for the corresponding word in the highest-scored derivation was checked against the gold standard. If no derivation was returned, the input string was successively shortened and analyzed until a derivation including the target word was recovered. This trimming of the input string was first done word-by-word from the end of the string leaving the words in front of the target word, and then carried out from the beginning of the string until a result was obtained. The results are shown in figure 13.[32]

Task	System	Errors	Correct (%)
NN1 vs VVB	CLAWS4	19/307	93.8%
	Dynamic Syntax	12/307	96.1%
NN2 vs VVZ	CLAWS4	15/206	92.7%
	Dynamic Syntax	16/206	92.2%

Figure 13. Dynamic Syntax Parser vs. CLAWS4 in N/V tagging

[29]In the BNC, present tense verbs (VVZ) are erroneously tagged as plural nouns (NN2) 6.23% of the time, while present plural verbs (VVB) are tagged as singular nouns (NN1) 5.43% of the time. These results are when considering only the first tag where multiple tags are given by CLAWS4.

[30]With the frequency of either tag in the corpus for that word being at least 20%.

[31]With the frequency of either tag being at least 5%.

[32]The baseline of choosing the most frequent tag for the two wordclasses given the wordform was calculated at 65.1% for NN1/VVB and 76.2% for NN2/VVZ.

The dynamic system made fewer errors on both tests, although the difference is too small to be statistically significant. There was very little overlap between the errors made by the two models from the two tests only four examples were mistagged by both systems. This suggests that the fact that the dynamic system has "learnt" its tag frequencies and collocation strengths from the CLAWS-tagged BNC does not mean that they make the same errors. The advantage that the dynamic model has is that the performance here is simply a by-product of its performance as a parser. The tagging performance should continue to improve as the grammar and the parsing performance improve, and the results show that it is already starting from a high standard.

6.2. Word Recovery Task

It has already been shown ([4], [29]) that syntactic models can outperform standard n-gram techniques in the task of language modelling, which corresponds to how well the model predicts the language. It would also be of great interest to see how a linguistically-motivated model compares with this baseline. Conversely, from the perspective of system development this fundamental measure of model performance is likely to be of most use in evaluating and measuring improvements to the model. However, the dynamic system is not a complete probabilistic model, and normalizing it in a reliable way would involve issues of considerable complexity. We decided therefore to employ an approximation method. We remove a word from a sentence, randomly generate a set of *n-1* competitors[33], and get the system to rank the resulting it n strings. As noted previously, in language teaching this task is known as cloze testing with a fixed choice of words and is held to be an accurate indicator of all-round linguistic ability. The results were compared with a trigram model trained on the same data, the 100m word BNC.[34] We used the *one-count* method of Chen and Goodman [5] as this offered close to optimal performance given the size of the training corpus.[35]

Since the BNC has been used extensively for development of the system over a number of years, it was not possible to designate any of the corpus as test data. Therefore we used a section of the Hector corpus, a comparable mixed corpus of British English, as test data. This was already divided into sentences. The results presented below are for those sentences (less than 30 words in length) where some result was returned by the parser (even if the derivation was not complete).[36]

---

[33]The set of competitors was generated randomly in proportion to word frequency. So frequent words were more likely to be included, but were only included once.

[34]Direct comparison of the two systems is made problematic by the differing expectations of format following standard practice to keep the trigram model compact capitalization and punctuation is removed, with only an end of sentence tag used. The dynamic system on the other hand benefits from having texts with standard orthography and punctuation. Each system was given the words in its preferred form, therefore, although the task was only to recover the words, not the punctuation.

[35]Chen and Goodmans *all- count* offers fractionally better performance, but is considerably more time-consuming to implement. The marginal improvement would not effect the general findings.

[36]This figure includes 90% of sentences of this length.

Word Set	Trigram errors/word	Dynamic errors/word	Trigram correct	Dynamic correct
10	1.17	0.77	62.1%	62.1%
20	2.68	1.69	56.0%	40.6%
50	5.72	4.55	50.0%	34.4%
100	8.33	7.94	40.9%	30.1%

Figure 14. Dynamic Syntax parser vs. trigram modelin Word Recovery Task

The results in figure 14 show both average number of errors (ie. higher-rated substitutions) per word and the percentage of correct guesses (ie. words where there was no higher-rated substitution) for different sizes of substitution sets.

The results clearly show that the dynamic model makes fewer errors overall, but the trigram model recovers more first place scores. Looking at the results in detail, the dynamic model is generally better on the less frequent words, as it captures collocation relations outside the window of trigrams and also makes use of grammatical zeroes. The trigram model, in contrast, is far stronger on frequent words and frequent sequences. It is an ongoing task to add additional factors to the dynamic probabilistic model to better capture these latter frequent sequences.

7. Conclusion

This paper has argued that it is profitable to reexamine the foundations of how we model natural language syntax. It has proposed that the novel approach of Dynamic Syntax offers a model that is in keeping with the established methodology for generative grammar and, at the same time, provides a competence grammar that is ideally suited to be used in a direct way in an overall model of language performance.

It has further been demonstrated that for many practical tasks, the Dynamic Syntax approach offers many advantages, not least in tackling the phenomenon of flexible constituent order, which continues to raise problems for models of syntax based on some notion of syntactic structure. It could be argued that the majority of languages around the world (and thus the majority of low-density languages) fall into this category.

References

[1] Apresjan, J. D. Principles and methods of contemporary structural linguistics, Mouton, The Hague, 1973.

[2] Brown, P. F., S. L. Della Pietra, V. J. Della Pietra, J. C. Lai & R. L. Mercer. *An estimate of an upper bound for the entropy of English*, Computational Linguistics, **18**, 31–40, 1992.

[3] Chafe, W. L. Meaning and the structure of language, University of Chicago Press, 1970.

[4] Chelba, C. & F. Jelinek. *Exploiting syntactic structure for language modeling.* In Proceedings of 36th ACL and 17th COLING, 225–231, 1999.

[5] Chen S. F. & J. Goodman. *An empirical study of smoothing techniques for language modeling.* In Proceedings of 34th ACL, 310–318, 1996.

[6] Chomsky, N. Syntactic structures, Mouton, The Hague, 1957.

[7] Chomsky, N. Aspects of the theory of syntax, MIT Press, 1965.

[8] Cowper, E. A. A concise introduction to syntactic theory, University of Chicago Press, 1992.

[9] Culicover, P. W. & R. Jackendoff. Simpler syntax, Oxford University Press, 2005.

[10] Fillmore, C. J. & P. Kay. Construction Grammar, Unpublished manuscript, University of California at Berkeley, Department of Linguistics, 1996.

[11] Franks, S. Parameters of Slavic morphosyntax, Oxford University Press, 1995.

[12] Garside R. & N. Smith. *A hybrid grammatical tagger:* CLAWS4, In Corpus Annotation, R. Garside, G. Leech & T. McEnery (eds.), Longman, London, 1997.

[13] Ginzburg, J. & I. A. Sag. Interrogative investigations: the form, meaning and use of English interrogatives, CSLI, Stanford, 2000.

[14] Goldberg, A. E. Constructions: a construction grammar approach to argument structure, University of Chicago Press, 1995.

[15] Harris, Z. A theory of language and information: a mathematical approach, Oxford, Clarendon Press, 1991.

[16] Hausser, R. Computation of language: an essay on syntax, semantics and pragmatics in natural man-machine communication, Springer-Verlag, Berlin, 1989.

[17] Hausser, R. *Complexity in Left-Associative Grammar*, Theoretical Computer Science, **106**, 283–308, 1992.

[18] Heaton, J. B. Writing English language tests, Longman, London, 1976.

[19] Hudson, R. Word Grammar, Blackwell, Oxford, 1984.

[20] Jackendoff, R. Semantic structures, MIT Press, 1990.

[21] Kathol, A. Linear syntax, Oxford University Press, 2000.

[22] Kempson, R., W. Meyer-Viol & D. Gabbay. Dynamic Syntax: the flow of language understanding, Blackwell, Oxford, 2001.

[23] Kilgarriff, A. & D. Tugwell. *Sketching words*, In Lexicography and natural language processing: a festschrift in honour of B.T.S. Atkins, M-H Corréard (ed.), EURALEX, 2002, 125–137.

[24] Matthews, P. H. Grammatical theory in the United States from Bloomfield to Chomsky, Cambridge University Press, 1993.

[25] McCawley, J. D. The syntactic phenomena of English, University of Chicago Press, 1998.

[26] Mel'čuk, I. Poverxnostnyj sintaksis russkix čislovykh vyraženij [*The surface syntax of Russian number expressions*], Wiener Slawischer Almanach Sonderband 16, Institut fur Slawisitik der Universitat Wien, Vienna, 1985.

[27] Milward, D. *Dynamic Dependency Grammar*, Linguistics and Philosophy, **17**, 561–605, 1994.

[28] Reape, M. *Domain union and word order variation in German.* In German in Head-Driven Phrase Structure Grammar, J. Nerbonne, K. Netter & C. J. Pollard (eds.), 151–197, 1994.

[29] Roark, B. *Probabilistic top-down parsing and language modeling*, Computational Linguistics, **27(2)**, 249–276, 2001.

[30] Schank, R. C., Conceptual information processing, Elsevier, Amsterdam, 1975.

[31] Schütze, C. T. The empirical base of linguistics: grammaticality judgments and linguistic methodology, University of Chicago Press, 1996.

[32] Steedman, M. The syntactic process, MIT Press, 2000.

[33] Suppes, P. *Semantics of context-free fragments of natural languages*, In Approaches to Natural Language, K.J.J. Hintikka, J.M.E. Moravcsik & P. Suppes (eds.), Reidel, Dordrecht, 370-394, 1973.

[34] Tomasello, M. Constructing a language: a usage-based theory of language acquisition, Harvard University Press, 2003.

[35] Tugwell, D. Dynamic Syntax, PhD Thesis, University of Edinburgh, 1999.

[36] Tugwell, D. *Language Modelling with Dynamic Syntax*, In Proceedings of Text, Speech and Dialogue 2006, Brno, Czech Republic, Springer, Berlin, 285–292, 2006.

Language Engineering for Lesser-Studied Languages
S. Nirenburg (Ed.)
IOS Press, 2009

doi:10.3233/978-1-58603-954-7-183

Computational Field Semantics: Acquiring an Ontological-Semantic Lexicon for a New Language

Sergei NIRENBURG[1] and Marjorie MCSHANE

Institute for Language and Information Technologies
University of Maryland Baltimore County

Abstract. We present a methodology and tools that facilitate the acquisition of lexical-semantic knowledge about a language L. The lexicon that results from the process described in this paper expresses the meaning of words and phrases in L using a language-independent formal ontology, the OntoSem ontology. The acquisition process benefits from the availability of an ontological-semantic lexicon for English. The methodology also addresses the task of aligning any existing computational grammar of L with the expectations of the syntax-oriented zone of the ontological-semantic lexicon. Illustrative material in this paper is presented by means of the DEKADE knowledge acquisition environment.

Keywords. semantics, computational semantics, lexical acquisition, low-density languages

1. Introduction

1.1. What constitutes a comprehensive set of resources for a particular language?

These days one usually starts the work of developing resources for a particular language with the acquisition of textual corpora, either monolingual or parallel across two or more languages. Such corpora serve as the foundation for the various types of corpus-oriented statistics-based work that have been actively pursued over the past 20 years, machine translation being one of the most prominent end applications. There is, however, a consensus among workers in natural language processing that having at one's disposal formal knowledge about the structure and meaning of elements of a language L is truly beneficial for a broad variety of applications, including even corpus-based ones. This being the case, the questions arise, *What knowledge should be acquired*? and *How should knowledge acquisition be carried out*?

Consider how knowledge acquisition might begin. One can start by describing L's writing system, including punctuation marks, then describe L's conventions concerning word boundaries, the rendering of proper names, the transliteration of foreign words, and the expression of dates, numbers, currencies, abbreviations, etc. All of these

[1] Corresponding Author: Sergei Nirenburg, Department of Computer Science and Electrical Engineering, ITE 325, 1000 Hilltop Circle, Baltimore, Maryland, 21250, USA; E-mail: sergei@umbc.edu.

together comprise what the late Don Walker called language *ecology*. Next comes morphology – information about word structure in L. One should cover paradigmatic inflectional morphology (*run* ~ *runs*), non-paradigmatic inflectional morphology (e.g., agglutinating inflectional morphology, as found in Turkish), and derivational morphology (*happy* ~ *unhappy*).

Next, the structure of the sentence in L should be described. This would include, at a minimum: the structure of noun phrases – i.e., noun phrase (NP) components and their ordering; the realization of subcategorization and grammatical functions, like subject and direct object; the realization of sentence types – declarative, interrogative, etc.; and specialized syntactic structures such as fronting and clefting.

At this point, issues of meaning will come to the fore. First, one will have to deal with "grammatical" meanings in L – meanings that can be realized in various languages as words, phrases, affixes or features. For example, the notion of possession can be expressed by a genitive case marker in Russian, by the preposition *of* in English, and by free-standing pronouns in either language (*my, your*, etc.). Similarly, the fact that a noun phrase is definite can be realized in English by the definite article (*the*), in French by a free-standing word (*le, la, les*) or prefix (*l'-),* and in Bulgarian by a suffix (*-to, -ta, -'t*, etc.). One could expect to have to account for about 200 such grammatical meanings in L. These language-specific realizations will be stored in the so-called *closed-class lexicon* of L, which is the portion of the lexicon that, under normal circumstances, cannot be productively added to by language users – except over very long spans of historical change.

Figure 1 shows a closed-class elicitation screen from the Boas knowledge elicitation system – a system that elicits computer-tractable knowledge about low-density languages from non-linguist speakers of the language.[2]

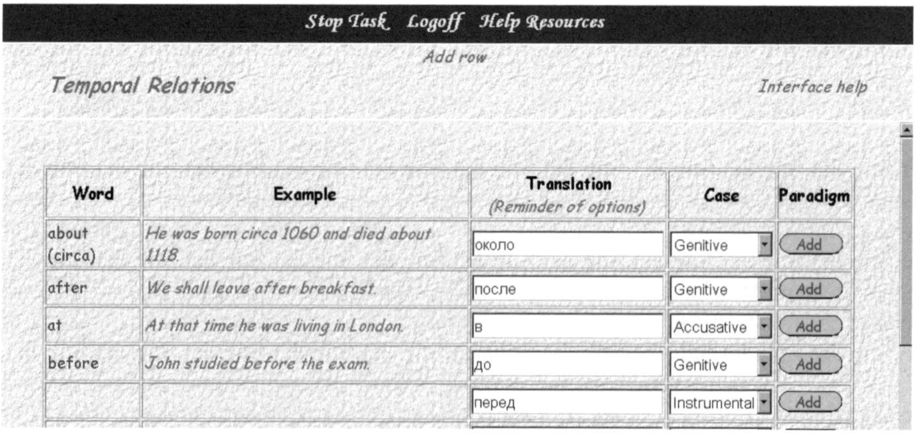

Figure 1. Closed-class lexical acquisition in the Boas system.

The first column provides an English "prompt" for the sense being elicited (the system assumes that all language informants know English), and the second column

[2] For further description of the Boas system see [6], [7], [8], [9], [14]. For another approach to gathering and processing knowledge for low-density languages, see [20].

provides an illustrative example of how this sense is used. The third column seeks one or more L equivalents for this meaning; note the "Add row" button at the top of the screen, which permits any number of additional rows to be added to the table if more than one realization of a given meaning is possible. The "Reminder of options" button links to a help page that describes all possible means of realizing closed-class meanings cross-linguistically: e.g., as a word, affix, case feature, etc. It also describes how various types of entities should be entered: for example, suffixes are preceded by a hyphen: *-to* is the suffix *to*. The fifth row, Case, is included for those languages that have inflectional case-marking. Since the screen shot was made from an elicitation session for Russian, this column is present and the inventory of cases in the pull-down menu is exactly those that are relevant for Russian. The last column permits the user to enter the inflectional paradigm for the given item, if applicable. Very often, if closed-class meanings have paradigms, they are idiosyncratic; therefore, users are asked to enter the paradigms for closed-class meanings explicitly. The information about a given language that permits the fourth and fifth columns to be catered to that language is elicited prior to the start of work on building the closed-class lexicon. This example shows the types of information that must be elicited in the closed-class lexicon and some practical decisions that were made in building a cross-linguistically robust knowledge elicitation system.

As mentioned earlier, the closed-class lexicon of any language is relatively small. The much larger portion of the lexicon is the *open-class lexicon*, which for many languages will contain nouns, verbs, adjectives and adverbs.[3] Unlike the closed-class lexicon, the open-class lexicon can be added to by language users – in fact new nouns and verbs are coined at a great rate, necessitating the constant updating of lexicons.

Figure 2 shows a screen shot of the Boas open-class elicitation environment, again using an example from Russian.

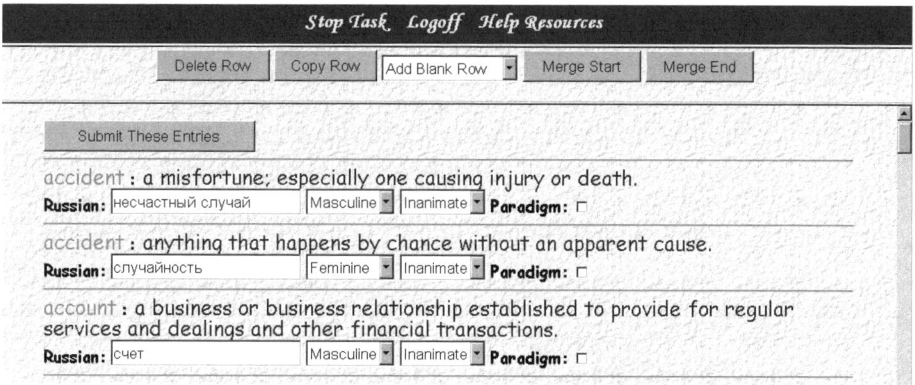

Figure 2. Open-class lexical acquisition in the Boas system.

Like the closed-class interface, the closed-class interface reflects information collected through pre-lexicon knowledge elicitation:

1) The informant posited two inherent features for Russian nouns: one with at least the values masculine and feminine, and the other with at least the value

[3] For different languages, different parts of speech might be utilized for both the closed-class and the open-class lexicon. We will not pursue the complex issue of part-of-speech delineation here.

inanimate (there are actually more feature values but they are not shown in this screen shot).

2) The informant has created inflectional paradigms for Russian, otherwise the "Paradigm" checkbox – which is used to indicate that there is an irregular inflectional paradigm – would not be present.

3) The informant does not think that any of the entries in L has irregular inflectional forms, since no checkboxes are checked. All words that have regular inflectional forms are interpreted based on rules created during the morphological stage of knowledge acquisition.

Since open-class acquisition is a big job, interface functions are provided to speed the process:

- *Delete Row* is used to remove a word from the list and put it into a trash bin. This is for words that cannot be translated or are not important enough in L to be included. The cursor must be in the text field of the given row before clicking on Delete Row. After clicking on it, the screen refreshes with that row missing. (These cursor and refresh comments apply to most functionalities and will not be repeated.)

- *Copy Row* is used when there is more than one translation for a given prompt. For example, there are two Russian words for English *blue* – one meaning *light blue* and the other meaning *dark blue* (there is no umbrella word for *blue*). Multiple translations must be typed in separate rows because they might have different inherent features, or one might be a word whereas another is a phrase, or one or both might have irregular inflectional forms.

- *Add Blank Row* is used to add a completely new entry for which variants in both English and L must be provided. Add Blank Row is actually not a button but a pull-down menu requiring the informant to indicate which part of speech the new item will belong to, since L might require different kinds of information for different parts of speech (e.g., nouns might have inherent features whereas verbs do not); therefore, it is important that a new row of the right profile be added. This function permits the informant to add, on the spot, entities that occur to him during work on the open class—like idioms, phrases, or compounding forms based on a word just translated.

- *Merge Start and Merge End* are a pair of functions that permit the informant to bunch word senses that have the same translation, thus reducing acquisition time, especially if a given entity in L requires additional work, like listing irregular inflectional forms.

Since speed is at the center of the interface design, keyboard-centered methods of working with the interface are encouraged. For example, tabbing takes the user from one action point to the next and if some variety of a Latin keyboard is being used, typing in the first letter of a given word in a drop-down menu will pull up that word.

In this paper, we discuss the acquisition of open-class lexical material. However, the type of lexical information to be focused on is "deeper" than that elicited in Boas. The difference is motivated by the fact that the Boas system was designed to feed into a quick ramp-up machine translation system. Since the focus was on *quick* ramp-up, relatively broad coverage was more important than deep coverage. Other systems, by contrast, benefit from depth of coverage, defined as precise and extensive syntactic and semantic information about each lexical item. It is lexical coverage for the latter types of high-end systems that is the focus here.

1.2. What is needed for processing meaning?

There are many opinions about what constitutes lexical meaning and what level of its specification is sufficient for what types of computational applications (see, e.g., [3]). In this paper we will follow the approach developed in Ontological Semantics, a theory of processing meaning that is implemented in the OntoSem semantic analyzer. In this approach, the goal of text analysis is creating unambiguous, formally interpreted structures that can be immediately used by automatic reasoning programs in high-end applications such as question answering, robotics, etc. A comprehensive description of the theory is beyond the scope of this paper. The most detailed description to-date is [19]. Descriptions of various facets of OntoSem can be found in [1], [2], [10], [12], [13], [15], [16].

OntoSem is essentially language-independent: it can process text in any language provided appropriate static knowledge resources are made available, with only minor modifications required of the processors. In what follows, we suggest a method for creating such knowledge resources for any language L. We concentrate on the knowledge related to the description and manipulation of lexical and compositional meaning. We demonstrate that the availability of a language-neutral ontology and a semantic, OntoSem-compatible, lexicon of English simplifies the task of acquiring the lexical-semantic components of the lexicon for L. Knowledge of non-semantic components of a language – notably, its morphology and syntax – must also be acquired, as it is important as the source of heuristics for semantic processing. The OntoSem resources provide help in formulating the syntactic knowledge of L because the system uses a lexicalized grammar, the majority of the knowledge for which is recorded in the syn-struc of lexicon entries.

There are four main knowledge resources in OntoSem: the lexicon, the ontology, the onomasticon (the lexicon of proper names) and the fact repository (the inventory of remembered instances of concepts: instances of real-world objects events as contrasted with the object and event types found in the ontology). We focus on the first two types of resources in this paper.

2. The OntoSem Ontology

The OntoSem ontology is used to ground meaning in an unambiguous model of the world. It contains specifications of concepts corresponding to classes of objects and events. Formatwise, it is a collection of frames, or named collections of property-value pairs, organized into a directed acyclic graph – i.e., a hierarchy with multiple inheritance.[4] Concepts are written in a metalanguage that resembles English (e.g., DOG,

---

[4] The use of multiple inheritance is not unwieldy because (a) the inheritance relation is always semantically "is-a", and (b) the ontology contains far fewer concepts than any language would have words/phrases to express those concepts. Contrast this with, for example, with MeSH (http://www.nlm.nih.gov/mesh/) and Metathesaurus (http://www.nlm.nih.gov/pubs/factsheets/umlsmeta.html), which are partially overlapping

WHEELED-VEHICLE, MENTAL-EVENT) but, unlike English words and phrases, concepts are unambiguous: DOG refers only to a domesticated canine, not a contemptible person or the act of tracking someone persistently. Therefore, although the concept DOG looks like the English word 'dog' (which is a convenient approach for the people building and maintaining the knowledge base) they are not equivalent.

The ontology is language-independent, and its links to any natural language are mediated by a lexicon. For example, the English lexicon indicates that one sense of *dog* maps to the concept DOG, another sense maps to HUMAN (further specified to indicate a negative evaluative modality), and yet another sense maps to the event PURSUE. Therefore, the ontology can be used to support language processing and reasoning in any language, given an ontologically linked lexicon for that language. The top levels in the OntoSem ontology are shown in Figure 3.

```
ALL
   EVENT
      MENTAL-EVENT
      PHYSICAL-EVENT
      SOCIAL-EVENT
   OBJECT
      INTANGIBLE-OBJECT
      MENTAL-OBJECT
      PHYSICAL-OBJECT
      SOCIAL-OBJECT
      TEMPORAL-OBJECT
   PROPERTY
      ATTRIBUTE
      RELATION
```

Figure 3. The top levels of the OntoSem ontology.

The PROPERTY subtree contains properties that are used to describe OBJECTs and EVENTs. In fact, the meaning of a concept *is* the set of property values used to describe it, such that concepts mean something with respect to other concepts within this model of the world. For people's use, a definition is provided for each concept, which not only provides a quick snapshot of the meaning but also acts as a bridge until all concepts can be described sufficiently to fully differentiate them from other concepts (the latter is, of course, a long-term knowledge acquisition effort).

An excerpt from the ontological frame for CORPORATION is shown in Figure 4. The upper section of the left-hand pane shows a subset of the features defined for this concept; those in boldface have locally specified values. The lower left pane is a snapshot of the parent(s) and child(ren) of this concept. The right-hand shows properties and their values; those in blue are locally defined whereas those in gray are inherited.

---

ontologies of medical terms developed by the National Library of Medicine. In these resources, many lines of inheritance (even 10 or more) are common, with the semantics of "parenthood" varying significantly. (For a description of our attempts to use these resources for automatic ontology population, see [17].

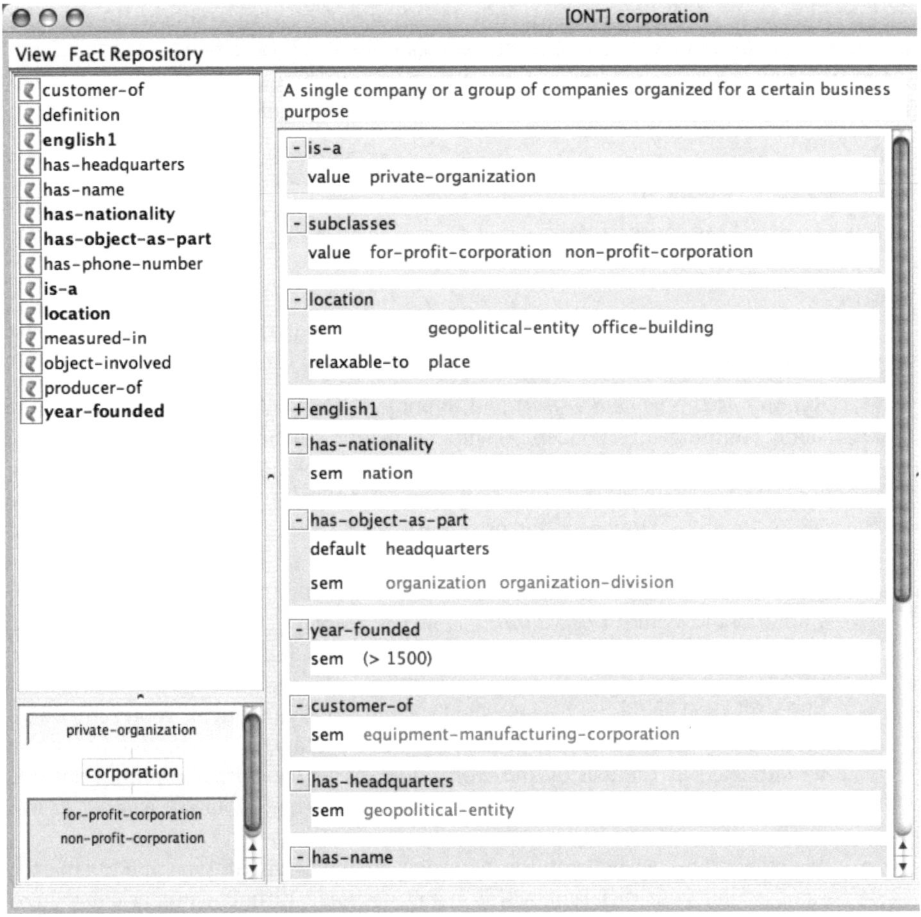

Figure 4. An excerpt from the OntoSem ontological frame for CORPORATION.

The precision and depth of property-based descriptions of concepts varies from domain to domain. For example, there are currently no property-based differences between the ontological siblings EAGLE and EMU since none of our applications have given priority to describing the animal kingdom; however, such distinctions must ultimately be included to permit artificial agents to reason with the same nimbleness that a human brings to the task. The machine learning of property values to distinguish between OBJECTs has actually been the focus of a recent experiment, as we attempt to bootstrap our hand-crafted resources using machine learning techniques (Nirenburg and Oates 2007).

Selectional restrictions in the ontology are multivalued, with fillers being introduced by one of five facets. The *value* facet is rigid and is used less in the ontology than in the sister knowledge base of real-world assertions, the fact repository. The facets *default* (for strongly preferred constraints) and *sem* (for basic semantic constraints) are abductively overridable. The *relaxable-to* facet indicates possible but atypical restrictions, and *not* blocks the given type of filler. For example, the AGE of

COLLEGE-STUDENT is described as default 18-22, sem 17-26, relaxable-to 13-80, with the latter accounting for kid geniuses and retirees going back to school.

Slot fillers can be concepts, literals or frames, the latter used not only for scripts (i.e., fillers of the property HAS-EVENT-AS-PART) but also for other cases of reification:

concept	property	facet	filler
CAR	HAS-OBJECT-AS-PART	sem	WHEEL (CARDINALITY default 4)

The number of concepts in the OntoSem ontology, currently around 9,000, is far fewer than the number of words or phrases in any language for several reasons:

1. Synonyms (*apartment* ~ *flat*) and hyponyms (*hat* ~ *beret*) are mapped to the same ontological concept, with semantic nuances recorded in the corresponding lexical entries. Theoretically speaking, any "synonym" could actually be analyzed as a "near synonym" (cf. [5]) since no two words are *precisely* alike. However, for practical reasons a slightly coarse grain size of description is pursued in OntoSem.
2. Many lexical items are described using a combination of concepts. For example, the event of *asphalting*, as in *The workers asphalted the parking lot*, is lexically described as COVER (INSTRUMENT ASPHALT), understood as "to cover with asphalt."
3. Many lexical items are described using non-ontological representational means like values for aspect or modality. For example, the inceptive phase can be indicated in English by the word *start*, as in *He started running*; and the volitive modality can be indicated by the word *want,* as in *He wanted to win the race.*
4. Meanings that can be captured by scalar attributes are all described using the same scale, with different words being assigned different numerical values. For example, using the scalar attribute INTELLIGENCE, whose values can be any number or range on the abstract scale {0,1}, *smart* is described as (INTELLIGENCE (> .8)) whereas dumb is described as (INTELLIGENCE (< .2)).
5. Concepts are intended to be cross-linguistically and cross-culturally relevant, so we tend not to introduce concepts for notions like *to asphalt* (cf. above) or *to recall* in the sense of a company recalling a purchased good because it is highly unlikely that all languages/cultures use these notions. Instead, we describe the meaning of such words compositionally in the lexicons of those languages that do use it.

3. The OntoSem lexicon

Even though we refer to the OntoSem lexicon as being a semantic lexicon, it contains not only semantic information: it also supports morphological and syntactic analysis and generation. Semantically, it specifies what concept, concepts, property or properties of concepts defined in the ontology must be instantiated in the text-meaning representation to account for the meaning of a given lexical unit of input. Lexical entries are written in an extended Lexical-Functional Grammar formalism using LISPcompatible format. The lexical entry – in OntoSem, it is actually called a *superentry* – can contain descriptions of several lexical senses; we call the latter *entries*. Each entry (that is, the description of a particular word sense) contains a number of fields, called zones. The skeleton for an OntoSem lexicon entry is illustrated below. The purpose of each zone is briefly explained as comments. Underscores show that values for these fields must be filled in. In some cases the values are strings ("__") and in other cases they are structures (__).[5]

```
(word
   (word-pos1                     ; part of speech & sense number
      (cat __)                    ; part of speech
      (def " __ ")                ; definition in English
      (ex " __ ")                 ; example(s)
      (comments " __ "))          ; acquirer's comments
      (syn-struc __ )             ; syntactic dependency
      (sem-struc __ )             ; semantic dependency
      (synonyms "__")             ; string(s) with (almost) the same meaning
      (hyponyms "__")             ; string(s) with a more specific meaning
      (abbrev "__")               ; abbreviation(s)
      (sublang "__")              ; subject domain, e.g., medicine
      (tmr-head __ )              ; semantic head of atypical phrasals[6]
      (output-syntax __)          ; overall syntactic category of atypical phrasals
      (meaning-procedure __ )) ; call to a procedural semantic routine
   (word-pos2 ...)
   ...
   (word-posN ...))
```

Figure 5. The structure of an OntoSem lexicon entry.

The OntoSem lexicon directly supports the dependency-oriented description of syntax of L, so if a dependency grammar for L exists, it can be adapted to the OntoSem environment. If such a grammar does not exist, the acquisition of the OntoSem-style lexicon for L will aid in developing such a grammar by providing subcategorization information for the lexicon entries of L.

The central zones of a lexicon entry are the *syn-struc*, which describes the syntactic dependency constraints of the word, and the *sem-struc*, which describes the word's meaning. In fact, these two zones, along with *cat*, are the only ones that **must** appear in each lexicon entry (the definition and example zones are for the convenience of acquirers). As an example, consider the seventeenth sense of *in* (Figure 6) in the OntoSem English lexicon, as shown in the DEKADE development environment (see [16] for a description of DEKADE).[7]

---

[5] Note that in the upcoming screen shots of OntoSem lexical entries the distinction between strings and structures is not overt, but it is understood by the OntoSem analyzer.

[6] The fields *output-syntax* or *tmr-head* tell the parser how to treat phrasal entries that are composed of a series of immediate constituents (e.g., np, adj) rather than syntactic functions (e.g., subject, direct object).

[7] Here and hereafter, in making screen shots we show only those fields that are relevant, often leaving out the last 7 fields of the entry, starting with *synonyms*.

```
(in-prep17
  (cat prep      )
  (def temporal; followed by month, year, century, etc. )
  (ex He came in January. His change of career in 2002 surprised us. )
  (comments DAY is possible only in the plural; this is covered in a different
            sense: "in the days prior to X"                                    )
  (syn-struc ((ROOT $VAR1) (CAT (OR N V))
             (PP ((ROOT $VAR0) (CAT PREP) (OBJ ((ROOT $VAR2) (CAT N)))))) )
  (sem-struc (^$VAR1 (SEM EVENT) (TIME (VALUE ^$VAR2)))
             (^$VAR2 (SEM (OR MONTH YEAR DECADE CENTURY))) )
```

Figure 6. One lexical sense of the word *in.*

The syntactic structure (syn-struc) indicates that the input covered by this sense of *in* should contain a constituent headed by a noun (n) or verb (v) followed by a prepositional phrase (pp). All syntactic elements in the syn-struc are associated with variables, which permit their linking to semantic elements in the sem-struc. The variable associated with the head word, here *in*, is always $var0; it does not have an explicit sem-struc linking since the whole entry is describing the meaning of $var0 in a particular type of context.

The sem-struc says that the meaning of $var1 ("meaning of" is indicated by a caret (^)) is some ontological EVENT whose time is the same as the time of the meaning of $var2. Moreover, it is specified that the meaning of $var2 must represent a MONTH, YEAR, DECADE or CENTURY. This entry predicts that one cannot say, for example, **in Monday*, since *Monday* is an instance of the ontological concept DAY.

The linking of syntactic and semantic elements is not always straightforward, as can be shown by a few examples:

- More than one entity can have a given case-role: e.g., in the sense of *argue* that covers the input *He argued with me about sports,* both the subject (*he*) and the object of the preposition (*me*) are AGENTS of an ARGUE-CONFLICT event. Similarly, when the sentence *They asphalted the road using huge trucks* is analyzed, a COVER event will be instantiated whose INSTRUMENTS are both ASPHALT and TRUCK ((CARDINALITY > 1) (SIZE > .9)). That is, the word *asphalt* is lexically described as COVER (INSTRUMENT ASPHALT); the instrumental interpretation of *huge trucks* is analyzed on the fly.
- A given entity can have more than one semantic role: e.g., in the sense of *coil* that covers the input *The snake coiled itself around the tree*, SNAKE is both the AGENT and the INSTRUMENT of COIL (the concept COIL also covers people coiling objects like rope, etc.).
- In some cases, elements of the syn-struc are nullified in the semantic structure, blocking their compositional analysis. This occurs most typically with prepositions within PP arguments or adjuncts of another head word. For example, in the lexical sense for *turn in*, as used in the input *He turned in his homework* (which is mapped to the concept GIVE), the meaning of *in* is nullified because its meaning is folded into the central mapping of *turn in* to the concept GIVE.

In the subsections to follow we describe and provide examples of a number of theoretical and practical advances reflected in the OntoSem lexicon.

3.1. Treatment of Multiword Entities (Phrasals)

Among OntoSem's lexical advances is the robust treatment of multiword elements, what we call phrasals. Phrasals in OntoSem can contain any combination of lexically fixed and ontologically constrained elements. Space does not permit a full description of all types of multi-word elements so rather than attempt a full categorization, we provide just a few examples for illustration.

Example 3.1.1 Two phrasal senses of the verb *blow* are shown in Figures 7 and 8. The first sense is for a transitive sense of *blow up*.

```
(blow-v1
   (cat v          )
   (def phrasal: blow up = cause to explode )
   (ex They blew up the bridge. The dynamite blew up the bridge. )
   (comments         )
   (syn-struc ((subject ((root $var1) (cat np)))
               (root $var0) (cat v)
               (prep-part ((root up) (root $var2) (cat prep)))
               (directobject ((root $var3) (cat np))))        )
   (sem-struc (explode
                (agent (value ^$var1))
                (theme (value ^$var3)))
               (^$var2 (null-sem +))    )
   (synonyms          )
   (hyponyms          )
   (abbrev         )
   (sublang         )
   (tmr-head          )
   (output-syntax          )
   (meaning-procedure (fix-case-role (value ^$var1) (value ^$var0)) )
)
```

Figure 7. An example of the part of speech *prep-part* in a lexicon entry.

The default case-role for the subject is agent, but if the meaning of $var1 cannot be agentive (e.g., *dynamite*), then the procedural routine "fix-case-role" is used to select a more appropriate case-role – here, instrument (see Section 3.2 for further description of procedural semantic routines).

There are three reasons why the phrasal *blow up* is not listed as a multi-word head word (as, e.g., *child care* would be):

(1) The first word can inflect and therefore must be productively analyzed, not "frozen".

(2) This phrasal can be used with two different word orders: the particle *up* can come before the object (*He blew up the bridge*) or after the object (*He blew the bridge up*). If this phrasal could only be used with the former word order, then instead of describing *up* as "prep-part" (prepositional particle), we would describe it as a preposition and use a standard prepositional phrase.

(3) Intervening material can come between the components: e.g., one can say *He blew the bridge right up*.

Sense 6 of *blow,* shown in Figure 8, shows *another* sense of the word *blow.*

```
(blow-v6
  (cat v        )
  (def phrasal: blow one's stack - get angry )
  (ex When he realized his accountant had been stealing funds,
      he blew his stack.                                        )
  (comments          )
  (syn-struc ((subject ((root $var1) (cat n)))
              (root $var0) (cat v)
              (directobject ((root $var2) (cat n) (root stack)))) )
  (sem-struc (anger
               (phase begin)
               (domain (value ^$var1))
               (range 1))
              (^$var2 (null-sem +))     )
```

Figure 8. An example of a lexically specified direct object.

Syntactically, this is a typical transitive sense except that the head of the direct object must be the word *stack* – or the plural *stacks*, since no number is specified. Semantically, however, the words *blow* and *stack* are not compositional—together they mean *get angry*. This meaning is shown by the scalar attribute *anger* whose domain (the person who is angry) is the meaning of the subject of the sentence, and whose range is the highest possible value on the abstract scale {0,1}. The feature "(phase begin)" shows that this phrasal is typically inceptive in meaning: i.e., the person just begins to be extremely angry. The meaning of $var2 is attributed null semantics since it is not compositional.

Example 3.1.2 The next example, sense 7 of the verb *see* (Figure 9), shows how the meaning of sem-struc elements can be constrained in order to permit automatic disambiguation.

```
(see-v7
  (cat v              )
  (def to consult professionally )
  (ex She saw the doctor about her chronic migraines. )
  (comments              )
  (syn-struc ((subject ((root $var1) (cat n)))
              (root $var0) (cat v)
              (directobject ((root $var2) (cat n)))
              (pp ((root $var3) (cat prep) (root about) (opt +)
                  (obj ((root $var4) (cat n))))))              )
  (sem-struc (consult
               (agent (value ^$var1))
               (beneficiary (value ^$var2) (sem work-role))
               (theme (value ^$var4)))
              (^$var3 (null-sem +))                              )
  (synonyms consult   )
```

Figure 9. Example of a semantic constraint in the sem-struc.

The key aspect of this structure is that the beneficiary – the person whom one sees – is ontologically a WORK-ROLE. So, if one sees the doctor (PHYSICIAN < MEDICAL-WORK-ROLE < WORK-ROLE) about a headache, sees a mechanic (MECHANIC < TRADE-ROLE < WORK-ROLE) about a clunk in one's car engine, or sees a lawyer (ATTORNEY < LEGAL-ROLE < WORK-ROLE) about divorce proceedings, this sense will be chosen. Of course, one can also *see* any of these people in the sense "visually perceive", which is sense see-v1 in our lexicon. This type of true ambiguity must be resolved contextually by the semantic analyzer.

3.2. Calls to Procedural Semantic Routines

Another advance in the OntoSem lexicon is the inclusion of calls to procedural semantic routines to resolve the meanings of entities that cannot be interpreted outside of context. Although deictic elements, like *you* and *yesterday*, are the most famous of such elements, the need for procedural semantics actually radiates much wider: for example, any time the English aspectual verb *start* (Figure 10) has an OBJECT rather than an EVENT as its complement, as in *She started the book*, the semantically elided event in question must be recovered. This recovery is carried out by the routine called "seek-specification", which attempts to determine the meaning of the head entry (some sort of EVENT) using the meaning of the subject and the meaning of the object as input parameters. The ontology is used as the search space. This routine will return READ and WRITE as equally possible analyses based on the fact that both of these are ontologically defined to have their DEFAULT THEME be DOCUMENT (BOOK < BOOK-DOCUMENT < DOCUMENT).

```
(start-v4
  (cat v          )
  (def unspecified event on specified object )
  (ex She started a book. )
  (comments transitive )
  (syn-struc ((SUBJECT ((ROOT $VAR1) (CAT N)))
              (ROOT $VAR0) (CAT V)
              (DIRECTOBJECT ((ROOT $VAR2) (CAT N)))) )
  (sem-struc (EVENT
               (AGENT (VALUE ^$VAR1))
               (THEME (VALUE ^$VAR2) (SEM OBJECT))
               (PHASE BEGIN))                          )
  (synonyms          )
  (hyponyms          )
  (abbrev          )
  (sublang          )
  (tmr-head          )
  (output-syntax          )
  (meaning-procedure (SEEK-SPECIFICATION (VALUE ^$VAR0) (VALUE ^$VAR1) (VALUE ^$VAR2)) )
)
```

Figure 10. An example of a call to a procedural semantic routine.

As presented earlier, another procedural semantic routine fixes case roles if the listed case role is not compatible with the type of semantic element filling that role. Still other routines are used to resolve the reference of pronouns and other deictic elements.

3.3. The Necessity of Constraining Senses

Perhaps the most important aspect of the OntoSem lexicon is that it attempts to constrain each lexical sense sufficiently to permit the analyzer to choose exactly one sense for any given input. Consider again the verb *make*, which currently has 40+ senses and counting. Most of its senses are phrasals, meaning that the syn-struc includes specific words that constrain the use of the sense. The following are just a few examples. The specific words that constrain the sense are in boldface, and the italicized glosses are human-oriented explanations of what each phrasal means. (Of course, in the sem-struc of the respective entries the meanings are encoded using ontological concepts with appropriate restrictions on the meanings of the case roles.)

- X makes **out** Y ~ *X can perceive Y*
- X makes **sure** (that) Y ~ *X confirms Y*
- X makes **away with** Y ~ *X steals Y*
- X makes **an effort/attempt to** Y ~ *X tries to do Y*
- X makes a **noise/sound** ~ *X emits a sound*
- X makes **fun of** Y ~ *X teases Y*

The senses of *make* that are not phrasals are also explicitly constrained to support disambiguation. Compare senses make-v1 and make-v2 shown in Figures 11 and 12.

Both are transitive senses but they take different kinds of direct objects: for make-v1 the direct object is a PHYSICAL-OBJECT, whereas for make-v2 it is an ABSTRACT-OBJECT.

```
(make-v1
  (cat v        )
  (def to engage in the activity that brings an artifact into being )
  (ex She made a cake (out of wheat flour). He made a movie. )
  (comments          )
  (syn-struc ((SUBJECT ((ROOT $VAR1) (CAT N)))
              (ROOT $VAR0) (CAT V)
              (DIRECTOBJECT ((ROOT $VAR2) (CAT N)))
              (PP
               ((ROOT $VAR3) (CAT PREP) (ROOT (OR OF FROM OUT_OF)) (OPT +)
                (OBJ ((ROOT $VAR4) (CAT NP))))))                          )
  (sem-struc (CREATE-ARTIFACT
               (AGENT (VALUE ^$VAR1))
               (THEME (VALUE ^$VAR2)))
              (^$VAR2 (MADE-OF (VALUE ^$VAR4)))
              (^$VAR3 (NULL-SEM +))                  )
  (synonyms create   )
  (hyponyms concoct
            devise
            prepare  )
```

Figure 11. The sense of *make* that means creating an artifact.

```
(make-v2
  (cat v        )
  (def to bring into being an abstract object )
  (ex She made problems for her teachers. )
  (comments          )
  (syn-struc ((SUBJECT ((ROOT $VAR1) (CAT N)))
              (ROOT $VAR0) (CAT V)
              (DIRECTOBJECT ((ROOT $VAR2) (CAT N)))) )
  (sem-struc (CREATE-ABSTRACT-OBJECT
               (AGENT (VALUE ^$VAR1))
               (THEME (VALUE ^$VAR2))) )
```

Figure 12. The sense of *make* that means creating an abstract object.

One does not see these constraints overtly in the lexicon entry because they are in the ontological description of CREATE-ARTIFACT and CREATE-ABSTRACT-OBJECT, respectively. That is, CREATE-ARTIFACT is ontologically described as having the THEME ARTIFACT and CREATE-ABSTRACT-OBJECT is ontologically described as having the THEME ABSTRACT-OBJECT. As such, the analyzer "sees" these constraints just as it would see the constraints if they were overtly specified in the sem-strucs of the lexical entries. This points up an important aspect of OntoSem resources: they are designed to be used together, not in isolation. As such, the often difficult decision of whether to create a new concept or use an existing concept with lexical modifications is not really a big problem: either way is fine since the resources are leveraged in tandem.

4. Lexical Acquisition for L Using the OntoSem English Lexicon

The main efficiency enhancing benefit of using an existing OntoSem-style lexicon to acquire a new lexicon is the ability to reuse semantic descriptions of words – i.e., the sem-struc zones. After all, the hardest aspect of creating OntoSem lexicons, or any lexicon that includes semantics, is deciding how to describe the meaning of words and phrases. To create a sem-struc one must, at a minimum:

- be very familiar with the content and structure of the ontology to which words are mapped
- understand which meanings are ontological and which are extra-ontological, like modality and aspect
- understand what grain size of description is appropriate: it would be infeasible to record *everything* one knows about *every* word if one sought to create a lexicon and ontology in finite time
- understand how to combine the meanings of ontological concepts and extra-ontological descriptors to convey complex meanings
- be able to detect the need for procedural semantic routines and write them when needed

We believe that as long as the acquirer understands the meaning of a lexicon entry in the English lexicon, he can express the same meaning in L – be it as a word or a phrase. This belief is predicated on the hypothesis of practical effability, the tenet that every idea can be expressed in every language at a certain realistic level of granularity. Without going into a long discussion of the philosophical underpinnings of this hypothesis, let us just observe that a meaning that can be expressed using a single word in L1 might require a phrase in L2 or vice versa. So it is immaterial that some languages may have forty words for snow while others have one or two – in those other languages, the meaning of the 40 words can certainly be expressed using phrases or even clauses. Indeed, the famous Sapir-Whorf hypothesis that states that our language in a large part shapes our view of the world, is, at least in part, predicated on preferring single-word meaning realizations to phrasal ones. This distinction is less important for the practical automatic understanding of text than it is for philosophical and psychological deliberations.

Let us consider some of the many eventualities an acquirer might face in creating an L lexicon sense from an English one:

- The English sense and the L sense are both single-word entities that have the syn-struc and the same sem-struc. Acquisition of the L sense is trivial: the English head word is simply changed to the L head word.
- The English sense is a single word but the L sense is multiple words. The L acquirer will have to decide if (a) the multiple words are completely fixed (like *child care*), in which case they can be entered as a multi-word head word with an underscore in between (*child_care*) or (b) the words can have inflections, intervening words, etc., in which case they must be acquired as a complex syn-struc.
- The English sense contains multiple words but the L sense is a single word.

- The English sense and the L sense are both argument-taking entities (e.g., verbs) but they require different subcategorization frames, meaning that the inventory of syntactic components needs to be modified. Of course, every time the variables in the syntactic structure are changed, one must check to see if any of the linked variables in the semantic structure require modification.

The above inventory is just a sampling of the more common outcomes, with the full inventory including more fine-grained distinctions. We will now illustrate the process of creating lexicon of L from the lexicon of English, moving from simpler issues to more complex ones and using examples from a variety of languages.

Example 4.1 The first noun entry alphabetically in the English lexicon is, not surprisingly, *aardvark.*

```
(aardvark-n1
   (cat n)
   (syn-struc ((root $var0)(cat n)))
   (sem-struc (AARDVARK))).
```

If L has a word whose meaning corresponds directly to the English word *aardvark*, one can simply substitute it in the header of the entry: in a Russian lexicon, the headword would be аардварк. Of course, AARDVARK in the sem-struc denotes a concept, not a word in any language. In the OntoSem ontology, the ontological concept AARDVARK is at present minimally described as a kind of mammal. However, if or when more information is added to the ontology describing the aarkdvark – its habitat, its preferred food, its enemies, etc. – this information will have to be added only once, in the ontology, and then it will be accessible and usable in applications covering any language for which an ontological-semantic lexicon is available.[8]

Example 4.2 The noun *table* has two entries in the English lexicon, glossed as comments below:

```
(table-n1      ; a piece of furniture
   (cat n)
   (syn-struc ((root $var0)(cat n)))
   (sem-struc (TABLE)))

(table-n2      ; a compilation of information
   (cat n)
   (syn-struc ((root $var0)(cat n)))
   (sem-struc (CHART))).
```

The corresponding entries in a Hebrew lexicon (in transliteration) will be recorded under two different head words:

[8] Compare this "savings" in acquisition to the approach adopted for the SIMPLE project, a comparison that is detailed in [11].

```
(shulhan-n1
   (cat n)
   (syn-struc ((root $var0)(cat n)))
   (sem-struc (TABLE)))

(luah-n1
   (cat n)
   (syn-struc ((root $var0)(cat n)))
   (sem-struc (CHART))
   (synonyms "tavla")
```

The acquirer will also notice that the Hebrew *tavla* is another way of expressing the meaning (the ontological concept) CHART. As a result, this word may be acquired in one of two ways – using its own entry or as a filler of the synonyms zone of the entry *luah*-n1, as shown above.

Example 4.3 The entry for *desk* is similarly simple:

```
(desk-n1
   (cat n)
   (syn-struc ((root $var0)(cat n)))
   (sem-struc (DESK)))
```

The corresponding entry in a Russian lexicon (given here in transliteration) will have to be headed by the word *stol* 'table' and, and the syn-struc will add the necessary modifier that constrains the sense: *pis'mennyj* 'writing'. The modifier is, of course, attributed null semantics in the sem-struc because its semantics is folded into the ontological concept this sense is mapped to: DESK.

```
(stol-n1
   (cat n)
   (syn-struc ((root $var0) (cat n)
      ((mods (root $var1) (root pis'mennyj))
   (sem-struc
      (DESK)
      (null-sem ^$var1)))
```

Example 4.4 Lexical entries for verbs involve more work, mostly because their subcategorization properties must be described. The entry for *sleep* is as follows:

```
(sleep-v1 (cat v)
  (syn-struc ((subject ((root $var1) (cat n)))
              (root $var0) (cat v)))
  (sem-struc
     (SLEEP (EXPERIENCER (value ^$var1)))),
```

This entry states that *sleep* takes a subject headed by a noun; that its meaning is expressed by the ontological concept SLEEP; and that the EXPERIENCER case role should be filled by the subject of *sleep* when an instance of SLEEP is generated in the text meaning representation of the input sentence. The corresponding entry in French lexicon will be very similar, with *dormir* substituted for *sleep* in the header of the entry. This is because French, just like English, has intransitive verbs, and *dormir* happens to be intransitive, just like *sleep*.

Example 4.5 If the lexical units realizing the same meaning in L and English do not share their subcategorization properties, the acquirer will have to make necessary adjustments. Consider the English entry *live*-v2:

```
(live-v2
   (cat v)
   (syn-struc
       ((subject ((root $var1) (cat n)))
        (root $var0) (cat v)
        (pp ((root in) (root $var2) (cat prep) (obj ((root $var3 (cat n)))))))
   (sem-struc
       (INHABIT
           (AGENT (value ^$var1))
           (LOCATION (value ^$var3)))
       (^$var2 (null-sem +))),
```

This states the following:

- This sense of *live* takes a subject (a noun) and an obligatory adjunct which is a prepositional phrase introduced by *in*.
- The meaning of this sense is expressed by the ontological concept INHABIT whose AGENT and LOCATION case roles are filled by the meanings of the subject and the prepositional object of *live*-v2, respectively.
- The meaning of the preposition itself should be ignored (attributed null semantics) because it is taken care of by the meaning LOCATION in the sem-struc.

In French, this meaning is expressed by the word *habiter*, which is a regular transitive verb. As a result, when acquiring the lexicon for French, the above entry will be changed to:

```
(habiter-v2 (cat v)
   (syn-struc
       ((subject ((root $var1) (cat n)))
        (root $var0) (cat v)
        (directobject  ((root $var2) (cat n))))
   (sem-struc
       (INHABIT
           (AGENT (value ^$var1))
           (LOCATION (value ^$var2))))
```

Even though this slight change to the syn-struc must be entered, this is still much faster than creating the entry from scratch.

Example 4.6 A still more complex case is when the meaning of a word sense does not precisely correspond to any ontological concept. Consider the notion of "marrying" in English and Russian. In English, men can *marry* women and women can *marry* men, using the same verb that maps to the concept MARRY.

```
(marry-v1
   (syn-struc
      ((subject ((root $var1) (cat n)))
       (root $var0) (cat v)
       (directobject ((root $var2) (cat n))))
   (sem-struc
      (MARRY                    ; to take as spouse
         (AGENT (value ^$var1))
         (AGENT (value ^$var2)))))
```

However, MARRY does not fully express the meaning of any single word in Russian. Instead, there is a Russian word for the case of a man marrying a woman (where the man is the AGENT) and another word for the case of a woman marrying a man (where the woman is the AGENT). If the man is the AGENT, the verb is *zhenit'sja*, whereas if the woman is the AGENT a phrasal is used: *vyjit zamuzh za,* literally, "to leave married to". The gender information is in boldface in both entries for orientation.

```
(zhenit'sja-v1
   (syn-struc
     ((subject ((root $var1) (cat n)))
      (root $var0) (cat v)
      (pp ((root na) (root $var3) (cat prep) (obj ((root $var2) (cat n))))))
   (sem-struc
     (MARRY
        (AGENT (value ^$var1) (gender male))
        (AGENT (value ^$var2) (gender female)))
     (^$var3 (null-sem +))))

(vyjti-v3
   (syn-struc
    ((subject ((root $var1) (cat n)))
     (root $var0) (cat v)
     (directobject ((root $var4) (cat n) (root zamuzh)))
     (pp ((root za) (root $var3) (cat prep) (obj ((root $var2) (cat n))))))
   (sem-struc
     (MARRY
        (AGENT (value ^$var1) (gender female))
        (AGENT (value ^$var2) (gender male)))
     (^$var3 (null-sem +))
     (^$var4 (null-sem +))))
```

Note also that the syntactic structure of these entries is different from that of English *marry*. In the first of these two entries (*zhenit'sja*) the syn-struc describes an intransitive verb with a PP complement introduced by the preposition *na*. In the second entry, the syn-struc describes the phrasal *vyjti zamuzh za,* expressed as the third sense of the verb *vyjti* (whose other senses include "get out" and "be depleted"). This sense includes the direct object *zamuzh* and a prepositional phrase headed by the preposition *za*. To reiterate, in both of the above entries, the ontological concept MARRY is locally modified by constraining the semantics of its agents. Note that this modification is local to the lexicon entry: the concept MARRY, as specified in the ontology, is not affected outside of the above lexicon entries.

Example 4.7 Perhaps the greatest motivation for "reusing" an existing OntoSem lexicon is avoiding the necessity of inventing the semantic representation of complex words from scratch. Above we have seen rather straightforward entries for which available ontological concepts can be utilized. However, when describing entries like conjunctions and adverbs, the actual analysis required to create a sem-struc, and the procedural semantic routines needed to support it, can be non-trivial.

Let us consider the case of adverbs more closely. Not surprisingly, they tend not to be included in ontologies or semantic webs (or, for that matter, in corpus annotation). However, they are as important as any other lexemes to a full semantic interpretation and, as such, receive full treatment in OntoSem lexicons. Take the example of *overboard*, whose sem-struc says that the event that it modifies must be a MOTION-EVENT whose SOURCE is SURFACE-WATER-VEHICLE and whose DESTINATION is BODY-OF-WATER.

```
(overboard-adv1
  (cat adv)
  (anno
    (def "indicates that the source of the motion is a boat and the
           destination is a body of water")
    (ex "They threw the rotten food overboard. He jumped overboard."))
  (syn-struc
   ((root $var1) (cat v)
    (mods ((root $var0) (cat adv) (type post-verb-clause)))))
  (sem-struc
    (^$var1   (sem MOTION-EVENT)
     (SOURCE  SURFACE-WATER-VEHICLE)
     (DESTINATION   BODY-OF-WATER))))
```

While this description is quite transparent, it requires that the acquirer find three key concepts in the ontology, which takes more time than simply replacing the head word by an L equivalent (e.g., Russian *za bort*). More conceptually difficult is an adjective like *mitigating*:

```
(mitigating-adj1
  (cat adj)
  (anno
   (def "having the effect of moderating the intensity of some property")
   (ex  "mitigating circumstances (i.e., circumstances that lessen the intensity
```

```
        of some property of some object or event that is recoverable from
        the context)"))
  (syn-struc
   ((mods ((root $var0) (cat adj))
    (root $var1) (cat n))
  (sem-struc
    (^$var1
      (effect (> (value refsem1.intensity))))
    (refsem1 (property)))
  (meaning-procedure (seek-specification (value refsem1) reference-procedures)))
```

This semantic description says: the noun modified by *mitigating* has the effect of lessening the intensity of some property value of some object or event; *which* property of *which* object or event needs to be determined using procedural semantic reasoning, using the function called in the meaning-procedures zone. There are three important points here: first, coming up with a semantic interpretation for this word is not easy; second, once we do come up with one, it would be nice to use it for more than one language; and, third, despite the fact that the recorded semantic analysis of this entity does not take care of all aspects of its interpretation, like those that must be contextually determined by procedural semantics, it does as much as a lexical description can be expected to do.

It is not only adjectives and adverbs that can present a choice space that takes time to sort through. Here are a few examples of select senses of words from other parts of speech, written in what we hope is an obvious shorthand:

fee (n.)
MONEY (THEME-OF: CHARGE)
violist (n.)
MUSICIAN (AGENT-OF (PLAY-MUSICAL-INSTRUMENT (THEME: VIOLA)))
file (n.)
SET (MEMBER-TYPE: DOCUMENT)
aflame (adj.)
the modified is the THEME of BURN
exempt (from sth.) (adj.)
the modified is the BENEFICIARY of an EXEMPT event whose THEME is the object of the *from*-PP
managing (adj.)
the modified is the AGENT of a MANAGEMENT-ACTIVITY (so 'managing editor' is an EDITOR (AGENT-OF MANAGEMENT-ACTIVITY))

In sum, any time that a semantic description requires more work than direct mapping to an ontological concept, there are gains to be had by interpreting that description as a language-neutral representation of meaning that can then be associated with the corresponding head words in different languages.

Example 4.8 What happens if the English lexicon does not contain a word or phrase that must be acquired for the lexicon of L? This case is identical to the task of acquiring the English lexicon in the first place. Consider, for example, the English verb *taxi*. It is applicable to aircraft and denotes the action of its moving on a surface. The ontology contains the concepts AIRCRAFT and MOVE-ON-SURFACE. When faced with the task of acquiring the entry for *taxi*-v1 for the English lexicon, the acquirer faces the choice of either putting the construct (MOVE-ON-SURFACE (theme AIRCRAFT)) in the sem-struc zone of the lexicon entry or opting for creating a new ontological concept, say, TAXI-EVENT, in which the same information will be listed. In the latter case, the sem-struc zone of the entry for *taxi*-v1 will be a simple reference to the new ontological concept TAXI-EVENT.

The choice of strategy in such cases may be beyond the purview of this paper, as it will depend on a particular application. The general rule of thumb is to try to keep the ontology as small as possible and at the same time make sure that it can help to describe the meaning of as many words and phrases in L as possible. This is a well-known desideratum in formal descriptions, cf. [4] for a succinct early explanation.

If, by contrast, available ontological knowledge is not sufficient for rendering the meaning of the new word, then the ontology itself must be augmented before a lexicon entry can be created. This, of course, makes the task of writing lexicon entries much more complex.

5. Final Thoughts

Acquiring resources for low- and mid-density languages is difficult since there tends to be little manpower available to compile them. For that reason, reusing resources that already exist should always be considered an option worth exploring. Of course, the temptation in working on low- and mid-density might be to avoid depth of analysis, instead relying only on large corpora and stochastic methods for text processing. For this reason, one must answer the question, What is all this semantic information good for? It is good for any application that can benefit from disambiguation, since the single most compelling reason to engage in knowledge-rich natural language processing is to permit applications to work on disambiguated knowledge, rather than highly ambiguous text strings. To our thinking, this includes *all* NLP applications, though we acknowledge this opinion as not universally held. Two other obvious beneficiaries of semantically analyzed text are automated reasoners and machine learners, both of which can benefit from more semantic features in the feature space. Apart from these practical uses of OntoSem resources, we believe that there are significant theoretical reasons for pursuing rigorous broad-scale and deep lexical semantics for NLP. Indeed, the stated goal of linguistics is to explain the connection of texts with their meanings. The broad goal of computational linguistics should then be developing computational means of establishing correspondences between texts and their meaning. If we are serious about reaching this goal, the development of semantic lexicons for the various languages and of the semantic metalanguage of description should be viewed as the core tasks of the field.

References

[1] Beale, Stephen, Sergei Nirenburg and Marjorie McShane. 2003. Just-in-time grammar. *Proceedings 2003 International Multiconference in Computer Science and Computer Engineering*, Las Vegas, Nevada.

[2] Beale, Stephen, Benoit Lavoie, Marjorie McShane, Sergei Nirenburg and Tanya Korelsky. 2004. Question answering using Ontological Semantics. *Proceedings of ACL-2004 Workshop on Text Meaning and Interpretation*, Barcelona.

[3] Cruse, D.A. 1986. *Lexical Semantics*. Cambridge University Press.

[4] Hayes, P.J., 1979. The naive physics manifesto. In: D. Michie (ed.), *Expert Systems in the Microelectronic Age*. Edinburgh, Scotland. Edinburgh University Press.

[5] Inkpen, Diana and Graeme Hirst. 2006. Building and using a lexical knowledge-base of near-synonym differences. 2006. *Computational Linguistics* 32(2): 223-262.

[6] McShane, M., S. Nirenburg, J. Cowie and R. Zacharski. 2002. Embedding knowledge elicitation and MT systems within a single architecture. *Machine Translation* 17(4): 271-305.

[7] McShane, Marjorie. 2003. Applying tools and techniques of natural language processing to the creation of resources for less commonly taught languages. *IALLT Journal of Language Learning Technologies* 35 (1): 25-46.

[8] McShane, Marjorie and Sergei Nirenburg. 2003. Blasting open a choice space: learning inflectional morphology for NLP. *Computational Intelligence* 19(2): 111-135.

[9] McShane, Marjorie and Sergei Nirenburg. 2003. Parameterizing and eliciting text elements across languages. *Machine Translation* 18(2): 129-165.

[10] McShane, Marjorie, Stephen Beale and Sergei Nirenburg. 2004. Some meaning procedures of Ontological Semantics. *Proceedings of LREC*-2004.

[11] McShane, Marjorie, Sergei Nirenburg and Stephen Beale. 2004. OntoSem and SIMPLE: Two multi-lingual world views. *Proceedings of ACL-2004 Workshop on Text Meaning and Interpretation*, Barcelona.

[12] McShane, Marjorie, Sergei Nirenburg and Stephen Beale. 2005. An NLP lexicon as a largely language independent resource. *Machine Translation* 19(2): 139-173.

[13] McShane, Marjorie, Sergei Nirenburg and Stephen Beale. 2005. Semantics-based resolution of fragments and underspecified structures. *Traitement Automatique des Langues* 46(1): 163-184.

[14] McShane, Marjorie and Ron Zacharski. 2005c. User-extensible on-line lexicons for language learning. Working Paper #05-05, Institute for Language and Information Technologies, University of Maryland Baltimore County.

[15] McShane, Marjorie, Sergei Nirenburg and Stephen Beale. 2005. The description and processing of multiword expressions in OntoSem. Working Paper #07-05, Institute for Language and Information Technologies, University of Maryland Baltimore County.

[16] McShane, Marjorie, Sergei Nirenburg, Stephen Beale and Thomas O Hara. 2005. Semantically rich human-aided machine annotation. *Proceedings the Workshop on Frontiers in Corpus Annotation II: Pie in the Sky*, ACL-05, Ann Arbor, June 2005, pp. 68-75.

[17] Nirenburg, Sergei, Marjorie McShane, Margalit Zabludowski, Stephen Beale, Craig Pfeifer. 2005. Ontological Semantic text processing in the biomedical domain. Working Paper #03-05, Institute for Language and Information Technologies, University of Maryland Baltimore County.

[18] Nirenburg, Sergei and Tim Oates. 2007. Learning by reading by learning to read. *Proceedings of ICSC-07*. Irvine, CA. September.

[19] Nirenburg, Sergei and Victor Raskin. 2004. *Ontological Semantics*. MIT Press.

[20] Probst, Katharina, Lori Levin, Erik Peterson, Alon Lavie, Jaime Carbonell. 2002. MT for resource-poor languages using elicitation-based learning of syntactic transfer rules. *Machine Translation* 17/4: 245-270.

Language Engineering for Lesser-Studied Languages
S. Nirenburg (Ed.)
IOS Press, 2009

doi:10.3233/978-1-58603-954-7-207

Applying the Meaning-Text Theory Model to Text Synthesis with Low- and Middle Density Languages in Mind

Leo WANNER[a,b] and François LAREAU[b]
[a]*Institució catalana de recerca i estudis avançats (ICREA)*
[b]*Universitat Pompeu Fabra, Barcelona*

Abstract. The linguistic model as defined in the Meaning Text Theory (MTT) is, first of all, a language production model. This makes MTT especially suitable for language engineering tasks related to synthesis: text generation, summarization, paraphrasing, speech generation, and the like. In this article, we focus on text generation. Large scale text generation requires substantial resources, namely grammars and lexica. While these resources are increasingly compiled for high density languages, for low- and middle density languages often no generation resources are available. The question on how to obtain them in a most efficient way becomes thus imminent. In this article, we address this question for MTT-oriented text generation resources.

1. Introduction

With the progress of the state of the art in Computational Linguistics and Natural Language Processing, language engineering has become an increasingly popular and pressing task. This is in particular true for applications in which text synthesis constitutes an important part – among other things, automatic text generation, summarization, paraphrasing, and machine translation.

Large coverage text synthesis in general requires substantial resources for each of the languages involved. While for high density languages, more and more resources are available, many of the low- and middle density languages are still not covered. This may be due to the lack of reference corpora, the lack of specialists knowledgeable in the field and in the language in question, or other circumstances. The question which must obviously be answered when a text synthesis application is to be realized for a low- or middle density language for which no text synthesis resources are available as yet: How can these resources be obtained in the most rapid and efficient way? This obviously depends on the exact kind of resources needed and thus, to a major extent, on the application and the linguistic framework underlying the implementation of the given system that addresses the application.

In this article, we focus on one case of text synthesis: the natural language text generation. We discuss the types of resources required for a text generator based on the *Meaning Text Theory*, MTT [1, 2, 3, and 4]. MTT is one of the most common rule-based linguistic theories used for text generation. This is not by chance: MTT's model is synthesis (rather than analysis, or parsing) oriented and it is formal enough to allow for an intuitively clear and straightforward development of resources needed for generation.

The remainder of the article is structured as follows. In Section 2, we present the basics of the MTT-model and the kind of resources it requires. Section 3 contains a short overview of the tasks implied in text generation. In Section 4, text generation from the perspective of MTT is discussed. Section 5 elaborates on the principles for efficient compiling of generation resources and Section 6 discusses how resources for new languages can be acquired starting from already existing resources. Section 7 addresses the important problem of the evaluation of grammatical and lexical resources for MTT-based generation. Section 8, finally, contains some concluding remarks.

As is to be expected from an article summarizing an introductory course on the use of Meaning-Text Theory in text generation, most of the material is not novel. The main information sources used for Section 2 have been [1, 2, 3, and 5]. For Sections 4, 5, and 7, we draw upon [6, 7, 8, and 9] and, in particular, on [10], which is reproduced in parts in the abovementioned sections. A number of other sources of which we also make use are mentioned in the course of the article.

2. Meaning-Text Theory and its Linguistic Model

MTT interprets language as a rule-based system which defines a many-to-many correspondence between an infinite countable multitude of meanings (or semantic representations, SemRs) and an infinite multitude of texts (or phonetic representations, PhonRs); cf., e.g., [1, 2, and 3]:

$$\bigcup_{i=1}^{\infty} \mathrm{SemR}_i \Leftrightarrow \bigcup_{j=1}^{\infty} \mathrm{PhonR}_j$$

This correspondence can be described and verified by a formal model – the Meaning-Text Model (MTM). In contrast to many other linguistic theories such as *Systemic Functional Linguistics* [11, 12], *Functional Linguistics* [13]; *Cognitive Linguistics* [14, 15], *Role and Reference Grammar* [16], etc., MTT is thus in its nature a formal theory.

An MTM is characterized by the following five cornerstone features:

(i) it is *stratificational* in that it covers all levels of a linguistic representation: semantic, syntactic, morphological and phonetic, with each of the levels being treated as a separate stratum;

(ii) it is *holistic* in that it covers at each stratum all structures of the linguistic representation: **at the semantic stratum**, the *semantic* (or *propositional) structure* (*SemS*) which encodes the content of the representation in question, the *communicative* (or *information*) *structure* (*CommS*) which marks the propositional structure in terms of salience, degree of acquaintance, etc. to the author and the addressee, and the *rhetorical structure* (*RhetS*) which defines the style and rhetorical characteristics that the author wants to give the utterance under verbalization; **at the syntactic stratum**, the syntactic structure (*SyntS*), the CommS which marks the syntactic structure, the *co-referential structure* (*CorefS*) which contains the co-reference links between entities of the syntactic structure denoting the same object, and the *prosodic structure* (*ProsS*) which specifies the intonation contours, pauses, emphatic stresses, etc.; **at the morphological stratum**, the *morphological structure* (*MorphS*) which encodes the word order and internal morphemic organization of word

forms, and the ProsS; **at the phonetic stratum**, the *phonemic structure* (PhonS) and the ProsS.[1]

(iii) it is *dependency-oriented* in that the fundamental structures at each stratum are dependency structures or are defined over dependency structures;

(iv) it is *equivalence-driven* in that all operations defined within the model are based on equivalence between representations of either the same stratum or adjacent strata;

(v) it is *lexicalist* in that the operations in the model are predetermined by the features on the semantic and lexical units of the language in question – these features being stored in the lexicon.

Depending on the concrete application in which we are interested, more or less strata, more or less structures are involved. As mentioned in Section 1, in this article, we focus on automatic text generation, i.e., on written, rather than on spoken texts. Therefore, the more detailed definition of the notion of the Meaning-Text Model can discard the phonetic representation, such that the definition reads as follows:

Definition: *MTT Model, MTM*

Let **SemR** be the set of all well-formed meaning (or semantic) representations, **SyntR** the set of all well-formed syntactic representations, **MorphR** the set of all well-formed morphological representations and **Text** the set of all texts of the language $\mathcal{L}$ such that any SemR $\in$ **SemR**, any SyntR $\in$ **SyntR**, and any MorphR $\in$ **MorphR** is defined by the corresponding basic structure and a number of auxiliary structures: SemR = {SemS, CommS, RhetS}, SyntR = {SyntS, CommS, CorefS, ProsS}, and MorphR = {MorphS, ProsS}. Let the basic structures be directed labeled graphs of different degree of freedom such that any directed relation *r* between a node *a* and node *b* in a given structure, *a*–*r*→*b*, expresses the dependency of *b* on *a* of type *r*. Let furthermore *a* and *b* be semantic units in a SemS $\in$ SemR, lexical units in a SyntS $\in$ SyntR, and morphemes in a MorphS $\in$ MorphR. Then, the MTM of $\mathcal{L}$ over **SemR** $\cup$ **SyntR** $\cup$ **MorphR** $\cup$ **Text** is a quadruple of the following kind

$$\text{MTM} = (M_{\text{SemSynt}}, M_{\text{SyntMorph}}, M_{\text{MorphText}}, \mathcal{D}), \text{ such that}$$

A grammar module M_i (with i $\in$ {SemSynt, SyntMorph, MorphText}) is a collection of equivalence rules, $\mathcal{D}$ is the set of dictionaries (lexica) of $\mathcal{L}$ and the following conditions hold:

$$\forall\ \text{SemR}_i \in \textbf{SemR}: (\exists\ \text{SyntR}_j \in \textbf{SyntR}: M_{\text{SemSynt}}(\text{SemR}_i, \mathcal{D}) = \text{SyntR}_j)$$
$$\forall\ \text{SyntR}_i \in \textbf{SyntR}: (\exists\ \text{MorphR}_j \in \textbf{MorphR}: M_{\text{SyntMorph}}(\text{SyntR}_i, \mathcal{D}) = \text{MorphR}_j)$$
$$\forall\ \text{MorphR}_i \in \textbf{MorphR}: (\exists\ \text{Text}_j \in \textbf{Text}: M_{\text{MorphText}}(\text{MorphR}_i, \mathcal{D}) = \text{Text}_j)$$

The syntactic and morphological strata are further split into a "deep", i.e., content-oriented, and a "surface", i.e., "syntax oriented" substratum, such that in total we have to deal with six strata; Figure 1 shows the resulting picture.

[1] In what follows, we will call the semantic, syntactic, morphological, and phonemic structures the "basic structures" of the corresponding stratum.

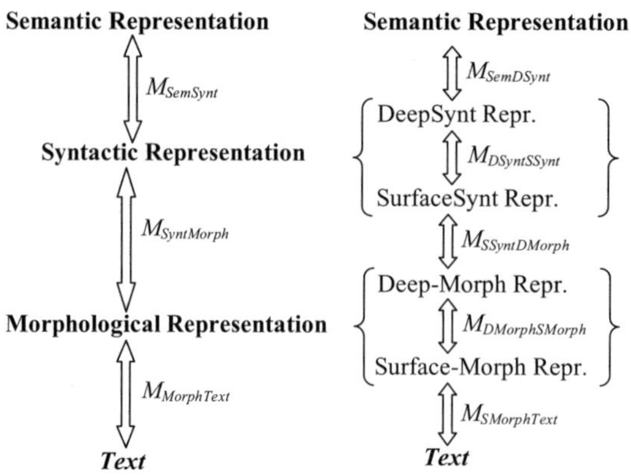

Figure 1: Meaning-Text Linguistic Model

In the remainder of the section, we briefly describe the individual strata, the modules of the MTM and the dictionaries the modules make use of.

2.1. Definition of the Strata in an MTM

As already outlined above, a linguistic representation at a given stratum of the MTM is defined by its basic structure and the co-referential, communicative, rhetorical, and prosodic structures as complementary structures that are defined over the corresponding basic structure. The rhetorical structure can also be treated as part of the *context of situation* [17] and the prosodic structure is irrelevant for written texts; we leave them thus aside in our rough introduction to MTT and focus on the first three structures, which are essential for our application.

2.1.1. Basic structures at the individual strata of an MTM

Let us introduce, in what follows, the definition of the basic structures of an MTM that play a role in text generation: the semantic, the deep-syntactic, the surface-syntactic, and the deep-morphological structures. Surface-morphological structures are similar to deep-morphological structures except that they already have all morphological contractions, elisions, epenthesis and morph amalgamation performed. Therefore, we do not discuss them here.

Definition: *Semantic Structure* (SemS)

Let S_{Sem} and R_{Sem} be two disjunct alphabets of a given language $\mathcal{L}$, where S_{Sem} is the set of *semantemes* of $\mathcal{L}$ and R_{Sem} is the set of semantic relation names {1,2,…}. A semantic structure, Str_S, is a quadruple (G, α, β, D_S) over $S_{Sem} \cup R_{Sem}$ with

- $G = (N, A)$ as a directed acyclic graph, with the set of nodes N and the set of directed arcs A;
- α: as the function that assigns to each $n \in N$ an $s \in S_{Sem}$
- β: as the function that assign to each $a \in$ A an $r \in R_{Sem}$
- D_S as the semantic dictionary with the semantic valency of all $s \in S_{Sem}$

such that for any $\alpha(n_i)$ $-\beta(a_k)\rightarrow\alpha(n_j) \in Str_S$ the following restrictions hold:

1. $\beta(a_k)$ is in the semantic valency pattern of $\alpha(n_i)$ in D_S
2. $\exists\, n_m, a_l$: $\alpha(n_i) -\beta(a_l)\rightarrow\alpha(n_m) \wedge \beta(a_k) = \beta(a_l) \Rightarrow a_k = a_l \wedge n_j = n_m$

The conditions ensure that a SemS is a predicate-argument structure.

Although SemS is language-specific, it is generic enough to be isomorphic for many utterances in similar languages. Consider, e.g., the following eight sentences:[2]

1. Eng. *Orwell has no doubts with respect to the positive effect that his political engagement has on the quality of his works.*
2. Ger. *Orwell hat keine Zweifel, was den positiven Effekt seines politischen Engagements auf seine Arbeiten angeht*
   lit. 'Orwell has no doubts what the positive effect of his political engagement on his works concerns'.
3. Rus. *Orvell ne somnevaetsja v tom, čto ego političeskaja angažirovannost' položitel'no vlijaet na kačestvo ego proizvedenij*
   lit. 'Orwell does not doubt in that that his political engagement positively influences [the] quality of his works'.
4. Serb. *Orvel ne sumnja u to da njegov politićki angažman deluje povoljno na kvalitet njegovih dela*
   lit. 'Orwell does not doubt in that that his political engagement acts positively on [the] quality of his works'.
5. Fr. *Orwell n'a pas de doute quant à l'effet positif de son engagement politique sur la qualité de ses œuvres*
   lit. 'Orwell does not have doubt with respect to the positive effect of his political engagement on the quality of his works'.
6. Sp. *Orwell no duda que sus actividades políticas tienen un efecto positivo en la calidad de sus obras.*
   lit. 'Orwell does not doubt that his political activities have a positive effect on the quality of his works'.
7. Cat(alan). *Orwell no dubta que les seves activitats polítiques tenen un efecte positiu en la qualitat de les seves obres*
   lit. 'Orwell does not doubt that the his political activities have a positive effect on the quality of the his works'.
8. Gal(ician). *Orwell non dubida que as súas actividades políticas teñen un efecto positivo na calidade das súas obras*
   lit. 'Orwell does not doubt that the his political activities have a positive effect on quality of-the his works'.

Some of the sentences differ with respect to their syntactic structure significantly, yet their semantic structures are isomorphic, i.e., they differ merely with respect to node labels. Figure 2 shows the English sample. The number 'i' of a semanteme stands for the 'i-th sense' of the semanteme's name captured by this semanteme.

Note that the structure in Figure 2 is simplified in that it does not contain, for instance, temporal information which corresponds to a specific verbal tense at the syntactic strata; it does not decompose the comparative semanteme 'better.5'; etc.

To obtain the other seven semantic structures, we simply need to replace the English semantemes by the semantemes of the corresponding language. This is not to say that the semantic structures of equivalent sentences are always isomorphic. They

[2] The original French sentence is from [3].

can well differ both within a single language (cf. [18] for semantic paraphrasing within one language) and between languages – for instance, when the distribution of the information across the same semantic representation is different as in the case of the Indo-European vs. Korean/Japanese politeness system [7].

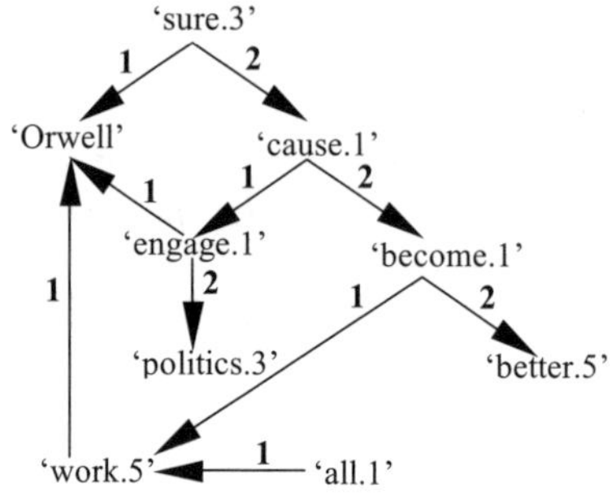

Figure 2: Semantic structure of sentence 1

Definition: *Deep-syntactic Structure* (DSyntS):

Let L_D , R_{DSynt} and G_{sem} be three disjunct alphabets of a given language $\mathcal{L}$, where L_D is the set of deep lexical units (LUs) of $\mathcal{L}$, R_{DSynt} is the set of DSynt relations {I, II, III, …} of $\mathcal{L}$ and G_{sem} the set of semantic grammemes of $\mathcal{L}$.

A DSyntS, Str_{DSynt}, is a quintuple $(G, \alpha, \beta, \gamma, D_L)$ over $L_D \cup R_{DSynt} \cup G_{sem}$, with

- $G = (N, A)$ as a dependency tree, with the set of nodes N and the set of arcs A
- α as the function that assigns to each $n \in N$ an $l \in L_D$
- β: as the function that assigns to each $a \in A$ an $r_{ds} \in R_{DSynt}$
- γ: as the function that assigns to each α(n) a set of semantic grammemes
- D_L: as the dictionary with the syntactic valency of all $l \in L_D$

such that for any $\alpha(n_i) -\beta(a_k) \rightarrow \alpha(n_j) \in Str_{DSynt}$ the following restrictions hold:

1. $\beta(a_k)$ is in the syntactic valency pattern of $\alpha(n_i)$ in D_S
2. $\exists\, n_m, a_l$: $\alpha(n_i) -\beta(a_l) \rightarrow \alpha(n_m) \wedge \beta(a_k) = \beta(a_l) \;\Rightarrow a_k = a_l \wedge n_j = n_m$

The set of deep-lexical LUs contains the LUs of the vocabulary of the language $\mathcal{L}$ to which two types of artificial LUs are added and three types of LUs are excluded. The added LUs include: (i) symbols denoting *lexical functions* (LFs), (ii) *fictitious lexemes*.

LFs are a formal means to encode lexico-semantic derivation and restricted lexical co-occurrence (i.e., collocations); cf., among others, [19, 20, 21, and 22]: SMOKE ⇒ SMOKER, SMOKER ⇒ HEAVY [~], SMOKE ⇒ HAVE [*a* ~$_N$], …[3] Each LF carries a functional label such as S_1, Magn and $Oper_1$: S_1(SMOKE) = SMOKER, Magn(SMOKER) = HEAVY, $Oper_1$($SMOKE_N$) = HAVE.

Fictitious lexemes represent idiosyncratic syntactic constructions in $\mathcal{L}$ with a predefined meaning – as, for instance, <$X_{count.noun}$ N_{number}> meaning 'roughly N of X' in Russian.

[3] '~' stands for the LU in question.

The excluded LUs involve: (i) structural words (i.e., auxiliaries, articles, and governed prepositions), (ii) substitute pronouns, i.e., 3rd person pronouns, and (iii) values of LFs.

Semantic grammemes are obligatory and regular grammatical significations of inflectional categories of LUs; for instance, *nominal number*: singular, dual, …; *voice*: active, passive, …; *tense*: past, present, future; *mood*: indicative, imperative, …; and so on.

Compared to SemS, DSyntS is considerably more language-specific, although it is abstract enough to level out surface-oriented syntactic idiosyncrasies; cf. Figure 3 for the DSyntS of the sentences 1 (English) and 3 (Russian) from above. $Oper_1$ and Bon are names of LFs. The subscripts are the grammemes that apply to the lexeme in question.

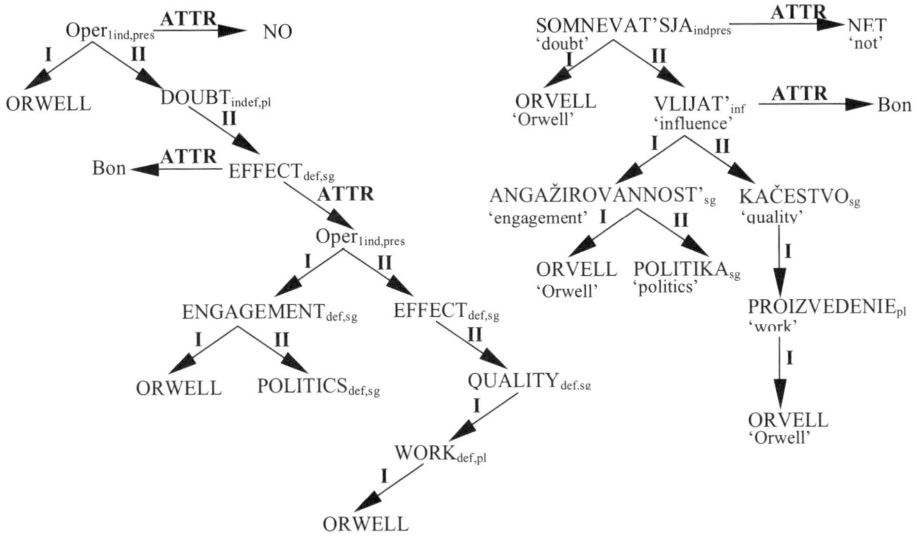

Figure 3: DSyntSs of the sample sentences 1 and 3 above

Divergences between semantically equivalent DSyntSs can be of lexical, syntactic, or morphological nature [23, 6, and 7].

Definition: *Surface-syntactic Structure* (SSyntS)

Let L, R_{SSynt} and G_{sem} be three disjunct alphabets of a given language $\mathcal{L}$, where L is the set of lexical units (LUs) of $\mathcal{L}$, R_{SSynt} is the set of SSynt relations and G_{sem} the set of semantic grammes.

A SSyntS, Str_{SSynt}, is a quintuple $(G, \alpha, \beta, \gamma, D_L)$ over $L \cup R_{SSynt} \cup G_{sem}$, with

- $G = (N, A)$ as a dependency tree, with the set of nodes N and the set of arcs A
- α as the function that assigns to each $n \in N$ an $l \in L$
- β: as the function that assigns to each $a \in A$ an $r_{ss} \in R_{SSynt}$
- γ: as the function that assigns to each $\alpha(n)$ a set of semantic grammemes
- D_L: as the dictionary with the syntactic valency of all $l \in L$

such that for any $\alpha(n_i) -\beta(a_k)\rightarrow\alpha(n_j) \in Str_{SSynt}$ the following restrictions hold:

1. $\beta(a_k)$ is in the syntactic valency pattern of $\alpha(n_i)$ in D_L
2. $\exists\, n_m, a_l$: $\alpha(n_i) -\beta(a_l)\rightarrow\alpha(n_m) \wedge \beta(a_k) = \beta(a_l) \Rightarrow a_k = a_l \wedge n_j = n_m$

Consider in Figure 4 as example of an SSyntS, the surface-syntactic structure of sentence 7 (i.e., Catalan) from above.

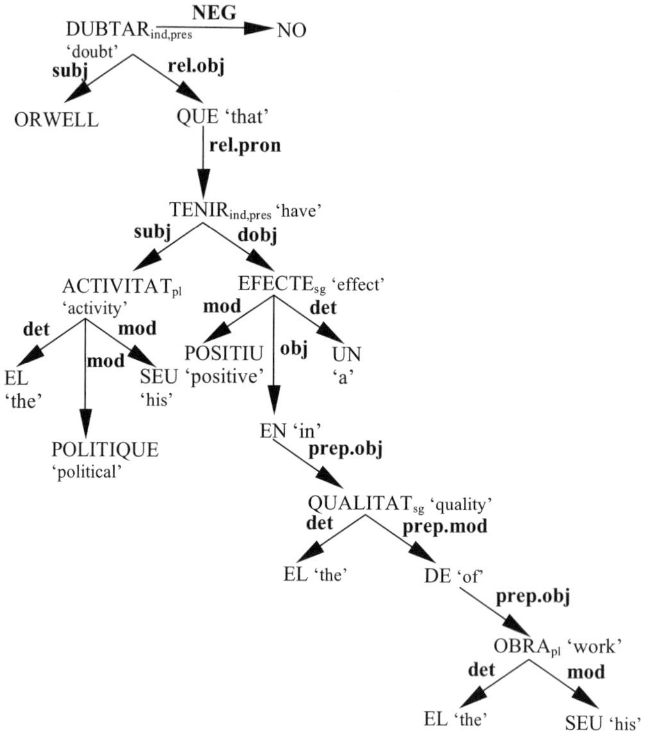

Figure 4: SSyntS of the sample sentence 7 above

Definition: *Deep-morphological structure* (DMorphS)

Let L and G_{sem} be disjunct alphabets of a given language $\mathcal{L}$, where L is the set of lexical units (LUs) of $\mathcal{L}$ and G_{sem} the set of semantic grammemes.

A DMorphS, Str_{DMorph}, is a quadruple $(G, \alpha, \kappa, \gamma, \rho)$ over $L \cup G_{sem}$, with

- $G = (N, <)$ as a chain, with the set of nodes N and the precedence relation '$<$',
- α as the function that assigns to each $n \in N$ an $l \in L$
- κ as the function that defines over N the set of constituents C
- γ: as the function that assigns to each α(n) a set of semantic grammemes
- ρ: as the function that defines for each pair c_i, $c_j \in C$ a precedence order relation.

The main function of a DMorphS is thus to provide a linearization of the dependency tree as given in the corresponding SSyntS. Following [24], we assume that in contrast to the preceding basic structures, DMorphS also reflects a phrase structure.[4] Consider, e.g., the Catalan DMorphS for our sample sentence:

$$\mathrm{ORWELL}_{sg} < [[\mathrm{NO} < \mathrm{DUBTAR}_{3p,sg,ind,pres}] < [\mathrm{QUE} < [\mathrm{EL}_{fem,pl} < \mathrm{SEU}_{fem,pl} < \mathrm{ACTIVITAT}_{fem,pl} < \mathrm{POLITIQUE}_{fem,pl}] < \mathrm{TENIR}_{3p,pl,ind,pres} < [\mathrm{UN}_{masc,sg} < \mathrm{EFFECTE}_{masc,sg} < \mathrm{POSITIU}_{masc,sg} < \mathrm{EN} < \mathrm{EL}_{fem,sg} < \mathrm{QUALITAT}_{fem,sg} < [\mathrm{DE} < [\mathrm{EL}_{fem,pl} < \mathrm{SEU}_{fem,pl} < \mathrm{OBRA}_{fem,pl}]]]]$$

Figure 5: DMorphS of the sentence 7 above

2.1.2. Co-referential structure

A co-referential structure (CorefS) consists of a set of (bidirectional) co-references between different nodes of a given basic structure that denote the same object. CorefS is defined over a DSyntS or an SSyntS; given that a SemS is an acyclic graph (rather than a tree), there is no need to repeat nodes that denote the same object: all relations can refer to one single node without that well-formedness conditions of the propositional structure are violated. As a consequence, CorefS is defined between deep lexeme nodes (in a DSyntS) and between surface lexeme nodes (in a SSyntS). For instance, in Figure 3, $\mathrm{CorefS}_{\mathrm{Dsynt}}$ would contain 'N_i[ORWELL] $\leftrightarrow$ N_j[ORWELL]' and 'N_i[EFFECT] $\leftrightarrow$ N_j[EFFECT]' (with i and j being the number of the corresponding nodes in the propositional structure).

2.1.3. Communicative Structure

The Communicative Structure (CommS) (or *information structure*) is central to text generation in that it determines the distribution of the information across a sentence and ensures the cohesion between the sentences. In contrast to commonly known proposals concerning information structure [26, 27, 28, and 29], CommS in an MTM is a very rich multidimensional structure that is defined over a basic structure:

Definition: *Communicative structure* (CommS)

Let Str_i be a basic structure at the stratum $\mathbf{S}_i$. The communicative structure $CommS_i$ defined over Str_i is a set of possibly overlapping labeled areas, such that the labels belong to eight different dimensions D_i (i = 1,2,…,8) as specified below and the following restriction holds: If in the $CommS_i$ two areas overlap, then, the labels of these areas belong to different dimensions. The set of dimensions is given by the following eight dimensions:

D1: {Theme, Rheme, Specifier}
D2: {Given, New}
D3: {Focalized, Non-focalized}
D4: {Foregrounded, Backgrounded, Neutral}
D5: {Presupposed, Non-Presupposed}
D6: {Emphasized, Non-Emphasized}
D7: {Unitary, Articulated}
D8: {Signaled, Performed, Communicated}

---

[4] For some languages, a more complex phrase-like structure is needed to determine the word order. Consider, for instance, the *topological field model* for German [25]; for the treatment of the field model in MTT, see [24].

For a detailed introduction to CommS in general and to all eight dimensions, see [5]; to give an impression of how important CommS is, it suffices to focus on the first four dimensions.

2.1.3.1. The Thematicity Dimension

The three-partite *Thematicity*-dimension is the primary dimension in text generation. *Rheme* identifies what is stated; *Theme* identifies about what Rheme is stated; and *Specifier* captures the circumstances under which the statement is made.[5] In complex structures, the Theme or Rheme elements may be recursive, i.e., contain embedded Thematicity partitions; cf. the Thematicity structure of SemS from Figure 2 in Figure 6, where Rheme is subsequently subdivided into more fine-grained Theme-Rheme partitions:

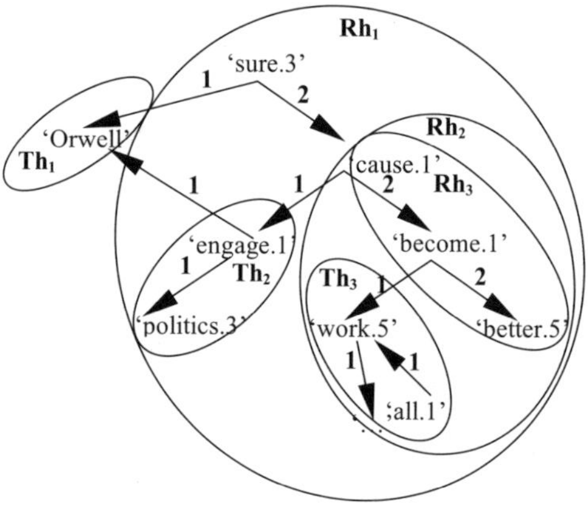

Figure 6: Thematicity distribution in SemR of sentence 1 (the outgoing arrow of 'work.5' points to 'Orwell')

Thematicity is so crucial for text generation because it provides information for the determination of the basic sentence structure: roughly speaking, the Theme-element is predestined to become the subject of a clause and the Specifier-elements attributive constructions.

2.1.3.2. The Givenness Dimension

The bipartite *Givenness*-dimension with *Given* and *New* as its elements is equally immediately reflected in the sentence structure and the morpho-syntactic features of its elements. *Given* is what the author presents as known to the addressee, and *New* is what the author presents to be unknown to the addressee. Figure 7 illustrates the influence of Giveness on generation. The left side contains simple semantic structures with different distributions of Given [G] and New [N]. The right side shows the effect of each distribution at the surface of the corresponding sentence.

['friends']$_N$ ←**1**– ['present']$_N$ –**2**→ ['show']$_N$ ≡ *Some friends present / make a presentation of a show.*
['friends']$_N$ ←**1**– ['present']$_G$ –**2**→ ['show']$_N$ ≡ *Some friends make **the** presentation of a show.*
['friends']$_N$ ←**1**– ['present']$_G$ –**2**→ ['show']$_G$ ≡ *Some friends make **the** presentation of **the** show.*
['friends']$_G$ ←**1**– ['present']$_G$ –**2**→ ['show']$_G$ ≡ ***The** friends make **the** presentation of **the** show.*

Figure 7: Expression of different Givenness distributions

[5] Note that outside the MTT, Thematicity is two-partite in that it consists of Theme and Rheme only.

2.1.3.3. The Focalization Dimension

The *Focalization*-dimension identifies elements of an utterance that are logically important to the author himself (i.e., are in his focus of attention). A standard syntactic means to express focalization of an element is its fronting. Consider the expression of focalization of the semanteme 'show' in the first of the semantic structures in Figure 7:

9. *It is a show some friends are making a presentation of.*

2.1.3.4. The Foregrounding Dimension

The *Foregrounding*-dimension identifies elements of an utterance that are psychologically primary to the author (the corresponding elements are *Foregrounded*) and those that are unimportant to him (the corresponding elements are *Backgrounded*). Common syntactic means for foregrounding is raising and for backgrounding – appenditive parentheses. Cf., for illustration, Figure 8.

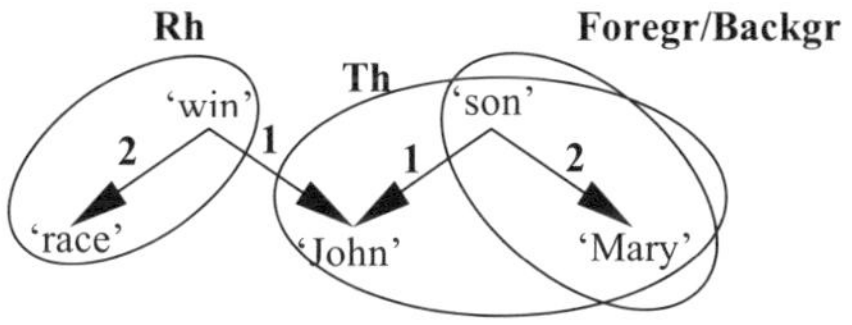

Figure 8: Foregrounded/Backgrounded elements in a SemS

If we foreground the fragment 'son' **–2→** 'Mary', the resulting sentence is 10; if we background it, the resulting sentence is 11:

10. *Mary's son John won the race.*
11. *John (who is Mary's son) won the race.*

2.2. Grammar Modules of an MTM

With the definition of the representations at the different strata at hand, we can define the grammar modules of an MTM.

Definition: *Grammar Module* $M_{Si,Si+1}$

Let $\mathbf{R}_i$ and $\mathbf{R}_{i+1}$ be the multitudes of well-formed representations of the linguistic model at the strata $\mathbf{S}_i$ and $\mathbf{S}_{i+1}$, respectively. Then, a (Grammar) Module $M_{Si,Si+1}$ consists of a set of elementary rules such that for any well-formed $R_i \in \mathbf{R}_i$ there is a subset of rules $M'_{Si,Si+1} \subseteq M_{Si,Si+1}$ such that

(i) each rule from $M'_{Si,Si+1}$ establishes a correspondence between a minimal fragment of R_i and a minimal fragment of $R_{i+1} \in \mathbf{R}_{i+1}$

(ii) each node and each arc of R_i is covered by at least and at most by one rule $M'_{Si,Si+1}$

For each pair of adjacent strata, a distinct grammar module has thus to be defined. The rules in the grammar modules are of a standard format: 'L ⇔ R | Conditions', i.e., they contain a lefthand side representation $R_i \in \mathbf{R}_i$, a righthand side representation $R_{i+1} \in$

$\mathbf{R}_{i+1}$ and a number of (optional) conditions that restrict the equivalence. Consider five sample rules from different grammar modules in Figure 9. Rules 1 and 2 are samples from the Sem ⇔ DSynt grammar module. Units in single quotes stand for semantemes; names beginning with a '?' are variables; 'Lex(α)' stands for the lexeme corresponding to the semanteme α. In Rule 1, the semanteme 'intensive' is mapped onto the LF Magn (of the lexeme that corresponds to the semanteme bound to the variable ?Xs), and the semanteme bound to ?Xs is mapped onto its lexeme. The predicate-argument relation between 'intensive' and ?Xs is mapped onto the DSynt-relation **ATTR**. Note also that the orientation of both relations is opposite. The rule applies only if the lexeme expressing the semanteme bound to ?Xs possesses a Magn-value. Rule 2 maps the semantic relation **1** onto the deep-syntactic relation **I** – if Lex(?Xs) has in its Government Pattern (GP) a first DSynt-actant, and, in case Lex(?Xs) is a verb, it is finite and no passive construction is foreseen.[6]

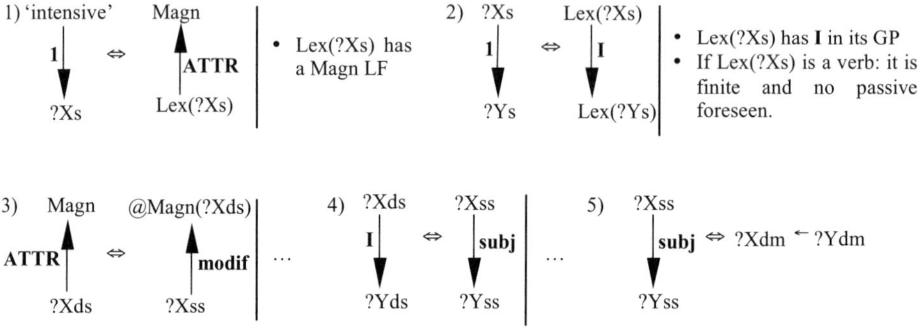

Figure 9: Sample grammar rules from different grammar modules

Rules 3 and 4 are samples of the DSynt ⇔ SSynt module. In Rule 3, the Magn-LF label corresponds to the value of Magn applied to the lexeme bound to ?Xds: '@LF(λ)' stands for the application of the LF to the lexeme λ and use of the value lexeme.[7] The deep lexeme ?Xds corresponds to the surface lexeme ?Xss, and the DSynt-relation **ATTR** corresponds to the SSynt-relation **modif**(ier). We dispense with the outline of the conditions for the application of this equivalence. Rule 4 exemplifies the correspondence between the DSynt-relation **I** and the SSynt-relation **subj**(jective) – including the correspondence between their arguments (again, certain conditions that we do not indicate here must be fulfilled).

Rule 5 defines the correspondence between the subjective relation and the precedence relation between the subject and its verbal governor – meaning that the subject comes linearly before the verb. Obviously, this rule is language-specific since in free word order languages, the order between all sentence elements is largely determined by the communicative structure.

As must have become clear, the rules imply correspondence links between nodes of the left hand side and those of the right hand side – although these usually are not made explicit. Thus, in the rules above, 'intensive' corresponds to Magn, '?Xs'

[6] Note that the choice of the passive is due to the communicative structure at the semantic side and is handled by another rule.

[7] For the interpretation of LFs as "deep lexemes" and as functions, see [30].

corresponds to 'Lex(?Xs)', etc. As we will note in Section 4, in a formal model for text generation, these links need to be made explicit.

2.3. The lexica in an MTM

Rich lexica play a key role in an MTM. These lexica are known as *Explanatory Combinatorial Dictionaries*, ECDs [21]. Each lexical entry in an ECD consists of a certain number of zones. The following three zones are of special relevance in the context of text generation: 1. the lexical definition of the LU in question, 2. the government pattern of the LU, 3. the lexical functions that apply to this LU.

The lexical definition presents the meaning of the LU. It can be more or less decomposed. Consider a possible definition of Eng. ADMIRATION:

> *Emotional attitude of X, favorable with respect to Y because of the action, state or property Z of Y, which X believes extraordinary.*

X, Y, and Z are the semantic actants implied in the definition; in terms of semantic roles, X is the Experiencer, Y is the Object (of the attitude), and Z is the Cause (of the attitude).

The government pattern (GP) of an LU specifies: (i) this LU's syntactic and semantic valency, (ii) the projection between the semantic and syntactic valencies, (iii) the subcategorization patterns of the LU. Semantic valency specifies the semantic actant slots determined by the meaning of the LU; syntactic valency does so with respect to syntactic actant slots. For the majority of the LUs, semantic and syntactic valencies are projected one-to-one onto each other – as in the case of ADMIRATION.[8] Table 1 shows a standard GP-table for Fr. ADMIRATION 'admiration'. 'N' stands for noun or nominal phrase, 'A_{poss}' for possessive adjective, and 'A' for adjective.

Table 1: Government Pattern for Fr. ADMIRATION

X = 1= I	Y = 2 = II	Z = 3 = III
1. de 'of' N 2. A_{poss} 3. A	4. de 'of' N 5. pour 'for' N 6. devant 'in front' N 7. envers 'towards' N	8. pour 'for' A_{poss} + N

The LFs that apply to an LU are listed together with their values. Cf. some LFs of Fr. ADMIRATION and of Eng. ADMIRATION in Table 2.[9]

Table 2: Sample LFs for Fr. ADMIRATION and Eng. ADMIRATION

$Able_1$	*sujet* 'subject', *enclin* 'tend', *porté à* [ART ~] 'carried to'	*open* [to ~]
$Able_2$	*digne* 'worth'	*be worthy* [*of* ~]
Ver_1	*justifiée* 'justified', *fondée* 'funded', *sincère* 'sincere'	*justified, well-founded, sincere, …*
$AntiVer_1$	*injustifiée* 'unjustified', *de commande* 'of the order'	*grudging*
$Oper_1$	*éprouver* 'feel', *ressentir* 'sense', *avoir* 'have', …	*feel* [~], *have* [~]
$IncepOper_1$	*tomber* [en ~] 'fall in'	*fall* [in ~]

[8] However, this is not always the case; cf. e.g, FLY, where Z=3 (the Instrument) is usually not expressed by a syntactic actant: *He flew from Barcelona to Montreal.*

[9] The translations of the French LF-values are literal.

$FinOper_1$	*perdre* [ART ~] 'lose'	*lose*
$Oper_2$	*attirer* 'attract' ,...	*compel, draw*
$ContFunc_0$	*durer* 'last'	*last*
$FinFunc_0$	*s'éteindre* 'extinguish', *s'evanouir* 'vanish', ...	*vanish*

3. The Basics of Text Generation

Text generation is the production of written material from a formal representation. The formal representation which serves as input can extremely vary: some text generators start from a surface-oriented syntactic structure, while others start from extra-linguistic numerical data series. Samples of MTT-generators are available for both extremes. Consider, e.g., [31] for a "shallow" syntactic generator and [32, 33] for "deep" generators. In order to cover the whole range of MTM-strata, we focus on the latter.

From the perspective of deep generation, text generation involves the following major tasks:

(1) *Content selection*: selection of the content that is to be rendered in a textual format from a given data or knowledge base.
(2) *Discourse structure planning*: construction of a text plan that determines in which order the discourse units are to be presented and how they are linked in order to ensure coherence.
(3) *Sentence planning*, which in its turn consists of several demanding subtasks:
   a. *Aggregation*: fusion of structures or content to avoid reduplication,
   b. *Sentence packaging*: determination of sentence boundaries,
   c. *Sentence structure determination*: selection of the overall syntactic structure of sentences,
   d. *Lexicalization*: Mapping of semantic units encountered in the content (semantic) structures onto lexical units.
(4) *Surface realization*: Spelling out of the morphological features associated with the lexical units.

Let us briefly introduce each of these tasks in order to be able to discuss then in Section 4 how an MTM is used for text generation.

3.1. Content Selection

The task of content selection assumes that not all content that is available to the generator is to be communicated to the reader. Strictly speaking, content selection is not a text generation task in the sense text generation has been defined above. Rather, it implies the assessment of the relevance of the given data or knowledge sources with respect to the addressee's profile, the context of the situation and the general state of affairs as judged by an expert of the field. It can be thus realized as an "expert system shell" prior to rendering the relevant data/knowledge structures into a textual format by a text generator, into a table format by a table generator or into a graphic form by a graphic generator.[10]

Nonetheless, content selection is traditionally considered a part of text generation. Often, it is combined with discourse planning into a more complex task, namely *text*

[10] The choice of the most appropriate mode for rendering the relevant information to the reader is another task in *multimodal* text generation.

(or *macro*) *planning*. How appropriate this combination is depends on the genre of the text under generation. For narration, it is natural to select the content as the story goes on; for reports on numerical time series, the content that is to be communicated is better chosen beforehand using expert knowledge. For instance, for air quality bulletins, the information on threshold exceedance, on highest and/or lowest concentrations of air pollutant substances, on remarkably sharp rises and falls of the concentrations due to changing meteorological conditions, etc. is predestined for communication [34]. Thus, if, as shown in Figure 10, the air quality index reaches at 16:00 the highest mark on a 6 grade scale, both the mark and its rating should be transmitted to the addressee.

time	11:00	...	16:00
AQ-index	3	...	6

AQ-index	1	2	3	...	6
rating	very good	good	fair	...	very bad

Figure 10: Numeric time series in the air quality domain

One of the formats for the codification of the selected content are the *Conceptual Graphs*, CG [35]. CGs are semantic networks with *concepts* as nodes and *semantic roles* (such as OBJ(ect), VAL(ue), R(e)S(u)LT, ATTR(ibute)) between the concepts as arcs. The concept nodes can be typed. Consider Figure 11 for the codification of the information highlighted in Figure 10 in grey as a conceptual graph.

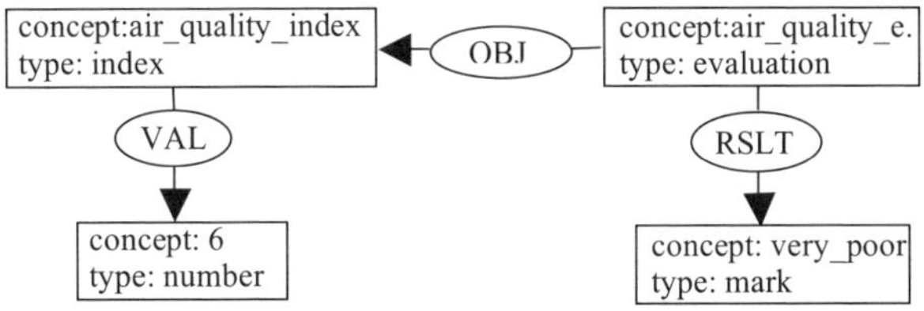

Figure 11: Codification of content in terms of Conceptual Graphs

3.2. Discourse structure planning

Two major strategies for discourse structure planning are known: (i) schema-driven planning [36] and (ii) Rhetorical Structure Theory (RST)-driven planning [37]. Schemata, or *scripts* [38], encode standard patterns of the discourse structure in terms of predefined sequences of rhetorical predicate constructions. Their use is convenient in the case of a static discourse and content structure – as, e.g., in weather report generation [32]: as a rule, the past, current and future atmospheric and meteorological conditions are always presented in the same sequence such that one general discourse structure (or schema) can defined and used for any input.[11] RST-driven planning implies a dynamic construction of a discourse tree or graph in which between the "discourse spans" coherence relations of the type ELABORATION, INTERPRETATION, CAUSE, JUSTIFICATION, etc. hold [39, 40]. For instance, between the two statements from Figure 11 'air_quality_index is 6' and 'air _quality_evaluation results in "very poor" ', the INTERPRETATION-relation holds;

[11] In practice, the discourse schemas are usually dynamic to a certain extent in that they can be adapted to the changing input data by changing the order of the appearance of some fragments or dropping them.

cf. Figure 12. Since INTERPRETATION is an asymmetric relation, it is directed. 'N' stands for governor or "nucleus", and 'S' for dependent or "satellite".

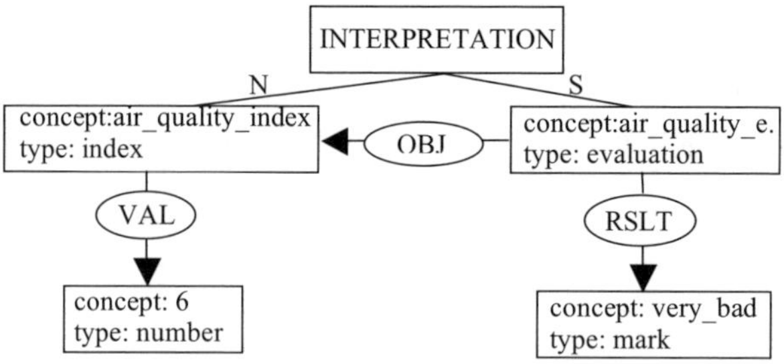

Figure 12: Illustration of the discourse relation INTERPRETATION

Schema-based and RST-based planning strategies can be combined [41, 42, and 43].

3.3. Sentence planning

Sentence (or *micro*) planning is certainly the most challenging task in text generation and still awaits its final solution. State of the art text generators – including MTT-based generators – address the individual subtasks of sentence planning in isolation, some of them rather *ad hoc* and shallow (as, e.g., sentence packaging and sentence structure determination), others in more depth (as, e.g., aggregation and lexicalization, and especially such aspects of lexicalization as referring expression generation).

3.3.1. Aggregation

As mentioned above, aggregation deals with the fusion of linguistic or knowledge structures to avoid reduplication of information and thus to achieve a higher degree of text conciseness; see, among others [44, 45]. A reduplication of information can be of contextual, conceptual, lexico-semantic, or syntactic nature; cf. the following examples:[12]

12. a. *Last year, John spent his summer holidays in Barcelona.*
    b. *In the summer of 2007, Mary spent her holidays in the capital of Catalonia.*
    c. *In the summer of 2007, James spent his leisure time in Barcelona.*
13. *Last year, John, Mary and James spent their summer holidays in Catalonia's capital Barcelona.*

Sentence 13 contains the information from 12a-c in a concise form. To be able to fuse 'last year' and '2007', we need to know that the year of reference is 2008 – which is contextual information. That summer holidays are during the summer and that Barcelona is the capital of Catalonia is extra-linguistic, i.e., conceptual information. The information that 'leisure time' and 'vacations' mean (roughly) the same is of lexico-semantic nature and the realization of the possessive construction *in Catalonia's capital Barcelona* instead of the repetition of *in Barcelona* and *in the capital of Catalonia* is of syntactic nature.

[12] To save some space, we give here examples in terms of actual sentences rather than in terms of the corresponding structures.

Each type of aggregation can be handled by aggregation rules at the corresponding level of linguistic representation.

3.3.2. Sentence packaging

The central task of sentence packaging is to partition a given semantic structure into sentences – without, however, having necessarily determined the structure of these sentences. This task is highly language-specific. For instance, English favours much shorter sentences than German and Russian. In current text generators, sentence packaging is solved more or less *ad hoc*. Most often, the conceptual structures (or, after discourse planning, the discourse spans) already implicitly predetermine the division of the content into clauses and subsequently sentences. For illustration, Figure 13 shows the semantic structure corresponding to the conceptual structure of Figure 12 and its packaging into two sentences.

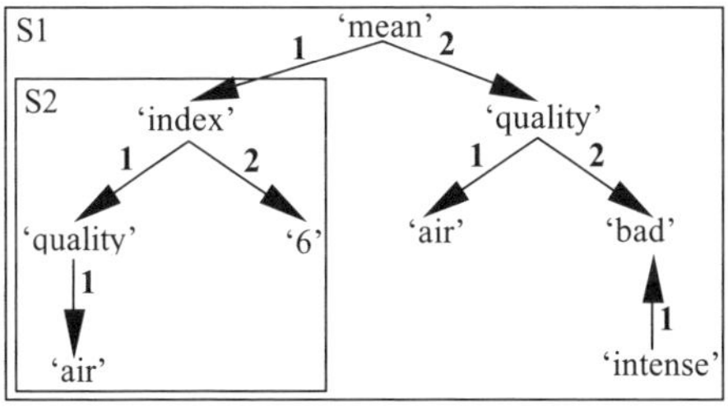

Figure 13: Sentence packaging in a semantic structure

3.3.3. Sentence structure determination

Sentence structure determination can be performed together with sentence packaging or after it. In any case, the structure of a sentence is decisively influenced by the communicative structure. As illustrated in Subsection 2.1.2 above, dimensions such as Thematicity, Focalization, etc. require specified elements to be realized as syntactic subject or object, to be fronted, raised, etc. Essential is also the information on the communicative dominance of an element in a given sentence structure. Thus, the dominance of the semanteme 'mean' in the S1 package of Figure 13 will lead to a sentence like *S2 means that the air quality is very poor*, while the dominance of the semanteme 'quality' will lead to a sentence like *Given S2*, *the quality of the air is very poor*.

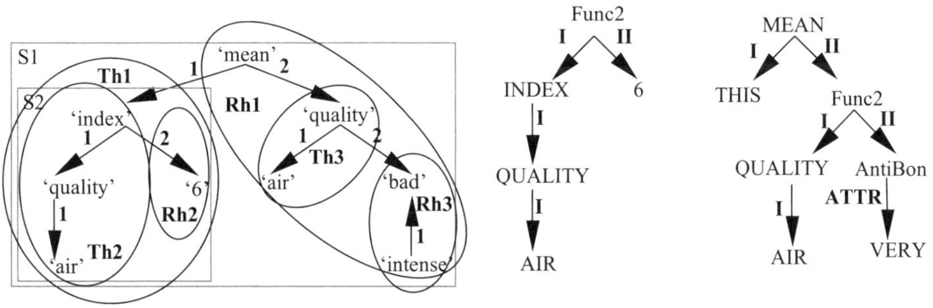

Figure 14: Interdependency between CommSemS and DSyntS

Some works, in fact, treat the role of the communicative structure in generation; cf., among others, [46, 47, 48]. However, the majority of the generators foresee a default sentence structure that mirrors the semantic or conceptual structure. To take our sample semantic structure from Figure 13 further, consider in Figure 14 (previous page) one of its possible communicative structures and the DSynt-structures that correspond to this communicative structure. The realization of 'index' –**1**→'quality' –**1**→'air' as Theme and '6' as Rheme in S2, leads to a DSyntS with the $Func_2$-LF as DSynt-head such that the NP headed by INDEX is the first DSynt-actant and '6' the second DSynt-actant. At the SSynt-stratum, the default realization of **I** is **subjective** and of **II** it is **dir.objective**. In S1, S2 is as a whole Theme, so the most adequate realization is the sentential reference THIS as DSyntA **I**. With Th3 and Rh3 embedded in Rh1, the corresponding DSyntS must foresee a clause realization of Th3+Rh3; $Func_2$ as governor fulfils the constraints.

3.3.4. Lexicalization

As mentioned above, lexicalization has been one of the most popular research topics in sentence planning or even in text generation in general. It is a two-partite task: 1. lexicalization proper, i.e., finding adequate names for the individual semantic units or configurations of semantic units, and 2. choice of referring expressions in the case of a multiple occurrence of a name in a sequence of sentences in order to ensure cohesion. In some frameworks – including MTM – both subtasks are performed at different stages of generation.

The lexicalization algorithms proposed in the literature differ widely [49]. Some assume a one-to-one association of words with semantic units such that lexicalization is realized as a search in the semantic resources – be they an ontology or a conceptual net [50, 51]; some match fragments of the semantic structure with definitions of lexical units [52]; and others do first a direct dictionary look-up and explore then the best lexicalization among available (quasi-synonymous) options [48, 53]. Note that in Figure 14, lexicalization is done in parallel with the sentence structure determination, i.e., DSyntS already contains deep lexemes.

For work on the choice of referring expressions as a separate task, see, e.g., [54, 55, 56, and 57].

3.4. Surface generation

Surface generation is the less demanding and best mastered part of text generation. Its scope may vary in that it may cover generation starting from ordered (surface-) syntactic structures or simply the instantiation of the morphological features associated with the individual lexemes. But usually, it does not go beyond a straightforward realization of predetermined surface structures.

3.5. Summary: The linguistic framework and the requirements of text generation

Various linguistic theories have been used as theoretical foundation of text or sentence generators. However, the tasks of generation require some features that are easier and more naturally provided by some theories than by others. Let us summarize the most important of these features and assess what they imply:

- As a rule, generation is required to start from an abstract representation or even from numerical data series
  - ⇨ given that abstract (conceptual or semantic) structures are predicate-argument structures, the use of a dependency theory is more straightforward.
- Involves planning of text structures
  - ⇨ requires supra-sentence modelling instruments
- Involves planning of sentence structures
  - ⇨ requires the availability of the communicative structure
- Must be able to vary and use idiosyncratic expressions and word combinations
  - ⇨ requires rich lexica that are fully integrated into the generation procedure
- Experience has shown that it is most adequate to treat the different tasks of generation separately
  - ⇨ favours a multistratal model
- Should be formally verifiable
  - ⇨ requires a formal framework beneath the generator
- Should be easily maintainable
  - ⇨ favours a modular organization

In the next section, we discuss how an MTM can be used for generation and to what extent it meets the above requirements.

4. Text Generation Using MTMs

MTT is one of the most popular linguistic theories in text generation because it possesses all of the required features – with the exception of the notion of discourse structure and text planning mechanisms, which need to be interfaced with an MTM-based generator kernel. Before we discuss how this is done, we need to reinterpret the MTM in the sense of a generator: as pointed out above, MTM is an equivalence or correspondence model, while generation presupposes a transition model. More precisely, we can view generation in the sense of an MTM as a sequence of transitions between representations of adjacent strata – starting from the semantic stratum, up to the surface-morphological stratum. Let us have a more formal look at the realization of this transition model.

4.1. Formal realization of the MTM

The following characteristics of the MTM when viewed as transition model are decisive for its realization; see [8]:

- transitions take place between two adjacent levels of representation; no intermediate representations containing fragments of representations from both levels are admitted;
- the correspondence between chunks of representations is static;
- access is available to the source structure and the target structure of the transition as well as to the context of both structures;
- the transition rules are (at least theoretically) bidirectional and can be used in parallel.

These characteristics suggest the use of *finite state transducers* [58], only that in the case of an MTM and text generation, we have to deal with *graph transducers* rather than with *string transducers*.

4.1.1. MTM-grammar modules for generation

In order to be able to use the MTM-grammars presented above for generation, the following three actions must be taken:

(i) the rules must be made more exhaustive, explicit and formal;
(ii) an algorithm that applies the rules of a given module to an input structure of the stratum $\mathbf{S}_i$ and transduces it into an output structure of the stratum $\mathbf{S}_{i+1}$ must be defined and implemented;
(iii) the format of the dictionaries and the access of the dictionaries by the transduction algorithm must be formalized.

In what follows, we present these three actions as realized in the MATE workbench [59, 60].

4.1.1.1. Grammar rule format in MATE

A grammar $G_{i\rightarrow i+1}$ to map a structure of $\mathbf{S}_i$ to a structure of $\mathbf{S}_{i+1}$ in MATE consists of a set of minimal grammar rules of the following general format; see [60, 39ff) for details:[13]

left side (ls):	$<g_i>$
right side (rs):	$<g_{i+1}>$
right context (rc):	$<g'_{i+1}>$
conditions (cd):	<Boolean expression over $\mathcal{D}$, $\mathbf{S}_i$, and $\mathbf{S}_{i+1}$>
correspondences (cr):	$\{n_{i,j} \Leftrightarrow n_{i+1,k}\}$

with g_i being a graph defined over the node and arc alphabets of $\mathbf{S}_i$, g_{i+1} and g'_{i+1} graphs defined over the node and arc alphabets of $\mathbf{S}_{i+1}$; $\mathcal{D}$ being the dictionaries, $n_{i,j}$ being a node $\in g_i$, and $n_{i+1,k}$ being a node $\in g_{i+1}$. The statement '$n_{i,j} \Leftrightarrow n_{i+1,k}$' establishes a link between the corresponding nodes in g_i and g_{i+1} in order to ensure that (i) information can be propagated from one node to another node across strata; (ii) isolated fragments of the target structure introduced upon the application of the rule can be unified to one connected well-formed structure. A rule is applied to an input structure defined over the alphabets of $\mathbf{S}_i$ if the specified conditions are fulfilled and if an isomorphic image of g'_{i+1} (the right context) has been identified in the target structure. As indicated, the conditions may be defined over all dictionaries and both strata $\mathbf{S}_i$ and $\mathbf{S}_{i+1}$.

The left side 'ls' of a rule in $G_{i\rightarrow i+1}$ consists either of an elementary linguistically meaningful graph defined over the alphabets of $\mathbf{S}_i$ or a graph that is transduced to an elementary linguistically meaningful graph defined at the right side 'rs' over the alphabets in $\mathbf{S}_{i+1}$. As a rule, an elementary meaningful graph consists either of a single node (a linguistic name) or a single arc (a linguistic relation) – although sometimes bigger structures are required. For illustration, consider sample rules for the first four types of transductions involved in MTT-based generation from a conceptual structure: a Con-Sem rule, a Sem-DSynt rule, a DSynt-SSynt rule, and a SSynt-DMorph rule.

[13] See also [10] for a more detailed exposition.

Rule 1 (a Cons-Sem rule):

```
ls: ?Xcon {PTIM->?T{con= "tomorrow"}}
rc: ?Xsem{tense=FUT}
cr: Xcon⇔?Xsem
```

Rule 1 maps the conceptual time relation PTIM between the concept denoted by the variable ?Xcon and the "universal" concept TOMORROW onto the tense feature 'FUT' of the semanteme denoted by the variable ?Xsem. Note that ?Xsem is specified in the right context slot, which means that the semanteme bound to ?Xsem is assumed to have already been introduced into the target structure by another rule.

Rule 2 (a Sem-DSynt rule):

```
ls: ?Xsem {?r->?Ysem}
rs: ?Xds{I->?Yds}
rc: ?Xds
cr: Xsem⇔?Xds; ?Ysem⇔?Yds
cd: lexicon::(?Xds.lex).(gp).(?r)=I
```

Rule 2 maps the semantic relation (denoted by the variable '**?r**') of the semanteme bound to ?Xsem onto the DSynt-relation **I** of the lexical unit L bound to ?Xds. The conditions ensure that this is in accordance with the government pattern of L. The node ?Xds must already be present in the target structure. The semantic node bound to ?Xsem corresponds to the deep-syntactic node bound to ?Xds and the node bound to ?Ysem corresponds to the node bound to ?Yds.

Rule 3 (a DSynt-SSynt rule):

```
ls: ?Xds {dpos=V; finiteness=FIN; mood=IND; tense=FUT}
rs: ?Xss{ slex=will
          dpos=lexicon::(will).dpos
          spos=lexicon::will).spos
          tense=PRES
          aux_completive->?Xss{finiteness=INF}
rc: ?Xss
cr: Xds⇔?Yss; ?Xds⇔?Xss
cd: lexicon::(id).(iso)=ENG
```

Rule 3 introduces for an English verbal lexeme (referred to by ?Xds) that carries in the DSyntS the grammemes FIN, IND, and FUT, the auxiliary WILL. WILL inherits from ?Xds via the correspondence link the grammemes of finiteness and mood, but not of tense – which is PRES. Note that in this case, one DSynt-node corresponds to two SSynt-nodes.

Rule 4 (a SSynt-DMorph rule):

```
ls: ?Xss {dpos=V
          subj->?Yss
          ?r->?Zss}
rs: ?Ytp{b->rc:?Ztp}
cr: ?Yss⇔?Ytp; ?Zss⇔?Ztp
cd: not ?r=circumstantial
```

Rule 4 defines the relative ordering between the subject (bound to ?Yss) of a verbal lexeme (referred to by ?Xss) and any other dependent of the verb (?Zss): the subject goes before. The circumstantial elements are excluded since they may come before the subject.

4.1.1.2. Transduction

The algorithm adopted by MATE's transduction engine to map a source structure G_s defined over the alphabets of the stratum $\mathbf{S}_i$ onto a target structure of the stratum $\boldsymbol{S}_{i+1}$ using the grammar $G_{i \rightarrow i+1}$ can be sketched as follows:

> Given, a graph system (G_s, $G_{i \rightarrow i+1}$,$\mathbf{G}_t$) with G_s as the source graph, $G_{i \rightarrow i+1}$ as the rule grammar, $g \in G_{i \rightarrow i+1}$, $g = (ls,rs,rc,cd,cr)$ and $\mathbf{G}_t$ as the set of target graphs, map G_s onto $G_i \in \mathbf{G}_t$ performing the following steps:
>
> 1. Binding: Identify all isomorphic images of $ls \in g$ ($\forall g \in G_{i \rightarrow i+1}$) in G_s and associate their elements with the corresponding elements of *ls*.
> 2. Evaluation of conditions: Evaluate the conditions for each bound image of *ls*.
> 3. Clustering: Build groups of rules, **CL**, with a group (or, cluster) $CL \in \mathbf{CL}$ containing all applicable rules that do not contradict each other and mapping G_s in its entirety.
> 4. Application: Create the images of $rs \in g$ ($\forall g \in CL$, $\forall$ $CL \in \mathbf{CL}$)
> 5. Unification: Unify the images of all *rs* that belong to the same cluster *CL*.

The goal of the algorithm is thus to create for a given G_s all possible well-formed structures $\mathbf{G}_t$ that correspond to G_s in accordance with $G_{i \rightarrow i+1}$, avoiding incomplete G_ts, i.e., G_ts that do not entirely cover G_s and structures that are corrupted because several rules with an overlapping left-hand side graph have been applied.

4.1.2. Generation dictionaries

The propositional structures at each stratum are characterized by a distinct node and arc alphabets. During the transitions, elements or configurations of elements of this alphabet are put into correspondence to (configurations of) elements of the alphabet at the adjacent stratum. As a result, generation dictionaries contain two types of information: (i) information concerning the elements of the alphabet of a given stratum, (ii) information concerning the correspondence between elements of alphabets of adjacent strata. Since MTT is a lexicalist (i.e., node alphabet-oriented) theory, the dictionaries concern node alphabet elements.

At least two dictionaries are available: 1. a "semantic dictionary", which contains the information required with respect to semantic units (especially the information how semantic units are mapped onto lexical units), and 2. a "lexical dictionary" with the information on lexical units. Other dictionaries, such as a morphological dictionary can also be introduced. For generation from extra-linguistic abstract (conceptual) representations, furthermore, an additional, conceptual, dictionary is required. In what follows, we discuss first such a conceptual dictionary and then a semantic and a lexical dictionary.

4.1.2.1. Conceptual dictionary

The conceptual dictionary contains, first of all, the type and argument structure of each concept and the concept-semanteme mapping information; cf., for illustration, the entry for the concept CONCENTRATION.

```
concentration: property_attribute {
    sem = 'concentration'
    MATR = {relation = 1 target = referent}
    VAL = {relation = 2 target = referent}
    ATTR = {relation = 1 source = referent}}
```

The concept CONCENTRATION has two argument slots: something that has a concentration (referred to as MATR in accordance with [35]) and a value (referred to as VAL), i.e., an absolute concentration figure. The concept may also be modified by a qualitative characterization of the concentration ("high", "low", etc.), referred to as ATTR. The corresponding semanteme 'concentration' takes MATR as its first semantic argument (indicated by the "relation=1" parameter embedded in MATR's value) and VAL as its second. The attributes "target=referent" and "source=referent" indicate the direction of the semantic relation (for MATR and VAL, the semantic predicate is 'concentration', which takes MATR's and VAL's corresponding semantemes as its arguments, while ATTR's semantic correspondent is a predicate taking 'concentration' as its argument).

4.1.2.2. Semantic dictionary

The semantic dictionary gives, for each semanteme, all its possible lexicalisations. For instance, for the meaning 'cause' it lists the LUs CAUSE[V], CAUSE[N], RESULT[V], RESULT[N], DUE, BECAUSE, CONSEQUENCE, etc. Note that we do not consider at this stage the valency of the LUs. Thus, it does not matter that 'X causes Y' means that 'Y results from X'; what interests us here is only that these two lexemes can both be used to denote the same situation, regardless of the communicative orientation (in a more comprehensive dictionary, the criteria for the choice of a specific lexicalization are specified). Cf., for illustration, the entry for the semanteme 'concentration' as specified in the semantic dictionary:

```
concentration {
    label = parameter
    lex = concentration}
```

The "label=parameter" attribute-value pair specifies the semantic type of a semanteme. We can also specify the semantic type of the arguments of a predicate; for instance, adding the attribute "1=substance" would force the first semantic argument of 'concentration' to be of type "substance".

4.1.2.3. Lexical dictionary

The lexical dictionary is the richest of the set of three generation dictionaries. It contains, for each LU, information on its part of speech, minimal sub-categorization information and the LFs that are applicable to the LU. Consider, for illustration, the entry for CONCENTRATION:

```
concentration {
// Grammatical characteristics:
    dpos=N // deep part of speech is N(oun)
    spos=common_noun // surface part of speech is common noun
// Government pattern (subcategorization):
    gp={
// Sem-DSynt valency projection:
    1=I  // first semantic actant corresponds to the first deep-syntactic actant
    2=II  // second semantic actant corresponds to the second deep-syntactic actant
// First syntactic actant can be realized as "ozone concentration":
    I={
            dpos=N // actant is a noun
            rel=compound // linked with compound relation
            det=no // takes no determiner
}
// First syntactic actant can be realized as "concentration of ozone":
    I = {
            dpos=N // actant is a noun
            rel=noun_completive // linked with noun_completive relation
            prep=of // takes preposition "of"
            det=no // takes no determiner
}
// Second syntactic actant can be realized as "concentration of 180 μg/m3":
    II={
            dpos=Num // actant is a number
            rel=noun_completive // linked with noun_completive relation
            prep=of // takes preposition "of"
}}
// Lexical functions:
    Magn = high
    AntiMagn = low
    Adv1 = in // "(we found) ozone in a concentration (of 180 μg/m3)"
    Func2 = be // "the concentration (of ozone) is 180 μg/m3"
    Oper1 = have // "ozone has a concentration (of 180 μg/m3)"
    IncepFunc2=reach // "the concentration (of ozone) reached 180 μg/m3"
    IncepOper1=reach // "ozone will reach a concentration (of 180 μg/m3)"
}
```

It is convenient to use two levels of granularity for the part of speech, referred to as "deep" and as "surface" part of speech ('dpos' and 'spos', respectively). This allows for quick reference to a whole family of parts of speech in grammar rules (for example, "N" refers to any proper noun, common noun, or pronoun). All specific grammatical characteristics of an LU are described as feature-value pairs (for example, its gender or its ability to take or not plural, definiteness, a certain tense, etc.). The sub-categorization must contain the projection of the semantic to the syntactic valency and all possible ways of syntactically connecting the LU with its dependents. Governed prepositions must be indicated here, as well as case assignment if it exists in the language being described. The part of speech of the dependents can be restricted (for instance, the first actant of CONCENTRATION must be a noun, while its second must be a number).

As already outlined above, LFs are an efficient means to refer to recurrent semantic and syntactic patterns of restricted lexical co-occurrence and lexico-semantic derivation. In the example above, Magn points to an LU which is a syntactic modifier and has a meaning of intensification (AntiMagn is its antonym). The LF Func_2 refers to a semantically emptied verb that takes the keyword (CONCENTRATION) as its subject and the keyword's second semantic actant as its object. The LF IncepOper_1 points to a verb meaning roughly 'start' which takes the keyword as its object and the first actant of the keyword as its subject.

In general, we can state that the more information on restricted lexical co-occurrence the lexical dictionary contains the more natural and idiomatic the generated text will be.

4.2. Applying MTM in Generation

Now that we have a more formal outline of an MTM, let us assess it from the viewpoint of the generation tasks talked about in Section 3.

4.2.1. Text planning in an MTM-based generator

The text planning task is covered by a module that operates on an extra-linguistic representation outside the linguistic generator kernel and that provides as output a *text plan*. The text plan serves as input to the linguistic generator. Given that the most abstract stratum this generator starts from is either the semantic or the conceptual stratum, the text plan is required to be expressed as/mapped on a semantic or on a conceptual graph representation. This does not mean, of course, that the planning module is required to operate on a semantic/conceptual representation.

In practice, both schema-based and RST-based planning mechanisms have been used in MTM-based generation; cf. [61, 62] for the first and [63, 42] for the second. Figure 15 displays a sample text plan as produced by the planning module described in [42].


```
<span id="UN65932" relation="topic-focus-elaboration" modes="text">
  <span id="UN65938" node="nucleus">
    <infounit id="UN65941">
              <topic id="UN65943" section="current" type="aq" subtypes="secondary" alert="false"/>
    </infounit> </span>
  <span id="UN65951" relation="negative-justification" node="satellite">
    <span id="UN65956" node="nucleus">
      <infounit id="UN65959" order="1.2">
          <rating id="UN65961" ref="SN65568" label="1/6" possessor="aq" region="Catalunya"/>
      </infounit> </span>
    <span id="UN65973" relation="list" node="satellite">
      <span id="UN65977" node="nucleus">
        <infounit id="UN65980" order="1.4.1">
          <concentration id="UN65982" possessor="O3"/>
        </infounit> </span>
      <span id="UN65991" node="nucleus">
        <infounit id="UN65994" order="1.4.2">
                  <concentration id="UN65996" possessor="SO2"/>
        </infounit> </span>
      <span id="UN66005" node="nucleus">
        <infounit id="UN66008" order="1.4.3">
                <concentration id="UN66010" possessor="CO"/>
        </infounit> </span>
    </span> </span> </span>
```


Figure 15: Fragment of a sample text plan used as input to the linguistic generator

Such a text plan can be readily mapped onto a conceptual graph structure that is "understood" by the linguistic MTT-based generator.

4.2.2. Deriving the communicative structure

As we have seen in Section 3, the communicative structure is very important in MTT-based text generation. However, when we start from an abstract conceptual representation or from a numeric time series, CommS is not available. It must be derived in the course of generation. Some preliminary work on how this can be done is described in [64]. The central assumption underlying this work is that the communicative structure of a statement is determined by:

(iv) domain communication knowledge concerning the context of the statement: each domain has its own way "to tell the story",

(v) the discourse structure relations in which the statement is involved: RST-like relations give clear hints with respect to the distribution of the communicative structure.

Based on this assumption, rules of the following kind are derived for generation from numeric time series:

IF 1. between DU^{Sta-} and DU^{Sta} CONTRAST holds

2. the contrasted elements are $v^{-} \in Sta^{-}$ and $v \in Sta$ of t wrt circumstantial c

3. $t \in Th^{Sta-}$, $v^{-} \in Rh^{Sta-}$, $c \in Rh^{Sta-}$

THEN $Th^{Sta} \leftarrow t$; $Th^{Sta} \leftarrow c$, $Rh^{Sta} \leftarrow v$

(with 'Sta' as statement under construction, 'Sta^{-}' as one of the preceding statements, 'DU^{Sta}' as the discourse unit containing the statement Sta, 't' as token captured by the time series, 'v' as value of the token at a given time, 'Th^{Sta}' as Theme of the statement Sta and 'Rh^{Sta}' as Rheme of the statement Sta).

Using rules of this kind for the other primary dimensions such as Giveness, Focalization, and Foregrounding, a rich enough CommS can be derived to guide the subsequent generation.

4.2.3. Coping with sentence-planning tasks in an MTM-based generator

In the MT-transduction model as implemented for text generation, most of the sentence-planning tasks are realized during the Sem-DSynt transition; some aspects of lexicalization (such as anaphoric reference introduction) are naturally handled during the DSynt-SSynt transition. The surface-realization is done starting from the DSynt-SSynt transition through all remaining subsequent transitions.

As far as aggregation is concerned, the MTM covers lexico-semantic and syntactic aggregation; contextual and conceptual aggregation must be carried out outside (prior to) the linguistic generator proper – for instance, when mapping the conceptual structure to the semantic structure. Consider, for illustration, a sample rule that handles first actant aggregation for English.[14]

[14] Note that lexico-semantic and syntactic aggregation can also be carried out at a single stratum, namely the DSynt-stratum. However, this would require a *structure rewriting model*, rather than a transduction model. The general usefulness of such a rewriting model is undisputable – for instance for paraphrasing or summarization exercises.

Rule 5:

```
ls: ?S{?X1sem
       ?X2sem}
rs: ?X1ds{COORD->?Ads{
                lex=AND
                II->?X2ds{}}}
rc: ?Xds; ?Yds
cr: X1sem⇔?X1ds; ?X2sem⇔?X2ds
cd: ?S{?X1sem{1->?Ysem}
       ?X2sem{1->?Ysem}}
```

This rule applies in case the same first semantic actant occurs twice with different governors. The result of the rule at the DSynt-side is a coordination of the DSynt-realization of these governors.

In Subsection 3.3, sentence packaging can be interpreted as taking place either at the semantic stratum as a structure rewriting procedure, or during the Con–Sem transition. With the semantic stratum as the most abstract linguistic stratum, MTT foresees the first option. However, when a generator starts from a conceptual structure, the second option is more practical and more natural. So far, MTT-based generators are not an exception when compared to other state-of-the-art generators with respect to sentence packaging: they tend to adopt a rather *ad hoc* strategy of sentence packaging: a main verb with its argument structure forms by default a sentence; the sentence can be extended by relative clauses modifying the arguments of the main verb. We dispense here with giving rule examples for sentence packaging.

The transition model in an MTM allows for lexicalization strategies of various complexities. A comprehensive semantic dictionary contains all possible lexicalizations of each semanteme; see Subsection 4.1.2.2. The criteria for the selection of one specific lexicalization are to be specified in terms of attribute-value pairs in the dictionary.

The task of sentence structure determination is carried out during the Sem-DSynt and DSynt-SSynt transitions. As pointed out in Subsection 3.3.3, it is largely guided by the communicative structure.

5. Principles for Compiling Generation Resources

One key to the solution of the problem of the shortage of resources for low- and middle-density languages is the maximal reuse of the resources available for other languages. Existing resources can be reused in two different ways: (a) by *resource porting* [65, 66] and (b) by *resource sharing* [67, 68, 69, 10]. *Porting* implies the adaptation (by copy and modification) of the resources developed for language $\mathcal{L}_1$ to language $\mathcal{L}_2$, while *sharing* implies the extraction of resources shared by all languages considered and their common maintenance. Intuitively, porting seems more suitable for largely diverging $\mathcal{L}_1$ and $\mathcal{L}_2$ and sharing for typologically similar languages.

In our work, we focused so far on resource sharing for grammatical resources and resource porting for lexical resources [10]. For effective resource sharing, it is crucial that already the design of the organization of the resources supports resource (re)use across languages. We adopt the following strategy: (i) extract recurrent rule patterns across languages and factorize them out into a "meta-grammar", (ii) modularize (or packaging) language-specific rules, (iii) shift the bulk of the grammarian's work to the lexicon, (iv) generalize recurrent lexical patterns and introduce an inheritance mechanism. This strategy has been successfully applied to the development of resources for Catalan, English, French, Polish, Portuguese and Spanish.

5.1. Extracting recurrent rule patterns across languages

In general, a contrastive analysis of multilingual grammatical resources quickly shows that many of the rules are shared by a subset of the languages, or even by all languages under consideration. For instance, Rule 1 in 4.1.1.1, maps the concept 'TOMORROW' onto the semanteme 'future'. In subsequent transduction stages towards the surface, 'future' is realized by language-specific morphological or lexical means, but at the semantic stratum, it merely encodes the meaning 'one day later than now' – which is not specific to any language. Similarly, Rule 2 makes no reference to any specific lexical unit (LU), nor does it refer to any language-specific grammatical relation (semantic and deep-syntactic relations are universal by definition). Rather, it implements the government pattern of any given LU with respect to its DSyntA **I** slot. Analogous rules are available for all DSyntA slots (**II**, **III**, ...). Rules of this kind are good candidates to universality – although no absolute statements with respect to the universality of any grammar rules can be made at the current state of research in language engineering.

In contrast, Rule 3 is only valid for English. It refers to a specific lexeme (WILL), and it even explicitly requires that the ISO identification code of the language be "ENG".

Between these two extremes, rules are encountered that apply to a set of languages – a family or any *ad hoc* set. For instance, Rule 4 is an example of a (word order) rule which by default holds for all languages we considered so far (even for Polish as a free-order word language shows a strong preference for ordering the grammatical subject before the verb it is governed), but is certainly not universal. Furthermore, in English, the determiner in most cases agrees with its governing noun only in number, while, for instance, in Romance and Slavic (in case a determiner other than article is available) languages, it agrees in number and gender (in Slavic languages, also in case). Therefore, we can specify one rule for all these languages – excluding English:[15]

Rule 6:
```
ls: ?Xss {dpos=N
          det->?Yss}
rs: ?Ytp{gender=?Xss.gender
         number=?Xss.number}
cr: ?Xss⇔?Xtp; ?Yss⇔?Ytp
cd: not(lexicon::(id).(iso)=ENG)
```

Another option would be to provide this rule family-wise, specifying in the conditions `language::(id).(family)=romance`.

The general principle is thus to minimize the number of language-specific rules (such as Rule 3) and maximize the number of generic rules. The degree of generalization that can be achieved for a module depends on the language and the strata that are involved. Languages with a complex agreement or many lexical markers for

[15] For instance, Dutch forms in this respect a common set with English. This means that if we would include Dutch into our resource list, we would need to modify the rule accordingly.

grammatical meanings (articles, auxiliaries, etc.) require a higher share of language-specific rules, while languages with a poorer morphology have a smaller share of language-specific rules.

Table 3 below copied from [10] shows the distribution of the language-independent and language-specific rules in a medium coverage generation grammar system that involves Catalan (CT), English (EN), Spanish (ES), French (FR), Polish (PL) and Portuguese (PT).

Table 3: Distribution of generic and language-specific rules in a generation grammar framework

Module	**Core**	CT	EN	ES	FR	PL	PT
Con ⇒ Sem	50	0	0	0	0	0	0
Sem ⇒ DSynt	59	8 (12%)	8 (12%)	7 (11%)	7 (11%)	11 (16%)	6 (9%)
DSynt ⇒ SSynt	64	13 (17%)	16 (20%)	11 (15%)	16 (20%)	7 (10%)	12 (16%)
SSynt ⇒ Dmorph	70	13 (16%)	3 (4%)	12 (15%)	19 (21%)	8 (10%)	14 (17%)
DMorph ⇒ SMorph	7	8 (53%)	5 (42%)	6 (46%)	10 (59%)	10 (59%)	6 (46%)
SMorph ⇒ Text	12	1 (8%)	1 (8%)	1 (8%)	1 (8%)	1 (8%)	1 (8%)
Language-specific rules (%), avr.		14%	(11%	(12%)	(17%)	(12%)	(13%)

As can be observed, the deeper the stratum, the more generic a grammar module tends to be. Thus, the Con-Sem module is entirely language-independent, but highly domain-specific – certainly also because the above six languages are very similar with respect to their semantic codification.

5.2. Packaging language-specific rules

For further optimization of the organization of the resources, each grammar module can be organized in terms of packages. A package is a set of rules that complement each other, or, on the contrary, are in competition. Each package handles one specific linguistic phenomenon. Formally, a package is defined by an abstract rule from which other rules depend. An abstract rule is always empty, but it may have conditions associated to it. These conditions are then inherited to all rules that depend on it. A package can be also composed of several sub-packages – as, for instance, the language packages: rules specific to a language are grouped into a separate package, which in its turn consists of a number of sub-packages for various language-specific phenomena.

In each grammar module, a "core" package is defined. It contains all essential rules that are needed to process a standard input structure. For instance, the core package of the SSynt-DMorph module includes rules for lexicalization and actantial and modifier relation handling. Packages for lexical co-occurrence, quantification, voice, etc. complement the core package.

With this package-oriented design, it is possible to: (i) localize easier fragments of grammatical resources that can be shared across languages, (ii) exchange fragments of the resources without worrying about the interdependencies with other fragments, (iii) assign the development of different packages to different grammarians, observing the expertise and interests of each of them.

The strategy of packaging can also be extended to the design of dictionaries. Thus, the lexical core should constitute the main package, while additional packages could be developed by terminologists as experts in specific areas of specialized discourse. Furthermore, sub-packages could be introduced for each zone of a dictionary (see Section 2.3 above) and for semantic/lexical fields or domains.

5.3. Shifting the bulk of the grammarian's work to the lexicon

One of the obstacles during the development of large coverage generation grammars – be it for low-density or high-density languages – is the complexity of the transductions if they are considered as a purely grammatical matter. One way to ease the work of grammar writing is to encode information that is in its nature lexical in the dictionary for the individual LUs. For instance, the mapping of the argument relations in a semantic and deep-syntactic structure onto corresponding relations or node configurations at the adjacent stratum has in former MTT-generators been usually realized in terms of grammar rules of the following type:

Rule 6*:
```
ls: ?Xsem {1->?Ysem}
rs: ?Xds{I->?Yds}
cd: ?Ysem.theme = yes
cr: Xsem⇔?Xds; ?Ysem⇔?Yds
```

Rule 7*:
```
ls: ?Xsem {2->?Ysem}
rs: ?Xds{II->?Yds}
cd: ?Ysem.rheme = yes
cr: Xsem⇔?Xds; ?Ysem⇔?Yds
```

However, these rules ignore that the correspondences they realize are the default projections as encoded in the government pattern (GP) of any predicate and should thus be specified in the dictionary in a general form:

```
"predicate" {
        gp={1=I; 2=II; 3=III; …; 6=VI}}
```

We assume that a predicate possesses at most six arguments, with the *i*-th semantic argument (denoted by an Arabic numeral) by default corresponding to the *i*-th syntactic actant (denoted by a Roman numeral).

Each individual predicative LU inherits this GP such that a repetition is avoided (see also next subsection). In case an LU has a deviating projection, this deviation is entered in its individual GP. Grammar rules can then make use of the GP information (both inherited and individual) as indicated in Rule 2 in 4.1.1.1.

Such a shift of the workload from the grammar to the lexicon is also in accordance with our experience, which tells us that for untrained personnel it is much easier and faster to write lexical entries than to write grammar rules.

5.4. Relying upon rich hierarchical dictionaries

As already pointed out above, rich dictionaries are crucial for the development of stable large coverage MTT-based generators. The information that needs to be included in such dictionaries has already been outlined in Section 4.1.2. For an efficient organization of this information, we use inheritance. The inheritance allows us to factorize all information shared by several entries into abstract entries, from which it is then propagated to the entries for the concrete LUs. Consider a fragment of the verbal hierarchy "predicate" → "verb" → "direct transitive verb". The predicate node provides the default projection of the semantic valency to the syntactic valency of a predicative unit; cf. above. A verbal lexeme is a predicate (i.e., inherits, if they are not overwritten, all features defined for the predicate unit). Furthermore, its surface and deep part of speech are respectively 'V' and 'verb' and, by default, in the case of the finite form, its first syntactic actant is realized as a syntactic subject, usually a noun:

```
"verb" : "predicate"{
dpos=V; spos=verb
gp={I={dpos=N; rel=subj}}}
```

Note that such abstract entries are not necessarily universal. For each language, we keep a separate hierarchy since the parts of speech and the morpho-syntactic behavior of the lexical units that carry them can vary cross-linguistically. For example, in Polish, the syntactic subject is assigned the nominative case, such that this information would be added to the abstract verb entry for Polish; the exceptions are taken care of within the entries for the verbs in question.

English direct transitive verbs inherit from the "verb"-class. Furthermore, they realize their second syntactic actant as a direct object, and it is by default a noun:

```
"verb_dt" : "verb" {
gp={II={dpos=N; rel=dobj}}}
```

Now, adding a direct transitive verb to the lexicon is just a matter of expressing its membership in the verb_dt class and adding verb-specific information. Consider, for illustration, the entry for the verb EXCEED, where we have added information on its lexical co-occurrence:

```
exceed : "verb_dt"{
Magn="by far"
Magn="far"
AntiMagn="a little"}
```

All information on the projection of the semantic to the syntactic valency, the part of speech and the surface realization of the actants has been inherited. This information can be overwritten. For example, [*to*] EXPECT has two possible sub-categorization patterns, none of which corresponds to the default pattern for verbs:

```
expect : "verb" {
gp={ II={dpos=V; finiteness=FIN; mood=IND; prep=that}}
gp={II={dpos=V; finiteness=INF; prep=to; rel=iobj}
raise={II={rel=dobj}}}}
```

The first pattern gives rise to such sentences as $[We]_{\mathbf{I}}$ *expect* $[that\ the\ ozone\ concentration\ will\ increase]_{\mathbf{II}}$. The second pattern encodes a subject-raising construction where the first actant of DSynt-actant **II** is raised to become the direct object of EXPECT, downgrading actant **II** to an indirect object position; cf.: $[We]_{\mathbf{I}}$ *expect* $[the\ ozone\ concentration]_{\mathbf{II}/\text{raised subject, dir.obj}}$ $[to\ increase]_{\mathbf{III}}$.

6. Deriving Generation Resources for New Languages

The resource design principles discussed in Section 5 ensure that (i) no parts of the resources are repeated, (ii) the resources are linguistically sound, and (iii) the acquisition and maintenance (evaluation, correction, and extension) of the resources can be carried out easily by grammarians without extensive experience in the linguistic theory underlying the generator. Especially the last item is of relevance to our context. The principles allow for a swift acquisition of resources for new languages – including low- and middle density languages. Few changes need to be made to the grammar rules, since most of the language-specific information is dealt with in the dictionaries. Rules that handle articles, auxiliaries and other lexical markers of grammatical meanings, as well as agreement and word-order rules do need to be modified, but they are usually rather simple. Hence, the major workload of adding a new language consists in the description of the LUs of the language in question – although the distribution of the workload obviously heavily depends on the characteristics of the new language. Thus, the extension of the resources developed for the six languages Catalan, English, French, Portuguese, and Spanish to Galician,[16] which is very similar to Spanish, hardly required any new grammar rules; the main workload consisted in the translation of the vocabulary, i.e., in porting of the lexical resources. Consider the Galician lexical entries corresponding to EXCEED and EXPECT from above:

```
exceder: "verb_dt"{
Magn=moito
AntiMagn="un pouco"}

esperar : "verb" {
gp={II={dpos=V; finiteness=FIN; mood=SUBJ; prep=que}}
gp={II={dpos=V; finiteness=INF; prep=a; rel=iobj}
raise={II={rel=dobj}}}}
```

Note the difference in the mood of ESPERAR 'expect': while in English, it is the indicative, in Galician (as in Catalan and Spanish) it is the subjunctive.

The extension of the same resources to, e.g., Basque, would be more costly, and to, e.g., Lezgian (just to name a language that is rather different from the languages with which we usually work), or any other typologically radically different language, even more so.[17]

[16] Galician is a Western Ibero-Romance language spoken in the North-West of Spain; the total number of speakers of Galician is about 3 to 4 million.

[17] According to Wikipedia, Basque has about 1 million speakers (for 700 000 of them, it is the first language) and Lezgian, which belongs to the Lezgic group of the Dagestan language family, about 451 000 speakers.

7. Evaluation of the Resources

Any language engineering resources must be subjected to a rigorous evaluation at each stage of their development. This is also true for resources being obtained by resource sharing and porting. Lareau and Wanner [10] propose for MTT-based generation resources a three stage evaluation: (i) micro evaluation of grammatical resources, (ii) macro evaluation of grammatical resources, and (iii) evaluation of the consistency of the dictionaries.

Micro evaluation concerns the evaluation of individual rules. For each rule (or each set of equivalent rules) a set of test structures is to be set up. These structures must be as simple as possible but still cover all phenomena the rule in question has to be able to cope with. In most cases, a single rule cannot be tested in isolation; its application depends on the application of some core rules. For instance, it is not possible to test only the construction of a given syntactic relation without also applying the rules that create the nodes linked by the relation. Therefore, for evaluation, it is necessary to keep track of rule dependencies. Hence, not only do we associate a set of test structures with each rule, but we also associate each test structure with the set of rules it activates. When a rule is modified, all executed test routines that involved it are reset and run again. Micro-testing thus verifies elementary components separately.

By the very nature of micro evaluation, it is difficult to have for it language-independent test structures. Thus, even if we want to test a generic DSynt-SSynt rule, the input test structure will have to be a DSynt-structure, which by definition contains LUs of a specific language. Therefore, only the rules of the Con-Sem module can be micro-tested with language-independent test structures (since our conceptual structures are the same for all languages) – although it can often be assumed that generic rules tested in one language will work just as well in other languages.

Macro evaluation aims to assess the coverage of the linguistic resources for a given application – as, for instance, the generation of air quality bulletins or soccer match commentaries. The test structures used for this task must cover the largest possible number of text plans the generator has to handle. The goal is here not to test specific rules, but to make sure that the system can handle the input structures with which it is expected to be provided. Macro evaluation is best applied after micro evaluation, as it verifies the interaction between the various components of the grammar.

In addition to micro and macro evaluation of the grammatical resources, it is necessary to make sure that all units of the node alphabet at a given stratum can be expressed in terms of a feature, unit, or unit configuration at the adjacent stratum. In the context of text generation which covers all strata of an MTM, we must also ensure that all concepts that might appear in the input structures can be expressed in any language. Concepts are mapped following the instructions in the conceptual dictionaries to language-specific semantemes, which in their own turn are mapped to LUs. These LUs point to prepositions in their sub-categorization patterns and to other LUs through lexical functions. All these links form a complex network where errors are hard to spot for a human, so we created a small MATE grammar that consists essentially of simplified lexicalisation rules. This grammar takes as input a list of structures, each containing one concept (one structure for every concept expected in the input of the system), and produces structures representing the lexical links encoded by the dictionaries. Then, a set of consistency-checking rules is applied to make sure that there is no pointer to non-existent entries, and that each entry contains all the necessary information (for example, that Catalan nouns have a gender, that every LU has a part of speech, that syntactic relation names are specified in the sub-categorization patterns, etc.). If an error is found, an appropriate message is added to the output.

8. Conclusions

We hope that it became clear why MTT is one of the most popular linguistic theories in text generation. Our goal in this article was twofold: firstly, to give a brief introduction to the MTT-model and to its use as basis of a text generator, and, secondly, to show how grammatical and lexical resources in the MTT-framework can be efficiently developed and extended to cover new languages – be they high-, or low-, or middle-density languages. However, given that so far we experimented only with low- and middle-density languages that are very similar to the high-density languages for which resources are available, we cannot make any reliable statement on how big the effort would be to extend our resources to radically different languages. There is no other way to know it than to get started. Researchers embarking on this endeavour can be sure of our support.

Acknowledgements

This paper has been read and commented upon by M. Alonso Ramos and I. Mel'čuk; many thanks to both of them for valuable comments and suggestions, which helped to improve the first version of the paper considerably. The remaining errors are, as always, our own responsibility.

References

[1] Mel'čuk, I. *Opyt teorii lingvističeskix modelej "Smysl-Tekst"*. Nauka, Moscow, 1974.
[2] Mel'čuk, I. *Dependency Syntax*. State University of New York Press, Albany, 1988.
[3] Mel'čuk, I. *Vers une linguistique Sens-Texte. Leçon inaugurale*. Collège de France, Paris, 1997.
[4] Kahane, S. The Meaning-Text Theory. In: V. Agel et al. (eds.). *Dependency and Valency. An International Handbook of Contemporary Research*, Vol. 1, 546-570. De Gruyter, Berlin/New York, 2003.
[5] Mel'čuk, I. *Communicative Organization in Natural Language*. Benjamins Academic Publishers, Amsterdam, 2001.
[6] Mel'čuk, I. and L. Wanner. Syntactic mismatches in machine translation. *Machine Translation* **20** (2006), 81-138.
[7] Mel'čuk, I. and L. Wanner. Morphological mismatches in machine translation. Submitted.
[8] Bohnet, B. Covering the Mapping from Semantics up to Morphology by Transducers. In K. Gerdes et al. (eds.) *Meaning-Text Theory 2007,* 129-138. Sagner, Munich, 2007.
[9] Bohnet. B. and L. Wanner. On Using a Parallel Graph Rewriting Formalism for Text Generation. In *Proceedings of the 8th European Natural Language Generation Workshop at the Annual Meeting of the Association for Computational Linguistics*. Toulouse, 47-56. 2001.
[10] Lareau, F. and L. Wanner. Towards a Generic Multilingual Dependency Grammar for Text Generation. In T. Holloway King and E.M. Bender (eds.) *Proceedings of the GEAF 2007 Workshop. CSLI Studies in Computational Linguistics* ONLINE. http://csli-publications.stanford.edu. Stanford, 2007.
[11] Halliday, M.A.K. *An Introduction to Systemic Functional Grammar*. Arnold, London, 1994.
[12] Halliday, M.A.K. and C. Matthiessen. *Construing Experience through Meaning: A Language Based Approach to Cognition*. Cassell, London, 1999.
[13] Dik, S.C. *The Theory of Functional Grammar*. Foris, Dordrecht, 1989.

[14] Croft, W. and D.A. Cruse. *Cognitive Linguistics*. Cambridge University Press, Cambridge, 2004.
[15] Langacker, R.W. *Foundations of Cognitive Grammar Vols. I, II*. Stanford University Press, Stanford, 1987/1991.
[16] Van Valin, R.D. *Advances in Role and Reference Grammar*. Benjamins Academic Publishers, Amsterdam, 1993.
[17] Matthiessen, C.M.I.M. and J.A. Bateman. *Text Generation and Systemic Functional Linguistics*. Pinter Publishers, London, 1991.
[18] Milićević, J. *La paraphrase*. Peter Lang, Berne, 2007.
[19] Mel'čuk, I. Phrasemes in Language and Phraseology in Linguistics. In M. Everaert et al. (eds.) *Idioms*, 167-232. Lawrence Erlbaum Associates, Hillsdale, NJ, 1995.
[20] Mel'čuk, I. Lexical Functions: A Tool for the Description of Lexical Relations in a Lexicon. In L. Wanner (ed.) *Lexical Functions in Lexicography and Natural Language Processing*, 37-102. Benjamins Academic Publishers, Amsterdam, 1996.
[21] Mel'čuk, I., A. Polguère and A. Clas. *Introduction à la lexicologie explicative et combinatoire*. Duculot, Louvain-la-Neuve, 1995.
[22] Alonso Ramos, M. *Las funciones léxicas en el modelo lexicográfico de I. Mel'čuk*. PhD Thesis. U.N.E.D., Madrid, 1993.
[23] Mel'čuk, I. and L. Wanner. Towards a lexicographic approach to lexical transfer in machine translation (illustrated by the German-Russian language pair). *Machine Translation* **16** (2001), 21-87.
[24] Gerdes, K. and S. Kahane. Phrasing it Differently. In L. Wanner (ed.) *Selected Lexical and Grammatical Issues in the Meaning-Text Theory*, 297-335. Benjamins Academic Publishers, Amsterdam, 2007.
[25] Engel, U. *Deutsche Grammatik*. Julius Gross, Heidelberg, 1988.
[26] Daneš, F. Functional Sentence Perspective and the Organization of the Text. In F. Daneš (ed.) *Papers on Functional Sentence Perspective*, 106-128. Academia, Prague, 1974.
[27] Sgall, P., E. Hajičová, and J. Panevová. *The Meaning of the Sentence in its Semantic and Pragmatic Aspects*. Reidel Publishing Company, Dordrecht, 1986.
[28] Lambrecht, K. *Information Structure and Sentence Form. Topic, Focus, and the Mental Representation of Discourse Referents*. Cambridge University Press, Cambridge, 1994.
[29] Erteschik-Shir, N. *Information Structure. The Syntax-Discourse Interface*. Oxford University Press, Oxford, 2007.
[30] Wanner, L. and M. Alonso Ramos. What Type of Entity Is a Lexical Function? In *Proceedings of the 2nd International Conference on the Meaning-Text Theory*, 518-528. Moscow, 2005.
[31] Lavoie, B. and O. Rambow. A fast and portable realizer for text generation systems. In *Proceedings of the 5th Conference on Applied Natural Language Processing*, 265-268, 1997.
[32] Coch, J., E. De Dycker, J.-A. Garcia-Moya, H. Gmoser, J.-F. Stranart and J. Tardieu MultiMeteo: adaptable software for interactive production of multilingual weather forecasts. In: *Proceedings of the 4th European Conference on Applications of Meteorology (ECAM 99)*. Norkøping, Sweden, 1999.
[33] Wanner, L., B. Bohnet, N. Bouayad-Agha, F. Lareau, A. Lohmeyer, and D. Nicklaß. On the Challenge of Creating and Communicating Air Quality Information A Case for Environmental Engineers. In *Proceedings of Environmental Software Systems: Dimensions of Environmental Informatics*. Prague, 2007.
[34] Nicklaß, D., N. Bouayad-Agha and L. Wanner. Addressee-Tailored Interpretation of Air Quality Data. In *Proceedings of EnviroInfo*, Vol. 2, 67-74, 2007.
[35] Sowa, J. *Knowledge Representation: Logical, Philosophical and Computational Foundations*. Brooks Cole Publishing Co, Pacific Grove, CA, 2000.
[36] McKeown, K. *Text Generation: Using Discourse Strategies and Focus Constraints to Generate Natural Language Text*. Cambridge University Press, Cambridge, 1985.
[37] Mann, W.C. and S. Thompson. Rhetorical Structure Theory: A theory of text organization. In L. Polanyi (ed.) *The Structure of Discourse*. Ablex Publishing Corporation, Norwood, New Jersey, 1987.
[38] Schank, R. & R. Abelson. Scripts, Plans, Goals and Understanding. Lawrence Erlbaum Associates, Hillsdale, NJ, 1977.
[39] Hovy, E. Automated Discourse Generation Using Discourse Structure Relations. *Artificial Intelligence* **63** (1993), 341-386.
[40] Moore, J. and C. Paris. Planning Text for Advisory Dialogues: Capturing Intentional and Rhetorical Information. *Computational Linguistics* **19** (1993), 651-694.
[41] Rösner, D. and M. Stede. Customizing RST for the Automatic Production of Technical Manuals. In R. Dale et al. (eds.) *Aspects of Automated Natural Language Generation*. Springer Verlag, Berlin, 1992.
[42] Bouayad-Agha, N. and L. Wanner. Text Planning of Air Quality Information. In *Proceedings of EnviroInfo 2007*, Vol. 2, 81-88, 2007.

[43] Bouayad-Agha, N., D. Nicklaß and L. Wanner. Discourse Structuring of Dynamic Content. In *Proceedings of the Spanish Conference on Computational Linguistics*. Zaragoza, 2006.
[44] Dalianis, H. Aggregation in Natural Language Text Generation. *Computational Intelligence*, **15** (1999), 384-404.
[45] Shaw, J. *Clause Aggregation: An Approach to Generating Concise Text*. PhD Thesis. Columbia University, New York, 2002.
[46] McKeown, K. and M. Derr. Using Focus to Generate Complex and Simple Sentences. In *Proceedings of the 10th International Conference on Computational Linguistics,* 501-504, 1984.
[47] Iordanskaja, L., R. Kittredge, and A. Polguère. Lexical Selection and Paraphrase in a Meaning-Text Generation Model. In C.L. Paris et al. (eds.). *Natural Language Generation in Artificial Intelligence and Computational Linguistics*, 293-312. Kluwer Academic Publishers, Dordrecht, 1991.
[48] Wanner, L. *Exploring Lexical Resources for Text Generation in a Systemic Functional Language Model*. PhD Thesis. Saarland University, Saarbrücken, 1997.
[49] Wanner, L. Lexicalization in Text Generation and Machine Translation. *Machine Translation*, **11** (1996), 3-35.
[50] Reiter, E. A New Model for Lexical Choice for Nouns. *Computational Intelligence*, **7** (1991), 240-251.
[51] McDonald, D. On the Place of Words in the Generation Process. In C. Paris et al. (eds.) *Natural Language Generation in Artificial Intelligence and Computational Linguistics*, 227-247. Kluwer Academic Publishers, Dordrecht, 1991.
[52] Stede, M. *Lexical Semantics and Knowledge Representation in Multilingual Text Generation*. Kluwer Academic Publishers, Dordrecht, 1999.
[53] Polguère, A. A "Natural" Lexicalization Model for Language Generation. *Proceedings of the Fourth Symposium on Natural Language Processing 2000*, 37-50. Chiangmai, Thailand, 2000.
[54] Bohnet, B. and R. Dale. Viewing Referring Expression Generation as Search. In the *Proceedings of the Nineteenth International Joint Conference on Artificial Intelligence*. Edinburgh, Scotland, 2005.
[55] Horacek, H. On Referring to Sets of Objects Naturally. In H. Bunt and R. Muskens (eds.). *Third International Natural Language Generation Conference*, 70 – 79. Springer Verlag, Heidelberg, 2004.
[56] Krahmer, E., S. van Erk, and A. Verleg. Graph-based generation of referring expressions. *Computational Linguistics*, **29** (2003), 53–72.
[57] Dale, R. *Generating Referring Expressions: Constructing Expressions in a Domain of Objects and Processes*. MIT Press, Cambridge, MA, 1992.
[58] Aho, A.V. and J.D. Ullman. Translations of a Context-Free Grammar. *Information and Control*, 1971.
[59] Bohnet, B., A. Langjahr and L. Wanner. A Development Environment for an MTT-Based Sentence Generator. *Proceedings of the First International Conference on Natural Language Generation*. Mitzpe Ramon, Israel, 260-263, 2000.
[60] Bohnet, B. *Textgenerierung durch Transduktion linguistischer Strukturen*. AKA, Berlin, 2006.
[61] Goldberg, E., N. Driedger, and R. Kittredge. Using Natural Language Processing to Produce Weather Forecasts. *IEEE Expert*, **9** (1994), 45-53.
[62] Bethem, T., J. Burton, T. Caldwell, R. Kittredge, B. Lavoie, and J. Werner. Generation of Real-Time Narrative Summaries of Real-time Water Levels and Meteorological Observations in PORTS®. In *Proceedings of the Fourth Conference on Artificial Intelligence Applications to Environmental Sciences*, San Diego, California, 2005.
[63] Coch, J. and R. David. Representing Knowledge for Planning MultiSentential Text. In *Proceedings of the 4th Conference on Applied Natural Language Processing*, 1994.
[64] Wanner, L., B. Bohnet, and M. Giereth. Deriving the Communicative Structure in Applied NLG. Proceedings of the *9th European Natural Language Generation Workshop at the Annual Meeting of the Association for Computational Linguistics*, Budapest, 111-118, 2003.
[65] Alshawi, H. *The Core Language Engine*. The MIT Press, Cambridge, MA, 1992.
[66] Kim, R. M. Dalrymple, R.M. Kaplan, T. Holloway King, H. Masuichi, and T. Ohkuma. Multilingual Grammar Development via Grammar Porting. In *Proceedings of ESSLLI Workshop on Ideas and Strategies for Multilingual Grammar Development*, 2003.
[67] Avgustinova, T. and H. Uszkoreit. An ontology of systemic relations for a shared grammar of Slavic. In *Proceedings of the 18th International Conference on Computational Linguistics*, 28-34, 2000.
[68] Bender, E., D. Flickinger, and S. Oepen. The Grammar Matrix: An Open-Source Starter-Kit for the Rapid Development of Cross-Linguistically Consistent Broad-Coverage Precision Grammars. In *Proceedings of the Workshop on Grammar Engineering and Evaluation at the 19th International Conference on Computational Linguistics*, 8-14, 2002.
[69] Bateman, J., I. Kruiff-Korbayova, and G.J. Kruiff. Multilingual resource sharing across both related and unrelated languages. An implemented, open-source framework for practical natural language generation. *Journal on Language and Computation*, **3** (2005), 191-219.

Language Engineering for Lesser-Studied Languages
S. Nirenburg (Ed.)
IOS Press, 2009

doi:10.3233/978-1-58603-954-7-243

Hybrid Machine Translation for Low- and Middle-Density Languages

Stella MARKANTONATOU, Sokratis SOFIANOPOULOS, Olga GIANNOUTSOU, Marina VASSILIOU
Institute for Language and Speech Processing

Abstract. The main aim of this article is to present the prototype hybrid Machine Translation (MT) system METIS. METIS is interesting in two ways. As regards MT for low and middle density languages, METIS relies on relatively cheap resources: monolingual corpora of the target language (TL), flat bilingual lexica and basic NLP tools (taggers, lemmatizers, chunkers). In terms of research, METIS uses pattern matching algorithms and patterns in an innovative way. In order to put the discussion of METIS in context and define the niche that this research prototype fills, the landscape of state-of-the-art Machine Translation, especially as regards low and middle-density languages, is briefly described.

Introduction

Machine Translation (MT) is by no means a novel field of research. The first attempts, with the newly invented computers, date back to the end of the 1940s. Over the years, there were periods that MT was at the center of scientific attention and periods of neglect [1]. Nowadays, work on MT is conducted by many groups spread all over the globe. After so many years, MT is not just research. Today one can find MT applications for commercial or personal use or use over the web that yield results of satisfactory accuracy for a number of language pairs and sublanguages [2], [3].

Despite those advances, the MT community is not yet in a position to propose a technology for randomly chosen language pairs and general language that yields reasonable results, hopefully drawing on reasonable (as opposed to large) amounts of resources. Parameters such as the ones listed below seem to measure the difficulty of MT system development for new language pairs:

- availability of funding
- availability of NLP resources
- affinity of the Source Language (SL) and target one (TL)

How to make MT viable with modest financial and NLP resources is an important question that is being actively researched because new language pairs, in particular, those involving middle and low density languages, are becoming important in the international financial and social arena.

This chapter mainly reports on the experience in developing METIS, a relatively resource-poor MT system. As the authors do not presuppose an audience familiar with linguistic problems that often turn up in translation, Section 1 provides a brief list of translation problems some of which are treated by METIS in an interesting way. However, the authors do not dwell extensively on the various resources and tools because they are extensively discussed elsewhere in this volume. Section 1 may be skipped by people familiar with MT problems,[1] and Sections 2 and 3, by people familiar with state-of-the-art MT. Sections 2, 3 and 4 contain brief descriptions of the current types of MT systems and focus on Hybrid MT, as this is the natural context for introducing the innovative features of METIS. In Section 5 the METIS system is presented in detail.

1. Why is MT Such a Hard Problem?

MT is a hard problem because human languages are complex and the societies that use them refer to different cultural backgrounds. Below, some hard linguistic problems, notorious among MT workers (for most of these problems see also [4]), are listed together with some hints about strategies for dealing with them.

a) Language is ambiguous

1. The *bank* on the other side of the town
2. She waved to the man *with the straw hat*
3. John talked to Peter about *his* nephew

Lexical ambiguity: Sentence (1) contains the ambiguous English word *bank*. Furthermore, no strong clue is provided in the sentence for choosing among the different senses of *bank*. This would have been a problem even for systems equipped with a lot of information concerning the use of the various senses of words.

Syntactic ambiguity: Sentence (2) illustrates the notorious 'PP attachment' problem, that is, whether the PP *with the straw hat* attaches to the verb *waved* or to the noun *man*. While there is no clue as to which is the best attachment, it may be the case here that, at least for some language pairs, the same ambiguity holds across the language pair and, therefore, there is no need to solve it. Here, similarity of Source (SL) and Target Language (TL) provides the solution.

Semantic ambiguity: Sentence (3) illustrates an anaphor resolution problem, as it is not clear from the text whether the possessive *his* refers to *John* or to *Peter*. Argumentation similar to that concerning sentence (2) may be applied here.

b) Apart from being ambiguous, languages do not contain absolute synonyms but do contain near ones, as is illustrated by the following Greek examples:

4. Ο σύγχρονος άνθρωπος έχει μεγάλο εγκέφαλο
   'Modern man has a large brain'
5. Έχει μυαλό

[1] The text partly draws on a seminar on hybrid Machine Translation for low and middle density languages given in the framework of the NATO Advanced Study Institute on Advances in Language Engineering for Low and Middle Density Languages, Batumi, Georgia, October 15-27, 2007. The seminar was addressed to an audience with varying degrees of familiarity with MT and NLP in general. Its aim was to outline the landscape of recent research on MT drawing on limited resources. A discussion of typical MT problems and MT system classification was thought necessary to clarify some of the issues and has been used in this chapter.

'He has brains'

6. Έχε το μυαλό σου στην δουλειά σου
   'Keep your mind on your work'
7. Παρήγγειλα αρνίσια μυαλά
   'I ordered lamb brains'

Such problems could be partially solved with lexica containing information about lexical affiliations, that is, the set of lexical contexts which co-occur with each sense. For instance, in sentence (6) the co-occurrence of the words *έχε, μυαλό, δουλειά* (*have, brain/brains mind, work* respectively) disambiguates the word *μυαλό* and directs the system to the right translation, i.e. *mind.* Such affiliations can, to a certain extent, be captured by statistical systems.

c) Different languages have different word order

8. *The children* read a whole lot of different texts **every day**
9. Διαβάζουν *τα παιδιά* **κάθε μέρα** ένα σωρό διαφορετικά κείμενα

Translation equivalents of the phrasal constituents between sentences (8) (English) and (9) (Modern Greek) are indicated through formatting. It is obvious that there are word order mismatches between English and Modern Greek. The usual solution to this problem is to enumerate the possible word order correspondences. This can be done either with Context Based MT (CBMT) systems that rely on bitexts or with Rule Based MT (RBMT) or CBMT systems that use rules, probably in addition to statistics [5]. Alternatively, pattern-matching techniques (METIS II, see Section 5.3) may be used.

d) Pro-drop phenomena

Morphologically rich languages, such as Modern Greek (10), may drop a pronominal subject as at least number and person information is encoded in the verb's morphology. Languages that are less rich morphologically, such as English, require that the subject be always present (11).

10. Modern Greek: πηγαίνω τώρα
    $go_{-1st-sg}$ now
11. English: *am going now

The necessary pronoun can be added using a rule. METIS adds a 'dummy' pronoun at translation retrieval time and adds morphological features to it at token generation time (see Section 5.5). The procedure is rule-based.

e) Different languages have different lexicalizing strategies (head switching phenomena)

12. Ο Γιάννης ανεβαίνει τρέχοντας τις σκάλες
    the John goes-up running the stairs
13. John runs up the stairs.

This is an example of a well-known typological difference [6] between languages that prefer to encode telicity/path on the verb and manner on the satellite (such as Modern Greek, sentence (12)) and languages that prefer to encode manner on the verb and path on the satellite (such as English, sentence (13)). This problem requires that the translation lexicon contains detailed information about the relation of the subcategorization properties of predicates across a particular language pair and that the texts are parsed in depth. Alternatively, MT based on a detailed analysis and alignment of bitexts at phrase level could provide the necessary information. Both technologies are expensive and not well developed yet.

f) Languages do not share the same subcategorization patterns

14. Μπήκα στο σπίτι (V+PP)
    enter$_{-1st-sg-past}$ in-the house
15. I entered the house (V+NP)

Argumentation similar to that in (e) above applies here as well. The mismatch should be encoded in the translation lexicon or be captured by alignment of bitexts. METIS deals with such cases by conflating the treatment of NPs and PPs and then, by applying statistical techniques to choose the right TL preposition.

g) Languages have discontinuous words

16. She congratulated the winner warmly.
17. Έδωσε θερμά συγχαρητήρια στον νικητή
    PRO give-$_{3rd\ -past}$ warm congratulation$_{-pl}$ to the winner

Here, the Modern Greek example contains a relatively flexible multi-word unit that corresponds to a verb in English. The unit contains a noun modifier that corresponds to a TL verb modifier. Such cases require lexica with multi-word units combined with some information that the units are somehow flexible (for instance, here the adjective *θερμά* is allowed to intervene between the verb and noun).

h) Languages do not share the same phrasal categories

18. Θέλω να φύγω
    want$_{-1-sg-pres}$ to go$_{-1-sg-pres}$
    'I want to go'
19. Θέλω να φύγει ο Γιάννης
    want$_{-1-sg-pres}$ to go$_{-3-sg-pres}$ the John
    'I want John to go'

Modern Greek does not have infinitives and uses fully tensed verbs in subordinate clauses. This mismatch could be captured by some rule or by alignment of bitexts at phrasal level. METIS uses a special rule (see Section 5.3).

i) Different languages have different cultural backgrounds

The term "medieval period" makes little or no sense when applied to Modern Greek history. Rather, Greeks would talk about the Byzantine period (up to mid 15th century) and then, the Turkish Occupation (mid 15th century to beginning of 19th century), if they talk about political history, or about the post-Byzantine period, if they talk about art and cultural life.

Such problems lie beyond state-of-the-art MT. Probably, they could be solved by systems equipped with very informative resources such as ontologies [7] as well as extremely sophisticated algorithms able to retrieve and exploit large amounts of textual information.

To summarize, mismatches between languages vary from simple to difficult ones. Simple mismatches can be treated in a rather straightforward manner with lexica and simple grammar rules or simple alignments in the case of parallel corpora. 'Harder' mismatches require complex lexica and complex structure modifying rules while issues having to do with contextual information are the hardest to be solved.

2. Types of MT Systems and Resources They Require

MT systems can be classified into general types depending on the type/depth of analysis of the SL and TL required. This classification has been successfully represented using the famous Vauquois pyramid [8]. In this chapter, we will use an 'updated' Vauquois pyramid [4], which is closer to state-of-the-art MT (Figure 1).

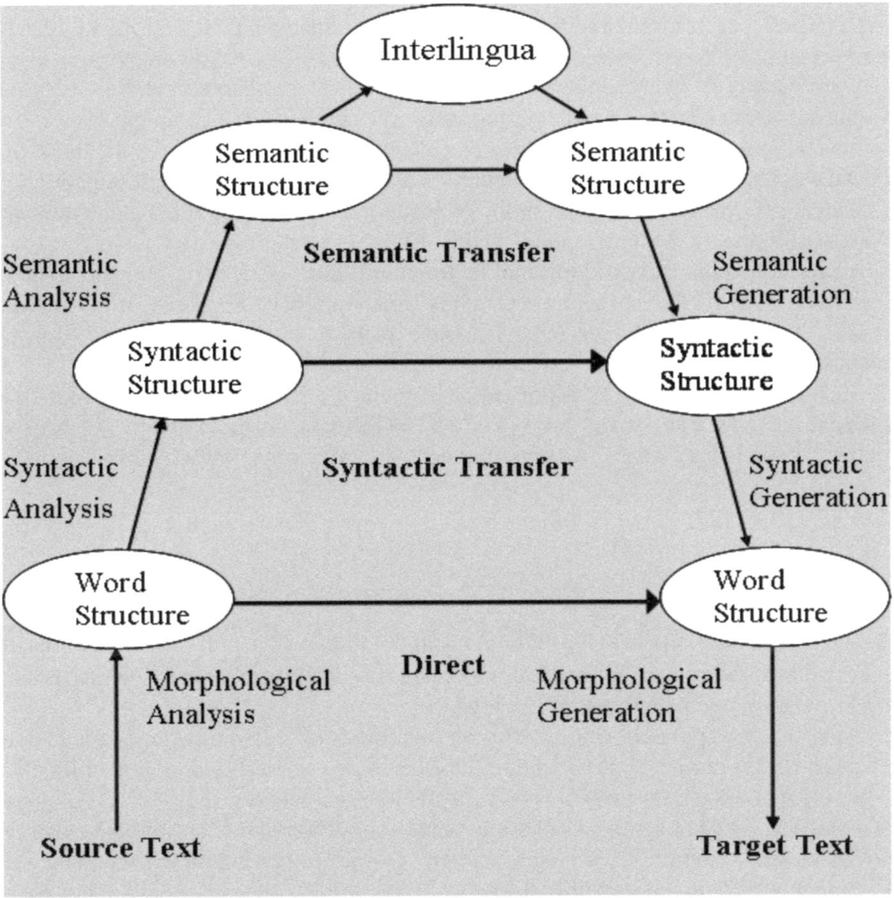

Figure 1. The updated Vauquois pyramid

According to this classification, we start from systems, placed at the bottom of the pyramid, that simply perform word-to-word or lemma-to-lemma substitution and move to higher-complexity systems as we approach the top. So, next up are systems that perform syntactic structure-to-syntactic structure substitution, then systems that perform semantic structure-to-semantic structure substitution and, finally, systems that map the SL input to a universal semantic language, the so-called interlingua. The idea is that a system 'climbs' up to some point of the pyramid during the analysis stage and then 'climbs' down during the generation stage. Language strings, both input and output ones, lie at the bottom of the pyramid while more abstract representations of linguistic knowledge are placed closer to the top. While moving to the bottom, the system goes through all the intermediate stages, those of semantic and syntactic generation down to the point of morphological generation. Mapping of the SL on the TL at the simplest level is called 'direct mapping', at syntactic level 'syntactic transfer' and, at semantic level 'semantic transfer'.

Obviously, more abstract representations require more complex resources, such as lexica, and tools. At the simplest level only bilingual lexica of tokens are required. If morphological analysis is performed, then tokenizers, part-of-speech taggers and lemmatizers are necessary as well as lemma-based lexica. To move to syntactic transfer, some sort of parser is required while morphological analysis is a prerequisite. Again, there are simple, robust tools for assigning a measure of syntactic analysis to a text (they are usually called 'chunkers') but, generally speaking, parsers can be NLP tools of considerable complexity. They too rely on increasingly complex lexica and grammars. Semantic analysis presupposes syntactic analysis and requires special lexica and parsers. A very abstract semantic analysis assigns an interlingua representation to a SL sentence. Generation proceeds in the opposite direction and requires generators and lexica of complexity that corresponds to the respective level of analysis.

Increasing complexity of tools and lexica entails increasing cost of development of these resources. To this cost, low reusability potentials must be added. It is for these reasons that it is unlikely for most language pairs to go beyond syntactic transfer systems.

In the next section we will present a different classification of MT systems that relies on the way translations are retrieved (rather than on the depth of analysis of linguistic knowledge). These two classifications are orthogonal to each other.

3. MT Paradigms

The aim of this section on MT paradigms is to help the reader to follow the discussion on hybrid MT (Section 4) for low and middle density languages. Interesting discussions on MT paradigms can be found in [9], [10].

The Vauquois pyramid (Figure 1) is an established, widely known classification of MT systems. It presents a classification of MT systems that relies on the identification of the linguistic analysis level where correspondences between the Source Language (SL) and the Target Language (TL) are established. Over the years of MT research, another classification of MT systems has been developed relying on the methods used to retrieve correspondences between SL and TL. So, MT today may be either Rule-based or Corpus-based or, eventually, Hybrid MT, if it draws on combinations of more than one of the other types of MT. Corpus-based MT may be Statistical or Example-based.

Types of MT systems

- Rule-based MT (RBMT)

- Corpus-based MT (CBMT)
  - Statistical MT (SMT)
  - Example-based MT (EBMT)
- Hybrid MT

Furthermore, a lot of tools are used to support the translation procedure. Of them, Translation Memories are the most well-known ones. Nowadays, a lot of attention is also paid to translation environments [2].

We have already pointed out that the Vaquois classification and the paradigm-based one are orthogonal to each other. If we try to put MT paradigms on the Vauquois pyramid, the following picture emerges:

- RBMT MT systems can be found at all levels of the pyramid: SYSTRAN is a widely known syntactic transfer-based system. The EUROTRA project worked on semantic transfer adopting an interlingua approach.
- SMT & EBMT are mostly cases of syntactic transfer.

Below, the pros and the cons of each paradigm are briefly presented.

3.1. Rule-based MT (RBMT)

RBMT relies on the full description of both SL and TL and of their correspondences at the lexical, morphological, syntactic and, sometimes, semantic level. Up to mid 1990s, it was the most popular approach.

Among the pros of RBMT one can list the following [11]:

- It is a good methodological choice if MT development work starts from scratch, that is, if there are no corpora, lexica or tools; this is because it requires only native speakers and linguists.
- Even with well-developed RBMT, the sources of mistakes are tractable and, often, repairable.

The cons of RBMT include the following:

- It takes a lot of development time and effort to produce reasonable quality of translations and this is the reason why…
- …RBMT is considered expensive
- RBMT relies on expensive resources (sets of rules, lexica). These resources cannot be reused for other language pairs. Of course, some 'generic' resources, such as parsers and taggers, can be reused for several translation pairs (provided that they are trained on or fed with linguistic knowledge appropriate for each language pair).

3.2. Corpus-based MT (CBMT)

The relatively recent availability of large corpora made Corpus-based MT an option. Large corpora have become indispensable tools in lexicography and linguistics. CBMT relies on a particular type of corpora, the so-called 'parallel corpora'. A parallel corpus contains texts and their translations, which are aligned at least at sentence level (but parallel corpora may be aligned at chunk or even word level).

The great promise of corpus-based MT approaches is the ability to induce 'hard-to-manipulate' linguistic information from the corpus rather than by explicitly representing it using a constantly growing collection of rules. The syntactic and semantic preferences of words (one of the reasons why the number of rules tends to explode in both hand-crafted and tree-bank induced grammars [12]) constitute a large part of the implicit information provided by the corpus. A similar argument can be made about word order. Thus, 'original' CBMT required that:

- much, and possibly all, linguistic knowledge was retrieved directly from natural language strings in the parallel corpora;
- mediating representations (such as linguistic annotations and rules) were minimized or, if possible, eliminated.

This 'purist' approach was soon abandoned for reasons of complexity, and linguistic representations were introduced at several levels of the procedure.

Two major branches have been developed within CBMT: Statistical MT (SMT) and Example-Based MT (EBMT).

3.2.1. Statistical MT

SMT became an active paradigm of research after the publication of the seminal paper by Brown and his collaborators [11]. It aims at translating a SL sequence into a TL one by maximizing the posterior probability of the target sequence given the source sequence.

Originally, posterior probability was modeled using target language models (n-grams of words). Nowadays, posterior probability is modeled as a combination of several models: phrase-based models and lexicon models for both translation directions, phrase and word penalties etc. Probabilities that describe correspondences between the source language and the target language are learned from a bilingual parallel text corpus and language model probabilities are learned from a monolingual text in the target language. Alignment is of utmost importance and has been the subject of plenty of research (for an overview, see [14]).

The main advantage of SMT is that it is considered relatively cheap because [11]:

- it takes less time and fewer resources to produce reasonable quality;
- it does not require expensive intermediate linguistic representations to produce reasonable results, as a lot of information is encoded in the strings;
- the core machinery is reusable (but this claim does depend on linguistic proximity of SL and TL)

The shortcomings of SMT include the following:

- it relies on bilingual corpora;
- Only a few and rather indirect methods have been devised thus far to control for errors [11];

- it has been shown [5] that resources such as bilingual lexica and, possibly, grammars are necessary to boost up quality;
- SMT systems deteriorate quickly when better quality is sought, as quality increases with corpus size.

3.2.2. Example-Based MT (EBMT)

EBMT incarnates the idea of translation by analogy as opposed to translation by (deep) linguistic analysis. The observation exploited here is that people translate on the basis of previous translations.

EBMT also relies on parallel corpora. The general idea is that the SL string is compared to the SL-side of the system, the best matching SL-sentence is selected and the aligned TL-side sentence is returned as the best translation.

EBMT provides the following advantages [11]:

- it is considered relatively cheap because it does not necessarily require expensive intermediate linguistic representations to produce reasonable results as a lot of information is encoded in the strings;
- correction of errors is relatively controllable;
- the core machinery is reusable (but this claim does depend on linguistic proximity of SL and TL)

Among the disadvantages of EBMT one can list the following:

- it relies on bilingual corpora;
- although stitching sentence fragments together remains a serious problem, working at sub-sentential level is also necessary; therefore ways for appropriately fragmenting sentences are needed;
- resources such as bilingual lexica and grammars are necessary to boost up quality;
- EBMT systems deteriorate quickly when better quality is sought as quality increases with corpus size.

It follows that 'purist' approaches are limited in one way or another, but experience shows that they can be cross-fertilized. Next, we will present some efforts for developing MT systems for low and middle density languages. It will be clear that developers draw on ideas from all paradigms.

4. Hybrid MT for Low and Middle Density Languages: Some Efforts

In this section we discuss some representative efforts to develop MT systems for low and middle density languages. The main issue is that of resources because many such languages are endowed with few or no resources at all. Manual development of resources seems to be the starting point for languages with no resources because it only requires trained people. On the other hand, if time and some financial resources are available, it seems that corpus collection should be the first priority. Corpora can be annotated manually or automatically and can be mined by appropriate algorithms to yield resources such as mono-/bi-lingual lexica, taggers, lemmatizers and chunkers/parsers (grammars).

In what follows, we first present efforts that rely on a certain amount of resources and then efforts that rely on very few resources. It will become clear that researchers are forced not to limit themselves to one MT paradigm but to make the most of different existing ideas, in short, they tend to develop *hybrid MT systems*.

One of the most serious problems in CBMT is that parallel corpora are sparse. Actually, parallel corpora of reasonable size and quality exist for only a few widely spoken languages. Therefore, one important research issue is the development of corpus-based MT systems on the basis of only a small amount of parallel corpora used as the training material for the system.

Popovic and Ney [5] compare the results of doing SMT between languages with large parallel corpora available (Spanish & English) and languages with very small bitexts available (Serbian & English). They note that small corpora are more controllable in terms of quality, are easy to construct and impose fewer training constraints on memory. In short, they argue for a hybrid MT technology that does not solely rely on large bitexts.

First, they notice that using a conventional dictionary substantially improves translation results between both pairs because this improves the quality of word alignment. Thus, a minimal introduction of rules (a lexicon can be viewed as a large collection of minimal rules) is shown to improve an SMT system regardless of the amount of training material available. Then, they notice that lemmatization of declinable parts of speech, such as adjectives, improves results in general and especially when little training material is available. Of course, this is easy to understand because lemmatization increases the probability of finding a matching lemma sequence as compared to the probability of finding matching token sequences.

Popovic and Ney conclude that an acceptable translation quality can be achieved with a very small amount of task-specific parallel text, especially if conventional dictionaries, phrasal books, as well as morphosyntactic knowledge, such as lemmatization tools, are available.

However, another important issue related to SMT, namely the ability of the user to control the behavior of the system, leads researchers to a significantly different conclusion, that is, not to adopt an SMT backbone. Hein and Weijnitz [11] compare the results of doing RBMT and SMT with Swedish, a medium density language. They notice that better results were achieved by the rule-based approach where the behavior of the system can be understood and errors can be corrected by improving the lexica and the grammars. SMT systems, on the other hand, make many unpredictable mistakes. Hein and Weijnitz [11] suggest that RBMT should be preferred but should be statistically backed up, for example, for the generation of rules or lexical entries in the translation lexicon. So, statistical backing up is 'pushed' to the resource creation sector while the main translation machine is rule-based.

The need for a hybrid approach that combines rule-based knowledge with SMT is also clear in the case of MT between typologically different languages. An interesting discussion is provided by Oflazer and El Kahlout [15], who translate between English and Turkish. Turkish is a heavily declined agglutinative language with subject-object-Verb (SOV) as a dominant order of clausal constituents. English, on the other hand, has an impoverished declension system and a rather rigid SVO order. Oflazer and El Kahlout [15] try to exploit Turkish sublexical structure because one Turkish word may align with an English phrase, sometimes a discontinuous one. They work with lexical morphemes (a canonical form of declinable morphemes, somehow equivalent to lemmata) in order to avoid the particularities introduced by certain properties of Turkish such as vowel harmony, and agreement. So they:

- segment Turkish words;
- define lexical morphemes in Turkish;
- tag English for lemmata and parts of speech;
- (for each sentence) extract the sequence of open class content words in both English and Turkish and align the two sets.

Better results are obtained if parallel corpora are segmented at lexical morpheme level and the content words are added to the corpus in order to bootstrap content word alignments. This is equivalent to using a flat bilingual dictionary as training material.

It is important that alignment be influenced by the language pair: the strategy adopted for the English – Turkish pair could be different if the SL was typologically similar to Turkish.

Monson et al. [16] report on building an NLP system for two resource-scarce indigenous languages: Mapudungun[2] and Quechua[3]. The researchers have confronted an interesting problem as no resources, no linguists and no fixed orthographic system were available for Mapudungun.

In their effort to hit two birds with one stone, they simultaneously developed resources and training materials for an EBMT system. To this end, they collected all parallel text they could find or create with native speakers. Of course, one of the two languages in a parallel corpus must be an established one (here, it was Quechua). The corpus was then used to extract a dictionary, a stemmer and then a morphological analyzer and some transfer rules. As in the case of Turkish, here too researchers were confronted with agglutinative languages. In such languages, morphology is actually quite similar to syntax; therefore the morphological analyzer is a kind of chunker as well. Given the small size of the corpora and the fact that both languages are heavily inclined, working with stems rather than tokens was preferred, in order to increase the probability of finding a proper match.

The above MT development efforts share some common features and conclusions:

- they all try to make do with little training material, i.e. parallel corpora because few or no such corpora are available for low and middle density languages;
- bilingual dictionaries are indispensable;
- lemmatization of the parallel corpus boosts up translation quality independently of corpus size;
- use of some syntactic information in the form of rules helps when the size of the corpus is small, and seems to make up for typological differences.

---

[2] "Mapudungun (mapu means 'earth' and dungun means 'to speak') is a language isolate spoken in central Chile and west central Argentina by the Mapuche (mapu is 'earth' and che means 'people') people" http://en.wikipedia.org/wiki/Mapudungun

[3] "Quechua (Runa Simi) is a Native American language of South America spoken today in various regional forms (the so-called 'dialects') by some 10 million people through much of the South America, including Peru, south-western and central Bolivia, southern Colombia and Ecuador, north-western Argentina and northern Chile" http://en.wikipedia.org/wiki/Quechua

5. METIS-II[4]: Corpus-based MT with Monolingual Corpora and Common NLP Resources

In this section we present METIS, an innovative hybrid MT research prototype. From the point of view of MT for low and middle density languages, METIS is promising because it makes do with simple resources. METIS is innovative because it combines two important features: first, it does not rely on parallel corpora at all (and, therefore, does not aim at reducing the size of the required parallel corpus) and second, it uses a set of simple resources:

- a large TL corpus;
- flat bilingual lexica with part-of-speech information;
- taggers, lemmatizers and chunkers; and
- small sets of rules at translation retrieval and token generation time.

We have already pointed out that parallel corpora are rare and available only for the widely spoken languages. Lack of parallel corpora, however, is not the only problem. Available corpora quite often represent only a certain register or sublanguage; hence, systems are tuned to a particular register, and ways should be developed to allow for a system to switch easily between different sublanguages. METIS offers a solution to this problem by resorting to monolingual corpora of the TL only.

Generation Heavy MT [17] also uses monolingual corpora of the TL but it relies on sophisticated tools and resources such as dependency parsers and lexica with rich subcategorization and categorial variation information. Resources required on the TL side are more sophisticated (and rare) than resources required on the SL side. Context-Based MT [18] also uses non-parallel corpora. It relies on a very large TL corpus (50 gigabytes to one terabyte) and a smaller, but still large, SL one, in addition to a large full-form bilingual dictionary.

METIS is of a hybrid nature because it draws on a variety of algorithms. Input data are pre-processed with rule-based and stochastic tools. Translations are retrieved with pattern-matching techniques coupled with statistical information, in addition to specific algorithms for the solution of combinatorial optimization problems (such as the assignment problem). A very small number of linguistic rules are also employed at translation retrieval stage. The METIS system works with patterns, i.e. phrasal segments of variant length (sentences, clauses, chunks, tokens), and makes use of a series of weights, on the basis of which the similarity between SL and TL patterns is calculated.

In short, METIS is different both at implementation level, given that it draws on a variety of algorithms, and conceptually, since translation is not viewed as a transfer procedure from the source language to the target one, but rather as a matching process of patterns between SL and TL, aiming each time at detecting the best match.

[4] METIS-II was an IST/FET Open project (IST-FP6-003768/FET) http://www.ilsp.gr/metis2/ A web application of the system is also available. This project was preceded by the proof-of-idea FET Open project METIS (http://www.ilsp.gr/metis/)

5.1. Patterns in METIS

A very special feature of METIS is that it introduces an innovative use of the term 'pattern'. METIS exploits patterns with pattern matching techniques.

In fact, several researchers in the corpus-based MT paradigm have reported on the use of patterns. Pattern-based MT systems generate patterns automatically from parallel corpora. Translation patterns are pairs of source and target patterns, with the source part used for comparison with the source sentence and the target part used as a generation rule. In EBMT systems, translation patterns are generalizations of sentences that are translations of each other and are produced by replacing some of the words of SL-TL sentence pairs by variables [19], [20].

The patterns used in METIS are not similar to the translation patterns mentioned above, because:

- there are no parallel corpora, therefore, there is no direct matching of the SL string with strings in the same language; and, more importantly,
- patterns are not viewed as fixed strings with or without slots for variables but as 'models' of TL strings, which are formed out of the input SL strings and receive their final form only after the corpus has been consulted using pattern matching techniques.

The METIS patterns contain syntactic information encoded in non-overlapping segments ("chunks"), which are generated for both languages with rule-based "chunkers." METIS uses the following set of chunk types: verb, noun, prepositional, infinitive and adjective phrases. The words in the METIS chunks are annotated with their lemma, part-of-speech tag and word form. Furthermore, chunks bear a label and are marked for headword. The label denotes the chunk's type, for example whether the chunk is a verb phrase or a prepositional phrase. The headword of the chunk is the one that determines the structure and the distributional properties of the chunk. For example, in the noun chunk *NP[the red door]* the head of the chunk is the word *door* which determines the structure of the chunk (for instance, an article and an adjective are placed before the noun) and its distributional properties (for instance, subject of a verb, object of a verb or preposition). We use this information to compare chunks for lexical, morphological and syntactic similarity (assuming that identity/similarity at all these levels entails semantic identity/similarity of chunks). Based on this kind of sub-sentential-level information, we have created a mechanism for measuring the similarity between a SL sentence and a TL one. These comparisons, coupled with information drawn from a bilingual lexicon, form the basic mechanism that has enabled us to translate without any parallel data.

The intuition behind patterns used in METIS is simple. The SL structure consists of a verb and satellite chunks that are either arguments of the verb or modifiers denoting time, place or manner. In the general case, we would like to recover in the TL the verbal meaning and the meaning conveyed by the satellite chunks. For instance, if an event is described in the SL as involving two participants and information about time and place, we would like the translation to report about the same event with the same number of participants and the same information about time and place. Crucially, however, we do not require that all these meaning components be of the same syntactic status across the language pair. This is partially achieved by having the pattern-matching algorithm use a set of similarity weights (see Section 5.2) to allow for inclusion of similar (but not identical) grammatical and syntactic categories in addition to identical ones. As a result, an AdjP may match with an AdjP, an NP or a PP in the descending similarity order.

Patterns are defined on the output of chunking of both the source and the target language. Depending on the stage of the matching algorithm, different types of pattern are used as the system concentrates on different types of information. It must be noted, however, that only a very small number of pattern types is required. Thus, for both the SL and the TL only three types of pattern are used: the Clause Pattern, the VG Pattern and the PP Pattern.

Only one regular expression, the **Clause Pattern**, is used to describe the structure of both Greek and English sentences. The Clause pattern describes the overall structure of a clause: the verbal group head and the number, labels and heads of the chunks (if any exist). In the regular expression (20), the use of Kleene star (*) ensures that all permutations are possible.

20. **Clause Pattern**
    (PP* token*)* VG (PP* token*)*[5]

The **VG pattern** describes the verb group. Other tokens such as adverbs, for example, will be part of it if found within the verb phrase. If found in isolation, they are not considered to form a pattern and will be treated in a different way.

The **PP pattern** describes both prepositional and noun chunks in terms of their constituent tokens. The generalization here is that a noun chunk can be represented as a prepositional one with an empty prepositional head. This representation captures phrase category mismatches between SL and TL, for instance in the case of different subcategorization patterns (Section 1). This is illustrated here using a somewhat simplified example (21).

21. [$_{pp}$ ∅ [$_{np\_nom}$ ο σκύλος]] [$_{vg}$ μπήκε] [$_{pp}$ στο [$_{np\_acc}$ δωμάτιο]]
    [$_{pp}$ ∅ [$_{np1}$ the dog]] [$_{vg}$ entered] [$_{pp}$ ∅ [$_{np2}$ the room]][6]

PP patterns can be simple or complex. Complex PP patterns consist of two nested simple PP patterns. Two such patterns have been defined: PP_OF and PP_POS. A PP_OF chunk describes the combination of a prepositional chunk with a genitive post-modifier (22). PP_POS chunks describe noun chunks modified by a Saxon genitive (23). Note that Modern Greek does not have Saxon genitives.

22. [$_{ppgof}$ ∅ [$_{np\_ac}$ τη συνάντηση] [$_{np\_ge}$ της επιτροπής]]
    [$_{pp\_of}$ ∅ [$_{np\_ac}$ the meeting] [$_{pp}$ ∅ [$_{np\_ge}$ the commission]]
    'the committee meeting'
23. [$_{pp\_pos}$ [$_{pp}$ ∅ [$_{np\_ge}$ the problem]] 's [$_{pp}$ ∅ [$_{np\_ac}$ solution]]]

---

[5] Tokens refer to adverbials and punctuation.

[6] NP1 and NP2 are chunk labels indicating the position of the TL PP patterns in relation to the VG pattern.

5.2. The METIS architecture

The METIS system architecture is illustrated in Figure 2 below. End users access the system through a web interface, where they select the preferred source language (Dutch, German, Greek or Spanish) and introduce the sentence they want to translate.

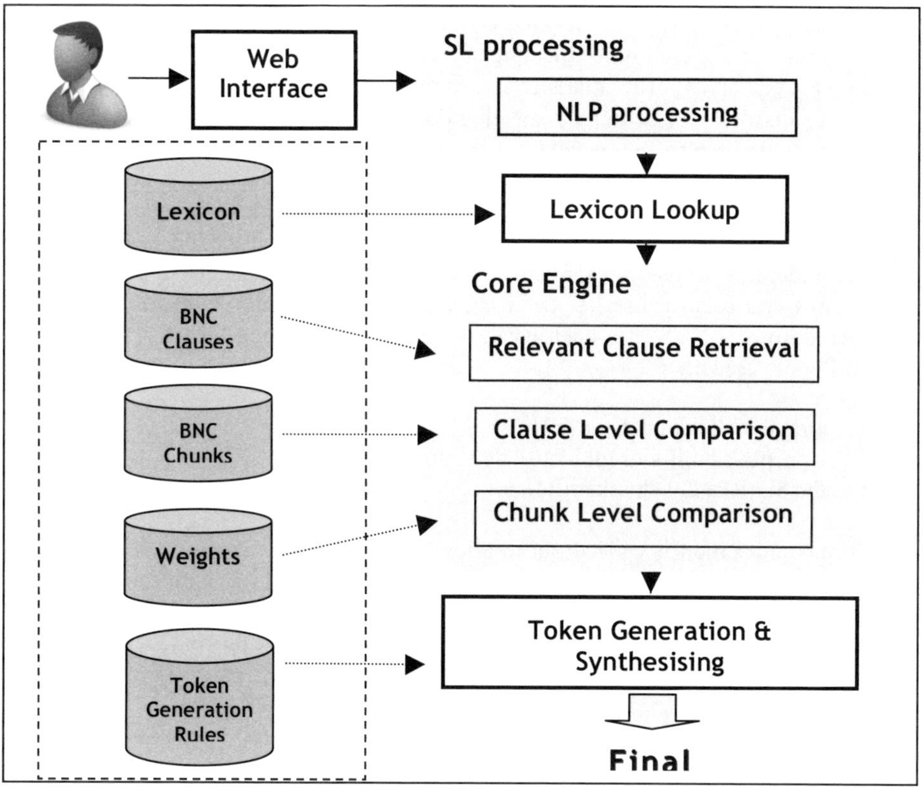

Figure 2. METIS architecture

Work starts with the pattern acquisition procedure, which involves the **SL processing** and the **Lexicon Lookup** procedures. Pattern acquisition uses a hybrid approach. The SL sentence is processed online: it is segmented into clauses and annotated for part-of-speech (PoS) and chunk information. For SL processing mainly off-the-shelf tools are used. They include stochastic PoS taggers [21] and rule-based lemmatizers and chunkers [22]. Some adjustments had to be made to both the SL and TL tools to improve compatibility of the resulting patterns. For instance, the output of the SL chunker has been slightly modified to boost the efficiency of the matching procedure. Pattern acquisition is completed with the Lexicon Lookup procedure. The lexica used are lemma-based and contain PoS information. The Lexicon Lookup procedure assigns a set of translation equivalent lemmata to each input lemma in the annotated clauses resulting from SL processing. In this way, a set of TL-like patterns is obtained. No score is assigned to multiple translation equivalents. Apart from lexical translation equivalents, no other equivalents, such as, for instance, alternative equivalents at phrase level or re-orderings of constituents are introduced because such issues are dealt with by the matching algorithm. Sentence (24) illustrates the output of the SL processing applied to a Modern Greek sentence containing only one clause. Sentence (25) illustrates the same sentence after lexicon look-up during which multiple translation equivalents were assigned to several words.

24. [ppgof ∅ [np_nm Ο υπουργός] [np_ge Οικονομικών]] [vgδιέλυσε] [ppgof ∅ [np_ac τη συνάντηση] [np_ge της επιτροπής]] [ppgof για [np_ac την κακοποίηση] [np_ge ανηλίκων]] (literal translation: The Finance Minister broke up the committee meeting about child abuse)[7]
25. [$_{ppgof}$ ∅ [$_{np\_nm}$ The minister/secretary] [$_{np\_ge}$ Finance/economics]] [$_{vg}$ break up/dissolve] [$_{ppgof}$ ∅ [$_{np\_ac}$ meeting/encounter] [$_{np\_ge}$ commission/committee]] [$_{ppgof}$ for/about [$_{np\_ac}$ abuse] [$_{np\_ge}$ child/juvenile]]

The set of TL-like patterns is fed to the core engine, which consults a relational database of TL patterns. TL patterns have been obtained from the TL corpus using a procedure identical to the one applied to the SL sentence: each sentence has been split into clauses and each clause has been tagged, lemmatized and chunked. The British National Corpus (BNC8) has been used, which is tagged using the CLAWS5 tagset. The NLP tools used are:

- a reversible lemmatizer [23];
- a purpose-built tool for clause detection;
- the ShaRPa 2.0 chunker [24].

Corpus indexation is carried out to allow for an efficient search for a best match. Thus, clauses have been indexed by the (finite) head verb, while chunks are classified according to their labels and head token.

The overall procedure is performed off-line once. The outcome, a set of TL patterns, is stored in a relational database containing

- clause patterns indexed by the main verb lemma and the number of the chunks contained;
- PP patterns indexed by the head lemma.

In the core engine, the pattern-matching algorithm attempts to detect the pattern similarities between the SL clause and the retrieved TL clauses at clause, chunk and token level, that is, a top-down approach has been adopted. This process, which is executed for each clause in a given SL sentence, employs a series of weights that encode bilingual lexical and syntactic information in a quantitative manner.

At the **token generation** stage, the output of the core engine, a TL clause in lemmatized form, is further processed and tokens are produced out of lemmata and PoS information through the application of a limited number of rules. Finally, all the translated clauses are combined into a single sentence at the **synthesizing** stage.

In the sections below, we present the translation procedure using an illustrative example. Readers who are only interested in a general description of the system may skip to Section 5.4, where we present the essential features of the algorithm.

---

[7] Heads of PP patterns are marked in bold.
[8] www.natcorp.ox.ac.uk/

5.3. Translation procedure illustrated

We now illustrate the translation procedure described above with an example drawn from a newspaper corpus. The SL is Modern Greek and the TL English. The example SL sentence is given in (26):

26. Σίγουρα χάσαμε ένα φίλο, αλλά επιβιώνουν τα κείμενά του
    definitely lost$_{\text{– 1st pl}}$ a friend but survive$_{\text{– 3rd pl}}$ the texts-his
    "We definitely lost a friend but his texts survive"

This sentence provides a good example for our discussion because it exhibits three characteristic mismatches between the SL, here Modern Greek, and the TL, here English. First of all, the first clause (CL1) lacks a phonetically realized subject. Modern Greek is a pro-drop language while English is not. Furthermore, in the second clause (CL2) the verb precedes the subject. This order (VSO) is frequently used in Modern Greek declarative sentences but is ungrammatical in the English ones. Lastly, the possessive determiner 'του' ('his') co-exists with the definite article and follows the noun. In English, there is only the possessive that occupies the position of the determiner/definite article. METIS, as we will see, successfully treats the first two mismatches.

Initially, the SL sentence, which consists of two clauses, as indicated below, is automatically annotated for PoS and lemma and chunked. Then, multiple translation equivalents (in the general case) are assigned to each SL clause lemma by the lexicon look-up procedure. In this way, a set of TL-like strings, or "patterns", is generated. In (27) this set is given in a compressed form (only the lemma, chunk and translation equivalents are indicated):

27. [$_{CL1}$ Σίγουρα (definitely|surely|certainly) [$_{NP\_NM}$ εγώ (I)] [$_{VG}$ χάνω (lose|miss)] [$_{PP}$ ∅ [$_{NP\_AC}$ ένας (a) φίλος (friend|boyfriend)]] αλλά (but) [$_{CL2}$ [$_{VG}$ ζω (live|be#alive)] [$_{PP}$ ∅ [$_{NP\_NM}$ ο (the) κείμενο (text) μου (my)]]

The pattern-matching algorithm handles each clause sequentially in four distinct steps and proceeds gradually from wider patterns to narrower ones, ensuring that the largest continuous piece of information is retrieved as such, while mismatching areas are identified. This top-down way of looking for matching patterns allows for fixing word order first at sentence level and then at chunk level. The translated clauses are combined into one sentence at the synthesizing stage, which signals the end of the translation procedure.

At the first step, the algorithm delimits the matching process within the clause boundaries. As a result, the TL clause database is searched for clause patterns similar to the TL-like pattern in terms of the verbal head and the number of contained chunks, which should equal or exceed by up to 2 the chunk number of the TL-like pattern. In this case, the algorithm looks for TL clause patterns having "lose" or "miss" as their main verb and containing 3 to 5 chunks.

The pattern-matching algorithm handles each clause sequentially in four distinct steps and proceeds gradually from wider patterns to narrower ones, ensuring that the largest continuous piece of information is retrieved as such, while mismatching areas are identified. This top-down way of looking for matching patterns allows for fixing word order first at sentence level and then at chunk level. The translated clauses are combined into one sentence at the synthesizing stage, which signals the end of the translation procedure.

At the first step, the algorithm delimits the matching process within the clause boundaries. As a result, the TL clause database is searched for clause patterns similar to the TL-like pattern in terms of the verbal head and the number of contained chunks, which should equal or exceed by up to 2 the chunk number of the TL-like pattern. In this case, the algorithm looks for TL clause patterns having "lose" or "miss" as their main verb and containing 3 to 5 chunks.

At the second step, the retrieved TL clause patterns are compared with the TL-like pattern at a lower level, namely, with respect to the type and heads of the chunks contained. The degree of the patterns' phrasal and lexical similarity is determined and the establishment of the chunk pattern order is achieved. Table 1 illustrates how the pro-drop phenomenon is treated (a dummy PRO is used for this purpose) and Table 2 shows how the VS order of the TL-like pattern is fixed to the right SV order by relying on information implicit in the corpus-retrieved sentence. More specifically, the system manages to establish the correct word order by matching a TL-like PP pattern in nominative (np_nm) with a TL PP pattern (NP1) that precedes the verb (Table 2). This matching is achieved by employing a set of weights, as explained in Section 5.5.3.

<table>
<tr><td>Source Sentence: Σίγουρα pp(np_nm(i)) vg(έχασα) pp(np_ac(έναν φίλο)) αλλά vg(επιζούν) pp(np_nm(τα κείμενα του))
Lexicon lookup: definitely|surely|certainly pp(np_nm(i)) vg(be finish|be lost|disappear|get lost|lose|miss|vanish|waste) pp(np_ac(a|an friend|boyfriend)) but vg(survive) pp(np_nm(the text my))</td></tr>
</table>

<table>
<tr><td>Source Clause:</td><td>definitely|surely|certainly pp(np_nm(i)) vg(be finish|be lost|disappear|get lost|lose|miss|vanish|waste) pp(np_ac(a|an friend|boyfriend))</td></tr>
<tr><td>Corpus Clause:</td><td>I 'm losing my best friend.</td></tr>
</table>

<table>
<tr><td>Score=100.0 %</td><td>pp([-{-}] np_nm([i{PnDmXx01SgNm}]))</td><td>vg([be{vb}finish{vvn-aj0}|be{vb} lost{ajvvn}|disappear{vv}|get{vv}lost{aj0vvn}|lose{vv}|miss{vv}|vanish{vv}|waste{vv}])</td><td>pp([-{-}] np_ac(a{at0}|an{at0}[friend{nn}|boyfriend{nn}]))</td></tr>
<tr><td>pp([-{-}] np_1([i{PNP}]))</td><td>100.0%</td><td>0.0%</td><td>19.0%</td></tr>
<tr><td>VG(be{VBB}[lose{VVG}])</td><td>0.0%</td><td>100.0%</td><td>0.0%</td></tr>
<tr><td>PP([-{-}] np_2(my{DPS}good {AJS} [friend{NN1}]))</td><td>12.0%</td><td>0.0%</td><td>100.0%</td></tr>
</table>

Table 1. Treating the pro-drop phenomenon

Source Sentence: Σίγουρα **pp(np_nm(**i**)) vg(**έχασα**) pp(np_ac(**έναν φίλο**))** αλλά **vg(**επιζούν**) pp(np_nm(**τα κείμενα του**))**
Lexicon lookup: definitely|surely|certainly **pp(np_nm(**i**)) vg(**be finish|be lost|disappear|get lost|lose|miss|vanish|waste**) pp(np_ac(**a|an friend|boyfriend**))** but **vg(**survive**) pp(np_nm(**the text my**))**

Source Clause:	**vg(**survive**) pp(np_nm(**the text my**))**
Corpus Clause:	Where interiors have survived ,

Score=84.38462%	vg([survive{vv}])	pp([-{-}] np_nm(the{at0} [text{nn}] my{dps}))
pp([-{-}] np_1([interior{NN2}]))	0.0%	**71.0%**
VG(have{VHB}[survive{VVN}])	**100.0%**	0.0%

Table 2. Treating word-order mismatches

Source Sentence:	Σίγουρα **pp(np_nm(**i**)) vg(**έχασα**) pp(np_ac(**έναν φίλο**))** αλλά **vg(**επιζούν**) pp(np_nm(**τα κείμενα του**))**
Lexicon lookup:	definitely|surely|certainly **pp(np_nm(**i**)) vg(**be finish|be lost|disappear|get lost|lose|miss|vanish|waste**) pp(np_ac(**a|an friend|boyfriend**))** but **vg(**survive**) pp(np_nm(**the text my**))**

Source Clause: definitely|surely|certainly **pp(np_nm(**i**)) vg(**be finish|be lost|disappear|get lost|lose|miss|vanish|waste**) pp(np_ac(**a|an friend|boyfriend**))**

Corpus Clause: pp(np_1(I**)) VG(**miss**) PP(np_2(**you**))** and **PP(np_2(**all my friends**))** there .

***Step 2 Score*: 96.19048%** ***Step 3 Score*: 97.94118%** ***Final Score*: 94.21009%**

Score=100.0%	-{-}	i{PnDmXx01SgNm}
-{-}	**-{-} 100.0%**	i{PnDmXx01SgNm} 0.0%
i{PNP}	-{-} 0.0%	**i{PnDmXx01SgNm} 100.0%**

Score=100.0%	miss{vv}
miss{VVB}	**miss{vv} 100.0%**

Score=94.117645%	-{-}	a{at0}|an{at0}	friend{nn}	PAD
-{-}	**-{-} 100.0%**	a{at0}!an{at0} 0.0%	friend{nn} 0.0%	null 20.0%
all{DT0}	-{-} 0.0%	**a{at0}!an{at0} 80.0%**	friend{nn} 0.0%	null 20.0%
my{DPS}	-{-} 0.0%	a{at0}!an{at0} 70.0%	friend{nn} 0.0%	**null 20.0%**
friend{NN2}	-{-} 0.0%	a{at0}!an{at0} 0.0%	**friend{nn} 100.0%**	null 20.0%

Table 3. Matching chunks

Source Clause: definitely|surely|certainly **pp(np_nm(**i**)) vg(**be finish|be lost|disappear|get lost|lose|miss|vanish|waste**) pp(np_ac(**a|an friend|boyfriend**))**

Final Clause: definitely!surely!certainly i miss a!an friend

Source Chunk:	pp([-{-}] np_nm([i{PnDmXx01SgNm}]))
Corpus Chunk:	pp([-{-}] np_1([i{PNP}]))
Final Chunk:	**pp([-{-}] np_1([i{PnDmXx01SgNm}]))**

Score=100.0%	-{-}	i{PnDmXx01SgNm}
-{-}	**-{-} 100.0%**	i{PnDmXx01SgNm} 0.0%
i{PNP}	-{-} 0.0%	**i{PnDmXx01SgNm} 100.0%**

Keeping chunk :pp([-{-}] np_nm([i{PnDmXx01SgNm}]))
Replacing [i{PNP}] with token:i{PnDmXx01SgNm}

Source Chunk:	vg([miss{vv}])
Corpus Chunk:	vg([miss{VVB}])
Final Chunk:	**vg([miss{vv}])**

Score=100.0%	miss{vv}
miss{VVB}	**miss{vv} 100.0%**

Keeping chunk :vg([miss{vv}])
Replacing [miss{VVB}] with token:miss{vv}

Source Chunk:	pp([-{-}] np_ac(a{at0}|an{at0} [friend{nn}]))
Corpus Chunk:	pp([-{-}] np_2(all{DT0} my{DPS} [friend{NN2}]))
Final Chunk:	**pp([-{-}] np_2(a{at0}|an{at0} [friend{nn}]))**

Score=94.117645%	-{-}	a{at0}|an{at0}	friend{nn}	PAD
-{-}	**-{-} 100.0%**	a{at0}!an{at0} 0.0%	friend{nn} 0.0%	null 20.0%
All{DT0}	-{-} 0.0%	**a{at0}!an{at0} 80.0%**	friend{nn} 0.0%	null 20.0%
My{DPS}	-{-} 0.0%	a{at0}!an{at0} 70.0%	friend{nn} 0.0%	**null 20.0%**
friend{NN2}	-{-} 0.0%	a{at0}!an{at0} 0.0%	**friend{nn} 100.0%**	null 20.0%

Processing Corpus chunk: pp([-{-}] np_2(all my [friends]))
Replacing [all{DT0}] with token:a{at0}!an{at0}
Removing term :my{DPS}
Replacing [friend{NN2}] with token:friend{nn}

Table 4. Replacement and/or modification of chunks

At the third step, which is illustrated in Table 3, the pattern matching algorithm performs a detailed comparison between the tokens contained in the TL chunk pattern and the respective TL-like ones, in order to establish degrees of lexical similarity and thus decide whether the TL chunk patterns will be retained, modified or replaced. Chunks with a score more than 98% are retained, those with a score between 80% and 98% are modified and those with a score less than 80% are replaced.

At the fourth step, illustrated with Table 4, solutions are found for the case when a chunk must be modified or replaced. In our example, the chunk "pp([-{}]np_2(a{AT0} good{AJ0} [friend{NN1}]))" is modified and the chunk "vg(have{VHB} [lose{VVN}])" is rejected and the database is searched for a more suitable alternative.The chunks that match best with the chunk patterns in the TL-like input string are located and, if necessary, are minimally modified on the basis of co-occurrence information induced from the corpus with statistical means. If no matching chunks are found, the system indicates the problem, processes the corresponding portion of the TL-like string with co-occurrence information and returns the result.

The result of the fourth step is a set of lemmatized TL clauses. This is put through the modules of token generation and synthesis to obtain the final translation, i.e. a TL sentence. Thus, the translation of CL1 is *definitely|surely|certainly we lost a friend* and of CL2 *but his the texts survive*. These two clauses are then synthesized into one sentence, yielding the final translation *definitely|surely|certainly we lost a friend but his the texts survive*.

It is evident from the above that METIS can effectively handle (a) the pro-drop phenomenon, since it manages to generate a subject, and (b) the subject-verb inversion, since it succeeds in establishing the correct SV order required in English.

We will give one more example to illustrate how METIS treats subcategorization mismatches of the type exemplified below:

28. Ο ρόλος του προπονητή τελειώνει όταν οι παίκτες μπαίνουν στο γήπεδο
the role the$_{_gen}$ coach$_{_gen}$ ends when the players enter into-the field
'The part of the coach ends when the players enter the field'

Here, the Modern Greek verb *μπαίνω* supports a PP complement while the English verb *to enter* supports a bare NP complement. To handle such cases, METIS conflates the representation of NPs and PPs and considers NPs as PPs with an empty prepositional head. We present Step 4 (Table 5) where the input PP chunk is compared with a TL PP chunk. All the prepositional heads from the SL are inherited. A statistics based algorithm is then applied to choose the right preposition (which may be the null one). The translation produced by METIS is *The part of the coach|trainer finishes When|While the players enter at|into the field.* A statistics based algorithm that measures frequency of co-occurrences of head words across chunks eventually decides that the right translation is *The part of the coach|trainer finishes When|While the players enter the field.*

Next, we present a detailed description of the Core Engine algorithm and the Token Generation and the Synthesizing modules.

5.4. The METIS Pattern-Matching translation approach

We have already pointed out that in METIS the translation problem is treated as an assignment one, that is, as a problem of discovering the best matching patterns (clauses, chunks and tokens) between SL and TL. So, METIS maps SL patterns onto patterns retrieved from the monolingual TL corpora, compares them and measures their similarity. The degree of similarity of two patterns is calculated on the basis of appropriate information depending on the types of the patterns compared. The METIS mapping process is top-down and mimics and exploits the recursive nature of language, moving from wider patterns to narrower ones. First it compares the SL and TL sentences and uses information about their overall structure to identify the correct order of chunks. Once the chunk order within the sentence is established, the process moves to a subsentential level and fixes word order within each chunk. This way, the algorithm first discovers the longest similar pattern and then identifies and corrects any residual mismatches.

<table>
<tr><td>Source Chunk:</td><td colspan="3">pp([at{prp}|in{av-prp}|into{prp}|on{av-prp}|to{av-prp}] np_ac([field{nn}]))</td></tr>
<tr><td>Corpus Chunk:</td><td colspan="3">pp([-{-}] np_2(the{AT0} [field{NN1}]))</td></tr>
<tr><td>Final Chunk:</td><td colspan="3">pp([at{prp}|into{prp}] np_2(the{AT0} [field{nn}]))</td></tr>
<tr><td>Score=83.4375%</td><td>at{prp}|in{av-prp}|into{prp}|on{av-prp}|to{av-prp}</td><td>field{nn}</td><td>PAD</td></tr>
<tr><td>-{-}</td><td>at{prp}!into{prp} 63.0%</td><td>field{nn} 0.0%</td><td>null 20.0%</td></tr>
<tr><td>the{AT0}</td><td>at{prp}!in{av-prp}!into{prp}!on{av-prp}!to{av-prp} 0.0%</td><td>field{nn} 0.0%</td><td>null 20.0%</td></tr>
<tr><td>field{NN1}</td><td>at{prp}!in{av-prp}!into{prp}!on{av-prp}!to{av-prp} 0.0%</td><td>field{nn} 100.0%</td><td>null 20.0%</td></tr>
<tr><td colspan="4">Processing Corpus chunk: pp([-{-}] np_2(the [field]))
Replacing [-{-}] with token:at{prp}!into{prp}
Replacing [field{NN1}] with token:field{nn}</td></tr>
</table>

Table 5. Subcategorization mismatches

Next, we present a detailed description of the Core Engine algorithm and the Token Generation and the Synthesizing modules.

5.5. The METIS Pattern-Matching translation approach

We have already pointed out that in METIS the translation problem is treated as an assignment one, that is, as a problem of discovering the best matching patterns (clauses, chunks and tokens) between SL and TL. So, METIS maps SL patterns onto patterns retrieved from the monolingual TL corpora, compares them and measures their similarity. The degree of similarity of two patterns is calculated on the basis of appropriate information depending on the types of the patterns compared. The METIS mapping process is top-down and mimics and exploits the recursive nature of language, moving from wider patterns to narrower ones. First it compares the SL and TL sentences and uses information about their overall structure to identify the correct order of chunks. Once the chunk order within the sentence is established, the process moves to a subsentential level and fixes word order within each chunk. This way, the algorithm first discovers the longest similar pattern and then identifies and corrects any residual mismatches.

In order to correlate the translation units (sentences and chunks) from the two different languages, we do not use any of the similarity measures used in other MT approaches. In METIS, the sentence and chunk similarity is calculated using a general pattern-matching algorithm and a series of weights, which mainly reflect grammatical information. The pattern-matching algorithm used is an implementation of the Hungarian algorithm, also known as Kuhn-Munkres algorithm, initially designed by H.W. Kuhn in 1955 and later revised by J. Munkres in 1957. It is an optimization algorithm which solves assignment problems in polynomial time. The algorithm takes as input an $n \times m$ cost matrix, where each value represents the cost of mapping the specific line element to the column element, and returns the optimal mapping of each line element to a single column element. The weights provide information about the similarity of part-of-speech tags and chunk labels across the SL and TL.

By addressing this matching problem as a general, weighted assignment problem, METIS manages to resolve translation issues without resorting to any linguistic TL generation rules. By employing a variety of weights, we are able to use the pattern-matching algorithm for structural matching at both clause and chunk level. How this is achieved is explained in the sections below.

5.5.1. The METIS core engine

We have described at length how the core engine of METIS system is fed with TL-like patterns and how it exploits information encoded in the TL-patterns and information from the TL corpus to solve disambiguation problems and to establish the correct order of clausal and chunk constituents. Figuratively speaking, we could say that with the METIS approach, rather than asking, as Nagao [25] and the EBMT paradigm did, 'tell me how you have translated it and I will repeat the translation', we provide the algorithm with a set of coarsely described translations and ask it to produce the one translation that best blends descriptions with corpus knowledge.

We have already illustrated the four steps of the algorithm for building up translations. Here, we will present the same steps in a more technical manner by explaining the algorithm. Earlier versions of the system, the algorithm and its performance are discussed in [26], [27] and [28].

5.5.2. Step 1: Retrieval of TL clauses/ translation candidates from the TL corpus

We have already explained that at the first step, the algorithm retrieves all the relevant clauses from the BNC database. We consider as relevant all corpus clauses that have the same verbal chunk head as the translated SL clause, and contain a number of chunks ranging within $[n, n+2]$, where n the number of chunks in the SL clause. At this step, all retrieved clauses that satisfy the search criteria have the same probability of being selected as the skeleton for the final translation. If no matches are found, the algorithm moves on to the next clause of the SL text. The algorithm evaluates the similarity of each retrieved clause with the SL clause turing the next two steps.

5.5.3. Step 2: Structural matching at clause level

At the second step, each possible translation of each of the clauses identified in the SL sentence, in our terminology each TL-pattern, is compared with all the TL clauses that have been retrieved from the TL corpus at Step 1. Comparison is based only on general chunk information, that is, on chunk labels and chunk head tokens and is performed by the pattern-matching algorithm. In this way, the pattern-matching algorithm achieves an optimum mapping of chunk patterns. It is at this step that establishment of the correct order of chunks in the clause takes place drawing on corpus information and on the calculation of the similarity of chunk labels and chunk heads in terms of the lemma and the PoS tag (see Table 6). The TL-pattern chunk sequence is rearranged to reflect the chunk sequence in the best matching TL clause. In this way, mismatches between SL and TL at the word order level are solved without any extra rules or information. For instance, a VSO declarative clause of Modern Greek, which generates a VSO TL-pattern, is re-arranged to an SVO clausal order, which is the grammatical order for English. Similarly, a noun-adjective sequence of Spanish or French is rearranged to an adjective-noun sequence in English or Modern Greek, which is the grammatical order in the NP for these two languages.

	PP	NP_AC	NP_NM	NP_GE	VG	ADJP
PP	100%	0	0	0	0	30%
NP_2	0	100%	60%	100%	0	30%
NP_1	0	60%	100%	30%	0	30%
VG	0	0	0	0	100%	0
ADJP	0	0	0	0	0	100%

Table 6. Weights used for chunk label comparison at clause level

As explained earlier, the Hungarian algorithm is used to calculate the similarity between a SL and a TL clause. A cost matrix is built for each SL-TL clause comparison pair in order to be used by the pattern-matching algorithm. Equation (1) is used for measuring the similarity of two chunks.

$$\begin{aligned} &ChunkScore_n = bcf_n \times LabelComp_n + tcf_n \times TagComp_n + lcf_n \times LemmaComp_n \\ &where\ bcf_n + tcf_n + lcf_n = 1 \end{aligned} \qquad (1)$$

In Equation (1), chunk similarity at clause level (*ChunkScore*) is calculated as the weighted sum of the chunk label comparison score (*LabelComp*), the chunk head lemma comparison score (*LemmaComp*) and the chunk head tag comparison score (*TagComp*). Each discrete chunk label is pre-assigned a set of cost factors to use when measuring similarity. These factors are the chunk label cost factor (*bcf*), the chunk head tag cost factor (*tcf*) and chunk head lemma cost factor (*lcf*).

The chunk head lemma comparison is calculated by simply comparing the lemmata, and is either 1 if they are the same or 0 if they are different. The chunk label and the PoS tag comparisons are calculated by looking up relevant tables of comparison weights. Table 1 illustrates a set of comparison weights that are used for the chunk label comparison (the chunk labels are the ones assigned by the Modern Greek and the English chunker used in METIS). Modern Greek chunk labels are indicated on the horizontal axis and English chunk labels on the vertical axis. We see that, for instance, a Modern Greek NP marked with the nominative case (NP_NM) that indicates a subject with nearly 100% accuracy, matches perfectly with an NP_1 of English, which is an NP placed before a finite verb.

When all SL clause chunks have been compared with the TL ones and the cost matrix is filled using Equation (1), the Hungarian algorithm returns the best clause structure by mapping each SL chunk to a single TL chunk and establishing the optimal chunk mapping. Next, Equation (2) is used to measure the similarity of two clauses. The clause comparison score at this step of the process is calculated by the weighted sum of the similarity scores of each SL-TL chunk pair, where *m* is the number of chunks in the SL clause, *ocf* (overall cost factor) is the cost factor of the SL chunk in the chunk pair and *ChunkScore* is the corresponding score, whose calculation we have already described. Each chunk label is pre-assigned a different cost factor, which reflects the importance of a chunk label over other chunk labels. This simply means that some chunks should contribute more to the comparison process when clause similarity is calculated.

$$ClauseScore = \sum_{n=1}^{m} \left\{ ocf_n \times \frac{ChunkScore_n}{\sum_{j=1}^{m} ocf_j} \right\} \quad , where\ m > 1 \qquad (2)$$

It could be claimed that weights correspond to “rules” traditionally employed by rule-based MT systems. However, there are certain important differences between rules and weights, as the latter are used in METIS. Crucially, weights are language-independent. Besides, weight values can be automatically determined and modified using machine learning algorithms, for instance genetic algorithms. The employment of these parameters makes it possible to establish the right constituent order and the appropriate matching of SL and TL patterns, without resorting to additional mapping rules. In Table 2 we have illustrated how weights rather than rules have been used to deal with word-order mismatches between Modern Greek as a SL and English as a TL.

When Step 2 has been executed, a list of SL-TL clause pairs is obtained. The list is sorted according to clause level similarity scores. For each of these clause pairs the chunk order has been established. Also, by comparing chunk head labels, some translation ambiguities may be solved as well. This list is then passed on to the next step of the algorithm.

5.5.4. Step 3: Word matching at chunk level

At Step 3, clause comparison is narrower and confined within the boundaries of the chunks. For each clause pair, each SL chunk is compared to the TL chunk to which it has been mapped. The comparison calculates the similarity of the words contained in the chunks based on lemma and part-of-speech information, which results in establishing the correct order of words within each chunk, based on the TL chunk. For instance, a Spanish Noun-Adjective sequence is matched with a Modern Greek or English Adjective-Noun one.

Again, chunk comparison is performed by the pattern-matching algorithm used for clause comparison in Step 2. In order to fill the cost matrix for chunk comparison, we calculate the similarity between the words of the SL chunk and the words of the TL chunk. Equation (3) illustrates the mechanism for calculating word similarity in METIS: it is the weighted sum of the lemma comparison and the PoS tag one. The *tcf* weight is the tag cost factor of the PoS tag of the SL word.

$$TokenScore_n = (1 - tcf_n) \times LemmaComp_n + tcf_n \times TagComp_n \qquad (3)$$

The cost matrix filled by applying Equation (3) is exploited by the Hungarian algorithm to identify the optimal word mapping, where each SL word is mapped to a single TL word. Eq. (4) is then used to compare words and calculate chunk similarity scores.

$$ChunkScore = \sum_{n=1}^{m} \left\{ ocf_n \times \frac{TokenScore_n}{\sum_{j=1}^{m} ocf_j} \right\} \text{, where } m > 1 \qquad (4)$$

In Equation (4), m is the number of words in the SL chunk and *ocf* is the overall cost factor of the PoS tag of the SL word.

After calculating all Step 3 similarity scores, we calculate a final comparison score of each SL-TL clause pair. This is the product of the scores of the two steps. The TL clause with the highest final score is selected as the basis of translation, while chunk and token order has already been established. Nevertheless, the final translation is derived from the specific corpus clause, only after the contained chunks have been processed with the purpose of eliminating any mismatches. The necessary actions are performed in the final step, Step 4, of the core engine.

5.5.5. Step 4: Final processing of chunks

At the end of the comparison process in Steps 2 and 3 a TL corpus clause is selected as the basis of translation. Chunk and token order has already been established. Nevertheless, the final translation is derived from the specific corpus clause only after the chunks contained in the clauses have been processed, with the purpose of eliminating any mismatches. This processing entails either modification of chunks or substitution of given chunks with other chunks in order to, eventually, form the final translation.

In case of substitution, the TL corpus is searched again for appropriate chunks in terms of label and tokens contained in them. This gives the system the opportunity to fully exploit the TL corpus data.

As already explained, the output of the pattern-matching algorithm is a lemmatized clause annotated for chunk and PoS information. This string serves as input to the token generation stage, where (a) token generation takes place and (b) agreement features are checked.

5.6. Token Generation

The token generation module receives as input lemmatized clauses annotated for chunk and PoS information. PoS information has been inherited from the SL input string. Chunk information has been accumulated from the corpus with the mapping procedure. The module draws on this information to produce word forms (tokens) and, at the same time, to fix agreement phenomena, such as subject-verb agreement.

For the generation task, METIS-II employs resources produced and used in the reversible lemmatizer/token-generator for English [23]. This lemmatizer/token-generator draws on the BNC and uses the CLAWS5 tagset.

The module is rule-based. Of course, the complexity of the module reflects the complexity of the target language in terms of morphology and agreement phenomena. English is relatively simple in both these respects. The rules apply on lemmata and yield tokens marked, as necessary, for tense, person, number, case and degrees of comparison (comparative and superlative degree).

The rule-of-thumb used to fix subject-verb agreement is that the morphological features of the SL main verb determine the morphological features of the TL subject. In this way, the generator is able to provide a suitable subject pronoun when a subject is missing in the SL clause. This is often the case with Modern Greek, which is a pro-drop language. Clauses exposing the pro-drop phenomenon are provided with a dummy pronoun early on in the translation procedure. The dummy pronoun is the head of a PP pattern, which is manipulated by the matching algorithm like any other PP pattern. The dummy pronoun receives specific features only at token generation time.

5.7. Synthesizing

As mentioned above, the METIS-II core engine creates separate translation processes for each clause. Each clause process is a separate thread, running in parallel with the others. When a clause thread has produced the translation, it reports back to the core engine.

After all SL clause threads have reported back, the corresponding target sentence is formed. Clauses are placed in the TL sentence in the same order as they are found in the SL sentence. In case of discontinuous embedding, the translation output consists of clauses placed next to each other.

5.8. Testing and Evaluating METIS

METIS has been tested and evaluated against SYSTRAN, a commercial, (mainly) RBMT system. SYSTRAN was chosen because it is one of the most well known and widely used MT systems and covers Modern Greek relatively well given the state of the art in MT. Furthermore, SYSTRAN covers several other language pairs and provides a homogenous evaluation framework for current work and for future work with other language pairs. However, it should be noted that not all language pairs have been developed for the same amount of time and that translation quality differs among language pairs covered by SYSTRAN.

Two evaluation sets of sentences were compiled: the training set that has been used throughout the project for development purposes, and the test set consisting of unseen data mined from a previously built bilingual corpus i.e. Europarl. The training set consisted of 200 sentences, which covered different text types and a range of grammatical phenomena such as word-order variation, complex NP structure, negation, modification etc. Vocabulary and syntactic constructions belonged to general language. The number of reference translations per sentence amounted to three (3).

The test set also consisted of 200 sentences, all drawn from the Europarl corpus. The number of reference translations was higher, namely five (5) per sentence.

Europarl consists of transcriptions of debates in the European Parliament and was chosen because it is widely used by the MT research community, in spite of the fact that in many cases the alignment was wrong.

Evaluation was carried out automatically with the BLEU, NIST and TER (Translation Error Rate) metrics. BLEU, originally defined by IBM [29] and used nowadays extensively in machine translation, is based on *n*-gram co-occurrences and provides a score range [0,1], with 1 being the best score. NIST [30], which is a modification of BLEU, is also based on *n*-gram co-occurrences, but employs a different range $[0, \infty)$. TER [31] is an error metric for machine translation that measures the amount of editing that a human would have to perform so that the translation evaluated matches exactly a reference translation. It is computed by dividing the number of edits by the average number of reference words for each sentence, thus, lower scores mean better translations. All three evaluation benchmarks require a reference corpus built from good quality human translations and employ a numeric metric, which measures the distance between the machine-translated sentences and the reference translations.

5.8.1. Evaluation results for the training set

Table 7 summarizes the scores obtained by SYSTRAN and the latest version of METIS-II for the training set. Table 8 illustrates the corresponding evaluation results. Modern Greek is the SL and English the TL

In the case of the training set, METIS-II outperforms SYSTRAN regarding two (BLEU and NIST) of the three metrics used (Table 7). The better performance of METIS-II for the training set is expected, given that system development was based on the particular corpus.

	METIS-II	**SYSTRAN**
BLEU	0.4590	0.3946
NIST	8.2496	7.7041
TER	41.058	37.258

Table 7. Scores obtained for METIS-II and SYSTRAN using the BLEU, NIST and TER metrics (training set, Modern Greek → English language pair)

More specifically, the mean accuracy of METIS-II, according to BLEU (Table 8), is higher than the SYSTRAN accuracy, while both systems are equal with respect to the maximum and minimum accuracies. Additionally, METIS-II achieved a perfect translation for 24 out of 200 sentences, while SYSTRAN translated perfectly only 15. The picture remains the same with the NIST metric (Table 8). METIS-II achieves a higher mean accuracy and also a better minimum accuracy, whereas both systems attain the same maximum accuracy.

Yet, in Table 7, we observe that, according to the TER metric, SYSTRAN performs better than METIS-II, since it receives a lower score (please recall that a lower TER score indicates a smaller number of edits, thus a better translation output). Nevertheless, they share the same maximum accuracy (Table 8); furthermore, METIS-II yielded 17 perfect translations out of 200 sentences, while SYSTRAN produced 14. Despite the fact that these numbers are comparable, the difference is still significant.

	BLEU		**NIST**		**TER**	
	METIS-II	**SYSTRAN**	**METIS-II**	**SYSTRAN**	**METIS-II**	**SYSTRAN**
Mean accuracy	0.3286	0.2794	**8.1131**	**7.1559**	**29.925**	**26.137**
Maximum accuracy	1.0000	1.0000	15.056	15.056	0.0000	0.0000
Minimum accuracy	0.0000	0.0000	0.4705	0.0518	114.286	93.750

Table 8. Comparative analysis of the evaluation results for METIS-II and SYSTRAN using the BLEU, NIST and TER metrics (training set, Modern Greek → English language pair)

5.8.2. Evaluation results for the test set

The scores obtained by SYSTRAN and the latest version of METIS-II for the test set (Modern Greek → English language pair) are illustrated in Table 9, while Table 10 contains a comparative analysis of the evaluation results.

	METIS-II	**SYSTRAN**
BLEU	0.2423	0.3132
NIST	6.8911	7.6867
TER	59.200	49.120

Table 9. Scores obtained for METIS-II and SYSTRAN using the **BLEU**, **NIST** and **TER** metrics (test set, Modern Greek → English language pair)

	BLEU		**NIST**		**TER**	
	METIS-II	**SYSTRAN**	**METIS-II**	**SYSTRAN**	**METIS-II**	**SYSTRAN**
Mean accuracy	0.1521	0.2331	6.7424	7.5123	58.0314	48.0218
Maximum accuracy	1.0000	1.0000	14.3741	14.4228	0.0000	0.0000
Minimum accuracy	0.0000	0.0000	0.6041	1.2389	117.647	109.091

Table 10. Comparative analysis of the evaluation results for METIS-II and SYSTRAN using the **BLEU**, **NIST** and **TER** metrics (test set, Modern Greek → English language pair)

As can be seen from Table 9, for the Europarl test set, the opposite conclusions are obtained: SYSTRAN outperforms METIS-II on all metrics. This is probably due to the fact that the Europarl corpus is unconstrained and contains more diverse phenomena than those treated in the training set.

As indicated in Table 10, SYSTRAN has a higher mean accuracy than METIS-II according to BLEU, but their maximum and minimum accuracies coincide. Moreover, both systems yielded the same number of perfect translations, namely 6 out of 200. As regards the NIST metric, SYSTRAN outperforms METIS-II in all respects, and the same is observed with respect to the TER metric, with the exception of the maximum accuracy. Furthermore, METIS-II produced 5 perfect translations out of 200 sentences, compared to SYSTRAN, which produced only 4.

Although the aforementioned results are not conclusive concerning the predominance of the one system over the other, a closer look at the translation outputs of the two systems can reveal their differences.

Generally, SYSTRAN seems to consistently fail in establishing the correct word order, in contrast to METIS-II, which nearly always permutes the constituents of a given sentence in accordance to the English word order. For instance, for the SL sentences (29) & (28) and (34) & (35), which are semantically equivalent except for the constituent ordering, METIS-II produces the same translation for both SL sentences, (31) and (36) respectively, even though it is supplied with no linguistic information regarding syntactic relations. SYSTRAN, on the other hand, respects the surface word order and does not succeed in capturing the existing semantic equivalence and eventually yields two different outputs for each group of sentences.

29. Όλοι οι φορείς συμμετείχαν στην επίσημη έναρξη του κοινωνικού διαλόγου
    all the bodies participated in the official opening of the social dialogue
30. Στην επίσημη έναρξη του κοινωνικού διαλόγου συμμετείχαν όλοι οι φορείς
    in the official opening of the social dialogue participated all the bodies
    'All bodies participated in the official opening of the social dialogue'

31. All carriers participated at the official beginning of social conversation *(METIS-II output for both (29) & (30))*
32. All the institutions participated in the official beginning of social dialogue *(SYSTRAN output for 29))*
33. In the official beginning of social dialogue participated all the institutions *(SYSTRAN output for (30))*
34. Το κολλαγόνο προσδίδει ελαστικότητα στο δέρμα
    the collagen lends elasticity to the skin
35. Το κολλαγόνο προσδίδει στο δέρμα ελαστικότητα
    the collagen lends to the skin elasticity
    'The collagen lends elasticity to the skin'

36. The collagen lends elasticity at skin *(METIS-II output for both (34) & (35))*
37. The collagen lends elasticity in the skin *(SYSTRAN output for (34))*
38. The collagen lends in the skin elasticity *(SYSTRAN output for (35))*

On the other hand, SYSTRAN is more effective in yielding the correct translation of prepositions, whereas METIS-II still falls short in this respect; however, its performance could be improved by further developing and better integrating the statistical method for disambiguating among the translation variants.

5.9. Future plans

METIS II holds the promise of being a viable solution for languages with few resources available. Of course, this task is simpler when the target language is a high density one. For the SL, established NLP technology is required (tagger, lemmatizer, chunker) plus a flat bilingual lexicon. The number of structure-modifying rules is minimal.

A set of improvements can be envisaged to include the following: (i) The system can be adjusted to handle more complex lexica. at the moment lemmata consist of one word. It would be very efficient to make METIS able to handle multi-word units (such as ‘contact lenses’, ‘X kicked the bucket’ etc.). (ii) Step 4 can be further enhanced with information about word co-occurrences derived from the TL corpus with statistical means. This algorithm is already operational, however, it is not yet mature.

One important feature of METIS that leaves ample space for improvements is the employment of adjustable weights. Adjustable weights are used in various stages of the translation process in order to make decisions that may lead to a different translation output. At this point of development, however, all the aforementioned weights have been initialized manually, based on intuitive knowledge. There are basically two lines of work, both related to machine learning, which are included in our future plans as regards weights: a) optimization of the initial weights, which have been set manually based on intuitive linguistic knowledge, and b) exploiting weights to customize the system to different domains and text types.

REFERENCES

[1] Hutchins, J. 2007. Machine Translation: a Concise History. To be published in Chan Sin Wai (ed.) *Computer Aided Translation: Theo*ry and Practice. Chinese University of Hong Kong, 2007 (http://www.hutchinsweb.me.uk/)

[2] Hutchins, J. 2008. Compedium of Translation Software. http://www.hutchinsweb.me.uk/Compendium.htm

[3] Thurmair, G. 2005. Improving MT Quality: Towards a Hybrid MT Architecture in the Linguatec ‘Personal Translator’. Talk given at the 10th MT Summit. Phuket, Thailand

[4] Dorr, B.J., Jordan, P.W. and Benoit, J.W. 1999. A Survey of Current Paradigms in MT. In M. Zelkowitz (ed) *Advances in Computers **49**,* London: Academic Press, 1-68

[5] Popovic, M., Ney, H. 2006. Statistical Machine Translation with a Small Amount of Bilingual Training Data. 5th SALTMIL Workshop on Minority Languages

[6] Talmy, L. 1985. Lexicalization Patterns: Semantic Structure in Lexical Forms. In Timothy Shopen (ed.) *Language Typology and Syntactic Description **3:** Grammatical Categories and the Lexicon,* , Cambridge: Cambridge University Press, 57-149

[7] Nirenburg, S. and Raskin, V. 2004. *Ontological Semantics.* Cambridge: The MIT press

[8] Vauquois, B. 1968. A Survey of Formal Grammars and Algorithms for Recognition and Transformation in Machine Translation, *IFIP Congress 68, Edinburgh*, 254-260

[9] Carl, M. and Way, A. (eds.). 2003. *Recent Advances in Example-Based Machine Translation.* Dordrecht: Kluwer Academic Publishers

[10] Hutchins, J. 2005. Towards a Definition of Example-Based Machine Translation. *Proceedings of the Example-Based Machine Translation Workshop held in conjunction with the 10th Machine Translation Summit, Phuket, Thailand,* 63-70

[11] Hein, A. S., Weijnitz, P. 2006. Approaching a New Language in Machine Translation. 5th SALTMIL Workshop on Minority Languages

[12] Gaizauskas, R. 1995. Investigations into the Grammar Underlying the Penn Treebank II. Research Memorandum CS-95-25, Department of Computer Science, University of Sheffield

[13] Brown, P., Cocke, J., Della Pietra, S., Della Pietra, V., Jelinek, F. , Lafferty, J., Mercer, R. , Roosin P. S. 1990. A Statistical Approach to Machine Translation. *Computational Linguistics* ***16. 2***, 79-85

[14] Melamed, I. D. 2001. *Empirical Methods for Exploiting Parallel* Texts. Cambridge: The MIT Press

[15] Oflazer, K., El Kahlout, I. D.. 2007. Exploring Different Representational Units in English to Turkish SMT. *Proceedings of the ACL/Second Workshop on SMT, Prague, June 2007*, 25-32

[16] Monson, C., Font Llitjos, A., Aranovich, R., Levin, L., Brown, R., Peterson, E., Carbonnel, J., Lavie, A. 2006. Building NLP Systems for Two Resource-Scarce Indigenous Languages: Mapudungun and Quechua. 5th SALTMIL Workshop on Minority Languages

[17] Dorr, B. and Habash, N. 2002. Interlingua Approximation: A Generation Heavy Approach. Interlingua Reliability Workshop. Tiburon, California, USA

[18] Carbonell, J., Klein, S., Miller, D., Steinbaum, M., Grassiany, T., Frey, J. 2006. Context-Based Machine Translation. *Proceedings of the 7th Conference of the Association for Machine Translation in the Americas, Cambridge, August 2006,* 19-28

[19] McTait, K. 2003. Translation Patterns, Linguistic Knowledge and Complexity in EBMT. In M. Carl & A. Way (eds.), 307-338

[20] Kitamura, M. 2004. Translation Knowledge Acquisition for Pattern-Based Machine Translation. PhD. Nara Institute of Science and Technology, Japan

[21] Labropoulou, P., Mantzari, E. and Gavrilidou, M. 1996. Lexicon - Morphosyntactic Specifications: Language-Specific Instantiation (Greek), PP-PAROLE, MLAP 63-386 report

[22] Boutsis, S., Prokopidis, P., Giouli, V. and Piperidis, S. 2000. A Robust Parser for Unrestricted Greek Text. *Proceedings of the Second International Conference on Language Resources and Evaluation* ***1****, Athens, Greece*, 467—482

[23] Carl, M., Schmidt, P. and Schütz, J. 2005. Reversible Template-based Shake & Bake Generation. Proceedings of the Example-Based Machine Translation Workshop held in conjunction with the 10th Machine Translation Summit, Phuket, Thailand, 17—26

[24] Vandeghinste, V. 2005. Manual for ShaRPa 2.0. Internal Report. Centre for Computational Linguistics, K.U.Leuven

[25] Nagao, M. 1984. A Framework of a Mechanical Translation between Japanese and English by Analogy Principle. In Elithorn, A. and Banerji, R. (eds.). 1984. *Artificial and Human Intelligence.* Amsterdam: North-Holland, 173-180

[26] Dologlou, I., Markantonatou, S., Tambouratzis, G., Yannoutsou, O., Fourla, A. & Ioannou, N. 2003. Using Monolingual Corpora for Statistical Machine Translation. *Proceedings of EAMT/CLAW 2003. Dublin, Ireland*, 61—68

[27] Tambouratzis, G., Sofianopoulos, S., Spilioti, V., Vassiliou, M., Yannoutsou, O. & Markantonatou S. 2006. Pattern Matching-based System for Machine Translation (MT). *Proceedings of Advances in Artificial Intelligence: 4th Hellenic Conference on AI, SETN 2006* ***3955****, Heraklion, Crete, Greece*, Lecture Notes in Computer Science, Springer Verlag, 345—355

[28] Markantonatou, S., Sofianopoulos, S., Spilioti, V., Tambouratzis, G., Vassiliou, M. and Yannoutsou, O. 2006. Using Patterns for Machine Translation (MT). *Proceedings of the European Association for Machine Translation Oslo, Norway*, 239—246

[29] Papineni, K.A., Roukos, S., Ward, T. & Zhu, W.J. 2002. BLEU: A Method for Automatic Evaluation of Machine Translation. *Proceedings of the 40th Annual Meeting of the Association for Computational Linguistics Philadelphia, USA,*. 311—318

[30] NIST. 2002. Automatic Evaluation of Machine Translation Quality Using n-gram Co-occurrences Statistics (http://www.nist.gov/speech/tests/mt/)

[31] Snover, M., Dorr, B., Schwartz, R., Micciulla, L. & Makhoul, J. 2006. A Study of Translation Edit Rate with Targeted Human Annotation. *Proceedings of Association for Machine Translation in the Americas*

C. Specific Language Groups and Languages

Language Engineering for Lesser-Studied Languages
S. Nirenburg (Ed.)
IOS Press, 2009

doi:10.3233/978-1-58603-954-7-277

Language Resources for Semitic Languages

Challenges and Solutions

Shuly WINTNER [a],
[a] *Department of Computer Science, University of Haifa, 31905 Haifa, Israel*

Abstract. Language resources are crucial for research and development in theoretical, computational, socio- and psycho-linguistics, and for the construction of natural language processing applications. This paper focuses on Semitic languages, a language family that includes Arabic and Hebrew and has over 300 million speakers. The paper discusses the challenge that Semitic languages pose for computational processing, and surveys the current state of the art, providing references to several existing solutions.

Keywords. Language resources, Semitic languages

1. Introduction

Language resources are crucial for research and development in theoretical, computational, socio- and psycho-linguistics, and for the construction of natural language processing (NLP) applications. This paper focuses on Semitic languages, which are reviewed in Section 2. Section 3 provides motivation for developing and utilizing language resources in broad context. The challenge that Semitic languages pose for computational processing is discussed in section 4. Section 5 surveys available resources for Semitic languages and provides references to existing solutions. The paper concludes with directions for future research.

This paper is based on (and significant parts are taken verbatim from) earlier publications [1,2,3].

2. Semitic languages

The Semitic family of languages [4] is spoken in the Middle East and North Africa, from Iraq and the Arabian Peninsula in the east to Morocco in the west, by over 300 million native speakers. The most widely spoken Semitic languages today are Arabic, Amharic, Tigrinya and Hebrew, although Maltese and Syriac are also notable as far as computational approaches are concerned. Extinct Semitic languages include Akkadian, Ugaritic, Phoenician, and many others. The situation of Arabic is particularly interesting from a sociolinguistic point of view, as it represents an extreme case of *diglossia*: Modern Standard Arabic (MSA) is used in written texts and formal speech across the Arab world, but is not spoken natively. Rather, colloquial Arabic dialects (Levantine, Cairene, Yemenite etc.) are used for everyday conversation, but lack an agreed-upon script [5, p. 267]. Several aspects make the Semitic languages stand out; we focus here on the *morphology* and the *orthography*, because these are aspects which benefited most from computational attention. Hopefully, syntactic features which are as interesting will be addressed computationally in the future.

The most prominent phenomenon of Semitic morphology is the reliance on *root-and-pattern* paradigms for word formation. The standard account of word-formation processes in Semitic languages [6] describes words as combinations of two morphemes: a *root* and a *pattern* (an additional morpheme, *vocalization*, is sometimes used to abstract the pattern further.) The root consists of consonants only, by default three, called *radicals*. The pattern is a combination of vowels and, possibly, consonants too, with 'slots' into which the root consonants can be inserted. Words are created by *interdigitating* roots into patterns: the consonants of the root fill the slots of the pattern, by default in linear order (see [7] for a survey).

As an example of root-and-pattern morphology, consider the root *k.t.b*, which denotes a notion of writing. In Hebrew, the pattern *haCCaCa* (where the 'C's indicate the slots) usually denotes nominalization; hence *haktaba* "*dictation*". Similarly, the pattern *maCCeCa* often denotes instruments; construed in this pattern, the root *k.t.b* yields *makteba* "*writing desk*". Aramaic uses the pattern *CeCaC* for active verbs, hence *ketab* "*write, draw*". In Maltese, *k.t.b+CiCCieC* yields *kittieb* "*writer*". In Arabic, the patterns *CaCCaC* and *CuCCiC* are used for perfect causative active and passive verbs, respectively, hence *kattab* and *kuttib* "*cause to write*" and "*cause to be written*", respectively. Root and pattern combination can trigger morphological alternations which can be non-trivial.

Other than the peculiar root-and-pattern process, the morphology of Semitic languages is concatenative. Inflectional morphology is highly productive and consists mostly of suffixes, but sometimes of prefixes or circumfixes, and sometimes of pattern changes (as in the case of broken plurals, discussed below). For example, Yemenite uses the prefixes *a-*, *tu-* and *yu-* for singular inflections of imperfect verbs, as in *aktub, tuktub, yuktub* "*write*"; it uses the suffixes *-na, -akum, -akun, -u, -an* for plural inflections of perfect verbs, as in *katabna, katabakum, katabakun, katabau, kataban*; and it uses the circumfixes *tu... i, tu... u, tu... ayn* for other imperfect inflections, e.g., *tuktubi, tuktubu, tuktubayn* [5, pp. 292-293].

Nouns, adjectives and numerals inflect for number (singular, plural and dual) and gender (masculine or feminine). A peculiarity of some Semitic languages, including Arabic and its dialects, is a word-internal plural form known as *broken plural*. In many languages, some nouns have an external (suffix) plural form, some have 'broken' plurals and some a combination of the two, and this is purely lexical (i.e., not determined by any feature of the singular noun). Hence the Classical Arabic *manzilun–manaazilun* "*station–stations*", or *malikun–muluukun* "*king–kings*"; and Tigrinya *berki–abrak* "*knee–knees*", or *bet–abyat* "*house–houses*" [8, p. 432].

In addition, all these three types of nominals have two phonologically distinct forms, known as the *absolute* and *construct* states; the latter are used in compounds [9,10]. For example, Hebrew *simla* "*dress*" vs. *simlat*, as in *simlat kala* "*bridal gown*"; Tigrinya *ẖezbi–ẖezb* "*inhabitants–inhabitants of*"; Maltese *mara* "*wife*" vs. *mart*, as in *mart Toni* "*Tony's wife*".

The proto-Semitic three-case system, with explicit indication of nominative, accusative and genitive cases, is preserved in MSA but not in the contemporary dialects of Arabic or in Hebrew. For example, Classical Arabic "*believer*" (singular, masculine, definite) is *almu'minu, almu'mini* or *almu'mina*, depending on whether the case is nominative, genitive or accusative, respectively.

Nominals can take possessive pronominal suffixes which inflect for number, gender and person. For example, MSA *kitaabu-hu* "*his book*" or Hebrew *simlat-a* "*her dress*". Verbs inflect for number, gender and person (first, second and third) and also for a combination of tense and aspect, which differs across different languages. Verbs can also take pronominal suffixes, which in this case are interpreted as direct objects, and in some cases can also take nominative pronominal suffixes. For example, MSA *ra'ayta-ni* "*you saw-me*" or Hebrew *lir'ot-am* "*to see them*".

The various Semitic languages use a variety of scripts [11,12, chapter 7]; still, some problems are common to many of them, including MSA and Hebrew. Two major features characterize the writing systems of both MSA and Hebrew: under-specification and the attachment of particles to the words which happen to follow them. The standard Hebrew and Arabic scripts use dedicated diacritics to encode most of the vowels, as well as other phonemic information (such as gemination and, in the case of Arabic, case endings). These diacritics are either altogether missing or only partially specified in most contemporary texts. This results in highly ambiguous surface forms, which can be vocalized and interpreted in a variety of ways. For example, the Hebrew form *šbt* can be pronounced *šavát, šabát, šévet* or *šebát*, among others.

Furthermore, the scripts of both languages dictate that many particles, including some prepositions, the coordinating conjunction, some subordinating conjunctions, the definite article and the future marker (in Arabic), all attach to the words which immediately follow them. Thus, a Hebrew form such as *šbth* can be read as an unsegmented word (the verb "*capture*", third person singular feminine past), as *š+bth* "*that+field*", *š+b+th* "*that+in+tea*", *šbt+h* "*her sitting*" or even as *š+bt+h* "*that her daughter*". This, again, adds to the ambiguity of surface forms.

3. The utility of language resources

Developments in computational linguistics and natural language processing result in the creation of a variety of resources and tools which are invaluable for research in the humanities and the social sciences, as well as for the production of natural language processing (NLP) applications. These include linguistic corpora, lexicons and dictionaries, morphological analyzers and generators, syntactic parsers, etc. The utility of language resources is outlined in this section, abstracting away from any particular language; available resources for Semitic languages are discussed in Section 5.

Corpora which record language use are instrumental resources for theoretical, computational, socio-, and psycho-linguistics, as well as for other fields such as literary research and psychology [13,14,15]. They provide means for computing word frequencies, discovering collocations, investigating grammatical constructions, detecting language change, exploring linguistic universals, and training natural language applications which are based on machine learning (this is the computational paradigm which allows computer programs to "learn" from data). Corpora can reflect written or spoken language, and can contain raw data, as well as human- or machine-produced annotations. Annotated corpora [16] can encode phonological information (e.g., synchronizing the transcription with audio recordings); morphological information (e.g., specifying the lexemes or the roots of words); syntactic information (e.g., associating a phrase-structure or a dependency-structure tree with each sentence); semantic information (e.g., specifying the sense of each word or the argument structure of verbs); and meta-information (e.g., the age and gender of the speaker). They can also be *parallel*, that is, consist of similar texts in more than one language, where correspondences across languages are explicitly marked as paragraph-, sentence- or word-alignment links [17]. Of course, the largest, fastest-growing corpus is the Web [18].

Standard lexicons, dictionaries and thesauri for various languages are available in digital format; this facilitates search and retrieval and enables the use of lexical resources in computational applications. This also provides means for novel organizations of lexical resources, both monolingual and multi-lingual. An example is WordNet [19]: it is a lexical database in which words are grouped by synonymy, and several lexical-semantic relations (e.g., hypernym–hyponym; meronym; etc.) are defined over the synonym sets (*synsets*). Multi-lingual extensions of WordNet, such as EuroWordNet [20] or MultiWordNet [21], synchronize the structure of these lexical databases across languages. Another example of a modern approach to the lexicon is FrameNet [22,23], an on-line resource that documents the range of semantic and syntactic combinatory possibilities of word senses through annotation of example sentences.

Shallow morphological processing involves *tokenization*, which segments a stream of text into individual *tokens*, taking care of issues such as punctuation, foreign characters, numbers etc.; and *stemming*, which reduces possibly inflected forms into standard forms, which are not necessarily lemmas. Deeper processing consists of full *morphological analysis*, which produces all the possible readings of the tokens in a text, along with morphological and morpho-syntactic features (e.g., root, pattern, number, gender, case, tense, etc.); and *generation*, which is the reverse operation. For languages with complex morphology, this is a non-trivial task [24]. In particular, morphological analysis of Semitic languages is ambiguous: a given surface form may be analyzed in several ways. Morphological *disambiguation* selects the correct analysis of a surface form in the context in which it occurs; this is usually done using heuristics, since deterministic algorithms for this task are not usually known. The combination of morphological analysis and disambiguation is extremely useful for tasks such as keyword search in context (KWIC) or producing a concordance, as it facilitates retrieval of word forms which are consistent with a specific analysis. It is also considered a necessary first step in many natural language processing applications. A related task, part-of-speech (POS) tagging, assigns a POS category to text tokens, taking into account their context. For Semitic languages, this is only an approximation of full disambiguation since more than one analysis may share the same POS.

Natural language applications that involve deeper linguistic processing, such as machine translation systems, are not yet on par with human performance. However, language technology is successfully used in areas such as machine-aided translation, information retrieval and extraction, automatic summarization, speech analysis and generation, learning and education.

4. Processing Semitic languages: The challenge

Some of the peculiar properties of Semitic languages that were discussed above are challenging when computational processing of these languages is concerned. This section discusses some of the difficulties.

A major complication in computational approaches to Semitic stems from the fact that linguistic theories, and consequently computational linguistic approaches, are often developed with a narrow set of (mostly European) languages in mind. The adequacy of such approaches to other families of languages is sometimes sub-optimal. A related issue is the long tradition of scholarly work on some Semitic languages, notably Arabic [25] and Hebrew [26], which cannot always be easily consolidated with contemporary approaches.

Inconsistencies between modern, English-centric approaches and traditional ones are easily observed in matters of lexicography. In order to annotate corpora or produce tree-banks, an agreed-upon set of part-of-speech (POS) categories is required. Since early approaches to POS tagging were limited to English, resources for other languages tend to use "tag sets", or inventories of categories, that are minor modifications of the standard English set. Such adaptation is problematic for Semitic languages. To begin with, there are good reasons to view nouns, adjectives and numerals as sub-categories of a single category, *nominals*. Furthermore, the distinction between verbs and nominals is blurry. [27] discuss a similar issue related to the correct tagging of modals in Hebrew. Even the correct citation form to use in dictionaries is a matter of some debate, as Arabic traditional dictionaries are root-based, rather than lemma-based [28].

These issues are complicated further when morphology is considered. The rich, non-concatenative morphology of Semitic languages frequently requires innovative solutions that standard approaches do not always provide. The most common approach to morphological processing of natural language is *finite-state technology* [29,30]. The adequacy of this technology for Semitic languages has been frequently challenged [31]. While finite-state morphological grammars for Semitic languages abound [32,33,34,35,36,37], they require sophisticated developments, such as flag diacritics [38], multi-tape automata [35] or registered automata [39].

The level of morphological ambiguity is higher in many Semitic languages than it is in English, due to the rich morphology and deficient orthography. This calls for sophisticated methods for disambiguation. While in English (and other European languages) morphological disambiguation amounts to POS tagging, Hebrew and Arabic require more effort, since determining the correct POS of a given token is intertwined with the problem of segmenting the token to morphemes. Several models were proposed to address these issues [40,41,42,43].

5. Language resources for Semitic languages

Development of language resources is expensive and time-consuming, and only few languages benefit from state-of-the-art tools and resources. Among the Semitic languages, MSA and Hebrew have the best-developed resources, although even they lag behind European languages. Resources for other Semitic languages are scarce. This section discusses some of the challenges involved in the production of language resources for

Semitic languages, and provides references to existing works. For reviews of existing resources for Arabic, including links to on-line resources, see [44,45].

In recent years, many language resources are distributed via two channels: the Linguistic Data Consortium (LDC, `http://www.ldc.upenn.edu`) and the European Language Resources Association (ELRA, `http://www.elra.info`). Many of the resources discussed below are available from these two repositories. Resources and tools for Hebrew are distributed through the Knowledge Center for Processing Hebrew (MILA, `http://mila.cs.technion.ac.il`), which should serve as a good starting point for anyone who is interested in state-of-the-art language technology for this language. As for Arabic, a limited reference point is the web site of the Association for Computational Linguistics Special Interest Group on Computational Approaches to Semitic Languages, `http://www.semitic.tk`. Many resources are referred to from the web-sites of Columbia University's Arabic Dialect Modeling Group (`http://www.ccls.columbia.edu/cadim`); the European Network of Excellence in Human Language Technologies (`http://www.elsnet.org/arabiclist.html`); and the Network for Euro-Mediterranean Language Resources (`http://www.nemlar.org`). Resources for Maltese are available from the Maltese Language Resource Server (MLRS, `http://mlrs.cs.um.edu.mt`).

5.1. Corpora

The LDC distributes several corpora of Arabic. The most comprehensive is the *Arabic Gigaword* corpus [46], which consists of over 200,000 documents taken from several news agencies, comprising in total over 1.5 billion words. Subsets of this corpus are also available with annotations: the LDC distributes three separate issues of the *Arabic Treebank* (ATB), consisting all together of over half a million words, in which words are morphologically analyzed and disambiguated, and where syntactic trees decorate each and every sentence [47,48,49]. In the last of those corpora, the annotation includes full vocalization of the input text, including case endings. A different treebank which is also distributed by the LDC is the Prague Arabic Dependency Treebank (PADT) [50]. Smaller in scale than the ATB (but still over 100,000 words), this corpus decorates a subset of the Arabic Gigaword data with multi-level annotations [51] referring to morphological and "analytical" level of linguistic representation.

In addition to textual corpora, the LDC distributes a variety of spoken language corpora, often along with the transcription of the spoken utterances. For Arabic, these include broadcast news, as well as spoken (usually telephone) conversations in Egyptian, Levantine, Gulf and Iraqi Arabic. Similarly, ELRA distributes spoken corpora of colloquial Arabic from Morocco, Tunisia, Egypt and Israel, as well as broadcast news and some text corpora.

Furthermore, LDC distributes a number of parallel Arabic-English corpora of various sizes [52,53,54,55], and a small English-Arabic treebank [56].

Hebrew corpora are predominantly distributed by MILA [57,2]. These include newspaper and newswire articles (over twenty million word tokens), as well as two years of parliament proceedings (over ten million tokens). These corpora are available as raw text, or with full morphological analysis, potentially disambiguated (automatically). A small subset (almost 100,000 words) is manually disambiguated. In addition, a small treebank of 6,500 sentences is also available [58]. ELDA distributes a few small databases of spoken Hebrew, as well as a large-scale phonetic lexicon comprising over 100,000 words. A much larger-scale project whose aim was to collect a representative corpus of spoken Hebrew was planned but never materialized [59]. Finally, a small corpus of child language interactions in Hebrew, transcribed and morphologically annotated, is part of the CHILDES database [60].

A Maltese National Corpus (MNC) is being constructed as part of MLRS [61], a development of the earlier Maltilex project [62]. The MNC is made up of a representative mixture of newspaper articles, local and foreign news coverage, sports articles, political discussions, government publications, radio show transcripts and some novels. It consists of over 1.8 million words and almost 70,000 different word forms, making it the largest digital corpus of Maltese in existence. A corpus management system has been constructed which supports different categories of users and multiple levels of annotation.

5.2. Lexical databases

One of the most commonly used lexicons of Arabic is distributed with the Buckwalter Arabic Morphological Analyzer by the LDC [63]. It consists of 78,839 entries, representing 40,219 lemmas, augmented by lists of hundreds of prefixes and suffixes and rules that control their possible combinations. The most comprehensive lexicon of Modern Hebrew, consisting of over 20,000 entries, many with English translations, is distributed by MILA [64]. A comprehensive Aramaic lexicon [65], along with English word translations, and some processing tools such as KWIC, is available on-line at `http://cal1.cn.huc.edu/`. A similar resource for Amharic is available at `http://www.amharicdictionary.com/`. A lexical database is also under construction for Maltese under the auspices of the MLRS project [61]. The first step has been the extraction of a full-form wordlist (approximately 800,000 entries) from the corpus side of the project. A Web-based framework is now in place to support the addition of linguistic information, by linguists, to lexical entries.

Several bilingual dictionaries for Semitic languages exist on-line. Some notable examples include an English-Maltese (`http://aboutmalta.com/language/engmal.htm`); an Arabic-English-French-Turkish dictionary (`http://dictionary.sakhr.com`); and the Arabic-Hebrew dictionary of [66] (`http://www.arabdictionary.huji.ac.il`). Many smaller-scale, sometimes domain-specific, lexicons and dictionaries for Semitic languages are listed at `http://www.yourdictionary.com/languages/afroasia.html`

More sophisticated lexical databases are only beginning to emerge for Semitic languages. There are preliminary designs for an Arabic WordNet [67,68], and progress is underway. A medium-scale WordNet for Hebrew, of some 5,000 *synsets* representing over 7,500 lemmas, is distributed by MILA [69]. It was developed under the MultiWordNet paradigm and is therefore aligned with English, Italian, Spanish and other languages; [69] discuss some of the difficulties involved in aligning lexical databases across languages, with emphasis on Semitic. Finally, a FrameNet for Hebrew is planned but its development had not yet started [70] .

5.3. Morphological processing

Several natural language processing applications for Semitic languages are hindered by the fact that texts must be morphologically pre-processed. Even shallow applications, such as information retrieval (e.g., as done by search engines) or KWIC, must be aware of word structure and orthographic issues.

Recent years saw increasing interest in computational approaches to Arabic morphology [33,71,38,72,35,73,74,75,76]. The state of the art, however, is most likely the morphological analyzer of Buckwalter [63], which combines wide coverage with detailed, linguistically informative analyses. Similarly, while many morphological systems were developed for Hebrew [77,78,79], the current state of the art is based on the HAMSAH morphological grammar [37] whose implementation is currently distributed by MILA [2]. For both languages, these modern analyzers are based on linguistically motivated rules and large-scale lexicons; they are efficient, easy to use and constantly maintained.

As far as morphological disambiguation is concerned, current approaches are based on machine-learning techniques, and cannot guarantee perfect success. For Arabic, early attempts at POS tagging [80,81] are now superseded by the full morphological disambiguation module of [41], whose accuracy is approximately 95%. For Hebrew, early approaches [82,79,40] are superseded by full disambiguation modules with accuracy of 88.5% [42] to 91.5% [43].

Morphological resources for other Semitic languages are almost non-existant. Few notable exceptions include Biblical Hebrew, for which morphological analyzers are available from several commercial enterprises; Akkadian, for which some morphological analyzers were developed [32,34,83]; Syriac, which inspired the development of a new model of computational morphology [35]; Amharic, with few recent initiatives [36,84,85,86]; and dialectal Arabic [87,88,89].

Also worth mentioning here are few works which address other morphology-related tasks. These include a system for identifying the roots of Hebrew and Arabic (possibly inflected) words [90]; programs for restoring diacritics in Arabic [91,92,93]; determining case endings of Arabic words [94]; and correction of optical character recognizer (OCR) errors [95].

5.4. Other resources

Computational grammars of natural languages are useful for natural language processing applications, but perhaps more importantly, for validating and verifying linguistic theories. Very few such grammars exist for Semitic languages. Early approaches include a phrase-structure grammar of Arabic [96] and a unification grammar of Hebrew [97]. Recently, a wide-coverage Slot Grammar for Arabic has been developed and released [98]. The current state of the art in parsing Arabic, however, is not overly impressive, and existing parsers use machine-learning approaches (training on either the Arabic Treebank or the Prague Arabic Dependency Treebank). [99] discuss the possibility of leveraging MSA resources to produce parsers of Arabic dialects.

Arabic has been the focus of much recent research in *machine translation*, especially translating to English. Much of this work is done in a statistical setup, in which parallel corpora are used to induce translation hypotheses, and (English) language models are used to select the most likely among the hypotheses. This endeavor resulted in the creation of several resources which can be useful for researchers in the humanities and social sciences. Most significant among those are probably the many parallel corpora discussed above. Of interest are also some works on *transliteration* of Arabic words, in particular proper names, to English [100,101,102]. Full machine translation systems, which could be invaluable for a variety of applications, are still not sufficiently high-quality, but several Arabic-to-English systems are currently being developed and their performance constantly improves [103,104,105,106,107]. There is also a small-scale effort to develop a Hebrew to English machine translation system [108]. Many systems are developed by commercial companies, and range from translation memories and machine-aided human translation software to full machine translation.

Acknowledgments

I am grateful to Nizar Habash, Noam Ordan and Mike Rosner for advice and comments.

References

[1] Shuly Wintner. Hebrew computational linguistics: Past and future. *Artificial Intelligence Review*, 21(2):113–138, 2004.
[2] Alon Itai and Shuly Wintner. Language resources for Hebrew. *Language Resources and Evaluation*, Forthcoming.
[3] Shuly Wintner. Computational approaches to Semitic languages. In Joseph Raben and Orville Vernon Burton, editors, *Encyclopedia of Humanities and Social Science Computing*. University of Sydney, Sydney, Forthcoming.
[4] Robert Hetzron, editor. *The Semitic Languages*. Routledge, London and New York, 1997.
[5] Alan S. Kaye and Judith Rosenhouse. Arabic dialects and Maltese. In Hetzron [4], chapter 14, pages 263–311.
[6] John J. McCarthy. A prosodic theory of nonconcatenative morphology. *Linguistic Inquiry*, 12(3):373–418, 1981.
[7] Joseph Shimron, editor. *Language Processing and Acquisition in Languages of Semitic, Root-Based, Morphology*. Number 28 in Language Acquisition and Language Disorders. John Benjamins, 2003.
[8] Leonid E. Kogan. Tigrinya. In Hetzron [4], chapter 18, pages 424–445.
[9] Hagit Borer. On the morphological parallelism between compounds and constructs. In Geert Booij and Jaap van Marle, editors, *Yearbook of Morphology 1*, pages 45–65. Foris publications, Dordrecht, Holland, 1988.
[10] Hagit Borer. The construct in review. In Jacqueline Lecarme, Jean Lowenstamm, and Ur Shlonsky, editors, *Studies in Afroasiatic Grammar*, pages 30–61. Holland Academic Graphics, The Hague, 1996.
[11] Peter T. Daniels. Scripts of Semitic languages. In Hetzron [4], chapter 2, pages 16–45.
[12] Henry Rogers. *Writing Systems: A Linguistic Approach*. Blackwell Publishing, Malden, MA, 2005.
[13] Kenneth W. Church and Robert L. Mercer. Introduction to the special issue on computational linguistics using large corpora. *Computational Linguistics*, 19(1):1–24, March 1993.
[14] Anthony McEnery and Andrew Wilson. *Corpus Linguistics*. Edinburgh University Press, Edinburgh, 1996.
[15] Graeme Kennedy. *An introduction to corpus linguistics*. Addison Wesley, 1998.
[16] Roger Garside, Geoffrey Leech, and Anthony McEnery, editors. *Corpus Annotation: Linguistic Information from Computer Text Corpora*. Longman, London, 1997.
[17] Philipp Koehn, Joel Martin, Rada Mihalcea, Christof Monz, and Ted Pedersen, editors. *Proceedings of the ACL Workshop on Building and Using Parallel Texts*, Ann Arbor, Michigan, June 2005. Association for Computational Linguistics.

[18] Adam Kilgarriff and Gregory Grefenstette. Introduction to the special issue on the Web as corpus. *Computational Linguistics*, 29(3):333–347, September 2003.

[19] Christiane Fellbaum, editor. *WordNet: An Electronic Lexical Database*. Language, Speech and Communication. MIT Press, 1998.

[20] Piek Vossen. EuroWordNet: a multilingual database of autonomous and language-specific WordNets connected via an inter-lingual-index. *International Journal of Lexicography*, 17(2):161–173, 2004.

[21] Luisa Bentivogli, Emanuele Pianta, and Christian Girardi. MultiWordNet: developing an aligned multilingual database. In *Proceedings of the First International Conference on Global WordNet*, Mysore, India, January 2002.

[22] Charles J. Fillmore and B. T. S Atkins. Starting where the dictionaries stop: The challenge of corpus lexicography. In B. T. S. Atkins and A. Zampolli, editors, *Computational Approaches to the Lexicon*, pages 349–396. Clarendon Press, Oxford, 1994.

[23] Colin F. Baker, Charles J. Fillmore, and John B. Lowe. The Berkeley FrameNet Project. In *Proceedings of the ACL/COLING-98*, Montreal, Quebec, 1998.

[24] Richard W. Sproat. *Morphology and Computation*. MIT Press, Cambridge, MA, 1992.

[25] Jonathan Owens. The Arabic grammatical tradition. In Hetzron [4], chapter 3, pages 46–58.

[26] Arie Schippers. The Hebrew grammatical tradition. In Hetzron [4], chapter 4, pages 59–65.

[27] Yael Netzer, Meni Adler, David Gabay, and Michael Elhadad. Can you tag the modal? you should. In *Proceedings of the ACL-2007 Workshop on Computational Approaches to Semitic Languages*, June 2007.

[28] Joseph Dichy and Ali Farghaly. Roots and patterns vs. stems plus grammar-lexis specifications: on what basis should a multilingual lexical database centered on Arabic be built. In *Proceedings of the MT-Summit IX workshop on Machine Translation for Semitic Languages*, pages 1–8, New Orleans, September 2003.

[29] Kimmo Koskenniemi. *Two-Level Morphology: a General Computational Model for Word-Form Recognition and Production*. The Department of General Linguistics, University of Helsinki, 1983.

[30] Kenneth R. Beesley and Lauri Karttunen. *Finite-State Morphology: Xerox Tools and Techniques*. CSLI, Stanford, 2003.

[31] Alon Lavie, Alon Itai, Uzzi Ornan, and Mori Rimon. On the applicability of two-level morphology to the inflection of Hebrew verbs. In *Proceedings of the International Conference of the ALLC*, Jerusalem, Israel, 1988.

[32] Laura Kataja and Kimmo Koskenniemi. Finite-state description of Semitic morphology: A case study of Ancient Akkadian. In *COLING*, pages 313–315, 1988.

[33] Kenneth R. Beesley. Arabic finite-state morphological analysis and generation. In *Proceedings of COLING-96, the 16th International Conference on Computational Linguistics*, Copenhagen, 1996.

[34] François Barthélemy. A morphological analyzer for Akkadian verbal forms with a model of phonetic transformations. In *Proceedings of the Coling-ACL 1998 Workshop on Computational Approaches to Semitic Languages*, pages 73–81, Montreal, 1998.

[35] George Anton Kiraz. Multitiered nonlinear morphology using multitape finite automata: a case study on Syriac and Arabic. *Computational Linguistics*, 26(1):77–105, March 2000.

[36] Saba Amsalu and Dafydd Gibbon. A complete finite-state model for Amharic morphographemics. In Anssi Yli-Jyrä, Lauri Karttunen, and Juhani Karhumäki, editors, *FSMNLP*, volume 4002 of *Lecture Notes in Computer Science*, pages 283–284. Springer, 2005.

[37] Shlomo Yona and Shuly Wintner. A finite-state morphological grammar of Hebrew. *Natural Language Engineering*, Forthcoming.

[38] Kenneth R. Beesley. Arabic morphology using only finite-state operations. In Michael Rosner, editor, *Proceedings of the Workshop on Computational Approaches to Semitic languages*, pages 50–57, Montreal, Quebec, August 1998. COLING-ACL'98.

[39] Yael Cohen-Sygal and Shuly Wintner. Finite-state registered automata for non-concatenative morphology. *Computational Linguistics*, 32(1):49–82, March 2006.

[40] Roy Bar-Haim, Khalil Sima'an, and Yoad Winter. Choosing an optimal architecture for segmentation and POS-tagging of Modern Hebrew. In *Proceedings of the ACL Workshop on Computational Approaches to Semitic Languages*, pages 39–46, Ann Arbor, Michigan, June 2005. Association for Computational Linguistics.

[41] Nizar Habash and Owen Rambow. Arabic tokenization, part-of-speech tagging and morphological disambiguation in one fell swoop. In *Proceedings of the 43rd Annual Meeting of the Association for*

Computational Linguistics (ACL'05), pages 573–580, Ann Arbor, Michigan, June 2005. Association for Computational Linguistics.

[42] Meni Adler and Michael Elhadad. An unsupervised morpheme-based hmm for hebrew morphological disambiguation. In *Proceedings of the 21st International Conference on Computational Linguistics and 44th Annual Meeting of the Association for Computational Linguistics*, pages 665–672, Sydney, Australia, July 2006. Association for Computational Linguistics.

[43] Danny Shacham and Shuly Wintner. Morphological disambiguation of Hebrew: a case study in classifier combination. In *Proceedings of EMNLP-CoNLL 2007, the Conference on Empirical Methods in Natural Language Processing and the Conference on Computational Natural Language Learning*, Prague, June 2007. Association for Computational Linguistics.

[44] Mahtab Nikkhou and Khalid Choukri. Survey on Arabic language resources and tools in the Mediterranean countries. Technical report, NEMLAR, Center for Sprogteknologi, University of Copenhagen, Denmark, March 2005.

[45] Christiane Fellbaum. Arabic NLP resources for the Arabic WordNet project, 2006.

[46] David Graff, Ke Chen, Junbo Kong, and Kazuaki Maeda. *Arabic Gigaword*. Linguistic Data Consortium, Philadelphia, second edition, 2006.

[47] Mohamed Maamouri, Ann Bies, Tim Buckwalter, and Hubert Jin. *Arabic Treebank: Part 1 v 3.0*. Linguistic Data Consortium, Philadelphia, 2005.

[48] Mohamed Maamouri, Ann Bies, Tim Buckwalter, and Hubert Jin. *Arabic Treebank: Part 2 v 2.0*. Linguistic Data Consortium, Philadelphia, 2004.

[49] Mohamed Maamouri, Ann Bies, Tim Buckwalter, and Hubert Jin. *Arabic Treebank: Part 3 v 1.0*. Linguistic Data Consortium, Philadelphia, 2004.

[50] Jan Hajič, Otakar Smrž, Petr Zemánek, Petr Pajas, Jan Šnaidauf, Emanuel Beška, Jakub Kracmar, and Kamila Hassanova. *Prague Arabic Dependency Treebank 1.0*. Linguistic Data Consortium, Philadelphia, 2004.

[51] Jan Hajič, Otakar Smrž, Petr Zemánek, Jan Šnaidauf, and Emanuel Beška. Prague Arabic Dependency Treebank: Development in data and tools. In *Proceedings of the NEMLAR International Conference on Arabic Language Resources and Tools*, pages 110–117, Cairo, Egypt, September 2004.

[52] Xiaoyi Ma, Dalal Zakhary, and Moussa Bamba. *Arabic News Translation Text Part 1*. Linguistic Data Consortium, Philadelphia, 2004.

[53] Christopher Walker, Stephanie Strassel, Julie Medero, and Kazuaki Maeda. *ACE 2005 Multilingual Training Corpus*. Linguistic Data Consortium, Philadelphia, 2006.

[54] David Graff, Junbo Kong, Kazuaki Maeda, and Stephanie Strassel. *TDT5 Multilingual Text*. Linguistic Data Consortium, Philadelphia, 2006.

[55] Dragos Stefan Munteanu and Daniel Marcu. *ISI Arabic–English Automatically Extracted Parallel Text*. Linguistic Data Consortium, Philadelphia, 2007.

[56] Ann Bies. *English–Arabic Treebank v 1.0*. Linguistic Data Consortium, Philadelphia, 2006.

[57] Alon Itai. Knowledge center for processing Hebrew. In *Proceedings of the LREC-2006 Workshop "Towards a Research Infrastructure for Language Resources"*, Genoa, Italy, May 2006.

[58] Khalil Sima'an, Alon Itai, Yoad Winter, Alon Altman, and N. Nativ. Building a tree-bank of Modern Hebrew text. *Traitment Automatique des Langues*, 42(2), 2001.

[59] Shlomo Izre'el, Benjamin Hary, and Giora Rahav. Designing CoSIH: The corpus of Spoken Israeli Hebrew. *International Journal of Corpus Linguistics*, 6(2):171–197, 2002.

[60] Brian MacWhinney. *The CHILDES Project: Tools for Analyzing Talk*. Lawrence Erlbaum Associates, Mahwah, NJ, third edition, 2000.

[61] Mike Rosner, Ray Fabri, Duncan Attard, and Albert Gatt. MLRS, a resource server for the Maltese language. In *Proceedings of 4th Computer Science Annual Workshop (CSAW-2006)*, pages 90–98, Malta, December 2006. University of Malta.

[62] Mike Rosner, Ray Fabri, Joe Caruana, M. Lougraïeb, Matthew Montebello, David Galea, and G. Mangion. Maltilex project. Technical report, University of Malta, Msida, Malta, 1999.

[63] Tim Buckwalter. *Buckwalter Arabic Morphological Analyzer Version 2.0*. Linguistic Data Consortium, Philadelphia, 2004.

[64] Alon Itai, Shuly Wintner, and Shlomo Yona. A computational lexicon of contemporary Hebrew. In *Proceedings of The fifth international conference on Language Resources and Evaluation (LREC-2006)*, Genoa, Italy, May 2006.

[65] Stephen A. Kaufman. *The Comprehensive Aramaic Lexicon, Text Entry and Format Manual*. Publica-

tions of The Comprehensive Aramaic Lexicon Project. The Johns Hopkins University Press, Baltimore, 1987.

[66] David Ayalon and Pessah Shinar. *Arabic-Hebrew Dictionary of Modern Arabic*. Hebrew University Press, Jerusalem, 1947.

[67] Mona Diab. The feasibility of bootstrapping an Arabic WordNet leveraging parallel corpora and an English WordNet. In *Proceedings of the Arabic Language Technologies and Resources*, Cairo, Egypt, September 2004. NEMLAR.

[68] William Black, Sabri Elkateb, Horacio Rodriguez, Musa Alkhalifa, Piek Vossen, Adam Pease, and Christiane Fellbaum. Introducing the Arabic WordNet project. In *Proceedings of the Third Global WordNet Meeting*. GWC, January 2006.

[69] Noam Ordan and Shuly Wintner. Hebrew WordNet: a test case of aligning lexical databases across languages. *International Journal of Translation, special issue on Lexical Resources for Machine Translation*, 19(1), 2007.

[70] Miriam R. L. Petruck. Towards Hebrew FrameNet. Kernerman Dictionary News Number 13, June 2005.

[71] Kenneth R. Beesley. Arabic morphological analysis on the internet. In *Proceedings of the 6th International Conference and Exhibition on Multi-lingual Computing*, Cambridge, April 1998.

[72] Riyad Al-Shalabi and Martha Evens. A computational morphology system for Arabic. In Michael Rosner, editor, *Proceedings of the Workshop on Computational Approaches to Semitic languages*, pages 66–72, Montreal, Quebec, August 1998. COLING-ACL'98.

[73] Jawad Berri, Hamza Zidoum, and Yacine Atif. Web-based Arabic morphological analyzer. In A. Gelbukh, editor, *CICLing 2001*, number 2004 in Lecture Notes in Computer Science, pages 389–400. Springer Verlag, Berlin, 2001.

[74] Kareem Darwish. Building a shallow Arabic morphological analyzer in one day. In Mike Rosner and Shuly Wintner, editors, *Computational Approaches to Semitic Languages, an ACL'02 Workshop*, pages 47–54, Philadelphia, PA, July 2002.

[75] Imad A. Al-Sughaiyer and Ibrahim A. Al-Kharashi. Arabic morphological analysis techniques: a comprehensive survey. *Journal of the American Society for Information Science and Technology*, 55(3):189–213, 2004.

[76] Nizar Habash. Large scale lexeme based arabic morphological generation. In *Proceedings of Traitement Automatique du Langage Naturel (TALN-04)*, Fez, Morocco, 2004.

[77] Uzzi Ornan. Computer processing of Hebrew texts based on an unambiguous script. *Mishpatim*, 17(2):15–24, September 1987. In Hebrew.

[78] Yaacov Choueka. MLIM - a system for full, exact, on-line grammatical analysis of Modern Hebrew. In Yehuda Eizenberg, editor, *Proceedings of the Annual Conference on Computers in Education*, page 63, Tel Aviv, April 1990. In Hebrew.

[79] Erel Segal. Hebrew morphological analyzer for Hebrew undotted texts. Master's thesis, Technion, Israel Institute of Technology, Haifa, October 1999. In Hebrew.

[80] Shereen Khoja. APT: Arabic part-of-speech tagger. In *Proceedings of the Student Workshop at the Second Meeting of the North American Chapter of the Association for Computational Linguistics (NAACL2001)*, June 2001.

[81] Mona Diab, Kadri Hacioglu, and Daniel Jurafsky. Automatic tagging of Arabic text: From raw text to base phrase chunks. In *Proceedings of HLT-NAACL 2004*, May 2004.

[82] Moshe Levinger, Uzzi Ornan, and Alon Itai. Learning morpho-lexical probabilities from an untagged corpus with an application to Hebrew. *Computational Linguistics*, 21(3):383–404, September 1995.

[83] Aaron Macks. Parsing Akkadian verbs with Prolog. In *Proceedings of the ACL-02 Workshop on Computational Approaches to Semitic Languages*, Philadelphia, 2002.

[84] Saba Amsalu and Dafydd Gibbon. Finite state morphology of Amharic. In *Proceedings of RANLP*, pages 47–51, Borovets, Bulgaria, September 2005.

[85] Sisay Fissaha Adafre. Part of speech tagging for Amharic using conditional random fields. In *Proceedings of the ACL Workshop on Computational Approaches to Semitic Languages*, pages 47–54, Ann Arbor, Michigan, June 2005. Association for Computational Linguistics.

[86] Atelach Alemu Argaw and Lars Asker. An Amharic stemmer: Reducing words to their citation forms. In *Proceedings of the ACL-2007 Workshop on Computational Approaches to Semitic Languages*, Prague, June 2007.

[87] Nizar Habash, Owen Rambow, and George Kiraz. Morphological analysis and generation for Arabic

dialects. In *Proceedings of the ACL Workshop on Computational Approaches to Semitic Languages*, pages 17–24, Ann Arbor, Michigan, June 2005. Association for Computational Linguistics.

[88] Kevin Duh and Katrin Kirchhoff. POS tagging of dialectal Arabic: A minimally supervised approach. In *Proceedings of the ACL Workshop on Computational Approaches to Semitic Languages*, pages 55–62, Ann Arbor, Michigan, June 2005. Association for Computational Linguistics.

[89] Nizar Habash and Owen Rambow. MAGEAD: A morphological analyzer and generator for the Arabic dialects. In *Proceedings of the 21st International Conference on Computational Linguistics and 44th Annual Meeting of the Association for Computational Linguistics*, pages 681–688, Sydney, Australia, July 2006. Association for Computational Linguistics.

[90] Ezra Daya, Dan Roth, and Shuly Wintner. Learning to identify Semitic roots. In Abdelhadi Soudi, Guenter Neumann, and Antal van den Bosch, editors, *Arabic Computational Morphology: Knowledge-based and Empirical Methods*, volume 38 of *Text, Speech and Language Technology*, pages 143–158. Springer, 2007.

[91] Rani Nelken and Stuart M. Shieber. Arabic diacritization using weighted finite-state transducers. In *Proceedings of the ACL Workshop on Computational Approaches to Semitic Languages*, pages 79–86, Ann Arbor, Michigan, June 2005. Association for Computational Linguistics.

[92] Imed Zitouni, Jeffrey S. Sorensen, and Ruhi Sarikaya. Maximum entropy based restoration of Arabic diacritics. In *Proceedings of the 21st International Conference on Computational Linguistics and 44th Annual Meeting of the Association for Computational Linguistics*, pages 577–584, Sydney, Australia, July 2006. Association for Computational Linguistics.

[93] Nizar Habash and Owen Rambow. Arabic diacritization through full morphological tagging. In *Human Language Technologies 2007: The Conference of the North American Chapter of the Association for Computational Linguistics; Companion Volume, Short Papers*, pages 53–56, Rochester, New York, April 2007. Association for Computational Linguistics.

[94] Nizar Habash, Ryan Gabbard, Owen Rambow, Seth Kulick, and Mitch Marcus. Determining case in Arabic: Learning complex linguistic behavior requires complex linguistic features. In *Proceeings of the The 2007 Joint Conference on Empirical Methods in Natural Language Processing and Computational Natural Language Learning (EMNLP-CoNLL 2007)*, Prague, June 2007.

[95] Walid Magdy and Kareem Darwish. Arabic OCR error correction using character segment correction, language modeling, and shallow morphology. In *Proceedings of the 2006 Conference on Empirical Methods in Natural Language Processing*, pages 408–414, Sydney, Australia, July 2006. Association for Computational Linguistics.

[96] Ayman Elnaggar. A phrase structure grammar of the Arabic language. In *Proceedings of the 13th conference on Computational linguistics*, pages 342–344, 1990.

[97] Shuly Wintner and Uzzi Ornan. Syntactic analysis of Hebrew sentences. *Natural Language Engineering*, 1(3):261–288, September 1996.

[98] Michael McCord and Violetta Cavalli-Sforza. An Arabic slot grammar parser. In *Proceedings of the ACL-2007 Workshop on Computational Approaches to Semitic Languages*, Prague, June 2007.

[99] David Chiang, Mona Diab, Nizar Habash, Owen Rambow, and Safiullah Shareef. Parsing Arabic dialects. In *Proceedings of the 11th Conference of the European Chapter of the Association for Computational Linguistics*, pages 369–376, Trento, Italy, April 2006.

[100] Yaser Al-Onaizan and Kevin Knight. Translating named entities using monolingual and bilingual resources. In *Proceedings of the Annual meeting of the Association for Computational Linguistics*, 2002.

[101] Yaser Al-Onaizan and Kevin Knight. Machine transliteration of names in Arabic text. In *Proceedings of the ACL workshop on computational approaches to Semitic languages*, 2002.

[102] Andrew Freeman, Sherri Condon, and Christopher Ackerman. Cross linguistic name matching in English and Arabic. In *Proceedings of the Human Language Technology Conference of the NAACL, Main Conference*, pages 471–478, New York City, USA, June 2006. Association for Computational Linguistics.

[103] Abraham Ittycheriah and Salim Roukos. A maximum entropy word aligner for Arabic-English machine translation. In *Proceedings of Human Language Technology Conference and Conference on Empirical Methods in Natural Language Processing*, pages 89–96, Vancouver, British Columbia, Canada, October 2005. Association for Computational Linguistics.

[104] Anas El Isbihani, Shahram Khadivi, Oliver Bender, and Hermann Ney. Morpho-syntactic Arabic preprocessing for Arabic to English statistical machine translation. In *Proceedings on the Workshop on*

Statistical Machine Translation, pages 15–22, New York City, June 2006. Association for Computational Linguistics.

[105] Fatiha Sadat and Nizar Habash. Combination of Arabic preprocessing schemes for statistical machine translation. In *Proceedings of the 21st International Conference on Computational Linguistics and 44th Annual Meeting of the Association for Computational Linguistics*, pages 1–8, Sydney, Australia, July 2006. Association for Computational Linguistics.

[106] Andreas Zollmann, Ashish Venugopal, and Stephan Vogel. Bridging the inflection morphology gap for Arabic statistical machine translation. In *Proceedings of the Human Language Technology Conference of the NAACL, Companion Volume: Short Papers*, pages 201–204, New York City, USA, June 2006. Association for Computational Linguistics.

[107] Mehdi M. Kashani, Eric Joanis, Roland Kuhn, George Foster, and Fred Popowich. Integration of an Arabic transliteration module into a statistical machine translation system. In *Proceedings of the Second Workshop on Statistical Machine Translation*, pages 17–24, Prague, Czech Republic, June 2007. Association for Computational Linguistics.

[108] Alon Lavie, Shuly Wintner, Yaniv Eytani, Erik Peterson, and Katharina Probst. Rapid prototyping of a transfer-based Hebrew-to-English machine translation system. In *Proceedings of TMI-2004: The 10th International Conference on Theoretical and Methodological Issues in Machine Translation*, Baltimore, MD, October 2004.

Language Engineering for Lesser-Studied Languages
S. Nirenburg (Ed.)
IOS Press, 2009

doi:10.3233/978-1-58603-954-7-291

Low-Density Language Strategies for Persian and Armenian

Karine MEGERDOOMIAN
The MITRE Corporation, McLean, Virginia, USA

Abstract. This paper presents research on the feasibility and development of methods for the rapid creation of stopgap language technology resources for low-density languages. The focus is on two broad strategies: (i) *related language bootstrapping* can be used to port existing technology from a resource-rich language to its associated lower-density variant; and (ii) clever use of linguistic knowledge can be employed to *scale down* the need for large amount of training or development data. Based on Persian and Armenian languages, the paper illustrates several methods that can be implemented in each instance in the goal of reducing human effort and avoiding the scarce data issue faced by statistical systems.

Keywords. low-resource languages, machine translation, linguistic development, Persian, Armenian

Introduction

Low-density languages, for which few online or computational resources exist[1], raise difficulties for standard natural language processing approaches that depend on machine learning techniques. These systems require large corpora, typically aligned parallel text or annotated documents, in order to train the statistical algorithms. As most of the languages in the world are considered to be low-density [1], there is an urgent need to develop strategies for rapidly creating new resources and retargeting existing technologies to these languages.

Recent methodologies have been developed for using web data to automatically create language corpora, mine linguistic data, or build lexicons and ontologies, while other approaches have focused on creating more efficient and robust techniques for identifying and locating existing web-based data for low-density languages [2]. Researchers have also exploited the application of available resources for developing systems or tools for low-resource languages by eliciting a corpus or language patterns [3,4], by bootstrapping resources for other languages [5,6], or by developing methods that require a smaller set of annotated data ([7,8], among others). This paper argues that different low-density languages require distinct strategies in order to rapidly build computational resources. By studying three specific cases – Tajiki Persian, conversational Iranian Persian found in weblogs and forums, and Eastern Armenian – we illustrate methodologies for cleverly reusing existing resources for these new

[1] The terms *low-density, lesser used, lesser studied*, and *minority languages* are often used interchangeably in the literature. These terminologies are not necessarily equivalent as certain majority languages commonly used in a society may still lack online resources and technologies (cf. Section 3). The terms *sparse-data, resource-poor* or *low-resource languages* are better suited to describe the languages discussed in this paper.

languages. The focus of this paper is on non-probabilistic methods for system development; however, the main argument that a more intimate knowledge of the context and characteristics of each language should be taken into account prior to development is also relevant for statistical approaches.

1. Strategies for low-density languages

As Maxwell and Hughes [1] point out, the obvious solution for dealing with the data acquisition bottleneck for low-density languages is to concentrate on the creation of more annotated resources. This is, however, an extremely time-consuming and labor-intensive task. A complementary approach, therefore, is for the research community to improve the way the information in smaller resources is used. To accomplish this goal, Maxwell and Hughes suggest two possible strategies:

(i) Scaling down: Develop algorithms or methods that would require less data; and
(ii) Bootstrapping: Transfer relevant linguistic information from existing tools and resources for resource-rich languages to a lower-density language.

In the case of statistical systems, scaling down could consist of downscaling state of the art algorithms by reducing the training data required for various tasks such as POS tagging, named entity recognition, and parsing. One such approach is active learning, where the annotation is performed and enhanced on samples that will best improve the learning algorithm thus requiring less annotation effort [9]. In addition, bootstrapping approaches have been implemented in cross-language knowledge induction, sometimes using comparable rather than parallel data (see [10] and references therein). In this paper, we introduce novel methods using non-probabilistic techniques and addressing both of these strategies. Bootstrapping is explored for related language pairs, where the existing resources and systems developed for a higher-density language can be used with little effort to build resources for the low-density variant. This approach is combined with the development of linguistic knowledge components that do not require large corpora and are thus especially suitable for low-resource languages. However, the paper advocates proper analysis of the linguistic context prior to actual development and illustrates methods for minimizing the human effort involved by focusing on linguistic properties that will provide the most gain for the new language system.

The paper targets three scenarios: Section 2 focuses on Tajiki Persian, which is a lower density variant of standard Iranian Persian. These languages have developed independently due to historical and political reasons and use distinct writing systems, yet the literary written forms of the two related languages remain almost identical. In Section 3, we look at the effect of *diglossia* in Iran where two distinct and significantly different variants of the language coexist. The "literary" form of Persian has traditionally been used in almost all forms of writing, while the "conversational" variant typically used in oral communication, is nowadays appearing more and more frequently in weblogs and forums. Existing computational systems for Persian have been developed for the literary language and face challenges in processing the conversational variant. Finally, Eastern Armenian is considered in Section 4. The computational resources for this language are extremely scarce and it is unrelated to other resource-rich languages.

The paper argues that in each instance, a different strategy should be implemented to obtain the most beneficial results. This requires some preliminary analysis of context, language relatedness, and availability of existing resources for the related languages. In the first two instances consisting of Tajiki Persian and conversational Iranian Persian, a form of *related language bootstrapping* can be employed, with an eye on the existing gaps and specific characteristics of the low-density language. In the case where no related language resources can be located as in the case of Eastern Armenian, there is a need to build a system based on linguistic knowledge. In this instance, however, the portability and modularity of the language processing system is crucial as we are now able to reuse components and tools to create and extend existing resources.

2. Tajiki Persian

There exist three distinct main varieties of Persian spoken in Iran (sometimes referred to as *Farsi*), Afghanistan (also known as *Dari*), and *Tajik* spoken in Tajikistan as well as by the substantial Tajik minority within Afghanistan. There is currently a rich set of computational resources for Iranian Persian such as online corpora, parallel text, online lexicons, spellcheckers, morphological analyzers, machine translation engines, speech processing systems, and entity extraction tools. The online resources for Tajiki Persian, however, are extremely scarce and computational systems have not been developed for this lower-density variety of Persian. Iranian Persian and Tajiki Persian have developed independently, resulting in linguistic differences especially in the domains of pronunciation and lexical inventory. In addition, Iranian Persian is written in an extended version of the Arabic script, referred to as the Perso-Arabic writing system, whereas Tajiki Persian uses an extended version of the Cyrillic script. The literary written forms of these two languages, however, are almost identical. It is therefore possible to take advantage of the relatedness of these languages in order to create certain resources and build stopgap systems for Tajiki Persian with very little effort.

This section presents recent work that attempts to build a preliminary Tajik-to-English machine translation system by building a mapping transducer from Tajik in Cyrillic script to its Perso-Arabic equivalent, which is then fed through an existing Iranian Persian MT engine [11]. The mapping correspondences between these two writing systems, however, are nontrivial and the distinct patterns of language contact and development in Tajiki Persian and Iranian Persian give rise to a number of ambiguities that need to be resolved.

2.1. The Writing Systems of Persian

Iranian Persian (henceforth IP) uses an extended version of the Arabic script; it includes, in addition, the letters for پ /p/, گ /g/, ژ /zh/ and چ /ch/. Although Persian has maintained the original orthography of Arabic borrowings, the pronunciation of these words have been adapted to Persian which lacks certain phonemes such as interdentals and emphatic alveolars. Hence, the three distinct letters س, ص, and ث are all pronounced /s/. One of the main characteristics of the script is the absence of capitalization and diacritics (including certain vowels) in most written text, adding to the ambiguity for computational analysis. Further ambiguities arise due to the fact that in online text, certain morphemes can appear either attached to the stem form or separated from it by an intervening space or control character.

Tajiki Persian is based on the Cyrillic alphabet. It also includes several additional characters that represent Persian sounds not existent in Russian. These are ҳ= /h/, ҷ = /j/, қ = /q/, ғ = /gh/, ӯ = /ö/, ӣ = /i/. Tajiki text is much less ambiguous than its corresponding IP script as all the vowels are generally represented in this writing system and capitalization is used for proper names and at the beginning of sentences. The orthography corresponds more directly to the Persian language pronunciation. For instance, the sounds /s/ and /t/ are represented with the Cyrillic character 'с' and 'т' respectively, regardless of the original spelling. The divergent pronunciation of the two language variants is also represented in the writing. Hence, the two distinct pronunciations of *shir* 'milk' and *sheyr* 'lion' in Tajiki Persian are also depicted in the orthography as шир and шер, respectively, preserving a distinction previously held in Classical Persian, while in Modern Iranian Persian they are both written and pronounced identically as شیر (*shir*). On the other hand, IP makes a distinction between *pul* 'money' and *pol* 'bridge', whereas Tajiki Persian pronounces both as пул (*pol*) [12].

Идеяи таъсиси телевизюни муштарак ду соли кабл, дар дидори руасои чумхури се кишвар пешниход шуда буд.

ایده تاسیس تلویزیون مشترک تاجیکستان، ایران، افغانستان دو سال قبل در دیدار روسای جمهوری سه کشور پیشنهاد شده بود.

Figure 1. Sample Tajiki and Iranian Persian writing systems (*source:* BBC Persian)

2.2. Issues in Mapping

The correspondence between Tajiki and Iranian Persian scripts is not always trivial. In certain instances, a basic letter correspondence can help achieve a correct map from Tajik into Iranian Persian as shown in Table 1. Consonants typically display a one-to-one correspondence in the two scripts. In addition, the most frequent representation of the /a/ sound is the letter 'o' in Tajik and the *alef* character 'ا' in IP as shown.

Table 1. Direct mapping of Tajiki to Farsi script

китобҳо	کتابها	*ketâbhâ*	'books'
коршиносони	کارشناسان	*kârshenâsâne*	'experts of'
мардум	مردم	*mardom*	'people'
вокунише	واکنشی	*vâkoneshi*	'a reaction'
корманди давлати	کارمند دولتی	*kârmande dowlati*	'government worker'

However, ambiguities arise at several levels. For instance, the Iranian Persian writing system includes three distinct letters representing the /s/ sound, four characters corresponding to /z/, two letters for /t/, and two different letters pronounced as /h/, due to the original orthography of the borrowed Arabic words. Hence, a basic mapping to the most common character results in divergences from standard orthography. For instance, the Tajik word Фурсат 'opportunity' may be mapped into the Perso-Arabic script as فرست (with a *sin* character), as فرثت (with a *se*) or as فرصت (with a *sat*), but only the latter is the correct Iranian Persian spelling. This word is actually more ambiguous than shown since the /t/ sound, the last character, is itself ambiguous between *te* 'ت' or *ta* 'ط'; thus this Tajiki word has six possible mappings, of which only one is correct.

Another major divergence comes from the distinct representations of the diacritic vowels – /æ/, /e/ and /o/ – in everyday writing. These vowels can be written in many ways in Perso-Arabic script. The Tajiki letter 'и', for instance, generally maps to the /e/ diacritic in Persian (also known as *zir*) which is often not represented in the written form, hence in the word китоби only the four letters 'к', 'т', 'о' and 'б' will be mapped. However, 'и' can also be mapped to 'ی' (*ye*) in the IP script as in фаронсавиҳо 'the French' which is written as فرانسویها (*færansæviha*) in Perso-Arabic.

Certain positional cues, however, can help disambiguate the character in Perso-Arabic script. For instance, the /æ/ sound is typically represented as 'a' in Tajik but is not written in Iranian Persian as can be seen in the transliteration of the Perso-Arabic orthography of the first example in Table 2. Yet, it can also appear as an *alef* in Perso-Arabic script if it appears in the beginning of the word as in the second example shown, or as a *'h'* if it is at the end of the word as illustrated in the third example in the table.

Table 2. Contextual cues in mapping

Tajik	Perso-Arabic	Transliteration	English
п**а**йом**а**дҳои	پیامدهای	pyamdhay	'consequences of'
анҷуман	انجمن	**a**njmn	'organization'
қоъид**а**	قاعده	qaed**h**	'regulation'

There are also factors beyond the level of the word. In written IP, if a suffix follows a word ending in the sound /e/ (which is written with the letter *he* 'ه'), it can never be attached to the preceding word. The suffixes in Tajiki Persian, however, appear attached to the end of the word. Examples are the plural morpheme /ha/ written attached in Tajik (қоъида**ҳо**) and detached in Iranian Persian (**قاعده‌ها**), or the auxiliary verb /æst/ 'is' again represented attached to the verb in Tajik (шуда**аст**) and written independently in IP (شده است). Even more problematic is the fact that a number of compound nouns are written as a single unit in Tajiki Persian while their subparts remain detached in the Perso-Arabic script in IP. For instance, the compound noun *riyasæt-jomhuri* 'the presidency' (literally "the directorship of the republic") is represented in Tajik as раёсатҷумҳурии, whereas it consists of two independent words in IP: ریاستجمهوری. Furthermore, Iranian and Tajiki Persian have differing patterns of contact, which in turn leads to different patterns of borrowed words. The choice of orthography makes a difference, as well: whereas Western terms borrowed into Iranian Persian must be reformulated in Perso-Arabic, the use of Cyrillic in Tajik allows for Russian terms (as well as other languages in contact from former Soviet republics, such as Uzbek) to be preserved in the original orthography instead of adapting to the Tajiki pattern. For instance, the month October in Iranian Persian is a borrowing from French and is represented as اکتبر /oktobr/ while it is written as in Russian октябр in Tajiki Persian.

Further ambiguities arise if the input source does not take advantage of the extended Tajiki script. For instance, BBC Persian documents written in Tajiki Persian use the same character 'г' to represent both /g/ and /gh/ (the latter is written as ғ in the extended Tajiki script). The unavailability of the full extended script inevitably gives rise to further ambiguities in mapping.

The issues discussed in this section suggest the need for an intelligent mapping algorithm and strategies for disambiguating the obtained results. In addition, a morphological analyzer component is needed to handle the segmentation issues presented.

2.3. System description

Based on the abovementioned descriptive study of the correspondences between the Tajiki Persian and Iranian Persian writing systems, a proof-of-concept Tajik system can be developed based on existing IP tools in order to serve as a stopgap measure until language-specific resources can be built. To begin with, an extensive finite-state transducer (FST) is written that converts Tajik text to Perso-Arabic script. The point of such an FST is to overgenerate, since as described above, many segments may represent several potential spellings in the target script. The potential combinatorial explosion is controlled using contextual rules that help to disambiguate the output, exemplified in Figure 2, as well as available Iranian Persian resources (lexicon, morphological analyzer).

```
# Add alef under diacritic at the beginning of the word
define initialA [(Aa) <- a || .#. _ ];

# Represent the /a/ sound at the end of the word (marked
# by WD tag) as 'he'
define silentH [h <- a %^WD];
```

Figure 2. Contextual rules for mapping Tajiki 'a'

Where there is still ambiguity between forms even after a lookup, a variety of disambiguation strategies such as statistical language modeling using Iranian Persian corpora could also be employed. Lexical divergences such as borrowings from Russian will need to be handled in a pre-processing step of looking up Cyrillic terms in a special lexicon with their corresponding Persian terms. As these terms are merged in with the FST/lookup table output, the results of the transformation improve. Finally, the output is run through a commercially available Persian to English machine translation engine. The final end-to-end system thus results in a rapidly developed

Tajik to English MT system without the benefit of Tajik-language resources. The rest of this section provides further details on the various components in the system.

The transliteration is developed using Xerox Finite-State Technology [13]. A basic grammar is written allowing any combinations of Tajiki characters to form a word. The grammar is compiled into a finite-state transducer (FST) where the lower side consists of the input string and the upper side provides the transliterated form of the word. A number of contextual rules are composed on the FST, as exemplified in Figure 2, thus performing the required orthographic and phonological alternations on the word forms based on the position of the character within the word. If contextual cues are unable to produce a single mapped output, the transducer creates all possible results for each input token, which is then disambiguated at the next stage in the process. For each input token, the resulting transliterated Iranian Persian words undergo morphological analysis and lexicon look-up to determine possible lexical items [14]. If an analysis is found, then the form is used. If there is no analysis, the word is matched against an unstemmed wordlist culled from various Persian corpora. If still no match is located, a number of "rules of thumb" are employed to select a likely alternative based on letter frequencies. Figure 3 shows the results of disambiguation when the morphological analyzer/lexicon combination works successfully.

1 alternatives (12 originally)
سخنگوی sxngv+Noun+sg+ez [speaker;spokesman;]

1 alternatives (1 originally)
بانک bank+Noun+sg [bank;]

1 alternatives (32 originally)
تاجیکستان taJykstan+PropN [Tajikistan;]

1 alternatives (12 originally)
پرداخته‌است prdaxtn+Verb+ind+perf.past+3sg [pay;attend;]

Figure 3. Disambiguated analyses

2.4. Evaluation

The results of the preliminary evaluation show that the current system is able to achieve 89.8% accuracy for an input corpus that uses the extended version of the Tajiki script. The transliterated document can then be used with the Language Weaver Persian-to-English MT system to create translations of the original Tajiki text.

Our current test corpus consists of approximately 500,000 words from articles taken from Radio Ozodi (the Tajik broadcast of Radio Free Europe). As a beginning testbed, this seemed ideal, since the domain largely matches the training corpora of commercial Persian MT systems such as Language Weaver Persian, and unlike several other sources, the full range of Tajik diacritics are used; later refinements will have to take into account defective orthography used by many electronic sources. At this early stage, a small test set of 6,156 tokens was run through the morphological analyzer and lexical lookup and evaluated against a golden truth corpus. The results show that the current system is able to achieve 89.8% accuracy in transliterating a document in Tajiki script to its Iranian Persian equivalent. In other words, in the case of 89.8% of input tokens, there was at least one correct transliterated form which was used as input to the MT component. The average token returned with 6.27 alternative spellings. Further analysis on the larger corpus is needed to determine the accurate level of precision and recall for various input documents.[2]

2.5. Summary

This section presented a methodology for the rapid creation of language technology resources for Tajiki Persian by taking advantage of existing resources and systems developed for the higher-density variety of Iranian Persian. It is expected that in the long term, stopgap systems like the one proposed here will be replaced with fully-developed MT based on the cultivating of resources, parallel corpora, rule development, and so forth. In the meantime, a comprehensive finite-state transducer is developed based on a preliminary study of the similarities and differences of correspondences in the two writing systems which, combined with simple scripts to integrate the results with existing Iranian Persian resources, provides a first draft Tajik to English machine translation system. The results documented are still at the preliminary stages; nevertheless, the approach has been proven effective for rapidly building translation capabilities for a language with scarce resources, in case a related higher-density language with a distinct writing system is available. The transliteration transducer requires very little human effort and a very small corpus is needed for testing purposes. In addition, it is hypothesized that this methodology can be used across a variety of unevenly dense languages with distinct scripts, such as Hindustani (Hindi, Urdu), the Turkic languages (Turkish, Azeri, Uzbek, Uighur), and Kurdish (Kurmanji and Sorani).

3. Persian Weblogs

Since its beginnings in 2001, the Persian blogosphere has undergone a dramatic growth making Persian one of the top ten languages of the global blog community in 2007 [15]. The Persian blogosphere[3] has opened the door to journalists, intellectuals, and University students who use blogs to evade government censorship or social and political restrictions, as well as conservative individuals who discuss various religious or political topics online [16]. This new medium has also provided a forum for bloggers to express their opinions and thoughts in their everyday speech rather than the traditional literary language. This creates a new challenge for the analysis of Persian language websites as current grammars and academic textbooks of Persian focus mainly on the literary dialect and existing text-based computational systems often fail to analyze or process conversational Persian.

3.1. Language of blogs

The *diglossic* situation of Persian, whereby two distinct varieties of the language coexist in the society, is also reflected in the language found in the Iranian blog

[2] For a more detailed discussion of results, see [11].

[3] The focus of this paper is on weblogs in Iran and among the Iranian expatriate community and the proliferation of Persian language blogs in Afghanistan is not studied.

community. Traditionally, Persian literature and news media have been written in the literary dialect which holds a higher prestige over the conversational form of the language. Although the latter has been used in some works of modern literature, its usage is generally limited to the informal, conversational domains and is rarely seen in written form. With the advent of blogs, the restrictions against the use of the conversational dialect in writing have been challenged and, despite strong criticisms from intellectuals and professional journalists, bloggers often use the conversational Persian variant in their posts.

Preliminary exploration of the language of Persian blogs shows parallels with English Blogspeak. As noted by Crystal [17] for English, the content of a site (e.g., information, political opinion, education, personal diary) strongly influences the general character of the language being used leading to linguistic variation on the Internet. This observation holds for the Persian language websites as well. Hence in both English and Persian, the language of blogs that address personal thoughts, opinions, and issues has been characterized as a conversational style in writing. Non-standard spelling that reflects the colloquial pronunciation of words is often used. Blog entries are usually written in short sentences and include a large number of hyperlinks. Deviant spelling is common and standard orthography is often ignored, opting instead for a more intimate style. Emotions are expressed with emoticons, ellipsis, repetition of letters and punctuation marks, and emphasis is shown with capitals and special symbols. Jargons and neologisms abound in Blogspeak, especially based on technical or computer-related terms.

Persian Blogspeak differs from that of English, however, due to its strong diglossic situation. While syntactic or grammatical variation is less frequent in English, the distinction between the literary and conversational language is especially poignant in Persian, affecting morphology and syntax as well. Persian Blogspeak often includes properties corresponding to the conversational language such as shortened verbal stems, frequent use of attached pronoun forms, and affixes that are not part of the standard formal grammar. There are more instances of free word order, idiomatic expressions, loan words, and an inordinate amount of orthographic variance partly due to the flexibility and ambiguity of the Perso-Arabic script. This section presents an overview of some of these characteristics and the ambiguities and challenges they raise for computational processing.

Persian morphology is affixal, consisting mainly of suffixes and prefixes, which generally follow a regular morphotactic order. Ambiguities arise in a computational analysis due to the use of the Arabic script since certain vowels are not marked in written text and spacing between words and morphemes is sometimes inconsistent. Furthermore, some affixes can represent different morphemes. For instance, the suffix -ی '-*i*' as in مردی (*mærdi*) can be an indefinite article (a man), a relativizing particle (the man (that)), the second person singular form of the copula verb 'to be' (you are a man), or a derivational form creating adjectives out of nouns (manhood, manliness)[4]. In addition, the lack of capitalization and short vowels can add to the ambiguity since the word can also be analyzed as the Nigerian province 'Maradi' or the verbal form *mordi* 'you died'.

Conversational forms of morphemes give rise to further ambiguity. For instance, *zænha* 'women' would be pronounced as *zæna* in the conversational variant. Since the /æ/ vowel is not usually written in Persian script, it would have the form زنا [zna] in a

[4] There is less ambiguity in speech since the stress pattern can distinguish some of the constructions.

text. Without the overt vowel in the first syllable, however, the word is now ambiguous between *zæna* 'women' and *zena* 'adultery'. Another instance of ambiguity arising from the conversational orthographic form can be found with words that end in the sound /e/ which is written as a 'h'. In conversational speech, the word-final /e/ assimilates (or merges) with the following /æ/ sound of some affixes. For example, the word *khune* 'house' when used with the pronominal suffix *–æm* becomes *khunæm* in the spoken language, meaning 'my house'. It is often represented as in خونم [xvnm] in the written form on blogs, which becomes ambiguous with the word *khunæm* meaning 'my blood' written exactly the same way. There is no ambiguity in the spoken language since the stress pattern of the words distinguish the two constructions: *khunÆm* 'my house' vs. *khUnæm* 'my blood'; yet the orthographic forms remain ambiguous.

The use of conversational language in writing introduces a number of affixes that can never be found in traditional literary text, such as the definite suffix '*e*' as in *ketab**e*** 'the book' or *forushænde**he*** 'the salesperson'. The area that has undergone the most change is probably the verbal domain, where not only the inflectional endings are modified but many of the verbal stems are also shortened. Hence, the literary form *miguyænd* 'they say' has become *migæn*, or *miændazæd* 'he/she throws' is pronounced *mindaze*, making it impossible for a system trained on literary text to analyze the conversational forms. In addition, conversational language makes more use of affixes where the literary language would use separate tokens. This is illustrated in the examples in Table 3 contrasting literary and conversational forms for the same sentences, with contrasting elements shown in bold.

Table 3. Conversational and literary corresponding forms in Persian

Literary form	**Conversational form**
استرس امتحان **مرا گرفته است** *(estrese emtehan **mæra gerefte æst**)* stress-of exam **me caught is** 'The stress of the exam has got me'	استرس امتحان **گرفته تم** *(estrese emtehan **gereftætæm**)* stress-of exam **caught-3sg-me** 'The stress of the exam has got me'
گرگ **او را می خورد** *(gorg **u ra mikhoræd**)* wolf **him Obj is-eating** 'The wolf is eating him'	گرگه **میخورتش** *(gorge **mikhorætæsh**)* wolf-def **is-eating-3sg-him** 'The wolf is eating him'

Since the writing in blogs more directly reflects the way people speak, changes in the pronunciation of Persian are represented in blog text as well. Examples include:

- the alternation of /an/ to /un/ in words like *nan* 'bread' → *nun*, *zendani* 'prisoner' → *zenduni*, or *tehran* 'Tehran' → *te:run*[5]
- the assimilation of /n/ to /m/ before /b/ as in *shænbe* 'Saturday' → *shæmbe* or *tænbæl* 'lazy' → *tæmbæl*
- the elimination of /t/ in /st/ clusters in words like *bæstæni* 'ice cream' → *bæssæni*, or *kojast* 'where is it?' → *kojas*

Blogs contain a large number of loanwords, especially from English which currently exerts a big influence on Persian because of computers and technology. Scientific and technological terms are widely used on blogs. This is in particular

[5] /:/ represents a lengthened vowel.

intensified when the Iranian government tries to crack down on the blogs, and bloggers begin posting ways to break the filtering technologies and provide technical support to each other online. These words of course follow the morphological rules of Persian and can take affixes as in *filteringeshun* (فیلترینگشون) = *filtering* 'filtering' + *eshun* 'their' ('their [attempts at/act of] filtering'). Examples of technical terms borrowed from English are: *anlayn* (آنلاین), *pablish* (پابلیش), *chætrum* (چتروم), *imeyl* (ای‌میل), *monitowr* (مونیتور), *es-em-es* (اس‌ام‌اس), *di-vi-di* (دی‌وی‌دی), *vindoz* (ویندوز), *afis* (آفیس), *fotoshap* (فتوشاپ), *kibord* (کیبورد). Other English and older French loans are also quite common: *pazel* (پازل) 'puzzle', *partner* (پارتنر) 'partner', *holokast* (هولوکاست) 'holocaust', *nostalzhi* (نوستالژی) 'nostalgy', *seksualite* (سکسوالیته) 'sexuality'.

One of the more striking aspects of Blogspeak, however, is the amount of neologisms or new words created by bloggers, typically using a loan word as the base combined with Persian language word-formation patterns. They include frequent words such as *linkduni* (لینکدونی) which literally means a storage place for links and corresponds to the English term 'blogroll', *tabusazi* (تابوسازی) meaning the act of making something taboo, or *filtershekæn* (فیلترشکن) literally meaning filter-breaker and referring to anti-filter software. Similarly, a number of new verbs have been formed by combining a loanword with a light verb such as *kærdæn* 'to do' or *zædæn* 'to hit'[6]. Examples of these new constructions are *chæt kærdæn* (چت کردن) 'to chat', *hæk kærdæn* (هک کردن) 'to hack', and *imeyl zædæn* (ای‌میل زدن) 'to email'. More recently, verbs are formed on the simple verb construction pattern instead of the compound forms above by adding the *–idæn* infinitival morpheme, forming the verbs *klikidæn* (کلیکیدن) 'to click', *danlodidæn* (دانلودیدن) 'to download', and *lagidæn* (لاگیدن) 'to blog'.

Misspellings are very common in weblogs, but sometimes they are done on purpose as for the many forms of spelling the word *seks* (سکس) 'sex' in order to be able to discuss a very taboo subject in Iranian society among the youth without being subject to filtering by the government. Bloggers write this word with the various characters representing the /s/ sound in Persian: صکص, ثکث, ثکص. In addition, the spelling of some words of Arabic origin are being modified by bloggers to represent their current pronunciation in Persian. Examples are the words that end in a "tanvin" as in لطفا [lTfa] 'please' which is now sometimes spelled with a /n/ as in لطفن [lTfn] to reflect the actual pronunciation *lotfæn*. Similarly, موسی [mvsy] 'Moses' and حتی [Hty] 'even' are now often spelled as موسا [mvsa] and حتا [Hta] to represent their pronunciations as *musa* and *hæta*, respectively.

As these examples show, the variant forms introduced by writing the conversational form of Persian add to the complexity and ambiguity of computational processing. As discussed earlier, there are also syntactic distinctions between the literary and conversational variants of Persian as conversational text contains more instances of scrambling (permutations of word order), topicalization, idiomatic expressions, and cultural inferences. This diversity is accentuated by variants of orthographic forms found online as each social group has defined its own standards or writing approaches: (i) the traditional orthography taught at school and recommended by the Persian Language Academy has strict rules of spelling and spacing; (ii) journalist and intellectual bloggers have recently proposed their own guidelines for

[6] Light verb constructions are very pervasive in Persian and consist of a preverbal element (noun, adjective or preposition) followed by a verb that is somewhat bleached in meaning called a "light verb".

Persian orthography that differ from the traditional rules; and (iii) bloggers using conversational language, mostly the youth, write the words as they are pronounced in spoken Persian and do not have any set standards.

3.2. Computational Processing of Blogspeak

As most existing computational systems of Persian have been developed for formal writing usually found in news reports, we expect that they would fail to successfully process the elements found in conversational blog text. This section describes the results of an evaluation performed on an existing morphological analyzer to confirm that the presence of conversational forms strongly hinders computational processing of Persian text. It is reasonable, however, to take advantage of these existing resources for building tools to process Persian Blogspeak which includes both literary and conversational variants. Although syntactic structures are also affected, the fundamental distinction between modern conversational Persian and literary Persian lies at the word level, ranging from choice of lexical items and inflection of word forms to orthographic variance. This suggests that it may be advantageous to extend an existing morphological analyzer for Persian to cover the conversational forms of the language.

Table 4. Ground truth files: Percent of conversation forms in each post

Topic	Total Entries	Conversational Entries in Text						% of Conv. in text
		Verb	Non-Verbal	Closed Class	Loans	Foreign Words	Interj	
News	271	0	0	0	0	0	0	0.00%
News	141	0	0	0	0	0	0	0.00%
Politics	219	8	0	3	1	0	0	5.5%
Politics/Book	467	45	13	20	3	0	2	17.8%
Politics	340	31	19	20	3	0	2	22.1%
Journal	391	33	16	34	0	0	5	22.5%
Journal	725	55	51	49	13	1	4	23.9%
Tech/Book	326	25	14	15	20	5	2	24.9%
Journal	16	0	0	4	0	0	0	25.0%
Tech/ Blogs	147	20	5	18	8	1	0	35.4%
Tech/ Blogs	150	14	8	20	11	3	0	37.3%
TOTAL NUMBERS:	**3193**	**231**	**126**	**183**	**59**	**10**	**15**	**19.5%**

A morphological analysis tool that can process conversational text found in blogs and offer the literary Persian equivalent will be able to associate blog vocabulary with dictionary forms which could ultimately benefit applications from Part-of-Speech (POS) tagging to machine translation and entity extraction. Such a task, however, may require a lot of human effort given the large amount of variance in conversational text. It is therefore beneficial to first perform a study to determine the most efficient way of extending the morphological system, allowing us to cleverly bootstrap existing resources. This section describes the results of such a study.

For the purpose of the evaluation, we selected a unification-based Persian morphological analyzer that was developed for processing literary Persian text [14]. The study was run on a small sample of blog posts collected from popular Persian blog sites[7] containing various topics ranging from personal journals to discussions of societal issues, to technical and computer-related subjects. Each post was manually annotated for Part of Speech information in order to develop a ground truth totaling 3,193 entries (including compounds). The number of entries in each document displaying conversational text characteristics was computed and can be seen in Table 4. As can be seen from the table, the two news-related posts did not contain any conversational forms at all. Some conversational morphology was found in the files related to politics, but the posts categorized as journals have a higher rate of conversational morphology and lexical items. Discussions of technical issues (often related to filtering and ways to avoid them) contain a large number of loans and foreign words. The results of the evaluation were judged based on accuracy and ambiguity level and are illustrated in Figure 4.

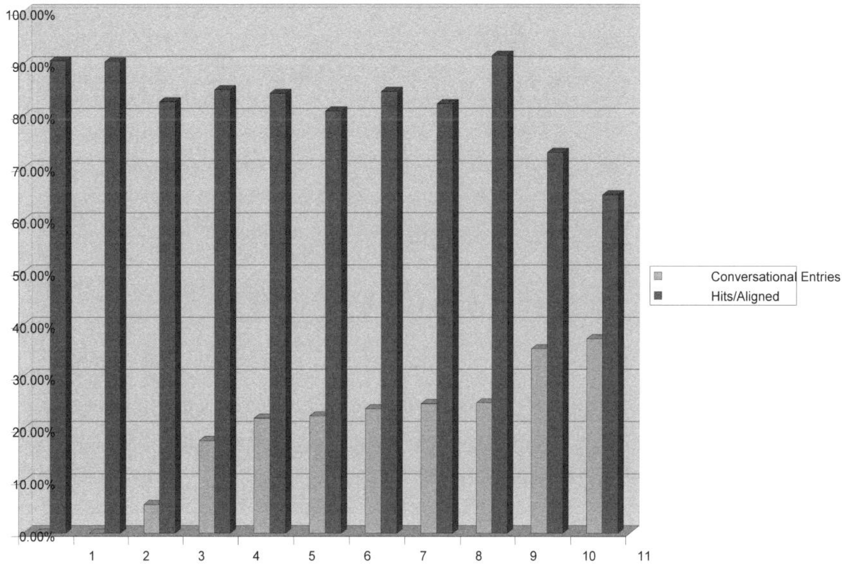

Figure 4. Correlation of conversational entry and accuracy of POS tag per correctly aligned entry

For each post, the system results were compared to the ground truth files by taking into account the number of correct alignments of the word entries, the number of correct POS tags, and the ambiguity the system generated in each instance – where ambiguity is defined as the number of POS tags in the system output, divided by the total number of entries in the output. The results shown in Figure 4 indicate a clear correlation between the percent of conversational entries in a blog post vs. the hits per correctly aligned entries in the document. The figure illustrates that the morphological analyzer tends to get better scores for the news items that have very low or null conversational entries. The lowest accuracy scores were obtained for the last two files that have the highest number of conversational forms. The only obvious exception to this pattern is file #9, which had a relatively high number of conversational forms but showed high accuracy scores; this file was a very short blog post consisting of only two

[7] The sites were www.khorshidkhanoom.com, www.z8un.blogfa.com, and www.4shanbe.blogfa.com.

sentences (16 entries). Figure 5 also shows that, as the level of conversational forms in the text increases, the ambiguity also seems to increase. This indicates that the morphological system encounters more unknowns in the text and thus generates more guesses as to their POS tag. The correlations noted in the results thus suggest a direct correspondence between the number of conversational forms in a text and the difficulty of analysis for the system.

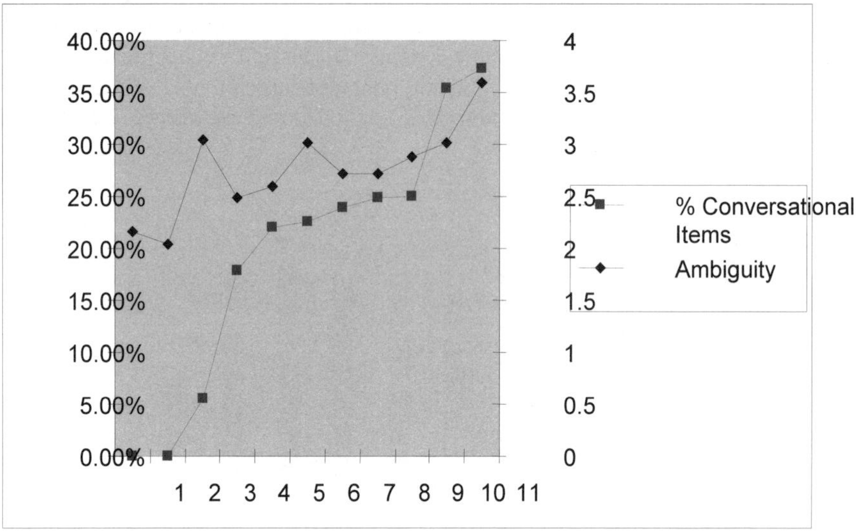

Figure 5. Correlation of conversational entries and ambiguity per system analysis

The total accuracy score obtained for all blog posts was 84%. A close examination of the results showed that a large majority of the correctly tagged entries (97%) were of literary form, while only 3% were conversational entries which were guessed correctly by the system. From the mistagged entries, on the other hand, a majority of 78% were conversational entries, as illustrated in Table 5.

Table 5. Breakdown of accuracy results

	Literary	**Conversational**
Correctly Tagged	97%	3%
Incorrectly Tagged	22%	78%

The results suggest that the presence of conversational forms in text does play a significant role in morphological analysis for tools developed primarily based on literary Persian. The statistical results suggest a direct correlation between the number of conversational forms and reduced performance. In addition, a closer examination shows that the majority of mistagged elements are of conversational form. A system that provides guesses based on word forms can provide better results although the ambiguity is increased as more (unknown) conversational forms are encountered in text. Based on these results, one can conclude that the presence of conversational forms negatively impacts the output of the morphological analyzer. The study also suggests that starting from an existing morphological analyzer for Persian, an analyzer can be developed to recognize the various conversational forms encountered in blog text. A closer examination, however, shows that in order for the extended system to be efficient, the additions can be performed in stages beginning with modifications that bear the most result. Table 6 provides a breakdown of the literary and conversational system tags for a small representative sample based on Part-of-Speech category. Note that these represent the number of entries tagged with a particular POS in the ground truth; hence we have counted each entry whether it was previously encountered or not (e.g., the postposition mistagged 7 times was the same one, namely the object marker *ro* in its conversational form).

Table 6. System tags analyzed per POS category

POS	Literary Matched	Literary Mismatched	Conversational Guessed	Conversational Mismatched
Noun	100	6	5	1
Verb	35	0	1	26
Adjective	22	1	0	3
Adverb	27	1	1	1
Proper Name	9	5	0	0
Pronoun	9	0	0	3
Preposition	42	0	1	3
Postposition	0	0	0	7
Conjunction	43	1	0	0
Determiner	11	0	0	1
Numeral	7	0	0	1
Quantifier	5	0	0	1
Relativizer	13	0	0	0
Question Word	4	0	0	0
Interjection	0	0	0	2
Loan Word (Noun)	0	0	3	0

Table 6 shows that the POS category missed most often is the verb in conversational form, which indicates that adding verbal conjugation rules for conversational language would provide the most value. On the other hand, nouns are typically guessed correctly by the system based on their inflectional morphology. The table also shows that the addition of frequent conversational items, such as the postposition *ro* and certain closed class items, could significantly improve the analysis results for blog text containing conversational language. Such a study helps us develop a more efficient strategy for extending the existing system as it is clear that we can improve the system stage by stage as some changes provide more value than others.

3.3. Summary

This section described a second instance of related languages, in this case the literary and conversational forms of the same language, and discussed a strategy for bootstrapping existing resources to improve processing of the new low-density variety. It was argued that a preliminary analysis of the distinctions and similarities between the language variants and a test study to identify a hierarchy of challenges raised by the low-density variant can be extremely beneficial in developing a bootstrapping strategy.

A descriptive study of conversational Persian found in weblogs identified a number of important differences at the word level in particular – such as the creation of new words, an extended set of borrowings especially in the technical domain, and orthographic representations that more directly reflect the pronunciation of words – which affect both lexical elements and morphological affixes. Thus, a focus on the morphological component would arguably provide the best results in capturing the new conversational forms encountered in text. As no previous research had been carried out to show whether conversational variants do in fact hinder morphological analysis, an evaluation was performed on a small corpus of blog text. A closer study using an existing system, however, helped identify specific gaps showing that the addition of some knowledge (e.g., verbal paradigm, frequent items, certain lexical categories) provides more value than others. This allows the extension of existing rules or lexicons to be performed in stages to provide rapid improvements with least human effort.

With the advent of social media such as blogs, forums and chatrooms, more and more people tend to use their spoken language in writing, which may show enormous differences with the traditional written form. We expect that the strategy proposed for Persian blog text can also be applied successfully to a large number of languages that display strong forms of diglossia as in the case of Arabic languages or the many languages in India.

4. Eastern Armenian

The third case scenario is Eastern Armenian, an Indo-European language with a severe lack of existing computational systems or tools. In addition, Eastern Armenian is written in the Armenian alphabet and therefore does not share the writing system of existing higher density languages. There are no computational grammars developed for this language and traditional grammars, as is often the case, are very prescriptive and incomplete. Several computational resources (e.g., a morphological analyzer and a corpus) are currently being developed for Western Armenian, a related language albeit with significant linguistic differences. It may therefore be possible to take advantage of existing Western Armenian tools to bootstrap these computational components for Eastern Armenian in the near future. There exists no syntactic component, as far as we are aware, for either variant of Armenian. Hence, in this paper we treat Eastern Armenian (henceforth EA) as an instance of a low-density language that is not in any way related to a resource-rich language with respect to parsing components. The main reusable elements in this case become the existing tools such as the segmenter, morphological analysis system, lexicon look-up tool, parser system, etc. This shows the absolute importance of modular and language-independent tools for development. In addition, the section presents a methodology for linguistic development for partial parsing.

4.1. Linguistic development

A common sentiment in natural language processing is that the development of knowledge-base systems is labor-intensive and time-consuming: "Statistical NLP models have a distinct advantage over rule based approaches to [rapidly retarget existing technologies to new languages], as they require far less manual labor" [19]. With very few exceptions, these claims are not substantiated by empirical evidence (cf. [20] but also [21,22]).

It is indeed true that, given pre-annotated or pre-aligned corpora, probabilistic technologies can be developed much more rapidly than a knowledge-base system. However, the creation of corpora that can be used to train statistical systems are extremely labor-intensive as illustrated in the following paragraph describing the development of a Cebuano corpus [23, p. 82]:

> The production of "parallel text" tells that story well. The University of Maryland produced nearly a million words of verse-aligned parallel text the first day, by the simple expedient of obtaining a Cebuano bible and aligning the verse numbers with those in an English bible that was already at hand. The University of Southern California Information Sciences Institute (USC-ISI) hired native speakers of Cebuano to produce translations, producing several thousand words within a week. But it was not until the team at Carnegie Mellon University found the newsletter of the Philippine Communist Party on the Web in both Cebuano and English that a large amount of truly representative example translations became available.

In particular in the case of low-density languages, for which very few resources exist, the development of parallel text and annotated corpora from scratch is rather a daunting task. On the other hand, we argue in this section that for resource-poor languages, development of knowledge-base components by a trained linguist, such as shallow parsers, with emphasis on providing generalizations for the most important structures in the language is highly valuable and can result in a first draft system with little effort. This section offers a blueprint for development of a partial parser without the need for a large set of hand-constructed rules.

Partial parsing refers to techniques used for recovering syntactic fragments instead of providing all of the information contained in a traditional syntactic analysis. As described in Abney [24], "The idea is to factor the parse into those pieces of structure that can be reliably recovered with a small amount of syntactic information, as opposed to those pieces of structure that require much larger quantities of information, such as lexical association information." A partial parser typically recognizes the key elements of a clause such as clausal boundary markers and simplex (i.e., non-recursive) clauses such as noun phrases (NP), preposition or postposition phrases (PP), and possibly simple verb phrases. Although partial parsers may also detect subjects and predicates, deeper analysis such as attachment resolution is not included at this stage of processing.

Partial parsing is especially useful for languages that display free word order, i.e., the clausal constituents do not always appear in a strict relative order in the sentence. In addition, the results of partial parsing can be used for bootstrapping – extracting information from a partially parsed corpus for use by more sophisticated parsers – or they could be used in applications such as entity extraction. This technique is therefore sometimes used as a preprocessing step. In what follows, we will focus on some important aspects of partial parsing development that are common in many low-density languages in order to build a first phase syntactic parser.

4.1.1. Grammar Books

When faced with a new language, clearly the first place to begin is with reference and grammar books. Unfortunately, in most instances, traditional grammars fail to provide all the relevant information needed for computational purposes. These grammar books oftentimes tend to define prescriptive rules (sometimes based on an older, literary version of the language) rather than providing descriptions of the modern language. The paradigms introduced are often incomplete for system development (e.g., not all lexical elements following a certain paradigm would be listed or the grammar book may not list certain irregular forms or exceptions). In addition, many grammar books fall short of making the correct generalizations and in most cases, grammarians do not explore distinctions between the spoken and written forms of the language under study. More importantly, grammar books that have not been developed for text analysis fail to discuss orthographic issues and variances which are crucial for computational analysis. It is therefore important to locate speakers of the language and a set of relevant corpora combined with keyword searches online to complement grammatical descriptions in reference books.

4.1.2. Phrasal boundaries

A first step in partial parsing is to reliably detect phrasal boundaries in text. One general method is to use function words to delimit clauses. In addition, a number of lexical items or morphological elements tend to appear at the beginning or end boundaries of certain phrases. For instance, pronouns in Persian within a noun phrase always occupy the last position at the NP boundary. In addition, certain affixes or function words are used to link the phrasal constituents in languages. These elements can easily be identified following a study of the basic NP and PP structures in the low-density language. This section presents a contrastive examination of the linking element in Tajiki Persian, Iranian Persian, and Eastern Armenian.

One of the important distinctions between the Tajiki and Iranian Persian writing systems involves the recognition of phrasal boundaries. Boundary recognition is a significant problem in Iranian Persian which uses the Perso-Arabic script, as there is no capitalization and the main morpheme linking the elements of a noun phrase is pronounced as /e/ which, being a diacritic, is typically not represented in orthography. As expected, this gives rise to very ambiguous results in applications such as MT and entity recognition which involve some level of phrasal parsing. In Tajiki Persian, however, the linking morpheme is represented in text, clearly indicating phrasal boundaries in a sentence. This distinction is illustrated in Ex. (1).

(1) نشست سران کشورهای ساحلی خزر شروع شد
‘The session of the heads of the coastal countries of the Caspian (Sea) began’

The nominal elements in the sentence are linked to each other with the so-called “ezafe” morpheme, which is pronounced as /e/ after consonants and /ye/ after vowels as shown in the transcribed version in Ex. 18.

(2)	*neshæst-**e***	*særan-**e***	*keshværha-**ye***	*saheli-**e***	*xæzær*
	session-**ez**	heads-**ez**	countries-**ez**	coastal-**ez**	Caspian

When a word in the noun phrase does not carry this affix, it marks the phrasal boundary. Hence, in this example, *xæzær* ‘Caspian’ is the end of the NP as shown in the parsed version in (3). However, the /e/ morpheme is typically not written in text, resulting in parsing ambiguity as any of the nouns may present a potential NP boundary for the system.

(3) [شروع شد] [نشست سران کشورهای ساحلی خزر]
[$_{NP}$ *session-**ez** heads-**ez** countries-ez coastal-**ez** Caspian*][$_{VP}$ *beginning became*]

Tajiki Persian orthography, on the other hand, explicitly writes the "ezafe" morpheme (и). Ex. (4) illustrated this for the same sentence, clearly demarcating the phrasal boundary.

(4)	Нишаст**и**	сарон**и**	кишварҳо**и**	соҳил**и**	Хазар	шуруъ	шуд
	*session-**ez***	*heads-**ez***	*countries-**ez***	*coastal-**ez***	*Caspian*	*beginning*	*become*

Hence, Tajiki Persian documents provide information on capitalization and boundary recognition which is not available to systems dealing with Iranian Persian text. In the case of Eastern Armenian, a language with very rich inflectional morphology, the linking elements within the NP constituents are also clearly demarcated by use of the genitive case morpheme as shown in Ex. (5).

(5)	Եվրոպական	երկրների	հանդիպումը	տեղի	ունեցավ
	European-gen	countries-gen	meeting-nom	place	had

'The meeting of the European countries took place.'

4.1.3. NP and PP structure

In order to determine the basic NP structure for partial parsing purposes, we would need to establish where the various constituents of the noun phrase appear relative to each other. Noun phrases, even in languages displaying relatively free word order, are quite rigid in structure. For instance, NPs in Persian (both the Tajiki and Iranian variants) can be described as in the schema shown in Figure 6 where each element except for the head noun is optional. This schema can represent the sentence '*in do ta ketab-e kheyli kohne-ye to*' [lit. this two (unit) book-of very old-of you] which can be translated into English as "these two very old books of yours".

Determiner	Number (Classifier)	Noun	[(Adverb)	Adjectives]	Possessor
	OrdinalNum				
	SuperlativeAdj				
	Quantifier				

Figure 6. NP structure for Persian

The relative ordering of the elements within a noun phrase can be determined by any trained linguist by identifying the elements that appear in complementary distribution. Note that these are basic structures that cover most syntactic constructions encountered in a corpus and do not necessarily cover more complex realizations of the noun phrase which can be added at a later stage. The schema in Figure 7 shows the basic NP structure in Eastern Armenian. This schema can be used to parse the sentence in Ex. (6).

Determiner	Number (Classifier)	[(Adverb)	Adjectives]	Noun
Possessor	OrdinalNum			
	Quantifier			

Figure 7. NP structure for Eastern Armenian

(6) մեր երկու լավագույն աշակերտները
our two excellent students-nom
'our two excellent students'

Languages that have prepositions or postpositions generally tend to form PPs by combining the preposition or postposition with a noun phrase. This is indeed the case for Persian where preposition phrases are simply formed as P + NP structures. Eastern Armenian, on the other hand, has a mixed system consisting of prepositions, postpositions and case markers. These are exemplified in Table 7.

Table 7. Eastern Armenian preposition/postposition phrases and oblique cases

Preposition	դեպի համալսարան	toward university	'towards the University'
Postposition	սեղանի վրայ	table-gen on	'on the table'
Locative case	համալսարանում	university-loc	'in the University'
Ablative case	համալսարանից	university-abl	'from the University'
Instrumental case	դանակով	knife-inst	'with the knife'

4.1.4. Word order

In addition to the elements and structures described, preliminary word order analysis is required to be able to develop simple rules (e.g., regular expression rules) for recognizing simple sentences containing a subject, an object, and a verbal element. For instance, both Persian and Armenian are verb-final languages and follow the word order 'subject-object-verb' for simple sentences, although Eastern Armenian writing style typically follows the 'subject-verb-object' order. However, it is easier to identify the arguments and their functions within an Armenian text as the latter generally uses distinct affixation (e.g., case marking) to distinguish subjects, objects, and oblique nouns. Additional items, such as basic adverbials and indirect objects may also be included for the purposes of partial parsing.

4.2. Language Technology Characteristics

In order for language technology to be valuable for low-density languages, it needs to be designed following the basic principles of reusability and portability. Agirre et al. [18] state that "if we want [Human Language Technology] to be of help for more than 6000 languages in the world, and not a new source of discrimination between them, the portability of HLT software is a crucial feature." For this purpose, natural language processing tools should be modular and language-independent allowing them to be combined for building a text analysis system for a new language.

Portability requires a more modular and flexible architecture rather than a hard-wired ordering of algorithms or linguistic knowledge coded directly into the software. One way of accomplishing this is to develop knowledge such as language rules within an independent component using a metalanguage, such as the Xerox finite state tools for morphological analysis, unification-based grammars for parsing, or regular expression rules. In addition, a number of tools can be built language-independently so that they can be applied to new languages, such as interface tools for lexicon development or scripts for corpus analysis. A modular or componentalized approach to language technology will therefore enable us to arrange and develop the natural language processing system in the best possible way for any given application or language.

In the case of low-resource languages, modularity, language-independence, and portability are crucial features in a toolkit allowing it to rapidly be applied to the development of computational systems for these languages, thus minimizing both human effort and cost.

4.3. Summary

This section discussed the main linguistic elements to be considered for the development of a partial parser with a small regular-expression grammar to recover syntactic fragments quite reliably. It was argued that, in the absence of related higher-density languages, one can develop linguistic knowledge fairly quickly for basic components. In addition, the existence of portable, modular, and reusable tools is crucial for application to new low-resource languages. Eventually, patterns for detecting multiword expressions, the distinct word orders found in active and passive sentences, as well as verbal subcategorization information can be added to enhance the basic rules if needed. Alternatively, partially parsed text can be used to train statistical systems.

5. Conclusion

By building upon the characteristics of three low-density languages –Tajiki Persian, conversational variant of Iranian Persian, and Eastern Armenian – this paper argues that there does not exist one single method for rapidly developing computational systems for low-density languages. Instead, it was proposed that focused studies can be performed to detect relevant language-specific characteristics, which can then be used for applying linguistic knowledge, taking advantage of portable and modular components in order to create stopgap language technology resources. These goals can be achieved by emphasizing two broad strategies: (i) *related language bootstrapping* can be used to port existing technology from a resource-rich language to its associated lower-density variant; and (ii) clever use of linguistic knowledge can be employed to *scale down* the need for large amount of training or development data. The methods discussed can be implemented for low-density languages in the goal of reducing human effort and avoiding the scarce data issue faced by statistical systems.

Acknowledgements

I would like to thank the participants of the 2007 NATO Advanced Study Institute on Low-Density Languages for valuable comments and discussion. The work on Tajiki Persian described in this paper was done in collaboration with Dan Parvaz and was supported by an innovation grant by the MITRE Corporation. The study on Persian weblogs was supported by a sponsored project at MITRE.

References

[1] M. Maxwell and B. Hughes, 2006. Frontiers in Linguistic Annotation for Lower-density Languages. In *Proceedings of COLING/ACL2006 Workshop on Frontiers in Linguistically Annotated Corpora,* 29-37. Association for Computational Linguistics.

[2] B. Hughes, 2005. Towards Effective and Robust Strategies for Finding Web Resources for Lesser Used Languages. In *Proceedings of Lesser Used Languages and Computational Linguistics*. EURAC, Bolzano,.

[3] K. Oflazer, S. Nirenburg, and M. McShane, 2001. Bootstrapping Morphological Analyzers by Combining Human Elicitation and Machine Learning. *Computational Linguistics*, 27(1).

[4] Ch. Monson, A.F. Llitjós, R. Aranovich, E. Peterson, J. Carbonell and A. Lavie, 2006. Building NLP Systems for Two Resource-Scarce Indigenous Languages: Mapudungun and Quechua. In *LREC 2006: Fifth International Conference on Language Resources and Evaluation.*

[5] H. Somers, 2005. Faking it: Synthetic Text-to-Speech Synthesis for Under-Resourced Languages – Experimental Design. In *Proceedings of the Australasian Language Technology Workshop 2005.* Sydney, Australia, pp. 71--77.

[6] Ch. Xi, and R. Hwa, 2005. A Backoff Model for Bootstrapping Resources for Non-English Languages. In *Proceedings of Human Language Technology Conference and Conference on Empirical Methods in Natural Language Processing* (HLT/EMNLP). Vancouver, Canada, pp. 851--858.

[7] Ph. Resnik, 2004. Exploiting Hidden Meanings: Using Bilingual Text for Monolingual Annotation. In *Lecture Notes in Computer Science 2945: Computational Linguistics and Intelligent Text Processing*, Springer-Verlag, pp. 283-299.

[8] D. Yarowsky, G. Ngai, and R. Wicentowski, 2001. Inducing Multilingual Text Analysis via Robust Projection across Aligned Corpora. In *Proceedings of the First International Conference on Human Language Technology Research* (HLT), pp. 161–168.

[9] S. Tong, 2001. *Active Learning: Theory and Applications*. PhD Dissertation, Stanford University.

[10] A. Feldman, 2006. *Portable Language Technology: A Resource-Light Approach to Morpho-Syntactic Tagging*. PhD Dissertation, Ohio State University.

[11] K. Megerdoomian and D. Parvaz, 2008. Low-density Language Bootstrapping: The Case of Tajiki Persian. In *Proceedings of LREC 2008*, Marrakech, Morocco.

[12] J.R. Perry, 2005. *A Tajik Persian Reference Grammar.* Boston: Brill.

[13] K.R. Beesley and L. Karttunen, 2003. *Finite-State Morphology: Xerox Tools and Techniques*. Palo Alto: CSLI Publications.

[14] J.W. Amtrup, 2003. Morphology in Machine Translation Systems: Efficient Integration of Finite State Transducers and Feature Structure Descriptions. *Machine Translation*, 18(3), pp. 217--238.

[15] D. Sifry, 2007. The Technorati State of the Live Web: April 2007. Available at http://technorati.com/weblog/2007/04/328.html

[16] J. Kelly and B. Etling, 2008. Mapping Iran's Online Public: Politics and Culture in the Persian Blogosphere, Research Publication No. 2008-01. The Berkman Center for Internet and Society.

[17] D. Crystal, 2001. *Language and the Internet*. Cambridge: Cambridge University Press.

[18] E. Agirre, I. Aldezabal, I. Alegria, X. Arregi, J. Arriola, X. Artola, A. Díaz de Ilarraza, N. Ezeiza, K. Gojenola, K. Sarasola, and A. Soroa, 2002. Towards the Definition of a Basic Toolkit for HLT. In *LREC 2002: Workshop on Portability Issues in HLT.* Las Palmas, Canary Islands, Spain.

[19] O. Kolak & Ph. Resnik, 2005. OCR Post-processing for Low Density Languages. In *Proceedings of the Conference on Human Language Technology and Empirical Methods in Natural Language Processing.* Association for Computational Linguistics. Pages: 867 - 874

[20] G. Ngai and D. Yarowsky, 2000. Rule Writing or Annotation: Cost- efficient Resource Usage for Base Noun Phrase Chunking. In *Proceedings of ACL-2000*, Hong Kong, pp. 117-125.

[21] J.P. Chanod and P. Tapanainen, 1995. Tagging French – Comparing a Statistical and Constraint-based Method. In EACL-95.

[22] G. Labaka, N. Stroppa, A. Way and K. Sarasola, 2007. Comparing Rule-Based and Data-Driven Approaches to Spanish-to-Basque Machine Translation. In *Proceedings of MT-Summit XI*, Copenhagen.

[23] D.W. Oard, 2003. The Surprise Language Exercises. In *ACM Transactions on Asian Language Information Processing* (TALIP), Volume 2 , Issue 2 Pages: 79 - 84

[24] S. Abney, 1997. Part-of-Speech Tagging and Partial Parsing. In *Corpus-based Methods in Natural Language Processing,* Edited by S. Young and G. Bloothooft. Kluwer Academic Publishers, Dordrecht.

Language Engineering for Lesser-Studied Languages
S. Nirenburg (Ed.)
IOS Press, 2009

doi:10.3233/978-1-58603-954-7-313

Applying Finite State Techniques and Ontological Semantics to Georgian

Oleg KAPANADZE
Institute of Applied information Sciences – IAI, Saarbrücken, Germany

Abstract. In the first part of the paper application of the Finite State Tools to one of the Southern Caucasian languages – Georgian is discussed. The FST has been very popular in computational morphology and other lower-level applications in natural-language engineering. The basic claim of finite-state morphology is that a morphological analyzer for a natural language can be implemented as a data structure called a Finite State Transducer. They are bidirectional, principled, fast and compact. In Georgian, as in many non-Indo-European agglutinative languages, concatenative morphotactics is impressively productive within its rich morphology. The Georgian language lexical transducer presented is capable of producing (analyzing and generating) all theoretically possible options for the lemmata from identified 21 sets of Georgian nouns and for most of the lemmata from about 150 sets of verb constructions. The second part of the paper is devoted to application of ontological semantics to Georgian. In a general ontological semantics lexicon meanings of words and expressions are represented in terms of instances of concepts from the ontology. Each lexicon entry comprises a morphological category and its syntactic and semantic features' description. A syntactic structure reflects syntactic valency represented as a syntactic subcategorization frame of an entry. A semantic structure links the lexicon entry with the language-independent ontological-semantic static knowledge sources - the ontology and the fact database. In a Georgian version of the ontological lexicon, alongside the mentioned monolingual information, each entry is supplied with the English translation equivalents. Consequently, we consider it as a potential bilingual ontological lexicon for multilingual NLP applications. The paper covers specifics of lexicon entries' formal description in the bilingual lexicon and discuss possible solutions for "toleration" differences in morpho-syntactic structure in the framework of a Georgian-English Ontological Semantics Lexicon.

1. Introduction

While there are many academic grammars and dictionaries for the Georgian language, this does not mean that there exists support for computational applications involving this language, since these resources are not available in a form that makes them applicable for computational processing.

A natural language engineering system includes many smaller processing components that contribute to specific subtasks, and solve a specific language subproblem. A core component of all large-scale natural language processing system applications – and especially for highly inflectional languages that comprises inflection, derivation and compounding – is a broad-coverage morphological analyzer. The morphological analyzer supports all the other components of a larger system, for instance, those that carry out syntactic parsing, spelling correction, indexing, data mining or machine translation. A natural language will typically contain tens of thousands, or even hundreds of thousands of roots. A morphological analyzer must perform a complete analysis of an inflected word form and produce a citation form (a canonical form of a word used as a headword in dictionaries) and a set of morphosyntactic features (number, person, gender, case, etc) for using the respective information in different language technology applications.

The main task of the endeavour described in this chapter was to prepare "lingware" – grammar and lexis – for text analysis and generation of Georgian texts in the **Finite State Automata** paradigm on the basis of the knowledge available about other languages. Finite state techniques have been very popular and successful in computational morphology and other lower-level applications in natural language engineering. The basic claim of the finite state approach is that a morphological analyzer for a natural language can be implemented as a data structure called **a Finite State Transducer (FST)**. FSTs are bidirectional, principled, fast, and (usually) compact. Defined by linguists with the help of declarative formalisms and created using algorithms and compilers that reside within an existing finite state implementation, finite state systems present excellent examples of the separation of language-specific rules and language-independent engines.

In early formulations of formal language theory and its possible application to natural language processing, finite state approaches were dismissed as inadequate for handling interesting natural language phenomena. From the 1960s through most of the 1980s concentrated on more powerful, but less computationally efficient, context-free and context-sensitive grammars. But since the 1990s the finite state approach has been resurgent, as can be witnessed by numerous research and commercial applications and the amount of literature devoted to finite state techniques. Although it is generally recognized that finite state techniques cannot do everything in computational linguistics, their resurgence was due to a new insight into phonological rewrite rules or, more generally, alternation rules.

In applications where finite state methods are appropriate, they are extremely attractive, offering mathematical elegance that translates directly into computational flexibility and performance. An early finite state system, Two-Level Morphology, was developed by K. Koskenniemi (1983). It gave linguists a way to do finite state morphology before there was a library of finite state algorithms and before compilers for alternation rules were developed. Without a composition algorithm, rules could not be cascaded, but were instead organized into a single level, applying in parallel between the two "levels" of the model: the lexical level and the surface level. Many linguists have tried to use two-level morphology but had to give it up, often claiming that two-level morphology does not work for certain types of natural languages (Beesley and Karttunen, 2003). At present, there is a broad choice of finite state implementations and toolkits is quite broad and includes *PC-KIMMO*, (www.sil.org/computing/catalogg/pc-kommo.html), the *AT&T FSM Library* (www.researct.att.com/sw/tools/lextools/fsm), *AT&T Lextools* (www.researct.att.com/sw/tools/lextools), the *Fsa Utils 6 package* (http://odur.let.rug.nl/~vannoord/Fsa.html) and the *Xerox Finite-State Calculus* (www.xrce.xerox.com/competencies/content-analysis/fst/home.en.html).

We used the latter toolkit as an implementation environment for developing a Georgian language lexical transducer. This product has been successfully used to develop FSTs for English, French, Spanish, Portuguese, Italian, Dutch, German, Finnish, Hungarian, Turkish, Danish, Swedish, Norwegian, Czech, Polish, Russian, Japanese. Research Systems include Arabic, Malay, Korean, Basque, Irish and Aymara. The applications that were developed include tokenization (word separation in running text), spelling checking and correction, phonology, morphological analysis and generation, part-of-speech disambiguation ("tagging"), shallow parsing and syntactic chunking.

2. Analyzing the Morphology of Georgian

Georgian grammar is not the main focus of this discussion. However, to give the reader an insight into how the lexical transducer for the Georgian was constructed, some information about the grammatical categories of Georgian nouns and verbs is necessary. Georgian is a member of the Kartvelian language family. Its structure is quite different from the structures of typical representatives of other language families, such as Indo-European, Semitic or Turkic.

2.1. *The Structure of Georgian Nouns*

The noun wordform's structure in Georgian is as follows:

NOUN_Stem + ***PLURAL_MARKER*** + **CASE_MARKER** + ***Emph_Vocal*** + ***POSTFIX*** + ***mph_Vocal***

R + *ებ (eb) ~ნ/თ (n/T)* + **7 options** + *ა(a)* + *9 options* + *ა(a)*

The structural units in italics are optional. There are two variants of the plural marker: *ებ (eb)* - for the modern Georgian and the archaic *~ნ/თ (n/T)* variations in different cases of declension. There are 7 cases in Georgian with different allomorphs

Nominative : -ი (-*i*), **0**
Ergative: -მა (-*ma*), -მ (-*m*)
Dative: -ს (-*s*)
Genitive: -ის (-*is*), -ს (-*s*)
Instrumental: -ით (-iT), -თ (-T)
Ablative: -ად (-ad), -დ (-d)
Vocative: -ო (-o), **0,**

and 9 *POSTFIX*es:

postfix_adverbial_"like" -ვით (-*viT*)
postfix_Locative_"at" -თან (-*Tan*)
postfix_Locative_"on" -ზე (-*ze*)
postfix_Inessive_"in" -ში (-*Si*)
postfix_Elative "from" -დან (-*dan*)
postfix_"till" -მდე (-*mde*)
postfix_"until" -მდის (-*mdis*)
postfix_Benefactive_"for" -თვის (-*Tvis*)
postfix_Destinative_"to" -კენ (-*ken*)

Standard academic grammars of Georgian list up to 21 classes of noun stems, including: stems ending with consonants, stems ending with vocals, stems ending with the vocal -ი (*i*), truncated stems, reduced stems, etc. The rest of the classes adopt an original declension type. In the version of a noun lexical transducer presented here, the most frequent ones are stems ending with a consonant and stems ending with the vocal ა(*a*) at the end. They include 5,642 and 8,437 units/citation forms respectively. The Georgian Noun analysis and generation module based on FST tools uses flag diacritics, an extension of the Xerox finite-state implementation. It provides feature-setting and feature-unification operations that help to keep transducers small and enforce desirable constraints. The use of Flag Diacritics is an alternative to composing such constraints into the transducer that can cause an explosion in the size of the resulting transducer.

Here are some typical examples of noun analysis:

კაცებისათვის [kacebisatvis] *("for the men")*

stem=*კაც*, number=pl{* ებ *}, caes=genitive {* ის *}, Emph_Vocal= {*ა*}

postfix_Benefactive_for{* თვის *}, cat=N.

ქალაქამდე [qalaqamde] ("*until the city*")
***stem=*ქალაქ*, Emph_Vocal=* {ა}, *postfix_till*{ მდე }, *cat*=N.**

ბანკირმა [bankirma] ("*banker*")
***stem=*ბანკირ, *case*=ergative{ მა }, *cat*=N.**

2.2. *The Verb System of Georgian*

The Georgian verbal patterns are considerably more complex than those of nouns. As the background for the description, we draw on the widely accepted grammatical tradition, according to which five classes of verbs are distinguished in Georgian:

Transitive verbs (C1), sometimes known as active verbs. This group consists mostly of transitive verbs. A small number of class members are intransitive. Class 1 verbs generally have a subject and a direct object. Some examples are "eat," "kill" and "receive." This class also includes causatives (verbs denoting "making someone do something") and the causative verbal form of adjectives (for example, "make someone deaf").

Intransitive verbs (C2). Intransitive verbs only take a subject, not a direct object (though a few govern an indirect dative object). Most verbs in this class have a subject that does not perform or control the action of the verb (for example, "die," "happen"). The passive voice of Class 1 transitive verbs belong in this class too, for example "be eaten", "be killed" and "be received." In addition, the verbal form of adjectives also have their intransitive counterparts: the intransitive verb for the adjective "deaf" is "to become deaf." This class may be further subdivided as follows: type (a) known as the 'radical (or markerless) intransitives'; type (b) known as the 'prefixal intransitives'; and type (c) known as the 'suffixal intransitives'.

Medial verbs (C3), sometimes known as the active-medial verbs. They differ from Class 1 verbs in that most denote intransitive activities, and so never take a direct object, but unlike Class 2 verbs, medial verbs mark their subject using the *ergative* case. Most verbs of motion (such as "swim" and "roll") and verbs describing weather phenomena (such as "rain" and "snow") belong to this class. Although these verbs are described as not having transitive counterparts (such as "cry"), some of them still have direct objects, such as "learn" and "study."

Inversion verbs (C4), sometimes known as indirect verbs. These verbs mark the subject with the dative case and the direct object with the nominative, a pattern known as inversion. Most Class 4 verbs denote feelings, emotions, sensations, and states of being that endure for periods of time. Verbs that convey the meaning of emotion and prolonged state belong to this class. The verbs "want" and "can" also belong to this class. Other common examples of Class 4 verbs are "sleep," "miss," "envy" and "believe."

Stative verbs. These *stative* intransitives sometimes are called 'passives of state.' Stative verbs do not constitute a class itself, but rather refer to a state, and their conjugations are very similar to those of indirect verbs. For example, when one says, "the picture is hanging on the wall," the equivalent of "hang" is a stative verb. A key parameter in determining the conjugation pattern of a stative verb is its valency: whether it is monovalent (or absolute, that is, incorporating only a subject) or whether it is bivalent (or relative, that is, also making an indirect reference).

The verb structure of Georgian is complicated, especially when compared to that of most Indo-European languages. In English, for example, the verb system features tense, person and number. This is also generally true for Georgian, but linguists avoid using the term 'tense' because the details of the Georgian situation are not exactly similar. Rather than using the terms "tense", "aspect", "mood", etc. separately, the Georgian verb grammar is built according to a syntactico-morphological principle around a construct called **series** that is described using the concept of screeve, from Georgian მწკრივი *mts'k'rivi* ("row"), (Tschenkeli 1958). There are 3 series established according to the syntactic features of Subject or Subject/Object relations reflected in a verb form. A screeve is a set of verb forms inflected for person and number that helps to distinguish between different time frames and moods of the verbal system. Each screeve comprises six verb forms, as in English. However, in addition to being associated with a particular time reference, screeves are combinations of tense, aspect and mode characteristics. There are 11 screeves spread across 3 Series: 6 screeves in the first series, 2 screeves in the second and 3 screeves in the third. The first series is subdivided into two subseries – Present and Future. The series and screeves are listed in the table below.

	Indicative	**Past**	**Subjunctive**
Series I/ Present Subseries	Present indicative	Imperfect	Present subjunctive
Series I / Future Subseries	Future indicative	Conditional	Future subjunctive
Series II/ Aorist Series		Aorist	Optative
Series III/ Perfective Series	Present Perfect	Pluperfect	Perfect subjunctive

Table 1. The series of screeves in Georgian.

The **Present indicative** is used to express an event at the time of speaking. It is also used to indicate an event that happens habitually. The **Imperfect** screeve is used to express an incomplete or continuous action in the past. It is also used to indicate a habitual past action with particle ხოლმე (*xolme*) to indicate the meaning of *used to.* The **Present subjunctive** screeve is used to express an unlikely event in the present and is usually used in a relative clause. The **Future indicative** screeve is used to express an event that will take place in the future. The **Conditional** screeve is often used together with რომ (*"if"*). The **Future subjunctive** screeve is used to express an unlikely event in the future and is usually used as a dependent clause. The **Aorist** screeve is used to indicate an action that took place in the past. It is also used in imperatives. The **Optative** screeve is used in negative imperatives, in obligations, in hypothetical conditions and in exhortations. The Present Perfect *screeve* is used to indicate an action, which the speaker did not witness. The Pluperfect *screeve* is used to indicate an action which happened before another event. The Perfect Subjunctive *screeve* is mostly used to express wishes.

2.3. *Patterns of Subject/Object Case Marking.*

A characteristic feature of Georgian is that apparent subjects and objects are not always marked consistently. Indeed, the subject of a clause may be marked with the *Nominative*, *Ergative*, or *Dative* case. There are three patterns of case marking for the subject and direct object, the actual pattern for any verb being determined by the verb class and series, as summarized in the Table 2.

VERBS	SERIES	SUBJECT	DIRECT OBJECT	INDIRECT OBJECT
Class 1	I	Nominative	Dative	Dative
	II	Narrative	Nominative	Dative
Class 3	III	Dative	Nominative	-თვის (*-Tvis*)
Class 2	all	Nominative	(Dative)	Dative
Class 4	all	Dative	Nominative	—

Table 2. Case Marking in Georgian

Class 1 and Class 3 verbs share the same pattern of marking. The use of the *Ergative* case is limited to marking the subjects of Class 1 and Class 3 verbs in the aorist series. The most Class 2 and 3 verbs are intransitive, meaning that they do not have direct objects. In the case of Class 4 verbs, where the subject is marked with the dative and the direct object with the *Nominative*, the postposition -თვის *Ttvis* ("for") is used to mark any indirect object. The use of the dative case to mark the subject, while the direct object is marked by the *Nominative*, is known as 'inversion'. As for the Georgian verb's structure itself, it consist of an obligatory root, and a number of affixes or, indeed, no affix at all as in the Present indicative 2nd person singular წერ (*ts'er*) "you write".

Georgian is considered to be an agglutinative language, which means that affixes each express a single meaning, and they usually do not merge with each other or affect each other phonologically. Each verb screeve is formed by adding a number of prefixes and suffixes to the verb stem. Certain affix categories are limited to certain screeves. In a given screeve, not all possible markers are obligatory. The overall structure can be visualized as linear sequence of positions, or 'slots', before and after the root position, which is referred to as slot ***R***. According to one analysis, there are a total of 24 slots in addition to the root (cf. www.armazi.com/georgian). In practice, however, no verb will have all possible slots occupied. The simplified model we introduce bellow for the Georgian verb morphological transducer has a total of nine slots (three before the root, and five following it), and is based on a table of allomorphs of the Georgian verb morphemes.

A	B	C	R	D	E	F	G	H
0	**0**	**0**		**0**	**0**	**0**	**0**	**0**
aA(a)	v (v)	a(a)		**eb(eb)**	**ineb (ineb)**	**od(od)**	**a (a)**	**T(T)**
mo (mo)	x (x)	i(i)		**ob(ob)**	**in (in)**	**d (d)**	o (o)	s (s)
mi (mi)	**h (h)**	e(e)		av(av)	**al(al)**		e (e)	
da (da)	s (s)	u(u)		**am(am)**	**ul(ul)**		**i (i)**	
Ca (Ca)	**m (m)**			**i (i)**			**n (n)**	
Se (Se)	**g (g)**			**d (d)**			**nen (nen)**	
ga (ga)	**gv (gv)**						**var (var)**	
amo (amo)							**xar (xar)**	
Semo (Semo)							**iyav (iyav)**	
gamo (gamo)							**iyav (iyav)**	
Camo (Camo)							**iyo (iyo)**	
gadmo (gadmo)								

Each column (corresponding to a slot in a verb form) consists of morphological elements which are in complementary distribution in a verb form sequence. Their combinations generate an inflected finite verb form. The columns in the table are composed of the following verb components:

Column **A** – **Preverbs.** They can add either directionality or an arbitrary meaning to the verb. Preverbs appear in the future, past and perfective screeves; they are generally absent in the present screeves;

Column **B** - **Prefixal nominal markers.** They indicate which person performs the action (agent) or for which person the verb is done (beneficiary; goal);

Column **C** – **Pre-radical vowels.** They have a number of functions, but in some cases no apparent function can be assigned to the pre-radical vowel:

-ა (*-a*)
forms Class 1 denominatives
forms causatives
indicates that the action takes place on something (the 'superessive version');

-ე *(-e)*
refers to indirect objects, mostly with Class 2 verbs
refers to pluperfect screeve subjects;
-ი *(-i)*
indicates first and second person indirect objects when the action takes place for someone's benefit (the 'benefactive version')
marks inverted subjects in the first and second persons converting a transitive verb to an intransitive verb (or to passive voice)
indicates reflexivity
forms the future / aorist stem of Class 3 verbs;
-უ (- *u*)
indicates an indirect object in the third person
marks an inverted subject in the third person;

Column **R – verb roots;**

Column **D – Thematic Suffix or Present/Future Stem formants;** Thematic suffixes are present in the present and future screeves for Class 1-3 verbs, but are absent in the past and mostly absent in the perfective screeves;

Passive Marker. In Georgian, two morphological means of converting a transitive verb to an intransitive verb (or to passive voice) are to add the version marker **-ი-** (the one in Column C) and to add -დ- (-*d*-) to the end of the verb root for certain types of verb roots (so called "inverted nouns").

Column **E – Causative marker -** ინებ- (-*ineb*-) Georgian causativity is expressed morphologically (where in English it is predominantly expressed syntactically). The causative marker obligatorily co-occurs with the version marker **-ა-** (***-a-***) from the Column C. There is no single causative marker in Georgian;

Participle marker *-ულ- (-ul-), -ალ- (-al-)*;

Column **F – Imperfective marker** or stem augment -დ-(-*d*-), -ოდ- (-*od*-) is characteristic of the imperfect, conditional, present subjunctive and future subjunctive *screeves*;

Column **G – The screeve markers** come before the second pronominal marker slot. They are seldom sufficient in themselves to identify the *screeve* unambiguously. The *screeve* markers are usually omitted before the third person pronominal marker;

Suffixal nominal markers. Intransitive verbs, the past and perfective screeves of the transitive and medial verbs, and indirect verbs, employ sets of vowels: in the indicative, first/second person -ი (-*i*) (strong) or -ე (-*e*) (weak), third person -ო (-*o*) or -ა (-*a*) for the third person; in the subjunctive, the suffixal nominal marker is the same for all persons, generally -ე (-*e*) or -ო (-**o**) or, less frequently, -ა (-*a*);

Auxiliary verbs are only used in the present indicative and perfective screeves of indirect verbs and in the perfective screeve of transitive verbs when the direct object is in the first or second person. The forms of the verb *to be* for the first and second singular are: მე ვარ (*Me* ***var*** *"I* ***am****"*) and შენ ხარ (*Sen* ***xar*** *"You* ***are****"*). For example, მიყვარ-ს *miq'var-s* mean "I love him/her" (the -ს (-*s*) at the end of the verb indicating that it is the third person whom the speaker loves). In order to say "I love you," the ***s*** at the end has to be replaced with **ხარ (*xar*)** (as the direct object is the second person): მიყვარ **-ხარ** *miq'var-****xar*** ("I love you");

Column **H – Suffixal nominal marker** -ს- (-*s*-) use the transitive verbs for the third person singular in present and future screeves.
Plural Marker. Depending on which set of nominal markers is employed, the appropriate plural suffix is added. It can refer to either subject or object.
Here are some typical examples of Georgian verb analyses detailing the morphological structure of a finite verb and its syntactic valency:

ვყიდით ***vyidiT*** "we sell it"
Subj3/ვ + ყიდ ***+ them/ი +თ = atsmko/Subj1Pl + Obj3Sg***
Subj3/ვ +ყიდ+ them/ი + თ = atsmko/Subj1Pl + Obj3Pl,

where *Subj3/v* indicates 3rd person Subject represented as **"ვ"**, *a verbal stem* "ყიდ", thematic marker *them/*ი, represented as "ი" and a plural marker "თ". This patern belongs to a screeve "*atsmko*" (Present Indicative) with a first person plural subject, indicated by "*SubjPl*" and a third person singular or plural object, indicated by *Obj3Sg": "Obj3Pl"*.

The Class 2 prefixal passive verb დამეხატებოდეს ***damexatebodes*** ("it will be painted for me") is analyzed as

Prv/და + Obj1Sg/მ +Pas/ე + ხატ +ებ +ოდ + ე + ს = kavshirebiti-1/Subj3Sg + Obj1Sg,

with a Preverb "და " (*Prv)* an object marked with first person singular marker "მ " (*Obj1Sg)* passive marker "ე "*(Pas), verb root* "**ხატ**", thematic suffix "ებ", imperfective marker "ოდ", *screeve marker* "ე" and a third person singular subject "ს". This pattern equals to a screeve "*kavshirebiti-1*"(Future subjunctive) with a Subject 3 person singular indicated by "*Subj3Sg*" and an Object 1 person Singular "*Obj1Sg"*.

As it could be determined from the table of allomorphs of the Georgian verb morphemes we do not introduce a single rank for each grammatical categories of the Georgian verb. Instead, we aggregate markers of different grammatical categories in the Columns based on their maximal distance of occurrences from a verbal root. Besides, one could also notice homonymy within some formants in different columns (e.g. *preverb* "ა(*a*) " from the column A and the formant "ა(*a*) " as *a neutral version formant* and *a part of causative* circumfix in the column C; a *passive marker* "დ (*d*)" in the column D and an *imperfective marker* in the column F.)

For resolving the outlined morphological homonymy we use continuation classes and Flag Diacritics, a module of the XEROX FST framework. The latter is useful also for marking roots with idiosyncratic morphotactic behavior, constraining circumfixes, and handling other cases that are feature-based rather than phonological.

3. An Ontological Semantics Lexicon for Georgian Language

The above FST-based morphological parser is a component of the lingware for Georgian language which is typically combined with the other resources in NLP applications. One such resource is a semantic lexicon that connects words in a language with their meanings represented in a formal language. In this section we describe our work on developing a Georgian Ontological-Semantic Lexicon (GOL) which has been developed using a methodology and an infrastructure elaborated by the Institute for Language and Information Technologies, University of Maryland Baltimore County. The basics of ontological semantics are presented in Chapter X of this volume. In this section we will concentrate on our experience in modifying the standard ontological-semantic lexicon to serve the needs of the processing of Georgian. Consider a simple example of the English Ontological Semantics lexicon entry:

```
(river-bed
 (river-bed-N1
  (POS N)
  (syn-struc
   ((ROOT $VAR0) (CAT N)))
  (sem-struc (river-bed))))
```

The first difference from the source English Ontological Semantics lexicon entries, which you can observe in the GOL, is a feature ***par*** for introducing a type of paradigm for noun declension and verb conjugation, an essential characteristic for the Georgian lexicon entries. The second difference, which is indicated also in bold cursive, is a case feature (***case ...***) that may have 7 different values for Georgian and is not introduced in the Lexicon English version due to its irrelevance for the English grammar point of view. Note that this feature is needed only for compounds in which a component is in a particular case form. Simple nouns are recorded in the lexicon in their citation form (the lemma), and the form in which they appear in text is determined by a syntactic parser.

```
(napiri [napiri]
 (napiri -N1
  (POS N)
  (par 1)
  (anno
   (def "")
   (ex "river-bank-N1; mdinaris napiri
                      [mdinaris napiri]
               lit.   river+Gen_Case_mark bank))
      (syn-struc
      ((n((root $var1) (cat n) (case gen) (root mdinare)))
        (ROOT $VAR0) (CAT N)))
  (sem-struc
   (RIVER-BANK)
   (^$var1 (null-sem +)))))
```

For the verb lexicon entries the both lexicons as an English as well as a Georgian one have more complicated structures:

```
(amoaqvs  [amoaqvs]
 (amoaqvs-v1
  (cat v)
  (par 2010)
  (morph )
  (anno
      (def "to remove a text unit from a text")
      (ex "cut-v6; They cut (out) four paragraphs from my essay;
      man ori Tavi amoiRo disertaciidan
      [man ori Tavi amoiRo disertaciidan]"))

(syn-struc
((subject ((root $var1) (cat np)))
 (root $var0) (cat v)
 (directobject ((root $var2) (cat np)))
  (pp-adjunct
   ((root dan [dan]) (root $var4) (cat psp)
    (obj ((root $var3) (cat n))))))

(sem-struc
   (REMOVE
    (agent (value ^$var1))
    (theme (value ^$var2) (sem TEXT-UNIT))
    (source (value ^$var3) (sem TEXT)))
        (^$var4 (null-sem +)))))
```

For the Georgian version we have added the same feature ***par***. Besides in the **ex**-field you can see a gloss in English and a translation equivalent (***cut-v6***) for the Georgian lexicon entry. The main difference for the verb entries in ***syn-struc*** between English and Georgian version is introduction of a ***direct-object*** and an ***indirect-object*** argument for GOL. A systemic difference observed in this example is thee ***pp-adjunct*** which stands in English for a Prepositional-Phrase-Adjunct, whereas for Georgian it is a Postfix-Phrase-Adjunct, that corresponds to a phrase headed by a postfix-marked word form (in the example above represented by ***dan [dan]***). If we follow this observation, we need to include all the Georgian postfixes in GOL as a lexicon entry (which indeed has been done), or alternatively (if the framework does not support this solution) to compile a lexicon for postfixes associated with the main Ontological-Semantic lexicon.

In the original conception of the ontological-semantic lexicon there is no direct correspondence between pairs of languages; all connections are made through the mediation of the ontological metalanguage for describing meaning. GOL was, however, conceived as a resource for a bilingual Georgian-English text processing applications, which necessitates direct juxtaposition of lexical units in the two languages. Consequently, in what follows we concentrate on how to use the facilities of the ontological-semantic lexicon for this purpose and discuss the problems lexical unit transfer between English and Georgian (that is "finding translation equivalents in the context") in the GOL framework.

The first example of the structural differences when looking for a Georgian equivalent concerns the 7th sense of the English verb ***use,*** the one represented in the English language construction ***used + to do smth.*** To recreate this meaning Georgian needs a different construction: ***Verb form in a past tense form + xolme*** *[xolme]* (particle denoting iteration). Consequently, for integration of this construction into GOL we introduced the ***xolme*** *[xolme]* particle as a lexicon entry alongside with feature ***(tense past)*** for verb form. In general, this can transfer the English language construction ***used + to do smth***. into the corresponding Georgian phrase:

```
(xolme   [xolme]
 (xolme-part1
  (cat particle)
  (morph )
  (anno
   (def "used as an aux.")
       (ex " used-v7; igi xatavda xolme {qalaqs}
                     [igi xatavda xolme {qalaqs}]
                      He used to paint {a town}"))
  (syn-struc
   ((np ((root $var1) (cat n)))
    (root $var2) (cat v) (tense past)
    (part((root $var0) (cat part)))))
  (sem-struc
   (^$var2
    (phase continue)
    (time (< (find-anchor-time)))
    (AGENT (value ^$var1))))
   (meaning-procedure
     (fix-case-role (value ^$var1)(value ^$var2)))))
```

Another example of a structural difference is the case when we need to treat verbs with different syntactic valency in Georgian and English languages. Thus, one of the senses of the English verb ***report*** is "to make known" which corresponds to the Georgian moaxsenebs [moaxsenebs] that takes a subject, a direct object and an indirect object. A simple solution we suggest here is a null-sem, or a zero correlate for an indirect object in the semantic structure, so that TMRs for those verbs will have the same description:

```
(moaxsenebs [moaxsenebs]
 (moaxsenebs-v1
  (cat v)
  (par 1229c3)
  (morph )
  (anno
   (def "make known")
   (ex „ report-v1;
       man generals moaxsena mimdinare mdgomareoba
       [man generals moaxsena mimdinere mdgomareoba]
  lit. „He has reported to the General a current situation"))
  (syn-struc
   ((subject ((root $var1) (cat n)))
    (root $var0) (cat v)
```

```
  (indirectobject ((root $var3) (cat n)))
  (directobject ((root $var2) (cat n)))))
(sem-struc
 (INFORM
  (AGENT (value ^$var1))
  (THEME (value ^$var2)))
 (^$var3 (null-sem +)))
```

It is clear that such a simple solution is not always available. Below we discuss some cases that require considerable changes in ***syn-struc*** for the Georgian entries. The first case involves the need to use a construction where English uses a simple word form. For example, an English verb ***commercialize*** is translated in Georgian using a causative construction. For instance the sentence "They commercialized sport" is rendered as ***maT sporti komerciad aqcies*** [maT sporti komerciad aqcies] (lit.: "*they sport comerce*+abl_case_mark *made*"]. The head verb of the construction is introduced as a lexical entry in GOL and the English word ***commerce*** is represented by the equivalent special root in the ablative case, which is "null-sem-ed" in the sem-str:

```
(aqcevs [aqcevs]
 (aqcevs-v1
  (cat v)
  (par 0522a)
  (morph )
  (anno
       (def "to apply methods of business for profit, to change
       so as to make profit")
       (ex "commercialize-v1; maT sporti komerciad aqcies
                              [maT sporti komerciad aqcies]
            lit.: " they sport  comerce+abl_case_mark  made"))
  (syn-struc
   ((subject ((root $var1) (cat n)))
    (directobject ((root $var2) (cat n)))
    (adj (root $var3)(cat adj)(case abl)(root komercia)))
    (root $var0) (cat v)))
  (sem-struc
   (CHANGE-EVENT
     (agent (value ^$var1))
     (theme (value ^$var2) (sem ORGANIZATION))
     (purpose PROFIT))(^$var3 (null-sem +)))))
```

Another such case is when an English lexicon entry for a noun contains a direct pointer to an ontological concept in the ***sem-struc*** while in Georgian one needs to use a ***adj+noun*** construction. For this purpose we introduce the syntactic structural unit ***(adj)*** with a special root argument that is "null-sem-ed" in corresponding ***sem-struc.***

Ex.: intangible-asset ~ aramaterialuri aqtivebi
[aramaterialuri aqtivebi]

As a lexicon entry for GOL we introduce ***noun*** of the type 21th declension (these nouns in Georgian are *pluralia tantum*). The ***syn-struc*** unit **adj** with root $var1 has a special root argument aramaterialuri [aramaterialuri], which is eliminated (that is "null-sem-ed") in ***sem-struc.***

```
(aqtivi [aqtivi]
 (aqtivi-n21
  (cat n)
  (par 1)
  (morph )
  (anno
   (def "")
       (ex "intangible-asset;
            aramaterialuri aqtivebi
            [aramaterialuri aqtivebi] "))
(syn-struc
  ((adj((root $var1) (cat adj) (root aramaterialuri)))
       (root $var0) (cat n) (number pl)))
(sem-struc
   (INTANGIBLE-ASSET)
   (^$var1 (null-sem +))))
```

Another interesting case is presented by the English term " accounts-receivable," for-which in GOL suggests a phrase debitorebi angariSsworebis mixedviT [debitorebi angariSsworebis mixedviT] that consists of three nouns with different case markers. Besides, the head noun must take a plural argument, though, it is an ordinal noun of the first declension that can in principle also appear in singular.

```
(debitori [debitori]
 (debitori-n1
  (cat n)
  (par 1)
  (morph )
  (anno
   (def "")
   (ex " accounts-receivable-n1;
        debitorebi angariSsworebis mixedviT;
        [debitorebi angariSsworebis mixedviT]"))
  (SYN-STRUC
   ((root $var0) (cat n) (number pl)
     (n((root $var1) (cat n) (case gen)))
     (adv((root $var2) (cat n) (case ins)))))
  (SEM-STRUC
      (ACCOUNTS-RECEIVABLE)
       (^$var1 (null-sem +))
    (^$var2 (null-sem +))))
```

A similar case we have with the English lexical entry ***disease***-N2 which is defined in the English lexicon as "plant disease". The corresponding GOL entry is represented by two variables – one with a special root as mcenare [mcenare] ("plant") in an archaic plural form, which is mandatory. A corresponding semantic structure, as in previous cases, is "null-sem-ed".

```
(daavadeba [daavadeba]
```

```
(daavadeba-n2
 (cat n)
 (par 3)
 (morph )
 (anno
  (def "plant disease")
  (ex " disease-n2; mcenareTa daavadeba "))
  (syn-struc
   ((n((root mcenare) (root $var1) (cat n) (pl arch)))
    (root $var0) (cat n)))
  (sem-struc
    (PLANT-DISEASE)
    (^$var1 (null-sem +)))))
```

In contrast to the above examples, there are also cases when the English phrasals and some specific senses are translated by a single lexicon entry in GOL. As an example consider an English gloss "to give [a patient] a check up." This sense in Georgian is lexicalized into the main verb of a clause with a subject as an agent.

```
(gasinja [gasinja]
 (gasinja -v1
  (cat v)
  (morph )
  (anno
   (def "to be the agent of some event")
       (ex "He gave the patient a check up;
       man gasinja avadmyofi [man gasinja avadmyofi]"))
```

The ***syn-struc*** for the Georgian lexicon entry is as follows:

```
(syn-struc
((subject ((root $var1) (cat n)))
  (root $var0) (cat v)
        (directobject ((root $var2) (cat n)))))
```

A ***sem-struc*** for the corresponding English lexicon unit is as follows:

```
(sem-struc
 (^$var2 (sem EVENT)          {check up}
  (agent (value ^$var1))      {He}
  (theme (value ^$var3))))    {patient}
```

$var2 is essential for the TMR in English is not used in the Georgian one. A corresponding ***sem-struc*** for the Georgian lexicon entry should be as follows:

```
(sem-struc
  ((sem EVENT)
   (agent   (value ^$var1))
   (theme (value ^$var2))
```

or a more specific type of EVENT. In both cases we have just partial overlap with English and Georgian versions of the ***sem-struc***. Consequently, it is not clear whether the lexicon entries with this sort of difference in semantic structure could be considered as translation equivalents by the MT translation engine.

The situation is much more complicated in the case of an English language construction ***to become + adj.*** In Georgian this meaning is lexicalized in certain types of verbs. For example an English sentence ***He became angry*** has the following syntactic and structures:

```
(syn-struc
   ((subject ((root $var1) (cat n)))     { He }
     (root $var0) (cat v)                 {became}
     (adj ((root $var2) (cat adj))))      {angry}

(sem-struc
   (CHANGE-EVENT
     (theme (value ^$var1))
        (effect (value refsem1)))
        (refsem1
      (RELATION
              (domain (value ^$var1))
                 (range (value ^$var2)))))
   (meaning-procedure
    (seek-specification (value refsem1) (value ^$var1)
                        (value ^$var2))))
```

This meaning is lexicalized into the Georgian verb brazdeba [brazdeba]. Its syntactic structure is described using just one variable, since it is a single-valency verb:

```
(brazdeba [brazdeba]
 (brazdeba-v1
  (cat v)
  (par 1044a1)
  (morph )
  (anno
   (def "")
   (ex " become-v2; He became angry;
                        igi brazdeba

                        [igi brazdeba]")

   (comments "In Georgian this meaning is lexicalized without an
   adjective"))

   (syn-struc
    ((subject ((root $var1) (cat n)))
     (root $var0) (cat v))
```

The above examples provide a brief illustration of the types of modifications we had to introduce into the ontological-semantic lexicon in order to adapt it to bilingual English-Georgian text processing. Needless to say, many additional cases of such modifications were detected and treated in our work. The Georgian Ontological-Semantic lexicon with the attached FST lexical transducer may be used as a basis for **Machine Translation** to supply a Machine Translation system's engine with a tagged, lemmatized and chunked text corpus of Georgian. The FST Transducer's Georgian version, however, may also provide the basis for a variety of probabilistic systems, as it would facilitate training statistical parameters as well as fitting into a Statistical/Hybrid development environment for future full-blown Georgian MT systems.

References

Aronson, Howard I. 1990. Georgian : a reading grammar. Corrected edition. Columbus, Ohio: Slavica Publishers.

Beesley K., L. Karttunen. 2003. Finite State Morphology. CSLI Publications. Center for Study of the Language and Information, Leland Stanford Junior University.

Koskenniemi, K. 1983. Two-level morphology: A general computational model for word-form recognition and production. Publication 11, University of Helsinki, Department of General Linguistics, Helsinki.

Nirenburg, S. and V. Raskin. 2004. Ontological Semantics. MIT Press.

Tschenkéli, Kita. 1958. Einführung in die georgische Sprache. 2 vols. Zürich: Amirani Verlag.

Subject Index

Language Engineering for Lesser-Studied Languages
S. Nirenburg (Ed.)
IOS Press, 2009

Author Index